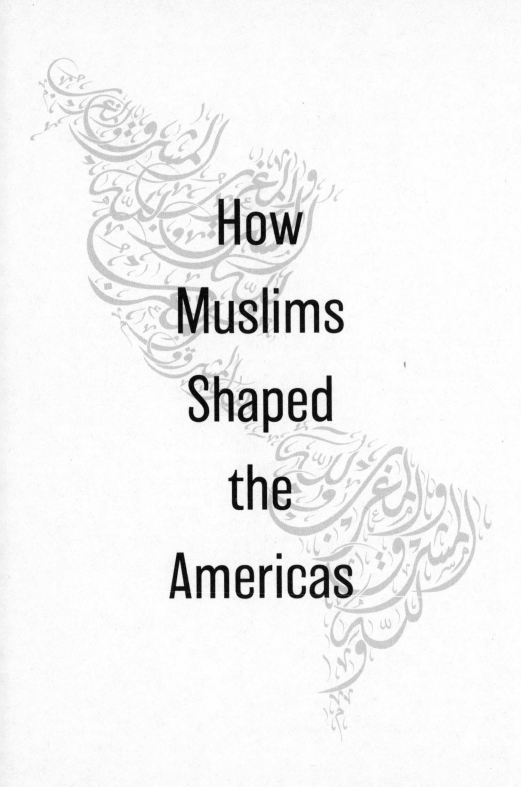

How
Muslims
Shaped
the
Americas

PRAYING
TO THE
WEST

OMAR
MOUALLEM

Published by Simon & Schuster

New York London Toronto Sydney New Delhi

SIMON &
SCHUSTER
CANADA

Simon & Schuster Canada
A Division of Simon & Schuster, Inc.
166 King Street East, Suite 300
Toronto, Ontario M5A 1J3

This Simon & Schuster Canada edition September 2021

SIMON & SCHUSTER CANADA and colophon are
trademarks of Simon & Schuster, Inc.

For information about special discounts for bulk purchases,
please contact Simon & Schuster Special Sales at 1-800-268-3216
or CustomerService@simonandschuster.ca.

Interior design by Lewelin Polanco

Manufactured in the United States of America

1 3 5 7 9 10 8 6 4 2

Library and Archives Canada Cataloguing in Publication is available on file.

ISBN 978-1-5011-9914-1
ISBN 978-1-5011-9921-9 (ebook)

For Noe Delilah and Elias Blue,
the closest thing to fate I know.

In memory of the Quebec City mosque victims:

Ibrahima Barry

Mamadou Tanou Barry

Khaled Belkacemi

Aboubaker Thabti

Abdelkrim Hassane

Azzedine Soufiane

Contents

Part 3 - وسط   *Wasat (Moderation)*

Part 4 - بدعة   *Bida (Innovation)*

Author's Note

The Islamic table of elements is far more complex than Sunni and Shia. Since Prophet Muhammad's death in 632, countless reformers have tried to steer his message in new directions, resulting in dozens of denominations, schools of thought (*fiqh*), and movements. This book covers only a fraction of them. I suggest that readers seek out additional information about the diversity and evolution of Muslim branches.

I've included a glossary for uniquely Islamic terms, including Muslim holidays, prayer times, honorifics, and the names of the five daily prayers. My intention with this book, however, has been to demystify and normalize the Muslim presence in the West. I avoided using common Arabic words, such as *Allah* when there's a perfect English-language equivalent, to emphasize not just Islam's commonalities with Christianity but its continuation of Abrahamic religions, as Prophet Muhammad intended. I have also avoided using contentious terms that Muslims do not commonly use, such as *jihadi*, *Wahhabi*, and *Islamic terrorism*, when there are more neutral equivalents, such as *violent extremists*, *ultraorthodox*, or *Salafi*, and *Islamist terrorism*. (The last refers to a specific political ideology.)

At the same time, I intentionally titled the four parts of this book using contentious Islamic terms, such as *Jihad* (struggle) and *Bida* (innovation), in hopes of neutralizing their politicized contexts, and reclaiming them from controversy. Similarly, I've opted to de-Americanize the word *America*. In this book, *the Americas, Greater America*, and sometimes *American* refer to all the people and land in the Western Hemisphere.

It's also worth noting that the chapters are neither sequenced in order of the founding year of Islamic movements nor explored within the timeline of my travels, which began in April 2017 and ended in December 2019, mere months before the COVID-19 pandemic restricted travel and access to religious temples. Rather, I've sequenced them in order of each community's roots in Greater America. For example, my first research trip to Inuvik, Northwest Territories, is the topic of the second to last chapter, while my last excursion, to northeast Brazil, is one of the first chapters.

Finally, I wish to briefly acknowledge that I researched, wrote, and published *Praying to the West* on many traditional lands of tribal nations and Indigenous communities. I'm indebted to their hospitality and the sacrifices of their ancestors, and grateful for the opportunity to be a guest of Turtle Island and beyond. I wish to acknowledge the communities here—with the caveat that these are imperfect transliterations of living languages. There are regional and familial differences in spelling and pronunciation and how the languages are spoken. I used the best resource available, Native-Land.ca, an Indigenous-led educational map for territory acknowledgments and colonial history, but the organization itself acknowledges that this is a work in progress. Thank you to Laura Redish, Leanne Betasamosake Simpson, and Marek Tyler for their assistance.

Anishinabek	Kalinago
Atakapa-Ishak	Karankawa
Bodéwadmi	Kizh
Coahuiltecan	Meskwaki
Chumash	Michif Piyii (Métis)
Gwich'in	Myaamiaki (Miami)
Haudenosaunee	Nakhóta (Stoney)
Huron-Wendat	nêhiyawak (Plains Cree)
Inuvialuit	Niitsítpiis-stahkoii (Blackfoot)

Očhéthi Šakówiŋ (Dakota Sioux)   Wabanaki Confederacy
Peoria   Warao
Sana   Wendake-Nionwentsïo
Tongva   Tupinambas
Tsuut'ina   Tzotzil and Tzeltal Maya

Introduction

The first time I learned I was Muslim was in preschool.

During an excursion to a pizzeria, which is what passed for a field trip in my hometown of High Prairie, Alberta, I consumed a few morsels of ham. My mom arrived with the other parents to pick me up from class, and I began to sing the praises of Hawaiian pizza. She cut me off with a gasp. "You're Muslim," she said loudly for my teacher to hear. "Muslims don't eat pork."

Abstaining from pork could be the first law of the Five Pillars of *Western* Islam. Unlike the actual pillars (pray daily, pay alms, fast through Ramadan, pilgrimage to Mecca, and declare Muhammad as a messenger of the one true God), they are defined by what you don't do: eat pork, celebrate Christmas, drink alcohol, gamble, and date. It's safe to say that I'll probably never complete the first set of pillars. But the second I dutifully observed until mid-adolescence. Then I pushed them over, one by one, over the course of ten years. The first to go up was the last to fall.

Which brings me to the second time I learned I was Muslim, a few years ago, at age thirty. I outed myself from the atheist closet by eating pork on a Food Network show. I immediately regretted it and decided to inform my mom before one of my relatives got to her first. I tried to explain my disposition to her, but again she cut me off: "You were born Muslim, and you'll die Muslim." I don't think she meant it as a threat, and certainly not as an offence, but that's how it felt.

After the Twin Towers fell on September 11, 2001, two days before my sixteenth birthday, I started becoming hostile to structural authority—governmental, institutional, and religious. Reflecting on it today, it probably had as much or more to do with how I wanted to be viewed than any firm views I might've held as a fledging writer and rapper. Throughout my twenties, I refashioned myself a professional skeptic in magazines, radio, and music, and I routinely disparaged religion and the religious. Part of my first date with my now wife was spent debating (or perhaps tormenting) a Christian street preacher. On my second date with Janae, we chilled with a documentary about human evolution.

Yet try as I might, I've never been able to shake free from the larger Muslim body, the *ummah*. When my parents pressured us to sign a sharia marriage contract to give them peace of mind, I was a begrudging Muslim. When Janae's friends, or the parents of previous girlfriends, warned that I might become an abuser and would absolutely dump them to marry a brown girl in time, I was an ashamed Muslim. When a literati type cornered me at a party to ask me why Muslims don't condemn Muslim terrorists, I was a polite Muslim. When the same man years later accused me of anti-Semitism, I was an irate Muslim.

Until recently, Muslim identity was imposed on me. But I feel different about my religious heritage in the era of ISIS and Trumpism, Rohingya and Uyghur genocides, ethnonationalism and misinformation. I'm compelled to reclaim the thing that makes me a target. I've begun to examine Islam closely with an eye for how it has shaped my values, politics, and connection to my roots. No doubt, Islam has a place within me. But do I have a place within it? Is there a seat in the ummah for nonbelievers?

In search of an answer, I started a journey to discover the oldest and most dynamic mosques in the Americas, as well as humbler temples that challenge the definition of Muslimhood. I wanted to demystify these houses of worship, for myself and others; humanize a minority in need of humanization; and document the diversity among denominations, nationalities, and individuals. I prayed in dozens of mosques from the edges of the Amazon to the Arctic Circle, capturing the multiplicity of practices and beliefs inside. Everywhere I went, I left behind a prayer. It was medicine, going down smooth or bitter, but always tasted like an antidote to the intolerance that once infected me and increasingly infects Westerners scarred by ignorance and fear.

But why the Americas? Anti-Muslim anxieties are more pronounced in Europe, after all. The population of Greater America's Muslims is statistically insignificant: some 10 million people spread across 16 million square miles, even if they occupy an outsized space in the media cycle and collective fears of the other 99 percent.

But it's that very isolation that has allowed American Muslims to develop into the most racially diverse religious group in the United States *and* the most diverse Muslim population in the world. In a city like Houston, over one hundred Muslim houses of worship go by many names: *masjid, jaamah, musalla, Husaynia, jamatkhana, temple.* The variation and banality of these landmarks at once debunk the myth of a monolithic Islam and the "clash of civilizations." When there are clashes, they're usually between the temple walls and coreligionists.

Isolated from Islamic scholarship by an entire hemisphere, Muslim traditions evolved uniquely alongside New World cultures until the postwar period. Globalization and Islamism, a relatively modern political movement, complicated Muslims' abilities to practice and define Islam on their own terms. As those practices begin to look standardized, they're being complicated again by the free flow of information in the social media age, gradually evolving into an inclusive Muslim movement with human rights at the forefront.

Perhaps American Islam is overlooked because Islam itself is seen as synonymous with the East. In fact, Prophet Muhammad modelled it on Abrahamic faiths, so it's no more Eastern and no less Western than Christianity, especially in the New World. Its American roots stretch back further than every nonindigenous faith except Catholicism (and maybe further back, according to disputed history of Chinese exploration).

Islam underpinned much exploration, colonization, and development in the New World. After the fall of Granada in 1492, the Spanish Reconquista served as a blueprint for conquistadors. Indigenous Americans were sometimes identified as *moriscos* and *moriscas* (Moors), their sacred sites as *mezquita* (mosques), and their suffering justified by an announcement of "The Requirement," a Spanish decree offering a chance at peaceful submission, or death, exactly what was used to convert, conquer, and expel the Moors. And all of this was before the transatlantic slave trade introduced as many as 3 million Muslims who earned such a reputation for rebellion that Spain made several futile attempts to ban their importation.

Islam continued to shape the Americas, apparent in place names such as Almenara, Brazil ("The Minaret"), and blues music. Thomas Jefferson wrote one of the US Constitution's most sacred clauses ("no religious Test shall ever be required as a Qualification to any Office or public Trust") with a hypothetical Muslim president in mind. Centuries later, Black and brown Muslims would swear on Jefferson's personal copy of the English Quran during their oath of public office.

Westerners treat Muslim communities as a new viral outbreak instead of an essential gene in modern America's DNA. But I can't blame the public for not knowing the richness of American Islam when I did not know it myself. Christian-dominated historians have forgotten, ignored, and erased Greater America's Islamic roots, but so have orthodox Muslim theologians attempting to "purify" American Islam.

The concept of an ummah, a whole Muslim body unified in their beliefs, promotes universal common grounds but it also fuels the false concept of a monolithic Islam. Even I have used it to paint Muslims with this broad brush, ignorant of the nearly eighty sects and innumerable cultural interpretations. Every mosque I visited proved the ummah is, at best, a nebulous concept. In the Persian heart of Los Angeles, I went to a quasi-secular mosque attempting to "bring people in from the nightclub," as well as an older generation who abandoned Islam as a survival tactic. Under an extravagant dome in Dearborn, Michigan, I found a prayer hall nearly abandoned by congregants favouring American ideals. In southern Mexico, mosques reconnected some to their Moorish roots and others to Indigenous traditions. And at an undisclosed location in Toronto, I saw women lead prayers, queer people give sermons, and met fellow atheists seeking spirituality.

Every mosque told a different story. Each story complicated my view of Islam, Muslims, and myself. Every congregation had its frictions, but rarely were these issues related to Muslim extremism. Differences over opinion usually stemmed from differences in age, ethnicity, gender, and sexual orientation. I expected that to an extent. What I didn't expect was the sense of belonging I'd feel with most congregations. I began to wonder: Can one be Muslim if he doesn't believe in its basic tenets but seeks comfort in Islam's select messages and practices? If the airport security and most people assume I'm Muslim, including my own family, does it matter? In other words: Am I still Muslim?

This book is about the third time I learned I was Muslim—and the first time that I decided it for myself.

1

جهاد

Jihad

(Struggle)

Praised be the name of the
  giver of salvation.
Blood must be shed. We must
  all have a hand in it.
Oh God! Oh Muhammad!
  Servant of the Almighty!

—*Arabic script worn by enslaved*
African in Brazil, 1835

1

What's My Religion?
Masjid al-Aqsa
(Jerusalem)

*W*hat is your religion?"

It'd been a long time since someone asked me that question, and I couldn't recall it ever being asked so bluntly and sternly. The young Israeli guard at the entrance to the Temple Mount appraised my passport like a secondhand watch, giving more attention to the name inside than the glimmering Canadian crest on the cover.

It was the last day of an assignment in Israel and the West Bank, and by now I was used to the extra scrutiny. When I landed at Ben Gurion Airport earlier that week, my colleague, Spencer (white man, white hair), glided through customs like a swan. Predictably, I was detained. Customs kept me for three hours in a walled-off section with a dozen other men, women, and children bonded more by our Islamic names than any one ethnicity. The prejudicial scrutiny continued at checkpoints inside and outside the West Bank, where we were researching a school for Palestinian refugees. It followed me to Old Jerusalem, where we planned some sightseeing on our last day in the Holy Land. The only surprising thing about the Temple Mount guard was his straightforwardness. It was almost admirable.

I was in the middle of depositing my belongings and loose

shekels into a plastic metal detector tray when the guard asked the question. For a second I thought I'd misheard, and this might've been the first sign of heatstroke. I'd been roasting under the Jerusalem sun for over an hour waiting for the gates to the al-Aqsa plaza to reopen for afternoon visitors.

After watching Spencer clear security and disappear into the crowded compound, I repeated the officer's question aloud to make sure I heard him correctly. "What's my religion?"

"What are you?" he rephrased.

As far as I could tell, he hadn't asked anyone in front of me about their faith. How important could my religion be if theirs was not? I'm used to being asked about my nationality as a traveller (or my parents' nationality, when "Canadian" doesn't satisfy). But "what's your religion"?

That one takes me back to my childhood, pre-9/11, when the good folk of High Prairie genuinely hadn't heard of Muhammad or his book. Funny, I had a more cogent answer at age seven, seventeen, or twenty-seven than I did then, at thirty-two. First, it was, "I'm Muslim"; then, "I'm agnostic"; and finally, "I'm atheist"—all said, naturally, with the self-importance of someone proclaiming themselves vegan. I started toning it down once I clued in to the veiled bigotry of the "new atheist" movement, and realized that my devotion to disbelief had become another type of zeal and blind faith. It was an ego trip with none of the spiritual nourishment. But where did that leave me? What did that make me?

"Are you Muslim?" asked the guard.

Now that's a question I'm asked plenty. People ask if I'm Muslim before offering me a beer, or with surprise after I accept it. Sometimes, though, they ask if I'm Muslim to make sure the coast is clear before making a bigoted remark, leaving me in the awkward position of defending beliefs I do not hold myself. We rarely get there, though, because, when asked, I try to answer in ways that account for religious traditions I cherish. Like the fact that nothing beats family meals like Ramadan family meals, or that I sometimes gather my strength by reciting the opening line of the Quran, or that I find few environments more calming than a mosque. All of this I try to sum up with one nebulous phrase, "I grew up in a Muslim household," and hope they know what that means.

But in that uncomfortable moment, on Temple Mount, *Haram al-Sharif* in Arabic, neither the Israeli officer nor the sweltering tourists behind me had time for my nuance and nebulae. So I told him, "I have no religion."

"No religion?" the officer snorted. With that, he waved me through a metal detector with an air of pity.

———

"What's your religion?" was a reasonable question to ask the brown kid who showed up at your door like a desert mirage, joined your children at the dinner table, passed on saying grace, or inquired about the contents of your meatloaf. It was an especially fine question to ask whenever he requested lenience in gym class because he was fasting or missed a day of school on religious grounds.

Twice a year for Eid al-Fitr and Eid al-Adha, the holiest days of the Islamic calendar, my family drove to the nearest mosque one hour away in Slave Lake, where a robust Muslim community has thrived since the 1960s. The mosque was a doublewide trailer that my parents helped purchase and renovate into a holy place named al-Ameen ("the faithful"). It sat outside the small town, past the edge of a forest, propped above a muskeg, and was prone to shift after every rainfall. Eighty worshippers squeezed between panel walls on holidays. The role of muezzin—he who recites the call to prayer—rotated amongst the uncles, but it was always the same portly elder in the role of imam—he who leads prayers. He was appointed on account of his recitation and public speaking skills. His uniform was pleated khakis and linen shirts; his pulpit, a simple prayer rug.

I was three when al-Ameen opened, so my place in communal prayers would have started in the open space between the male and female sections partitioned by house curtains. Fidgety kids are present in every synagogue, church, or town hall, but on a typical Friday the wide-open carpet of a prayer hall might as well be a sandbox. While our fathers solemnly prayed, my cousins and I chased each other and flopped around on the floor, stopping only when an uncle broke his meditation to glower. We gradually started to emulate our elders, pausing mid-somersault to prostrate, and eventually squeezed into a row.

Watching through the corners of my eyes, I imitated the adults around me and tried to synchronize each movement: place my hands over belly, whisper unintelligible Arabic, bow, straighten up, prostrate, kneel, prostrate again, stand, and repeat. As there was nary a high school graduate among the barbers, cleaners, and self-made businessmen, I doubt anyone present understood the poetry in our body language. Each pose of Islamic prayer is a stanza unto itself. *Salat* begins with one's assertion of his strength before collapsing under God's overwhelming glory, but ends on one's knees, in the space between independence and irrelevance.

The lowest position entranced me the most. Looking backward between my legs, my elders appeared like moths on a ceiling. I'd hold that view for as long as I could, struck by the sight of my dad on all fours, whispering to the floor with an intimacy and vulnerability he showed nowhere and no one else. But as I fell behind in my practice, I relished the position of prostration more because it hid me away. Prayer remained an act of imitation. I couldn't shake the feeling of being watched and judged by those around me, a fate much worse than being judged by God.

The only time I remember praying alone was after sneaking into the basement in the middle of the night to watch *Sliver* on Cinemax, on the rumour that Sharon Stone would show her boobs a lot. I returned to the bedroom I shared with my brother, wide awake with guilt. As dawn crept, I feared I'd never sleep again. Then it occurred to me: I could pray for forgiveness. I rolled out of bed and repeated "al-Fatiha" in my head during a rapid simulation of salat. If my brother could have heard my thoughts, the Quran's first verse, considered a summation of the book in seven lines, would have been mistaken for a Bone Thugs-N-Harmony song. Scared he'd wake up and tell me I was doing it all wrong (not that he knew better), I raced through worship and back into bed. Sure enough, I slept again.

Despite my spiritual confusion, I cherished our mosque enough to feel wounded when it burned down one Halloween night. It seems so suspicious today, but in 1996, my elders took investigators on their word that there was no foul play, just "faulty wiring." With that, they went straight to work on rebuilding it. The generosity of Christian neighbours helped them construct a temple in the centre of town. It had double the square footage, a social hall in the basement, and a domed minaret.

By the time it reopened, I was thirteen and beginning to fancy myself as outspoken. Relatives said I'd make a good lawyer. My parents, trying to see a silver lining in my disobedience, agreed. I actually wanted to be a writer and rapper, and I never passed on the chance to nurture these goals by calling out the US government in school essays and talent shows. It was impossible not to apply my critical faculties to religion itself, especially after September 11, 2001.

Al-Ameen, however, maintained its old soul inside its new body. Even during the brief tenure of an Egyptian-trained imam (and locally trained school janitor), it felt like the same family reunion year after year. If there was a political message or a worry about racist backlash to one of his impassioned sermons, then I missed it. The mosque sat undisturbed through the 9/11 attacks, the thirteen-year war with Afghanistan, and the 2014 terror attack on the Canadian Parliament. Not even a wildfire that destroyed nearly half the town's buildings, including a church directly next door, left a scar.

Then, in October 2016, a few weeks before Donald Trump won the presidential election, someone smashed al-Ameen's windows.

Broken windows were minor scares compared to the bomb threats, spray-painted swastikas, and arson that terrorized about a hundred Islamic centres across North America that year. The twelve months between the Paris attacks in November 2015 and the 2016 US presidential election saw an unprecedented number of attacks on mosques. I couldn't imagine a place that evokes fondness in me would trigger hatred in another. A quarter of non-Muslim Americans recently told Pew Research that they're entitled to block Muslim centres from opening in their neighbourhoods if they don't want them. More than one-third admitted to an unfavourable view of Islam. Another poll by Ipsos found that Americans, on average, estimated Muslims formed 17 percent of the national population. The reality? One percent.

But facts are quaint artifacts of a bygone era. Feeling surrounded by hostile forces is real when the most powerful man in the world says, "I think Islam hates us." Trump's rhetoric was nearly identical to that used by ISIS propagandists to whip up deranged young men to go on shooting and stabbing sprees. By now countless millions of people know exactly what horror such statements can produce. Still, I was shocked by what happened during President Trump's first month in office. Within a week of his inauguration, the president tried to make good on his promise of a Muslim ban, setting in motion a series of responses that would leave six men dead in a Quebec City mosque. (Their names are on the dedication page of this book.)

People often ask me what it was like living in a small, conservative town during the early years of the War on Terror. They're surprised to hear that it was fine. Our family restaurant was never ostracized. Our house was never vandalized. I felt no change in how I was viewed or treated. The only dramatic difference was inside me. Not so, the early years of Trumpism.

The changes inside and out are impossible for me to ignore. They've only grown more intense with my awareness of the Western world's complicity in Hindu nationalist mobs, Rohingya genocide, and, most shocking to me, Uyghur concentration camps. The lesson of "never again," taught to us in school and repeated by our leaders, seems all but forgotten.

———

Back on Temple Mount, the Dome of the Rock revealed itself like a giant squatting beneath a bright blue sky. Visible from every inch of Jerusalem, the fine details of each gold plate and mosaic tile became clear only when I climbed the plaza steps and stood in its shadow. Once I got past the stunning architecture though, my thoughts wandered to several things that had weighed on my mind that summer in 2017.

I thought about what I'd just witnessed over the past week in the West Bank: men were forced through turnstiles en route to prayer;

trash was thrown at shopkeepers from settlers above; "Jewish only" bus stops were maintained by armed citizens; Israeli soldiers penned in a family from leaving their property with chain-link fence. It was especially shocking because I'd spent the prior week in Poland and bore witness to the Auschwitz-Birkenau memorial and museum.

If the progeny of Europe's Holocaust victims could so easily forget the cruelty of ethnoreligious nationalism, so willingly overlook the humanity of the Other, then what hope is there for the rest of us? I thought of my soon-to-be-born daughter and wondered, as my wife and I often do, whether bringing her into this world was a selfish and brutal act. The Canada that Janae and I inherited through birthright is much the same today—an imperfect, unequal colonial project striving to live up to its multicultural mythology—but the democratic system that new Canadians receive seems vulnerable to the rise of authoritarianism sweeping the so-called West. Our hopelessly porous borders, however, have invited Trumpism and laïcité fundamentalism, by way of France, to energize an extremist minority. Worse, they have been legitimized by Far Right pundits and politicians.

Approaching the mosque, I thought most about my father approaching his house of worship in Edmonton. Since our family moved to the Alberta capital, he'd barely missed a Friday prayer at the big-city mosque. Retiring in a neighbourhood with a sizable Arab community awakened his spirituality, though I hadn't noticed it until after the massacre at the Quebec City Grand Mosque. Barely a Friday passed since without thinking about the risk of someone running through the arched doors of my family's local mosque with hateful intentions. (In 2019, my fears came closer. Security cameras caught the leader of a notorious hate group stalking the place before Friday prayers. He claimed to be seeking a washroom.)

Those who've threatened and assailed mosques in the West emulate a battle that began in 1099 at al-Aqsa. The papacy, struggling to hold its power, sent restless Europeans on a holy war to recapture Jerusalem. They savagely seized the city, "cleansed" the mosque with Muslim blood, and turned it into a palace and horse stables. The Dome became a church before being reconverted by the Ayyubid caliphate.

Their Muslim recapturing is still a rallying cry for Islamophobes and radical Islamists alike.

But for most Muslims, al-Aqsa represents something more funda-mental to their faith. Having been to the holy land as a trader, the Prophet revered Christ and wished to bring a similar message of grace and peace to fellow Arabs. The Kaaba in Mecca itself was a pagan tem-ple. Exiled to Medina, Muhammad oriented the direction of prayer, or *qibla*, of the world's first mosque toward the holy city of monotheism. He instructed his first followers to bow in the same direction as their Jewish brethren, toward a giant exposed rock on the Temple Mount known as the Foundation Stone. The embrace of Judeo-Christian landmarks and beliefs proves that Islam has always been a "Western religion."

Decades after the Prophet's death, the first Muslim empire erected the Dome to enshrine the jagged rock, but it remains Judaism's most sacred site, the stone from which Earth itself was created and on which Abraham offered his son to God. Scholarly Muslims would see no issue with these beliefs, but common ground was insufficient for those who deem Muslims unworthy stewards.

Al-Aqsa plaza has been a target of bomb plots and state-sanctioned aggression. Since 2000, the Islamic body overseeing the compound has banned non-Muslims from entering the site's mosques, including the Dome of the Rock. Hardly a month goes by that Jewish pilgrims don't storm al-Aqsa, sometimes by the hundreds and aided by armed forces. And for a moment, I thought I was about to witness another raid. The chatter of tourists suddenly dimmed as I crossed the compound. I fol-lowed their gaze to a group of Israeli officers with assault rifles at the ready. They encircled a smaller group of Orthodox Jews, apparently so afraid of random acts of violence they required two guards per person. Palestinian shopkeepers standing on the compound periphery shook their heads in silence.

I found my travel mate outside the Dome's bronze open doors arguing with security refusing him entrance.

"Sir," he pleaded, "I've read the Quran. I respect Islam."

Israeli authorities had allowed him onto the compound with a cursory glance, but he was now in East Jerusalem, under Palestinian rules, and the same first impression kept him outside the building. "I am sorry," said the security guard, shaking his head. "It is only open to Muslims."

My colleague looked at me to vouch for him. "Salamu alaykum," I said to the guard, who stepped aside for me to enter.

There you have it: with a simple greeting of wishing someone peace, I'm Muslim yet again. I shot Spencer a rare smug expression of brown privilege. (Karma caught up to me a few hours later with yet another rigorous airport screening.) I removed my shoes and walked across the crimson carpet, immediately drawn to the intricate fence surrounding the Foundation Stone.

I encircled the sacred stone until I reached a fissure that Crusaders had widened to carve out a passageway to a cave—the Well of Souls, the Holy of Holies, the supposed centre of the Earth. History thumped beneath my feet as I descended the steps—paved with marble by Christians, recarpeted by Muslims. Around me, a man and woman prayed toward a marble niche demarking the qibla. A few others sat against the jagged walls, thumbing rosaries as they whispered Allah's ninety-nine qualities.

At its most basic definition, a mosque is wherever Muslims gather for communal prayers. They may be small-town trailers, like the one from my childhood, urban storefronts, luxurious museums, or literal caves, like the one in which Muhammad established a religion of 2 billion adherents. Though the Well of Souls might be the world's tiniest mosque, its Christian-Judeo-Muslim shrines and violent history tell an epic story, one so pervasive that we can sum it up as the clash of civilizations without further explanation.

The story is understood when a Canadian prime minister proposes a "Barbaric Cultural Practices" hotline, when an American president says "Islam hates us," and when Quebec and two dozen US states try banning sharia, as if it had the might to overturn their constitutions.

It's the underlying narrative that provokes white supremacist and Islamist terrorism equally. It is the story understood by the disenfranchised recruited by radical Islamists, promising a sense of belonging, and urging followers to spill blood in the streets. The story Muslim leaders draw from when they call people to riot over a cartoon and when they ban nonbelievers from entering holy sites.

It's shameful that only Muslims, or pseudo-Muslims like me, can enjoy the tranquility of the Dome of the Rock today. After entering the cave, my instinct was to appreciate the ancient sanctuary alongside visitors sitting on the floor. But I suddenly remembered the religious protocol of making two rounds of prayer upon entering a mosque. Scared of being called out for it, I found a spot at the foot of one of the rectangular stalls embroidered into the carpet. I straightened my back and prepared to pray, but there was a problem: I'd never learned how.

I tried to remember the order of the movements I mimicked as a child. I watched other worshippers through the corners of my eyes, but everyone prayed at their own pace. Eventually, though, the words came to me. I cupped my hands behind my ears and whispered something I never thought I'd hear myself say again: "Allahu akbar." I clasped my hands, and "al-Fatiha," the only prayer I ever committed to memory, came rushing back to mind. I repeated it as I knelt, stood, and bowed.

When my head touched the rug, the scripture vanished from my mind. A sudden genuine urge to pray for something real replaced it. *To what* didn't matter, only that it be for something. Looking back between my legs, I saw a woman my mother's age sitting against the stone wall with a little girl. She whispered something to the kid that made them both smile. Not a concern among them. I closed my eyes and thought about my own daughter. Janae and I had picked out her name almost a decade prior, so by then, Noe Delilah felt as real as any member of my family. Should Noe ever want to join her grandparents at a mosque or attend one alone when she was older, I prayed she'd have an expression like that. Not a worry in the world.

Islam Interrupted
Mesquita Salvador
(Salvador, Brazil)

*V*isitors to the state of Bahia had described it to me as Brazil's Black Mecca. I understood that four out of five Baianos identify as Black or mixed race and that northeast Brazil was the birthplace of capoeira and samba (popularized in Rio de Janeiro by freed people after abolition). Still, the moniker didn't do it justice. In the capital, Salvador, I was treated to a sumptuous show of Africana unrivalled by Atlanta, Kingston, or other cultural capitals. Touristy shops sold African textiles, folk art, and beauty products. Women donned colourful head wraps without pretension. On every commercial street, gowned women peddled *acarajé*, a greasy black bean bun introduced by enslaved ancestors five centuries prior.

The charms of Salvador's polychromatic old town were almost enough to forget I was standing on the site of the New World's first slave market, that I was admiring the same beautiful harbour that ruined the lives of 1.7 million people, approximately a third of Brazil's enslaved Africans and a sixth of all transatlantic slaves. As the closest point to Africa, northeastern Brazil physically gestures toward the continent like an outreached hand. In Bahia, though, the continental drift feels like it happened yesterday.

If Bahia is the West's "Black Mecca," then November is its figu-rative Ramadan. During the first three weeks of Novembro Negro, TV networks fire up their pro-Black content, and art collectives unveil new works. More recently, tourism campaigns have begun to tempt travellers to Bahia as the next best thing to a West African getaway.

Novembro Negro crescendos with an annual march on Black Awareness Day. On November 20, 2019, I joined a large procession of Baianos for the fortieth annual march across the historical centre. "Come on! Why aren't you marching with us?" one particularly in-tense man shouted at bystanders. "Come out here and join the fight."

He turned to me. "They're scared of us."

"Why?" I asked, with help of a hired translator.

"Because there's a lot of us and we're putting up a fight like our ancestors," he replied.

Brazilians embrace their identity as a racial democracy as passion-ately, and self-deceptively, as Canadians embrace multiculturalism and Americans libertarianism. That identity is every bit rooted in Brazilian racial integration as it is propaganda. Even the former national an-them, written one year after abolition, contains the lyrics, "We cannot believe that in another age Slaves there were in so noble a country." It's the opinion of many right-wing Brazilians, including President Jair Bolsonaro, that Blacks are owed nothing for the wrongs of slavery. After all, most Brazilians have some African ancestry, or so goes the excuse.

The tall and muscular activist, wearing a white linen outfit, began to list all their struggles to me—favelas, femicide, police brutality, ho-mophobia. He stopped only because blaring reggae drowned him out. For two hours, the mood bounced between pronouncements of pain and pride, anger and joy. A fake bullet wound between the eyes of a boy on my right, street peddlers hawking wine and toys on my left.

A prominent feminist in pan-African colours led the parade from atop an idling truck. "We are the city with the biggest Black popula-tion outside of Africa, and we're still fighting for equality," she shouted into a microphone. Congolese might bristle at this oft-repeated claim, as most Afro-Brazilians might appear to them to be whites. Regardless, they feel connected to the Black power movement because, despite representing a national majority, they suffer anti-Black racism. Plastered on shirts and signs were the faces of Brazilian resistance icons such as Marielle Franco, a Black feminist politician assassinated months before the 2018 election, and global civil rights icons such as Nelson Mandela and Mumia Abu-Jamal.

Organizers of the demonstration appointed Jamal, an American activist and writer on death row since 1982, as their annual honouree. As far as I could tell, he was the closest thing to a Muslim symbol. A typical Black Lives Matter demonstration in Canada would have many hijabs and knitted caps, but I spied not one amid the West African wraps and Rasta beanies. The last national census counted thirty-five thousand Muslims in a population of 212 million citizens. That's comparable to the ummah of a typical Toronto suburb. Even the highest estimate of half a million Brazilian Muslims, unreliably based on self-reporting from leaders of 150 mosques, amounts to one-quarter of 1 percent of the populace.

Most Brazilian Muslims are Arabs living in southeastern cosmopolitan cities, including dozens of relatives from both sides of my family tree. My ancestors have been migrating to São Paulo since before my parents were born. Seven million Brazilians have Lebanese ancestry, more than the population of Lebanon itself, but they're as homogeneously Christian as the rest of Brazil. When I told my cousins about my visit, and why, their reactions quickly went from enthused to confused.

My friend Sandro, an Afro-Brazilian immigrant, and his wife, a journalist who worked in Brazil for years, were also surprised when I asked them for leads back in Canada. It was almost as if I'd suggested flying to South America to write about hockey. Curiously, though, Sandro did recall how his father disapproved of pork. "When I was very young, my dad once mentioned we are not supposed to eat pork because it's dirty," Sandro suddenly remembered. "I had no idea what he was trying to say. Maybe it was passed down from Islam without his knowledge."

If my objective was finding traces of Islamic culture, we could

have gone to any old city in Mesoamerica. Iberian colonizers proliferated Moorish culture through architecture and language. Why else
would Spaniards have named *California* after Calafia (*Khalifa* in Arabic), a fictional Black queen who led a Muslim army? She symbolized
the West before Europeans "tamed" her. South Americans speak Arabized Latin (the Spanish *ojalá* or *oxalá* in Portuguese, which means an
emphatic "hopefully," derived from *insh'Allah*). They designed their
most beloved landmarks in Moorish revivalist fashion; a resurrected
medieval Moor would probably mistake the Alamo for a mosque.

I was interested in the absence of Islam, and why. Muslims were
more than a visible minority when Brazil's first constitution was
drafted in 1824. They were an influential group of free and enslaved
teachers, preachers, and freedom fighters.

When most Brazilians call Salvador "the Black Mecca," they're unaware of the metaphor's literal essence. Not two centuries ago, the
city had numerous private mosques inside huts, rented rooms, and
the homes of imams whose freedom was sometimes purchased by a
congregation. Thousands of enslaved, faithful Muslims resided in the
city. They studied Quran, sewed religious garments, and sold Arabic
amulets at the risk of punishment. They planned for a better future together, and, in 1835, they chose one of the holiest nights on the Islamic
calendar to rise up.

Six hundred armed Africans—the equivalent of more than twenty
thousand Salvador residents today—swarmed the municipal palace
like warriors in white battle dress. Known as the Malê, a catchall for
Muslims, their rebellion, it has been argued, was the first jihad ever
attempted in the West. But even if it meets one of many definitions of
the word *jihad*, as a holy war justified by Islamic law, then it was certainly not the first. More important, the Muslims who organized it had
no intention of establishing a caliphate, as is often wrongly presumed
about jihad. This struggle was multiethnic and multifaith, as much an
insurgency as a war of independence.

The so-called Malê leveraged Islam for a unified resistance fifty years
before pan-Islamism emerged as a coherent anticolonial idea abroad
and more than a century before the movement had sway. Though

police deftly put down the Malê revolt, it forced whites to admit they were on borrowed time and accelerated abolition. What's more, it's one of the best-documented slave uprisings, with scores of written testimonies and confiscated religious objects preserved in archives.

Why, then, did the revolt, like so many other chronicles of the New World's first Muslims, end up in the ash heap of history?

A few days before attending Black Awareness Day events, I interviewed Latin America's preeminent historian of transatlantic slavery. João José Reis's book *Slave Rebellion in Brazil* rescued the Malê revolt from the dustbin in 1986. Its English translation inspired a series of books dedicated to rediscovering Greater America's lost Islamic history.

The slight and well-groomed professor invited me into his high-rise apartment decorated with designer furniture, arresting photography by his daughter, and African and Indigenous artworks. We wasted little time on small talk and jumped right into the topic of how early Muslims fostered their faith in harsh conditions and to what extent Europeans tried to prevent them. In 1522, after Wolof sugar planters turned their machetes on their masters, what would become known as the New World's first rebellion, the Spanish Kingdom declared one of many bans against transporting "slaves suspected of Islamic leanings." Over the centuries, Wolof, Hausa, Fulani, Yoruba, and other significantly "Malê" ethnicities were unfavourably regarded as plucky, literate, and erudite, while Islam itself still kept an adversarial role in Christian history and psychology. Considering how important the Crusades, Inquisition, and Reconquista were to defining the "clash of civilizations," I would have thought that Europeans would try harder to keep Islam, that most barbaric and viral ideology, off their new lawn.

"Why would slavers traffic Muslims in spite of being advised against it?" I asked.

"The Reconquista was a Spanish thing," the professor said, with some annoyance for my conflation of Latin American history. "The Portuguese had expelled the Moorish Muslims one hundred years before Grenada. There was antipathy, but the Moors never got a stronghold of the Portuguese part of Iberia. Portugal was its own thing and Spain was its own thing and Brazil, as of 1822 (independence), was a third thing. The vast majority of the slave traders were Brazilian-born Portuguese subjects."

In other words, time did what time does: it made people stupid. Brazilians didn't know Arabic from hieroglyphics, never mind a Muslim from a practitioner of Orixá (the native Yoruban faith central to many Western Black religions). Sometimes they might spot Muslims in their white garments, sitting around a sheet laid for God's metaphysical presence, chanting in a singular, hallowed voice. Sufism, that mystical strain of Islam still prominent in West Africa, probably looked pagan to the white elite who tolerated Black religions just enough to sow divisions between adherents.

There was a period of secularizing in nineteenth-century Brazil that turned their focus toward capitalism. After Europe abandoned free Haiti, the Portuguese colony (and eventual Brazilian monarchy) absorbed the island's lucrative sugar industry to become the world's top exporter. As the closest point between East and West, Brazilians acquired slaves easily. Sugar money made them even more in demand and affordable, to the point that even some slaves had slaves.

"That was the big wave of Muslims," explained Reis. The high demand for slaves had coincided with the fall of Hausaland, a liberal Muslim empire, and the start of a theocracy ruled by Fulani fundamentalists in Central Africa. Their caliphate spread west to Nigeria, where they captured and sold another wave of Yoruba Muslims to Brazilian slavers. In a short period, Bahian plantations saw an influx of Muslim prisoners of war—former soldiers, priests, and royals of glorious kingdoms.

Though the Malê were initially unpopular with fellow slaves, who sometimes found them prudish and arrogant, their written culture, global membership, and prestige won them converts. The growing Muslim membership would have been missed by most Brazilians, who presumed Malê owed their intellect to "foreign blood" (if they could distinguish Malê at all). In fact, Islam spread to West Africa largely by peaceful traders, teachers, and preachers. It was easier, though, to

think Blacks were conquered by Arabs than to fathom them as cosmopolitan scholars, poets, students of twenty-five thousand schools, or
hajjis who'd seen more of the world as pilgrims than most settlers saw
in a lifetime. Among them were students of Quran who'd memorized
an entire tome on the rules of civility, slavery, warfare, and when one
justifies or negates the other.

I wondered if that factored into the rebellion? Sharia prohibits
abuse, neglect, and overworking of slaves. It also permits slaves to own
property, marry, raise families, and take legal action if these rights are
violated.

I asked Professor Reis, Were Muslims rising up against the bar-
barity of their bondage as much as the bondage itself? Would their
Muslim slavers have sold them to Westerners had they known the
wickedness of the Middle Passage? "It's a myth that Muslims abhorred
slavery more than non-Muslims," he said. "The slave trade and slavery
was a natural thing of the world. They all participated. It was not a
problem."

The sentiment bothered me. To normalize the Atlantic slave trade,
to me, doesn't sound far off from something then presidential candidate Jair Bolsonaro had said to delegitimize affirmative action: "The
Portuguese didn't even step foot in Africa. The Blacks themselves
turned over the slaves." Could they really have imagined such an in-
dustrialized system of slavery that routinely worked people to death?
Would they have sold their enemies to the West had they known that
they'd be packed into a ship basement for months, surrounded by sea-
sickness, cholera, and corpses? Maybe. But to say it was "not a problem," as Reis had, and to assume that a Black slave owner, Malê or no,
having survived this uniquely cruel bondage, would then maintain the
status quo sounded patently like denial.

It reminded me of how I used to self-justify the Arab slave trade
to free myself of cultural guilt. Arab Muslim imperialists globalized
the sub-Saharan African slave trade, starting in the seventh century.
The Umayyad caliphate's East African incursion established the sub-
Saharan slave routes that gradually expanded across continents and
dramatically darkened the shade of most human chattel. From 650 to

1600, Arab slavers bought and sold 7 million Africans, mostly women, and continued trading well into the twentieth century. Some Libyans are trading sub-Saharan Africans right now. That *ab'd*, the Arabic equivalent of "negro," translates to "slave" proves how interwoven these ideas still are in my culture.

How I wish I'd known that *ab'd* was a slur when my younger self used it in conversations with my relatives. During the few times I took Quran classes with a tutor, the religious figures who captured my attention most were ex-slaves promoted to leadership by the Prophet himself. As I perceived the lessons, the Messenger of God liberated subjects from bondage. In reality, Muhammad only tried to entice their liberty with rewards. Perhaps Muhammad saw the industry as one might see Wall Street: a necessary evil too big to fail. At best, it could be regulated.

Apologists have argued that Muhammad believed his reformations would indirectly lead to abolition. Instead, they became part of an infallible legal framework that grew the slave economy. To meet the demands of the expanding empire, his successors and subsequent Arab nations are responsible for selling about 9.5 million sub-Saharan Africans into bondage, not far from the 12.5 million sold to Greater America (1.8 million of whom died in the passage). Their visibility has been erased by miscegenation, integration, revisionism, and time.

I used to buy the postracial myth of my ancestors' history. Muslims are, by miles, the most diverse religious community in the West. But that does not shield them from anti-Blackness. In a sense, Muslims and Brazilians are alike in that many of them believe they're living out a postracial fantasy.

To relive the Malê revolt, Reis suggested I take a walking tour of the old city with his former student and fellow professor, Carlos Francisco da Silva Jr. The young scholar picked me up on the morning of Black Awareness Day in his nice SUV. "Some people assume I stole my car," he said. "Once, police stopped me to ask my wife if she was okay."

"Is she Black?" I asked.

He laughed. "No. That's *why* they wanted to see if she's okay." Da Silva is technically mixed race. In West Africa, locals regarded him as "white," yet in Brazil, he embodies the glib idiom: if you don't know whether someone is Black, ask the police.

He drove downtown and led me to the bottom of a main street sloping down from the original government palace. "The conspiracy was plotted here, in one of these houses," he said, pointing to a row of low-rise apartments above mundane shops. From the vantage point of this wide three-point intersection, the rebels had multiple escape routes and clear paths to the halls of power. "This is why I believe the Malê's military background had a big part in the revolt. It was so strategic."

Save for the palace behind us at the top of the hill, not a piece of 1835 still existed within our purview. I tried to imagine the January 25 uprising unfolding within the current scene, picturing dozens of freed and enslaved Africans in the basement of the current cell phone store. They wore white robes and Yoruba amulets, each one containing a scroll with a short prayer or promise of victory. They'd just broken their fasts, and for many, it would be their last Ramadan meal. They knew that not all six hundred men would survive the battle at dawn, but they had faith in God that their families, at least, would soon re-build Bahia as a pan-African nation. Faith had already brought them together in the home of their teacher, Manoel, and helped various Muslim tribes and allies. As Sufis, whose doctrine and rituals empha-size divine presence, they may have even felt God in the room. God had showed them a sign when a Catholic festival fell on *Lailat al-Qadr*, the Night of Power, which commemorates Prophet Muhammad's first revelation. In a few hours, virtually all white Baianos would be celebrating at a cathedral far away, clearing the government district to become their battleground.

Suddenly there's a banging on neighbouring building doors as mil-itary guards attempt to break down the entrances. They've received separate tips from African wives who feared their husbands' insurgency would lead to mass execution. As patrolmen close in on Manoel's home, the rebels decide to act then, hours before their planned attack.

Da Silva took over my imagination as he described the scene of fifty rebels pouring out of the present-day cell phone store with swords and a few guns. "According to the reports, they shouted, 'Death to soldiers,'" he explained. They followed Islamic rules of engagement, insofar as they only attacked police and guards (the "soldiers"), avoided injuring noncombatants, and resisted destroying homes.

We climbed the hill, following in the footsteps of the rebels as they awoke sleeping infantrymen on their way to the municipal palace. After chasing police off the first battlefront, the Malê planned to free a religious leader jailed in the basement of city hall. "They had soldiers from both sides attacking them with guns, but they could only do close combat," said da Silva. The tables quickly turned against them in the battle's second movement. The third, fourth, and fifth skirmishes were deadlier. Eventually the Malê were walking into bullets.

"All in all, the rebellion was five hours," da Silva explained, back in the car. He drove to the lower city and pulled over to the side of an industrial road with a slight view of the sea. He appeared reflective as he described the dozens of rebels killed or who drowned while escaping back into that awful harbour. "The Malê revolt opens a window to understand the lives and expectations under bondage," he said. "It tells a story of resistance and organisation in the African diaspora." I asked if there was anything permanent commemorating their heroism. There wasn't. "Public interest in these stories ends on page two of Brazilian history," he said.

That was starting to change, thanks to the ways pop culture, local politics, and Vidas Negras Important (Black Lives Matter) were tapping the mythic power of the Malê as part of a broader Black power movement. The previous night, a miniseries about the Muslim revolt of 1835 premiered. Other tributes have come by way of Malê-themed samba school performances and drumming groups. Several works of fiction have paid homage to folk heroine Luisa Mahin, who supposedly aided the rebellion by smuggling Arabic messages inside her street food.

A physical memorial is underway. In 2019, Salvador city councilwoman Marta Rodrigues successfully advocated to rename a metro station under renovation after the Malê. We spotted the council-woman a few hours later in the annual demonstration, a scarf with pan-African–coloured stripes draped over her shoulders. "We want to give visibility to these heroes and heroines," Rodrigues said of plans for the station and a monument honouring Mahin and other heroes of the rebellion. "It was an important revolt, but Brazilians don't know how to tell this story and how it happened; how it gave us the persistence to fight; what it represents for us today."

What *does* it represent to them today? At every chance, I asked this question of Brazilians Black, brown, and white; protestors, taxi drivers, and first cousins; Muslims and not. "All I know is the Malê were mad about *something*, and they were protesting against *something*," said an Uber driver's activist friend. (Not knowing the first thing about the revolt, she texted him mid-drive.) My only cousin even vaguely aware of the revolt thought Malê were an ethnic tribe, not her coreligionists.

There hadn't appeared to be much effect on public consciousness, but out in the march, many demonstrators were well aware of the revolt—maybe even too aware. Several of them falsely believed that Zumbi dos Palmares, the warrior king of a rogue ex-slave colony and whose 1695 execution is honoured on Black Awareness Day, was one of the Malê. Others lit up at the very mention of the semi-fictional Luisa Mahin, whose name also appeared on uniforms worn by teenagers representing a female empowerment program. The girls crowded around Zumbi's statue for a photo-op with Olívia Santana, a charismatic politician who was running to become Salvador's first Black woman mayor.

I spotted Santana while her supporters clamoured to speak with her. The state deputy greeted me with a customary kiss and pushed back her box braids to hear my questions over the noise.

"What's the importance of the Malê to the Black power movement?" I asked.

Santana said the Malê were an inspiration to the Black population for absolute freedom, which helped open the pathway to liberation. Too often, she said, Brazilian history touts white abolitionists as democratic heroes, when in fact the original abolitionists were Black rebels.

Santana knew the Malê were Muslim, not an ethnicity. I asked if that was of historical importance. She shook her head. No. "Only in the aspect of freedom of religion and resisting intolerance against African religions." After a period of peace, followers of non-Christian faiths have noted a surge in threats and harassment. That same Black history month in Bahia, a Candomblé temple had mysteriously burned. Whether it is Allah or the Yoruba god Ogun the Malê worshipped, she seemed to argue, what matters is that today's non-Christians can relate.

Her dismissal surprised me. Much like Muslims in the Western world, the Black diaspora knows what it's like to be associated with society's ills, to be burdened by dehumanizing policies and treated with suspicion, and to walk the world all too aware of the stereotypes that precede you. Since Bolsonaro started campaigning, Brazil's barely visible Muslim population has also reported an unprecedented level of racism. Much of it is stirred up by evangelicals inside his base. He has not specifically targeted Muslims, but need not in order for Muslims to be casualties of his anti-immigrant rhetoric. Anti-Blackness is deeper rooted than Western Islamophobia, but the two are not unrelated and sometimes intersect.

The crackdown on Muslims after the Malê revolt pushed everything remotely Islamic into hiding. Catholic elites saw it as an impediment to indoctrination. The church relatively tolerated Candomblé, which today has 2 million adherents worldwide, because it syncretized with Christianity. So did Islam, of course, self-evident in the Quran's continuity with the New Testament, including the belief that Jesus was a miracle-performing messiah set to return on Judgment Day. Christian theology and culture is inherent in Islam's origins, but this made Islam more of a competitive threat.

The stricter practices of Muslims and their tendency to isolate further hindered their cultural continuity. Islamic fashion and Arabic literature faded with the banishment of mosques and Muslim preachers. What few believers held on to Muslim culture past the point of emancipation, in 1888, did not do so openly or pass it on to another generation. As it eroded from society, it vanished from memory, leaving only residue. Islam's remaining traces in Black communities are the white sacred clothes and ablutions of Afro-Brazilian faiths, some derivative words, and, possibly, the Candomblé practice of greeting someone with a hand over one's heart. Islam is now as camouflaged in Caribbean and Brazilian religions as it is in the Portuguese language and architecture.

Black Islam escaped dormancy only with a modest conversion movement in the 1990s. One of the first mosques to cater to new believers was Centro Cultural Islâmico da Bahia in Salvador. I went to the green residential building better known as Mesquita Salvador one Friday morning to interview its imam about why the faith found appeal in a dominantly Catholic, but increasingly evangelical, nation.

Abdul Hameed Ahmad, the imam known as *shaykh* (preacher) Ahmad, watched for me and my translator from the second-storey balcony and buzzed us in. Doors led to separate chambers of the cinder-block building, the male-only section prayer hall at the front, the smaller female section in the back, and his personal abode up a flight of stairs. We entered through the front and followed his voice up a spiral staircase to his office.

Shaykh Ahmad sported a white goatee and wore loose layman's clothes over his tall, brawny body. He had a serene lilt and thick Nigerian accent. Ahmad never heard the anachronistic term *Malê* until meeting a billionaire Lebanese Brazilian recruited to help resurrect their spirit in Bahia with the opening of the mosque in the early nineties. The rediscovery of national Muslim history, thanks to João José Reis's research, overlapped with a Muslim propagation movement, thanks to enriched Gulf Arab states. The São Paulo businessman received large sums from the United Arab Emirates to establish mosques for converts scattered around the country.

Shaykh Ahmad seemed like the perfect imam for Salvador's growing ummah. He is ethnic Yoruban. His parents were the first in his family to convert to Islam from the traditional polytheist faith infused in Candomblé. He understands what it means to live in multicultural and multifaith societies. But he's also a University of Madinah alumnus, so Brazilian culture poses serious challenges to his orthodox views.

"When he first asked me, I told him I wasn't interested. Nigeria was healthy at the time—stable economy and good education—and all I knew about Brazil was Carla Perez, a pop star that seemed to be half-naked all the time," recalled Ahmad. At the same time, though, the shaykh was struggling to break old habits of Nigerian Muslims. His ultraconservative education put him at odds with Sufi African practices. Brazilians would be a clean slate. He decided to try it out.

Shaykh Ahmad was not wrong to fear Western hedonism. If anything, he'd underestimated it. Shaykh Ahmad arrived in February at the height of Carnival. In his eyes, every woman appeared to be "quasi-naked." He immediately told his associates "this isn't for me," but they guilted him into trying it for a year. Gradually Bahia grew on him. "Everything was similar to my country. The customs, the food, the happy, generous people." More than anything, the nascent *jamaat*, or congregation, was desperate for leadership.

Many white converts are enticed by the romance of Moorish history. For Black and mixed-race Brazilians, though, the appeal is practical. It answers moral questions and promises domestic stability. "The parents in Black communities aren't bringing the kids up together," said the shaykh. "Islam says you must have a base education in the home, which depends on the parents. This is what we're trying to teach our brothers and sisters—that marriage isn't just a program for a wedding but the whole moral compass of your family." A possible ancestral connection through the story of the Malê can make it personal; however, undoing the legacy and trauma of slavery has more sway. Perhaps the greatest difference between Arab and European slave trades is that the former encouraged slaves to have traditional families, while the latter usually prohibited it. Denying them this institution still has consequences for their progeny.

Shaykh Ahmad politely asked to pause our conversation to prepare his afternoon sermon. He delivered it an hour later, a speech about the importance of family values, mutual respect, and education. He wore a yellow-threaded black robe and white turban with a long tail draped over his shoulder and sat on the rug next to a regal throne. It was the only ornate thing in an otherwise humble room, ventilated by wide-open doors.

About thirty men and women filled the prayer hall. They were strikingly diverse not just for the city but for any other Western mosque. Salvador's demographics predicted an all-Black congregation, but about half the jamaat might fall into the categories of white or mixed race. I'd soon learn that several of them were immigrants and foreign students, but if I had tried to guess who based on wardrobe alone, I would have been wrong. Some Brazilians dressed more African than actual Africans. Altogether, they depicted the fabled racial democracy that both Brazil and Islam covet but rarely achieve.

This, the shaykh later explained, was by design. A decade ago, a representative of the Nation of Islam paid him a visit in the hopes that he would adopt and promote their Black nationalist agenda. The effort was part of a larger attempt to make up for dwindling US membership in South America and the Caribbean. As Ahmad tells it, the American offered him all sorts of material and financial incentives, including a promise to prop him up as a public figure on a media channel the Black nationalist group planned for the region. In return, said Ahmad, the Nation group asked him to kick out non-Blacks. The shaykh refused. "I told them, 'If you want to help us, you're more than welcome, but this doesn't work in tandem with me because Islam is for everyone.'"

Ahmad doesn't deny the existence of racism in the Brazilian ummah. São Paulo is home to one of South America's oldest and most stunning mosques, and yet Black Muslims in the megacity felt so unwelcome that they formed one of their own. Nigerian British author Habeeb Akande's book *Illuminating the Blackness: Blacks and African Muslims in Brazil* reports Afro women in the mosque feeling ignored by Afro men, whom he concluded leveraged their religious membership to pursue white brides. It's a complicated reality, but one that Shaykh Ahmad tries to address with the Quran's stance on racial equality. Say what you want of the orthodox Sunni Islam he prescribes, it has pushed the modern ummah closer to Muhammad's postracial vision.

I met some congregants upstairs over cookies and tea. We talked about what brought them to Islam, or Brazil, or both. The natural-born Muslims were drawn across oceans by universities, while the natural-born Brazilians were drawn to make *shahada*, the Muslim proclamation, by a mix of traditional family values and countercul- ture. Two young women stood out in matching ill-fitted hijabs and slit designer jeans. Juliana Alexandre and Alíce Barreto told me they were not Muslims but undergraduates studying ethnography at a local university. Alíce was researching how the Malê revolt is taught in early childhood education, and Juliana, local Islam in general.

I talked to Juliana and Alíce about their early findings. Ten years after a federal law mandated lessons on Afro-Brazilian history, the stu- dents found little mention of the Malê's religion in any curriculum. "There was no content in books," said Alíce, speaking from personal experience. "It was all material I learned in university." She was sur- prised to learn about Muslim history sleeping under her feet and just as surprised to learn about a mosque in her hometown.

"I didn't believe that Islam could exist in the Western world," said Juliana. "I already had an affinity for the religion. I believe Islam is more than what 'they' say it is, what 'they' tell us, and what 'they' film. Truth is, I already looked for a mosque since I was young, but I didn't know about the Islamic centre. This was my chance to learn about the reli- gion."

"Are you going to convert?" Alíce asked. I sensed that Alíce had wanted to ask her friend this question for a while.

"I'm thinking about it. I haven't decided yet, but in virtue, it would be this totally radical change of habits."

"What sort of habits do you want to change?" I asked.

"I don't want to change the way I dress," she said with a laugh.

"And also—the boyfriend," Alíce quipped.

"That's not it," Juliana said demurely. "I want to change my per- spective on the world." Islam, she believed, offered a global view—not just where you're from but your place within the world—and validated the humanity of all. "I'm interested in its social equality. I believe this is different from the other religions." In Brazil, she said, colour classifies you into a social position. She felt "mechanized" to look for a better system.

Until meeting the young students, I had not seen any evidence that the religion of the Malê rebels held much significance for Brazilians—neither the believers in mosques nor the nonbelievers at protests. But Juliana made me reconsider that. From one class, she'd become interested enough in the potential faith of her ancestors to maybe one day become a believer. If public awareness is only beginning, how many converts might come out of public school, postsecondaries, and popular culture?

Of course, this was exactly what the designers of the New Christian World feared could happen. It's why kings tried to literally ban Islam from the Americas. When it was too late, they tried to ban it from sight. And when they lost control, they tried to ban it from minds.

But time has shown that those efforts have also failed. Now we know that Muslims have played a role in shaping the New World for as long as any post-Columbian American faith. If Islam was in the not-too-distant cultures of many of the slaves and enslavers, then Islamic history is also American history.

Branches to early Muslims may be broken and lost, but their cultural influences are strong and discoverable if we know what to look for. Our continent isn't as Christian as we think.

Purification
Calcutta No. 1 Masjid
(Calcutta Settlement, Trinidad and Tobago)

*W*hen foreign journalists travel to Trinidad for a story about the Caribbean nation's Muslims, it's usually with one question in mind: How did an island of barely a million people become a bigger exporter of ISIS loyalists than possibly the United States and Canada combined? Between 130 and 250 Trinidadians—as many as one in 450 Muslims—joined the former caliphate. This dubious distinction has eclipsed other things that the country's 112,000 Muslims would rather be known for.

The Republic of Trinidad and Tobago appointed the first Muslim head of a Western state in 1987, President Noor Hassanali, a man admired as that rare scandal-free politician in a borderline narco state. It was also the first Western country to declare a public holiday for Eid al-Fitr (the last day of Ramadan). Muslims are so evenly stitched into the social fabric that few Trinidadians know, or probably care, that Islam is the faith of famous soca musicians, sports heroes, and entrepreneurs. "But the narrative is ISIS and Muslim gangs," said Jalaludin Khan, my on-the-ground assistant.

Khan, a cultural heritage expert, promised to guide me to the oldest mosques in the Western Hemisphere, where a unique Muslim practice emerged from a British social experiment. The indentured Indian labourers, who first arrived aboard the *Fatel Razack* ("Victory of Allah the Provider") in 1845, came from a variety of castes, sects, and former kingdoms that would have barely intermingled before the Crown sent them to save their postabolition plantations from economic ruin. Cut off from formal religious authority for generations, these Indians (the term "South Asian," though geographically and politically correct, is uncommon in the Caribbean) aggregated Sunni, Shia, Sufi, Sikh, and Hindu thought into a unique Muslim culture.

I hoped to find the seeds of Indo-Caribbean Islam at historic mosques in Iere Village and Calcutta Settlement, each of them built by two of the 221 surviving passengers aboard the maiden voyage, as well as Port of Spain's first mosque, which was cofounded by Jalaludin's grandfather.

Despite my working with a respected consultant, historians and caretakers were wary of my arrival. "They want to know, *What are your real intentions?*" Jalaludin explained, as our driver navigated Port of Spain's morning rush hour. *"Are you with some state agency? Or someone with a specific narrative?"* Recently, a *National Geographic* documentary series approached community leaders with requests like mine, only to blindside them with questions about radicals and self-styled Muslim gangs like "Unruly ISIS."

That was not my focus, I assured him. I was, however, intrigued by the racial divide amongst Afro- and Indo-Muslims. Trinidadian Muslims share a language, nationality, holy book, and, for the most part, Sunni orthodoxy, yet their mosques are more segregated than the island itself, which has developed with a near-even split of Blacks in the north and brown people in the south. Was this by accident or design? To find out, I scheduled interviews with leaders of mosques across the racial and theological spectrum, including an imam who opens his door to gangsters, in hopes of helping turn their lives around, and Yasin Abu Bakr, the leader of Jamaat al-Muslimeen, a militant group responsible for another unfortunate national title: the only Islamist coup attempted in the Western world.

On July 27, 1990, Jamaat al-Muslimeen launched an insurrection when it stormed parliament and took every elected member hostage, including a wounded prime minister. Another unit seized a state television station. Abu Bakr declared the government of Trinidad and Tobago overthrown live on air, but he failed to win enough civilian support to make up for his vastly outnumbered militants. Parliament was recaptured after three days and twenty-four deaths. In the fallout, Black Muslims were stigmatized as "radicals." Though their delegitimization has faded with reconciliation and time, Black and mixed-race Muslims report being held back from religious leadership positions.

Before hitting the highway, we made an unannounced visit to Port of Spain's historic mosque. It's one of dozens of mosques overseen by ASJA (an Urdu acronym that roughly translates to "Volunteers of the Prophet's Customs"). ASJA is the largest Islamic organization in the country, overseeing eighty-plus mosques, schools, and centres. Jalaludin's family left ASJA for a more progressive network long before he was born, and his attempts to secure access before we arrived went ignored. As he repeatedly knocked on the entrance, I took in the impressive Indian architecture and *kalasha*-style domes more reminiscent of Hindu temples.

Just as we prepared to turn back, the door swung open. A mufti wearing a white gown and turban stood in the entrance. His smile nearly outsized his bushy white mane streaked with red dye. He looked overjoyed, as if expecting us all week. Behind him in the lobby, three men in near-identical uniforms shared his ebullience. I spied more men sleeping on thin mattresses in the prayer hall. None but the mufti spoke English. In a thick South Asian accent, he insisted we join them for a cup of tea.

"Is that the imam?" I asked Jalaludin as we removed our shoes.

He shook his head. "Tablighi Jamaat. Missionaries from Pakistan."

Known as the "Muslim Jehovah's Witnesses" on account of their politeness and persistence, Tablighi are apolitical reformists who believe that religious propagation is core to salvation. Led by a trained scholar, this particular group had been travelling the Caribbean islands for three months, relying on the charity of strangers for shelter. I'd only encountered Muslim missionaries once before and wouldn't have identified them had they not first misidentified my lumberjack beard as a religious symbol instead of a fashion trend.

I assumed there wasn't a need for foreign missionaries on an island with substantial Muslim demographics and infrastructure. Trinidad has one hundred and forty mosques, two Muslim television stations, and a satellite campus of Darul Uloom, India's most prestigious Muslim seminary. But, in fact, that's why Tablighi are so common in Trinidad. Unlike traditional missionaries, their goal is "correction," not conversion. They encourage incremental self-improvement for stated believers, from observing daily prayers at home to observing them at mosque, from studying Quran to leading Quran studies.

The only thing to surprise Jalaludin about our encounter was the venue. ASJA presents itself as a steward of Islam as it was practised by the indentured forefathers. Whether that's true is debatable, but in preserving Indo-Islamic rituals, ASJA resists the homogenizing force of fundamentalists, and thus has long been hostile toward Tablighi. Of course, Tablighi themselves are not ultraorthodox as a rule—any sincere Muslim man can join a mission—but Tablighi usually are fundamentalists for three reasons: first, it takes some zeal to leave behind your work and family for a six-month voluntary mission; second, a significant number of missionaries are from the Islamic Republic of Pakistan, where sharia is constitutionally enshrined with overwhelming public support; and third, the movement's origins itself:

Tablighi Jamaat is a pacifist offshoot of Deobandism, an Indian revivalist movement that aims to purify Islam by returning to the ways of the Prophet and his disciples, right down to the red dye in their beards and hemmed robes. (Muhammad used the former to conceal grey hairs and encouraged it for Muslims to differentiate themselves from Christians and Jews, who once forbade hair dye. As for the hem of their bottoms, it was most likely to prevent tracking sand through the mosque.)

So why were they there in a venue known to keep Tablighi missionaries at bay? On our way back to the car, Jalaludin noted a peculiar change to the sign. In fresh paint, it read "Jama Masjid 1361–1362," just as it had for as long as he could remember, but ASJA's logo was missing. It was clear that an ideological coup had occurred inside one of the country's most important houses of worship without many noticing.

My aides explained that since shoring up on the island in the late 1960s, missionaries have nudged the islands' Muslims toward "pure Islam." As many as two-fifths of Trinidad's Muslims are what you might call fundamentalists, according to a 1999 study titled "The Influence of Indian Islam in Fundamentalist Trends in Trinidad and Tobago." That's remarkable considering their Western lineage.

The tug-of-war between traditionalists and ultraorthodox fundamentalists came into sharp focus later that morning in Calcutta Settlement. The island's first Indian colony is home to the Americas' oldest mosque. Plainly known as Calcutta No. 1 Masjid, it was founded in 1863 by a *Fatel Razack* passenger and has been associated with ASJA for as long as it has been an association.

Its founders formed ASJA in the 1930s to shield against progressive practices gaining popularity. For the latter half of its existence, ASJA has protected its traditions from the political centre, pushed there by Deobandism and Salafism (a.k.a. Wahhabism), a slightly more austere, harsher, and ethnocentric Arabian movement. (Both have their quietists and extremists, and neither ideology causes one to take up terrorism any more than evangelicalism causes one to shoot an abortionist or Hasidism causes one to terrorize Palestinians.) Calcutta No. 1 Masjid became a focal point of religious politics in the 1960s. That's when its imam, a dynamic twenty-five-year-old, tried to reinvigorate the mosque with lessons he learned from travelling preachers.

"So you had a situation where they threw him out," explained Manwar Ali, a TV preacher and Calcutta resident whose recollection of the mosque stretched back to a time when worshippers tied donkeys outside. Sitting on an artful rug between Ali and the mosque's imam, I noticed the imam shoot Ali a disapproving look.

"They asked him to step down," Ali clarified. "He was trying to break away from what was traditional Indo-Pakistan practices that are associated *with* Islam, but when people started to study it and ask,

'What did Allah say on this practice?'—they found nothing. Let me give an example, without disrespecting the imam. Some people celebrate the Prophet's birthday, but other people will not."

"I want to be clear," the imam said, adjusting his kufi. "We still celebrate it here. At this masjid, we do celebration."

And so began a debate over what to do on Prophet Muhammad's birthday, whether to celebrate less important holidays, and the proper way to memorialize the dead. It went on like this until the imam had to run out the door, late for another appointment. I soon learned that Ali was no longer a member of the congregation. In fact, he'd been physically barred in 1990, locked outside on his way to Friday prayer, along with others whose doctrine had become too rigid. He'd been welcomed back for this interview, but we weren't alone for long until one of the caretakers forced us out. From the rearview mirror, I watched her lock the gate on Ali yet again.

We soared south toward the old cane fields that were first toiled by enslaved Africans, then indentured Indians, who eventually came to own the land and establish their colonies. Minarets, crosses, and Hindu temple towers dotted the highway as testaments to Trinidad's religious potency. In addition to the world's three largest religions, the Orisha faith and Shouter Baptism thrive on the island.

We arrived in Iere Village, one of the oldest Indian settlements, and awaited our hosts in the shade of a small mosque topped by three domes, like unstemmed red onions. I used the moment to ask Jalaludin about the presence of fundamentalist Islam. Its rigour surprised me. I was in the land of soca and Carnival, "liming and wining," a country set to decriminalize cannabis within months. Puritanism seemed anachronistic in the Caribbean, whether ultraorthodox Islam or charismatic Christianity, another growing movement. The most generous foreign media portrayed Trinidad's ISIS problem as a symptom of Black ghetto malaise, as miseducated and misled converts manipulated into violent acts by international insurgents.

"Are the majority of extremists poor or middle class?" I asked.

"To be honest, it's both," said Jalaludin. Several privileged Indians and Blacks joined the extremists. Engineers, professional athletes, and an Indian school principal from Calcutta Settlement. Entire families had uprooted themselves for the "promised land" in Syria and Iraq. "The majority might be the poor and converts, but some are older persons. I don't think the Muslim community has dealt with extremism at a national level. They just hope it will go away. But it needs ventilation. Why *do* young men want to join gangs or go to Syria?" he asked rhetorically. The various Islamic organizations, like ASJA or the Trinidad Muslim League, are so focused on running their schools and mosques that they're missing the bigger picture. "They need to work with other Muslim communities to understand the roots of the problem."

It seemed so obvious that the primary root was fundamentalism, which was clearly not exclusive to one racial demographic. ISIS's particular brand of extremism is based on a romantic obsession with re-enacting early caliphates. Propaganda *might* stir hatred, poverty and alienation *might* incentivize the move, and gang violence *might* desensitize a person to genocide, but puritanical thought precedes all.

Trinidad's fundamentalist phenomenon caught on with the 1960s arrival of Eastern missionaries, but they did not arrive out of the blue. They were summoned by a sequence of events that played out for a century prior. We were standing in the shadow of the opening scene.

Iere Village mosque belonged to the Ahmadiyya Muslim Community, a South Asian movement formed as a progressive antidote to nineteenth-century fundamentalism. Ahmadi doctrine believes in the inherent right of women to education and economic freedom, and does not believe in the militaristic definition of jihad. But its liberal reforms are overshadowed by Mirza Ghulam Ahmad's claim that he was Prophet Muhammad's successor. An offshoot downgraded his prophethood to messiah soon after his 1908 death, while the dominant branch insists that Ahmad is merely a minor prophet. Yet anti-Ahmadi persecution never softened. If there's a Muslim community most burdened by purifiers and fumigators, it's this one.

Despite Ahmadis's marginality (1 percent of continental American Muslims, if that, and much less globally), no movement was more influential to early American Islam, and, ipso facto, modern American Islam. Ahmadiyya inspired the Nation of Islam, fractured Detroit's first mosque, forced laypeople everywhere to interrogate the basis of their beliefs, and sparked a crusade to define Muslimness in the West, sometimes violently.

The mosque's caretaker, Shamalar Mohammed, arrived with her friend Iezora Edwards, a University of West Indies professor and congregant. "This is our humble *masjid*," said Shamalar, opening the French doors to a homey prayer room sunlit by wrap-around bay windows. We sat together on the green carpet. I immediately understood this to be a liberal place by its gender barrier; a sheer curtain with partial view of the pulpit divided the men's and women's sections equally.

"You think we could ever do this at an ASJA mosque?" I asked Shamalar and Edwards. "Sit on the floor of the men's section, men and women, your hair uncovered?"

Shamalar laughed. "They're gonna show me out." Still, the fact that there *was* a barrier, erected in 2010, proved that even the most liberal jamaat had embraced some of the patriarchal conservatism of the same ideologues who labelled them apostates. Were my hosts in Pakistan or Saudi Arabia, they could be punished for calling this mosque a "mosque," for even calling themselves Muslims. The sanctioning of Ahmadi persecution by those countries in the 1970s made them into *kafirs*—the Islamist version of Untouchables. "There was an international Ahmadiyya convention here," said Edwards, "and there was a bombing. Nobody died, but it was a huge thing."

In 1983, she explained, the Ahmadiyya held an international convention on the island. The order, which had recently relocated to London from Pakistan for safety, considered the Caribbean its American nucleus. A significant portion of Muslim Caribbean people, including about a fifth of all Muslim Surinamese, belonged to the sect. But the torrent of Eastern fatwas had begun to wear them out. Under pressure from members who worried for their children's safety, congregations began severing ties with the Ahmadiyya. Convention organizers hoped it would reactivate the movement, but the result was the opposite.

"All what I remember," said Shamalar in rich Trini patois, "is we went to the function in our nice Indian clothes because we have people from away. Sit down and you just have *boom, boom, boom*. Everybody just say 'run!'" Shamalar was eleven years old, searching the crowd for her father, Iere Village's imam, who was in the front row. It left a mark on him forever, she said, but her family never disavowed Ahmadi theology. To this day, Iere Village mosque is a family operation and primarily a family congregation. But for Edwards, a teenager at the convention, the bombing forced her parents to change mosques. They joined the town's ASJA congregation for peace of mind while quietly holding liberal values at home.

Not long after the bombing, an Ahmadiyya missionary was assassinated in front of his child, marking the end of the order's active mission. They turned inward, but mainstream organizations still dehumanize them. The local Darul Uloom seminary officially designates them kafirs, and the liberal Trinidad Muslim League, once the Ahmadiyya face of Trinidad, painstakingly revised its foundational story as a misadventure with heretics. The Othering is even at the state level. "Whenever you have representations to the government for policy-making regarding Muslims in Trinidad, the Ahmadiyya is left out and not recognized as 'official,'" said Edwards.

"What would your father think of this infighting?" I asked Shamalar.

"He likes united," she said. "No pulling and tugging. We want everybody to unite, whatever religion it is."

It was different in the 1850s, when Shamalar's great-great-grandfather arrived on the small island. For three-quarters of a century, Indians practised Islam with little more than the prayer rugs and literature they came with. Despite their ethnic and sectarian diversity, they'd become instant brothers and sisters in the Caribbean. The lines between them gradually blurred into a new form of Indo-Caribbean Islam, celebrated annually during Hosay. The now obscure parade combined a sombre Shiite holiday (*Ashura*) with Pakistani passion plays, Diwali lanterns, Sikh martial arts, and all the joie de vivre of Carnival.

Unity only made sense in the face of white Christian supremacy that tried to stamp out Hosay and other public Muslim and Hindu celebrations. Muslims remained ambivalent to their differences as they pooled their funds to move from bamboo sheds to wattle-and-daub buildings. "Once you were Muslim, it didn't matter what sect you were," said Edwards. "Structured religion had not started yet."

Edwards's ancestors became more conscious of their differences with the chance discovery of an Afghani mufti amongst the indentured. Upon hearing about the young and multilingual polymath, her great-great-grandfather helped raise funds to buy him out of his indentureship contract and elevate him to the status of *khalifa* (caliph). The ummah empowered him to adjudicate and interpret Islamic law for the whole island. "That's when they became more conscious of the Shia-Sunni difference," she said.

Caribbean borders loosened after indentureship was abolished, giving way to Muslim missionaries who brought new literature and energy. A prominent local mosque had requested a permanent imam from the London publishers of a glossy English Islamic magazine, unaware that they'd contacted the European headquarters of the Ahmadiyya. Trinidad's khalifa, acting as gatekeeper, welcomed another trained mufti for the growing community. He didn't think anything odd about the missionary beyond maybe his noble attire, likely because he didn't think about Ahmadis at all. The sect had not existed when his indentureship began. But he became suspicious and concerned after the finer details of the mufti's creed began trickling through his sermons. Most shocking was the belief that Jesus died rather unceremoniously in India, and that the movement's founder will instead return to signal the End of Days.

The mufti was chased back to Punjab around 1923, where, according to the khalifa, he realized the error of his ways and accepted Sunni Islam. He would've remained a historical footnote had he not inspired a young intellectual to follow him to Delhi, train as a scholar across the Muslim world, and return to the Caribbean with a mission to tune Muslim practices for Western values. Throughout the 1930s, Trinidadian-born mufti encouraged worshippers to read English Qurans (sacrilege to those who believe in its immaculate Arabic design) and condemned fathers who denied their daughters an education. He encouraged women to join religious boards, form new committees, and give lectures on Islam. On occasion, Trinidadian women gave Friday sermons to mixed congregations, seventy years before such landmarks would be documented in North America and Europe.

"We grew up understanding there were ideological differences, but there was a kind of broad-mindedness that I really appreciated," said Edwards, who returned to her childhood mosque years later because the ASJA imam refused to sanction her marriage to a non-Muslim. More recently, that same imam who wouldn't recognize her marriage also joined Edwards at the Iere Village congregation, following a fundamentalist coup of his mosque.

Many of those early twentieth-century reforms have been undone but they precipitated the state of Islam in Trinidad today. They fractured the ummah into liberal, centrist, and conservative organizations and locked them in a battle for influence and authority. The bombing is only the most extreme example of the polarization that followed. Another was the stigmatizing of Hosay, now barely kept alive by a couple of Shia families and their secular supporters. But for Edwards and Shamalar, the most lasting effect has been on Muslim women's bodies and spaces. "I grew up merrily along without hijab, and then there was a realization of Muslim consciousness," Edwards said. "Missionaries started coming quite a lot. My grandfather would host their lectures at his house. It was knowledge for Muslims. It was enlightenment."

What the women described to me isn't a local phenomenon. Most of my life I'd believed hijabs were as fixed to the faith as the Quran, only to learn that the word *hijab* never once refers to wardrobe in scripture. Rather it meant a literal or metaphysical partition, not unlike in mosques (which also didn't exist in the time of the Prophet). It entered the sartorial lexicon in my parents' lifetime, and the style we often call *the* hijab became fashionable only in mine. I was in disbelief when my mother explained to me that the garment once had many names for Muslim women's many styles and languages. When she was a girl, it was more a marker of old age than piety, and it was *not* compulsory in public opinion.

The idea that she should veil for God and for the betterment of society reached her after moving to Canada, ironically. It was part of an Islamist philosophy that every aspect of life—from wardrobe to politics—is enriched with Islamic doctrine. For decades, Arab autocrats and monarchs worked to quiet Islamism with violent repercussions, but the humiliation of losing the Arab-Israeli wars left many Muslims to see secularism as a failed experiment. And so this once unpopular and suppressed philosophy became more appealing with each generation. It's why my mother only dabbled in being "hijabi" for a couple of years in the 1980s, but my sister has been one since she was twenty and my nieces since their midteens. Each will have her own motivation, and, in the end, none are our business any more than why some pious men roll up their pant cuffs and dye their beards red, but all are rooted in the same political events that heightened Muslim consciousness.

The Islamic revival, sometimes called the Islamic awakening, is more pronounced in Trinidad for a few reasons. For one, the blending of Islamic sects had always created confusion over what is and isn't orthodoxy. It also intersected with the partitioning of Pakistan and India, which raised both Hindu and Muslim consciousness amongst the Indian diaspora. Islamism also fit comfortably within the Caribbean's anticolonial independence and Black power movements.

But another reason for Trinidad's Islamist streak is a decades-long formal arrangement between ASJA and the World Muslim League, Saudi Arabia's powerful nongovernmental organization for religious propagation. Buoyed by oil wealth, the kingdom seized on the anticolonial moment in order to spread Islamism through philanthropy. Over the course of four decades, the organization has poured tens of billions of dollars into 3,750 Islamic projects in Muslim-minority countries. ASJA was its first Western partner. In 1962, ASJA, hoping to crush its Ahmadiyya adversaries with conservative Sunni preachers, asked the World Muslim League to finance a missionary guild that would receive and distribute Eastern-educated teachers from island to island. Unlike Tablighi missionaries, these scholars were highly political and skilled orators capable of finding audiences outside mosques. It became quickly apparent that their "purer" teachings would endanger the dearly held traditions of Indo-Caribbeans. Even more threatening to ASJA's male leadership was the conversion of hundreds of Afro-Caribbeans, who crossed the colour line, entered their mosques, and were now speaking with their daughters.

ASJA quickly pulled out of the guild, but it was too late to close Pandora's box. Word of Trinidad's fertile ground spread to other foreign preachers who hoped to make a name for themselves, and one such preacher, Dr. Abdel Salaam, an Egyptian scholar, found an excellent student in a former police officer disillusioned by government corruption. That student would take the Islamic oath known simply as *shahada*—"There is no god but God, and Muhammad is the messenger"—at the guild's outpost in Port of Spain before reinventing himself as Yasin Abu Bakr, the architect of the 1990 coup.

The insurrection resulted in 114 arrests but zero convictions. The group's cofounder and leader was freed in 1992 after the courts forced Trinidad to honour an amnesty agreement it had signed with Abu Bakr's Jamaat al-Muslimeen for a peaceful surrender. He immediately went to work rebuilding Jamaat with $2 million ($500,000 in US dollars today) paid out by the government for unlawful property damage. (The $15 million, USD$3.8 million, owed by Jamaat to the state for the militia's damage to public buildings remains to be seen.) So to understand tensions between African and Indian Muslims and the long-term impact of the missionary guild, I went to see "the imam" himself.

Jamaat al-Muslimeen's compound looked active and well kept from a distance. Freshly painted cinder-block residences, palm trees, and landscaping gave it the appearance of a three-star resort along a busy road, a few kilometres north of Parliament. An investigative journalist I hired to assist me entered the compound through an open gate as easily as one drives through a car wash.

In fact, we had done just that. Yasin Abu Bakr's son runs Jamaat's auto shop and wash, and successfully so by the looks of it. A bright, octagonal mosque in the centre also kept an impressive appearance, but the same could not be said of surrounding ventures. A kindergarten and primary school operated by the imam's wives appeared sparsely attended. The secondary school has shuttered for a lack of finances, as has the printshop, woodshop, and canteen. There were plans for a supermarket inside an unfinished warehouse that I found hard to believe. Al-Muslimeen was far from its heyday.

After its members were released, al-Muslimeen fractured into two main camps. The "straight edge" members followed cofounder Bilal Abdullah, a university-educated lieutenant who compelled all members to work legal jobs or attend school. Abu Bakr, who had led the insurrection, formed the other camp, focusing on fast growth. As one imam and former member told me, "The major leaders had left and the 'bad boys' started to fall in after the coup." Because Jamaat al-Muslimeen held a position of accepting bad apples, he said, "their image changed in the eyes of the nation, and things went south real quick."

A senior aide escorted me to the imam's office, where we immediately hit a snag that almost precluded me from getting even one of my many questions answered.

"There must be some kind of reciprocity," said Abu Bakr, leaning comfortably to one side of a rolling chair. Wearing a loose West African–style top, he asked for $100 in exchange for his time. It would go to the group's school, he assured me. But what he called a donation, my government might call financing terrorism. More important, I called it a bribe. I'd never paid a source for their participation, and didn't plan to.

"I don't see where the conflict of ethics is," he said. "I do have some background as a journalist. I worked at the Canadian Broadcasting Corporation for six years in television production."

I'd heard conflicting stories about Bakr, the man born Lennox Philip—why the former police officer gave up his uniform, how he found Islam, and whether he found it in Trinidad, Canada, or Libya—but employee of the Canadian state broadcaster was a first.

I held fast to my journalistic values, but said I was willing to honour my Islamic values by making a $100 contribution to an independent charity as *zakat*.

"Zakat is an entirely different thing," he said, at once unimpressed and amused.

He was right. Zakat is a required 2.5 percent alms, and one of the Five Pillars of Islam. I had no idea what I was talking about.

"Are you Christian or Muslim?"

Would calling myself Muslim be lying? There's not one of the five pillars that I observe. My nearest belief to traditional monotheism is that nothing comes from nothing, hence there's got to be *something*. But I'd spent the week travelling from mosque to mosque and in each one praying, learning about Islam, and engaging in the culture. At the very least, I was as much Muslim as he was a former journalist.

"I'm Muslim," I said.

"You sure?"

This went on awhile. Finally, I reminded him that I was there to understand the history and evolution of Trinidad's ummah, and he could either speak to al-Muslimeen's impact or leave it to others to interpret.

"Before me, I don't know any Africans who are Muslims," he said. "With humility I say that I am the tree that all the others came from."

Despite old newspapers that claimed Abu Bakr discovered Islam in the 1970s while a student at Toronto's Ryerson University, multiple credible sources, not to mention the imam himself, told me that he'd converted earlier than that, inside a shed that once stood on this property.

Before Jamaat seized the land, it was headquarters of the missionary guild that ASJA had founded. There were plans for an Islamic community centre too, but they fell apart once ASJA severed ties with the guild and began campaigning against its own brainchild. Abu Bakr had no idea the land would one day become a battlefield, and that he would be the linchpin, when he started visiting the Egyptian scholar in 1969. The shaykh's physical features fascinated young Lennox, who was stunned to see more of himself in an Arab than expected. "When he removed his turban and showed me his hair, I realized he was an African," he recalled. "That was a bit of a shock to me. The Muslims who were here did not present that history to us."

He was fresh off the police force with plenty of free time, and the preacher was happy to fill it with lessons that appealed to the justice-seeking ex-cop. They discussed Egyptian race relations in depth and the struggle of Afro-Arabs that the Muslim Brotherhood promised to remedy.

Black converts like Abu Bakr found inspiration in Islam's nonracial egalitarianism but quickly learned it was more theory than practice. When converts suddenly appeared in mosques, said Abu Bakr, Indians panicked over their impurities. "They thought we would marry their daughters." That hysteria is still present; even amongst the growing mixed-race population, called "Dougla," Indian mothers are rare. "Of course, I broke that a long time ago, you know," Abu Bakr bragged. "I have two wives that are Indian."

He continued, "Jamaat al-Muslimeen means 'the Muslim community.' So we welcome everyone." In reality, few non-Blacks joined ranks. Those who did were ostracized. If family disavowment wasn't disincentive enough for most brown Muslims, then it was probably the core message of Black power. Imams Abu Bakr and Bilal Abdullah found inspiration in Muslim leaders who saw Islam as complementary to pan-Africanism, not the other way around. Libyan leader Moammar Gadhafi befriended them and financed their growing organization, providing al-Muslimeen with paramilitary training that would eventually serve them.

During the decade that led up to the revolt, al-Muslimeen had earned respect for "cleaning the streets" and whistle-blowing on corrupt officials assisting the drug trade. But popular support with working-class Blacks didn't inoculate al-Muslimeen from being routinely thwarted, disparaged, and scapegoated. Muslim elites blamed al-Muslimeen for the anti-Ahmadi terrorism, despite intelligence reports pointing to a sleeper cell of Jamaat ul-Fuqra terrorists, a US-Pakistani group informally linked to the Tablighi movement. The friction crescendoed after a land dispute that the government tried to settle by raiding and destroying al-Muslimeen's properties. To Abu Bakr, this was an act of war.

"So," I interjected, jumping ahead, "let's say the coup was successful; say you took over the government and became leader of Trinidad. What was your plan?"

He maintained that the plan was to hold an election in ninety days, so long as the military removed itself from al-Muslimeen's compound, as it was ordered to do by the courts. "So it was to have a new election, and not us introducing into society some Islamic government."

"There was no plan to govern by sharia?"

"No."

This has been a point of debate for nearly thirty years. If al-Muslimeen's own literature used the "Islamic code of warfare" to justify rebellion, then it's reasonable to think it would govern by other sharia tenets. But, then again, the Malê slaves also used Islamic warfare rules to organize a multifaith rebellion against the state of Bahia, and there's no evidence that their end game was a caliphate. Nothing about the imam suggested to me that he was a religious fundamentalist. His face was shaved. A well-worn English Quran sat atop a heap of mail. The courtyard was painted with the common Islamic crescent moon and star, which Salafist fanatics would deem to be a blasphemous innovation. His style of debate—not through a scriptural lens, but geopolitical and historical—made it abundantly clear that his Islamism wasn't so dogmatic.

It was a stark contrast to David "Buffy" Maillard, the lieutenant who chaperoned our interview and could very well succeed the eighty-year-old imam. The US-raised, mixed-race Trinidadian would be an unlikely leader, not in the least because he's white passing. Buffy is, by his own admittance, "the most fundamental and extreme person here."

Despite traces of an old-school hip-hop in his slang and chain necklace, the self-proclaimed reformed gangster doesn't listen to music, which he said God forbids. Following my interview with Abu Bakr, Buffy gave me a tour but implored me not to photograph him beside the crescent symbol. Again, forbidden. He allowed a cat to wander into the mosque, based on a hadith by a companion of the Prophet, known as "Father of the Kitten." But his beloved mother, the "best woman I ever met"? She was "burning in hell" because she was Christian.

When describing the imam to me, Buffy compared Abu Bakr to the Mujaddid, an imam sent by God to revitalize Islam at the turn of each century. "What he brought to the country was the purification of the dïn [faith]." In fact, the leader and lieutenant have had their ups

and downs since Buffy joined al-Muslimeen in 1992, shortly after Abu
Bakr earned his prison release, regrouped his loyalists, and began their
rebuild. "Men were pouring through the gates on *Jumah* [Friday] and
the whole place was covered with people," said Buffy, his black and
red gown billowing in the wind. "We had three to four hundred new
members every month, seventy-five to one-hundred shahada a week."
He said it was unsustainable and impossible to manage.

In the early 2000s, infighting over government projects intended
to uplift poor communities irreversibly ruptured al-Muslimeen. Since
then, some members and offshoots have been involved in Islamic extremism and gang violence.

Buffy also left the group briefly but soon returned, a self-styled
gang youth counsellor attempting to bring people back into the fold.
Al-Muslimeen, he said, isn't responsible for the inequities that drove
former members to act like mafia, but authorities disagree. Buffy and
the imam have been tried for extortion, conspiracy, and murder, and in
2011 Buffy was accused of plotting with others to assassinate the prime
minister. Due to lack of evidence, "witness memory loss," and hung
juries, charges were dropped against the twelve Trinidadians. (One
of them, Ashmead Choate, the Indian school principal from Calcutta
Settlement, became the Caribbean's most notorious ISIS recruiter and
later died fighting for the caliphate in Iraq.)

It made me incredibly uneasy to think of Buffy as a counsellor to
troubled youth. Religion alone isn't an antidote to street life, especially
one so devoid of mercy. I asked Buffy why *his* Islam was so harsh and
black-and-white.

"Islam *is* black-and-white," he barked back. "Islam is perfect. If you
don't believe that, you're not a Muslim, okay?"

I told him that his perspective worried me. The pursuit of perfec-
tion, or purity, primes Muslims for extremist groups that want to exploit
their good intentions. I argued that what begins as self-improvement
can transform into intolerance and eventually evil acts, as the definitions of jihad and kafir become flattened into, respectively, "war" and
"enemy."

Buffy shook his head at me. "It's the *perversion* of said purity that is to blame," he said. "I raised pit bulls for nineteen years. There are no bad pit bulls. They just have bad owners." In his analogy, ISIS leaders are malicious dog owners and their recruits hapless puppies. But this misses an essential point about pit bulls, and other domestic dogs, in general. They are modern human innovations. Pit bulls were bred generation by generation, each time selected for muscularity, jaw strength, and bite force. So, yes, extremists are bad trainers, but their recruits are preconditioned to accept a command for violence, and to maximize the damage they inflict.

———

My fascination with Trinidadian Islam began with a search for counterpoints to its bad rap, but my angle changed. After praying in half a dozen mosques across the social spectrum, it became impossible to ignore the truth. Muslim fundamentalism was more widespread than most Trinidadians would admit or allow themselves to believe. I even detected it in a Friday sermon at Trinidad Muslim League's flagship mosque with a large, progressive, and nondenominational congregation. Sitting near the front of the prayer hall, a single open chamber for both men and women, the impassioned imam segued from modelling the kindness of Muhammad to a call for men to copy the Prophet's wardrobe and "lift your pants above your ankles until midway."

It was benign and even refreshing to hear an imam fussing over male bodies for a change. And like most ultraorthodox principles, it derived from the noble aim to live out our lives as the Prophet and his disciples had. Nevertheless, it was a telltale sign of how comfortable the late Trinidadian president's own jamaat had become with ultraorthodox dogma.

When even the most liberal nonconformist group was preoccupied with defining "pure" Islam, it's not hard to see how such an environment might drive a fringe minority to radicalism in the name of self-improvement. On the long and shaky sliding scale of purity, a logical end point isn't wrestling with one's impurities but fumigating society of others'. It was inevitable, then, that I'd encounter this end point for myself.

On my last working day in Trinidad, I hired a driver to take me into Laventille, a notorious hilltop suburb of Port of Spain, not unlike a favela in Brazil, to meet Abdul Haaq. Also known as "Imam Sleepy," he was introduced to me by a Canadian who met the young, Black faith leader on a humanitarian mission. On the phone, the imam was open to speaking about his redemption in prison and reforming of gang youth with scripture.

He dropped me "a pin" on Google Maps to simplify directions to his mosque in a ghetto ironically named Beverly Hills. I was treated to a postcard view overlooking the coastal capital through my window, while a jumble of cement, wood, and corrugated steel blurred outside the driver's side. "I haven't been here in a long time," my driver said, as we wound our way up to the highest point of Laventille.

"How long?"

"Long time," he said, and nothing more. He parked beside a baby blue building. A zigzagging stairway led from the narrow road to the top storey. The construction was unfinished, but it was still the nicest building for a mile. A hand-painted sign was propped on the second-storey ledge. In Arabic and English it read: "Masjid Ul-Furqan." The name references the Quran's twenty-fifth chapter, "The Criterion," promising that all sins are forgivable when one repents, atones, and believes.

A goateed man in his early thirties walked onto the top of the landing from an open door. He wore rolled-up khakis and a white T-shirt printed with Islamic calligraphy. He appraised us from above before making his way down, stepping past flowers planted in paint buckets and a bench press as he approached me. He removed a well-chewed *sewak* twig from his mouth, introduced himself as Abdul Haaq, and invited me inside. My driver waited by his car.

I followed Imam Haaq up the precarious staircase into a spacious and attractive prayer room. A couple of guys stretched across an embellished rug, sleeping between fans blowing from opposite sides of

the hall. We sat against the far wall by a door that opened to nothing—
just a crippling downhill tumble.

Haaq assured me that my preconceived notions of Laventille are
media distortions. No doubt he's seen the worst of his community's
problems. He's often called on by Muslim neighbours to help resolve
issues since police often end up exacerbating them. One of his congregants was killed in a police raid, shot seven times at close range.
(He was unarmed; his mother watched.) "My purpose is to draw the
youth away from the gang culture. A person like me, I'm a leader.
I'm the imam. But they will make me into something I am not," he
said. "Being Black and Muslim, and living in areas like this, what they
consider 'crime infested,' makes me a target."

Perhaps sensing my nervousness, Haaq added, "A lot of people believe that you would just come here, and somebody would just come
with a truck like a madman and kill you. *For nothing.* That is what they
believe. But tourists come around here, maxi loads of white people
who drive around here, just to watch the view."

It's not just tourists either. Since the crime surge of the mid-2000s,
religious leaders have come to ghettoes seeking out lapsed Muslims
or delinquents who'd converted for all the wrong reasons. The most
recent were representatives of the Nation of Islam, trying to make
inroads after decades of dormancy, but the imam turned them away,
wanting nothing of their Black power screed. Islam should erase colour, not emphasize it.

His journey to Islam started the day he watched the city burn
during the 1990 insurrection. Haaq was six. He absorbed the excitement and optimism of adults around him, most of whom, like his
mother, migrated from St. Vincent and the Grenadines during the oil
boom. Once full of dreams, Laventille came to symbolize the ambivalence, neglect, and corruption that squandered Trinidad's fortune.
Maybe not down there, in Port of Spain's lowland, but up here, in areas
strained by indifference, Al-Muslimeen were heroes. When Haaq was
old enough to get around on his own, he started attending Abu Bakr's
Friday sermons. Haaq didn't care much for the overbearing political

messages, but he perked up whenever the imam referenced Quranic parables and warrior sagas. It appealed to the part of him that wished to study English in university if he could ever afford it.

One day, an Indian imam seeking out students in poor neighbourhoods invited Haaq and other youth to experience Jumah at a large mosque associated with Darul Uloom's seminary. There, teachers focused on applying the Prophet's teachings to daily life. Haaq earned a reputation as a quick study, and a few imams volunteered to tutor him. He'd never seen such kindness and interest shown to him before. "Once I'm interested in something, and I want to learn, I learn fast, soak in everything," said Haaq. "I never used to smile. Just that was my demeanour. But I used to smile when I get there in Darul Uloom," he said, flashing a chipped-tooth grin. As Haaq stayed like that for a beat, just grinning, his nickname, Sleepy, became suddenly apparent in his one half-closed eyelid.

Religion alone couldn't save him from the fate of so many young, Black men living in the deepest parts of Laventille. He pointed his chewing twig at a random steel roof in the distance, where his mother and uncle raised him with a stress on education and self-discipline. That's what got them out of the ghetto. But after she remarried, Haaq and his mom had a falling out over his abusive stepbrothers, and Haaq ended up back in Laventille.

In 2004, Haaq was caught with an illegal weapon and sentenced to two years in maximum security. There, he submerged himself in his Islamic studies, learning Quran and proper prayers. After the prison imam was released, Haaq took over his role, regularly leading inmates in weekly prayers. He delivered his first sermon on basic Islamic principles, such as cleanliness and knowledge seeking.

Back on the outside, he returned to his mentor, studying privately for five years, until opening Ul-Furqan. Now a husband and father of four, Haaq has earned a righteous reputation for guiding disadvantaged youth to Islam. Preachers eager to reach impressionable converts look to Ul-Furqan as a venue.

"We used to have Ashmead Choate," he said. "He came about three times."

My heart rate picked up on hearing the name. Ashmead Choate was one of Buffy's eleven other co-accused, the school principal responsible for recruiting fanatics to Iraq and then dying there in battle. A graduate of Islamic University of Madinah, Choate was infamously arrogant. He was known to preach that Muslims were at war with unbelievers, that anyone speaking against ISIS should be killed.

"What did you think of him?" I asked.

This time Haaq's smile gave me chills. "Oh, he was a knowledgeable fella. He know what he was coming with, and the thing with he, when he gave any *khutba* [Friday sermon], he used to watch me. In the whole place, the only person he looking at while he talking is me. I don't know why."

The ever perceptive imam detected my nerves again and began defending Choate and his recruits. "Man make their choice. All kind of people make choices. And on the Day of Judgment we will know who was right and who was wrong."

"You don't know for sure if he was right or wrong to go to Syria?"

"I believe that they have the evidences for making the hijrah," he said, referencing Muhammad and his early followers' flight from Mecca to Medina.

Haaq said he was neutral, but the romance of that term exemplified the very fantasy that radicals like Choate used to lure new members. I got the impression he knew more people who'd made "hijrah." Indeed, when I asked about the whereabouts of his longtime mentor, Haaq replied, "He leave, he went," and would not say more.

He'd encountered a spectrum of teachers over the years from so many schools of thought. There were Black nationalists, Salafi pacifists, affable Pakistani missionaries, and even ASJA members who came by with food on Ramadan. Why were these the brothers who showed Haaq "what Islam is"? I wondered.

"Them more knowledgeable than me. They study Islam," he explained. "Not to say these men backwards, not to say these men is tyrants, they're known to be upright men with regards to Islam, and they make a decision based on their evidences."

"Hearing about things ISIS has done," I said, "massacring the 'unbelievers,' the kafir, taking women as slaves, dehumanizing people who have a heart, who have families, who have a history, who have a life story, who have dreams, aspirations—it doesn't seem cruel to you? Doesn't seem morally wrong?"

"What about the Rohingya Muslims?" he asked defensively. Haaq graphically recounted horrors that he'd read had been done to them by radical Buddhists. "What about the Uyghur in China being put in concentration camps right now?"

"And what about the Muslims in my country, in Quebec, massacred in their mosque?" I snapped back. Did their slaughter and families' suffering cancel out the caliphate's atrocities? Of course not! Yet he argued that we shouldn't single out Muslim violence when the world was turning a blind eye to genocidal violence targeting Muslims. I agreed to a point, but not as a justification for retaliation, and certainly not retaliation against people in another part of the world who had nothing to do with the injustices.

After a deep breath, I tried another approach. "Yazidis are a minority, and they're already disadvantaged in the same way growing up in Laventille put you at a disadvantage. You don't feel what's been done to them is morally wrong?"

He repeated his stance that only God knows, but I couldn't drop it. It upset me that he could have black-and-white positions on music, alcohol, and gender mixing but was suddenly wishy-washy on the most fundamental of sins. "Your mother and uncle, they're not believers," I reminded him. "Wouldn't that bring you agony for a Muslim to do that to—"

"Of course!"

"So how do you remain neutral when your own mother could be one of *them*?" I asked, restraining myself from using the word he might use himself: *kafir*.

Haaq started to speak but fell silent. After five long seconds, he answered slowly—a comma between each phrase. "Based on how I grew up, based on the things that I see with my own eyes, and the life that I lived, I see a man who coming to take your life, and you could lose your life in the process, I have no feelings for he. But innocent people . . . I don't condone the killing of innocent people."

He didn't fully condemn his mentors or any of the thousands of Islamic State soldiers. He did, however, employ some critical thought to the caliphate's collapse. "Allah is the one who give and take, who does reward and punish. Perhaps these people are being punished." By his calculation, they must have been on the wrong side of Islam; otherwise God would have allowed the Islamic State to prosper.

I thanked him for his time and honesty and asked if I could make salat before leaving. "Go ahead," he said curtly. In the corner of my eye, I could see he'd turned his back toward me, holding on to the doorway, leaning forward as he watched over the world.

It wasn't until I turned my focus inward that I realized what I had just asked. I'd prayed more times in the last five days than I had in the last five years. There had been such an immediate assumption in Trinidad that I was an observant Muslim that by the end, I was beginning to think of myself as one. I felt compelled to pray, but why? Was it to calm my nerves or to prove my allegiance, acting as one might under the Islamic State whenever the *adhan*—the call to prayer—is sounded?

I started reciting the Fatiha. I whispered the opening line—*In the name of God, the most gracious, the most merciful*—and, for the first time, felt it in my bones. Understanding nothing else of the verse, I improvised a prayer for Abdul Haaq, speaking into the carpet, hoping my words would stick to the fibres. "Please, Allah," I whispered, "teach him to be merciful. Teach them all your mercy and tolerance."

It wasn't just a prayer for Imam Haaq's jamaat, but all of Trinidad's. They'd given dogma too much sway over their religious affairs. Fearing backlash from religious authorities—and each other—they've avoided confronting extremism that, over time, left hundreds of their kin dead, imprisoned, or in limbo. For decades, they've avoided making a choice: to tolerate puritanism at the risk of losing loved ones to extremism or to tolerate heresy at the risk of losing them to hell. But it's not too late. Both paths will call for prayer, but only one calls for collective action.

In Search of a Supreme Leader

Temple No. 1

(Chicago, Illinois)

$\mathcal{S}$ince Prophet Muhammad's death in 632, countless reformers have bent Islam to their will or consequently steered it in new directions. The history repeats a typical story: Muslims colonize a land and the natives absorb it to an extent. New beliefs rally into a resistance that conquers the elites, takes shelter, or disappears.

Some Old World cities are uniquely prone to schism. But in the New World, none are more volatile than Chicago, Illinois. The Chi offers a parallel story of Islam—fourteen centuries of ideological diversity sped up and packed into a one-century saga.

Soon after the first Ahmadiyya missionary arrived in the United States in the early twentieth century, the mufti relocated to the "Black Capital of America." According to historian Michael Gomez, author of *Black Crescent: The Experience and Legacy of African Muslims in the Americas*, Sadiq's message may have inspired a self-proclaimed prophet, Noble Drew Ali, whose hotly contested death spawned several more African American Muslim saviors. One of them was Nation of Islam founder Wallace Fard Muhammad, who amassed a modest number of followers in four years, then vanished without

a trace. This cleared a path for his protégé, Elijah Muhammad, to reform the Nation into the most influential Black American separatists
of the last half-century, until his rebellious son, Warith Deen Mohammed, overtook the Nation, dismantled and "Sunnified" it. (W. D. Mohammed then changed the spelling of his surname with an "e" and
"o," apparently to differentiate himself from his dad.)

Until the Immigration and Nationality Act of 1965, American
Islam was, as scholar Sherman Jackson wrote, "dominated by an indigenous black presence." They still comprise a fifth of the country's
5 million Muslims, which is astonishing considering there were so few
to begin with. Compared to enslaved people in Brazil and the Caribbean, only a fraction of those in British North America and the United
States were transported from Africa, about three hundred thousand in
total, of whom as many as one-third may have been Muslim based on
their origins. And yet no Black religion has been revived as fervently
in the United States, and without the benefit of continuity, no less.
Perhaps the intense Christianizing of African Americans is why Islam
resonated so strongly. It cohered with their Abrahamic faith, with the
added bonus of a possible ancestral connection and dissenting power.

The vigour of African American Muslim communities is attributed
to a handful of public figures: Master Wallace Fard, Elijah Muhammad, Malcolm X, Louis Farrakhan, and W. D. Mohammed. But what
about that first African American Muslim leader, that Chicago prophet
who planted the first seeds in the so-called Moorish Science Temple of
America? Noble Drew Ali's name is obscure even to Black Muslims,
and his practices may not even appear Muslim to them anyway. But
Ali was the first American to tailor Islam to the conditions of Black
people. In doing so, he precipitated everyone from Muhammad Ali
to Mahershala Ali and half a million other African American Muslim
converts.

Ironically, Noble Drew Ali denied his own Blackness until his last
breath, and beyond. Inside the slim archival folder on him kept by the
Chicago Public Library collection on African American history and
literature, I found a copy of his death certificate attached to a 1992 af-
fidavit to correct his recorded race from "American Black" to "Moorish

American." Efforts to make that change were unsuccessful, according to the official vital record that I purchased, but digital forgeries to the contrary are abundant on the internet.

I wasn't sure I'd even meet any self-identifying Moors when I flew to Chicago in June 2019 to investigate this all-but-dead religion. They seemed to only exist online, leaving behind digital crumb trails to support the notion that American descendants of African slaves are neither African American, negro, nor that God-forsaken B-word. "Black, according to science, means death," reads Ali's original pamphlet. They are "Moorish American," descendants of the greatest empire on Earth, even if they don't know it yet.

Most scholars identify Ali as one Timothy Drew, an orphaned North Carolinian who discovered Islam somewhere in the Northeast United States and founded the Moorish Science Temple sometime between 1913 and 1925. However, a new book by historian Jacob S. Dorman, *The Princess and the Prophet: The Secret History of Magic, Race, and Moorish Muslims in America*, says Ali was Walter Brister, a Broadway child star and enigmatic circus performer who faked his death and reinvented himself as a Muslim prophet in Chicago. "As the first Black child star on Broadway, and then the founder of the first Muslim mass movement in America, Walter Brister was incongruously both the forerunner of the blond tap-dancing cherub Shirley Temple and of the militant Black Nationalist icon Malcolm X," wrote the author.

Most people interested in Noble Drew Ali aren't academics, though. They tend to research him on YouTube, where they learn that Ali's revelations came to him on a trip to North Africa. There, Ali was stunned to learn that a high priest of Egyptian magic had identified him as the reincarnation of Jesus and all other prophets. The priest bestowed Ali with a lost section of the Quran, which Ali used to trace American "negros" to the Moorish empire.

The Moors had spread Islam to Europe—this is true. But according to the Holy Koran of the Moorish Science Temple of America, often called the *Circle 7*, the Moors also ruled the whole of western Africa and the Americas, and they still rule Morocco today. In other words, he and millions of other Americans were not negro but Indigenous

Moors, and thus exempt from American segregation laws, that is, as long as they had Moorish citizenship papers, which only Ali could notarize (for a small fee). Gradually the self-named supreme grand sheik appointed lesser grand sheiks to officiate tens of thousands of Moorish citizenship ceremonies across the Northeast.

The movement was both Black nationalism and denial; Ali's acolytes sincerely believed that they'd remain legally subhuman—three-fifths a citizen under the US Constitution—until proclaiming Moroccan nationality.

It's easy to see why his ideas connected a century ago amid peak levels of immigration and heightened ethnonationalism. Harder to see is why Americans today would embrace Ali's spiritual and nationalist beliefs.

Moorish Science was considered a dead religion until a crop of websites emerged in the last fifteen years, showing that it's extremely alive. Or, at least, extremely online. As my research of Moorish Science moved from scholarship to social media, I realized the internet was populated with high-ranking Moorish clergy. These "sheiks" and "sheikesses" don Moroccan-style headwear, maintain antiquated spelling and pronunciation of "Moslem" identity, and proselytize scripture that hasn't seen many eyes since the 1930s. I've now lost count of the various Moorish Temple leaders supposedly operating in virtually every North American big city—even in Edmonton, Alberta, my home.

The internet creates more space for fringe views, and the echo chamber accelerates them. But would I ever meet a Moslem IRL? It seemed more like cosplay to me—less a "movement" than an online community, like Flat Earthers and ASMR enthusiasts.

If Moorish Americans communed anywhere, it was in the city they call Mecca: Chicago—specifically, in Woodlawn and Gresham, South Side neighbourhoods where Moorish Science was briefly resurrected in the seventies and early eighties by the Almighty Black P. Stone Nation, a youth club turned Black empowerment group with criminal elements. Its leader, Jeff Fort, discovered the fringe faith in jail, and upon his release used the Moorish holy book, insignia, and Ottoman fashion to overhaul the Stones into a quasi-spiritual gang. He changed his name to Chief Malik (Arabic for "angel") and the group's name to El Rukn (Arabic for "the cornerstone"), which he ran like a cult, purging or hemorrhaging thousands of members.

Was it possible that some of his disciples still practiced Moorish Science? After Fort's imprisonment in the mid-eighties, the Rukns reverted back to the Black Stone Nation but never revived their spiritual aspects.

I hired Wilfred Spears, a street-smart researcher and media producer, to help me out. A "Stone" by birthright, Spears grew up in Gresham in the eighties and helped me understand where the Black Stone's community work ended and the criminality began. During our preliminary call, I asked him if he knew any Moorish Americans. To my surprise, he said, "Lot of guys call themselves Moors."

The day after I arrived in Chicago, Spears picked me up from my Airbnb in a Lamborghini Urus to meet the leader of the Moorish Science Temple of America at the historic Temple No. 1. At least, that's what Supreme Grand Sheik Kenu Umar Bey would have you believe.

I'd already uncovered two Temple No. 1s in Chicago, one in DC, and another in Atlanta. I eventually stopped counting at thirty, though only a handful offered an address, if they replied to my messages at all. Their websites and YouTube sermons focused more on proving their legitimacy to the throne. Umar Bey's apathy for Moorish politicking distinguished him from other supreme grand sheiks. His social media and online literature were more focused on Moorish history and constitutional rights.

As Spears drove us to Temple No. 1, I looked out my window at the action on East Seventy-Ninth, a tough street immortalized in raps by Kanye West and many others. Vandalism and shuttered stores aside, it was tamer than what my steady diet of hip-hop and twenty-four-hour news had led me to imagine. Spears reminded me that looks can be deceiving. Fox News might politicize it, rap might glamorize it, but Seventy-Ninth is no joke. People get shot in broad daylight every day.

And yet when I requested he stop at McDonald's for a bathroom break, Spears refused to pull over anywhere but a back alley. "You good, dawg," he said. "Nobody gonna fuck with you." On this side of America's most segregated metropolitan city, he explained, anyone as light-skinned as me is presumed police. Spears wanted to prove a point that pissing in a back alley was a privilege he did not possess. "Self-hate is crazy, bro," he said. "Muthafuckas trained to hate each other."

I hopped out of the car, relieved myself outside, and hopped back in unscathed. We arrived at Temple No. 1 five minutes later. A quiet middle-aged man wearing all red, from sneakers to fez, stood in front of the handsome old building, selling cups of ice and syrup to pass-ersby on a sweltering summer day. He introduced himself as the assistant to Supreme Grand Sheik Kenu Umar Bey, and invited me to wait inside while he summoned the chief.

The temple had the air of a Masonic Hall. Some ceiling tiles were painted with Moroccan five-point stars, while the walls were decorated with Islamic calligraphy, vintage photos, and an enlarged replica of the Divine Constitution of the Moorish American Nation, a set of bylaws that read more like doctrine or prophecy.

Umar Bey finally emerged from a doorway bordered by a collection of swords and hand tools. Youthful for a man in his early sixties, he wore light-blue jeans and a black fez. I had many questions for him, starting with why the internet was suddenly popping with Moorish literature. Had an obscure history simply stumbled into the internet age?

"We call it one of the Moorish hadith," he explained. "These are the sayings of the prophet Noble Drew Ali that in the year 2000 the Moors will come into their own." In other words, it was prophecy.

From what I'd deduced, growth began around 2005—the year YouTube was invented—but that's beside the point. I wanted to understand the motivations of Americans today—postsegregation, post–Voting Rights Act of 1965—to proclaim Moorish nationality, study the Moorish Constitution, and carry ID cards with Moroccan flags.

"Our nationality is our nature," he said with brewing intensity. "A rose is a rose and an apple is an apple. A Moor is a Moor, a Korean is a Korean, and a European is *not* white. You can forget that—that's a status. I'm not Black—that's the *status*."

I didn't get a lick of it, and yet there was something refreshing about his brand of identity politics, the emphasis of nationality over complexion. Race and colour are hardly windows into individual minds. One's cultural history is, at least, a good start.

But Moorish beliefs are still predicated on racist pseudoscience. In Ali's doctrine, our nationalities and tribes fall into two categories, "Asiatics" and "Europeans." The former, comprising Turks, Arabs, Asians, Africans, and American Indigenous—what we would today describe as people of colour—are natural Muslims prepared for this earth by God. The latter—what we would call white—invented Christianity in hopes of salvation.

"So where does that leave me?" I asked.

"I believe and I know for a fact that we have the same bloodline. Islam?"

This was the first of countless times he'd punctuate his speech with "Islam." Usually it had an upturned inflection, meaning "understand?" Other times, "Islam" was an affirmation like *amen*, but it was also a salutation and interjection. I got the hang of his creative *Islams* by the time he finished explaining our shared ancestry through ancient Moabites, though I wasn't any closer to understanding the genealogical science.

"If that's true," I said, "then my Lebanese ancestry means I'm an Asiatic European mix."

He was shocked by my self-debasement. "Why would you say that?"

I started to explain how this tiny continental passageway has been repeatedly conquered by Grecians, Romans, Armenians, Ottomans—

"I see your forehead," he interrupted.

"What?"

"You have a wide, flat forehead. You don't get that in a European. Your hair, it don't fall down, it stands up. You have a nose. You don't have a pencil. You have lips."

"I do have lips," I said with a laugh.

"I'm not trying to be funny, man! When you laugh, look, your cheeks go up. You don't smile, and your face go flat. You Asiatic—bottom line." I couldn't dispute his observations. Nobody had ever described my face so accurately. But my olive skin seemed like a solid indicator of some ethnic European ancestry.

I reasked my question with a more modern example of mixed heritage: my then one-year-old daughter. "If one of her parents is Asiatic and the other European, what's that make her?"

"What's your opinion?" asked Umar Bey. "She's European?"

"My daughter?"

"Your wife."

"Well, it's not an opinion. Her dad emigrated from the UK. Her mom, I dunno, she's pretty white."

He ignored my use of the term "white," which Moors loathe as much as "Black," and requested a picture of Janae. I pulled up her Instagram on my phone. The supreme grand sheik of the Moorish Science Temple of America quietly examined her blond hair, grey eyes, milky skin, and agreed: "She Europe." He handed back my phone. "She look like a sympathizer," he added, sounding optimistic.

What did it mean, then, for Umar Bey and me to be allied against Europeans while living amongst Europeans and sometimes breeding with Europeans? Truthfully, it was hard to make sense of his beliefs. I was more drawn to his personal relationship to the faith and what "proclaiming" his nationality had done for his self-esteem.

Umar Bey became a Moor in 1976, the year that Fort left prison as Chief Malik. Though he kept his story purposely vague, the sheik credited Chief Malik for his enlightenment. "I don't want to say it was like winning the lottery—that's materialistic. It was like saying, 'Wow, I got my skin back.'"

The mythology gave him a sense of ancestral glory. This was echoed later by one of his students, rapper King Zakir. "The power it had does something to you almost immediately," he told me. Discovering Moorish Science felt like uncovering a lost scroll about himself.

"There's so much propaganda that we don't know where we're from," said Zakir. "I knew I wasn't Black. I knew I wasn't African American."

The sense of history and self that was lost in the transatlantic slave trade might be the most difficult trauma to heal. Noble Drew Ali must have known that when he began to evangelize alternative history, encouraged ethnic fashion, and began to notarize Moorish ID cards. His genius was understanding that self-knowledge dignified a man or woman.

Ali was doubtlessly a bit of a hustler. And so was Umar Bey, however sincere his beliefs were. After showing off laminated endorsements of Moorish Science from President George W. Bush and Chicago mayor Rahm Emanuel, he tried to charge me fifty dollars for the interview. I instead let him overcharge me for a copy of the *Circle 7*.

At a restaurant later that night, I read the Moorish holy book with an eye for Muslim doctrine. As Jacob S. Dorman wrote in *The Princess and the Prophet*, "Ali's knowledge of Islam did not come from enslaved Muslim ancestors, but from images of Islam in popular entertainment such as circus magic." There's truth in that. Ali plucked from Orientalist tropes, and his knowledge of Islam did not come from enslaved Muslim ancestors, nor could it have. But it's overly simplistic to say there was nothing Islamic about Moorish Science.

I found conspicuous similarities between Moorish and Ahmadiyya revelations. In particular, the story of Jesus Christ surviving crucifixion, migrating to India, and dying of natural causes. The chapter was lifted from the *Aquarian Gospel* by an American Presbyterian pastor who claimed to be in possession of Jesus's "authentic" memoirs, but there's strong evidence that *Aquarian Gospel* borrowed from an English translation of *Jesus in India* by Mirza Ghulam Ahmad. Given that Noble Drew Ali had contact with Ahmadi missionaries in the 1920s, it's not a stretch to say that Ahmadi theology influenced Moorish Science as much as or more than Aquarianism, Kemeticism, Free Masonism, and Garveyism had. The most original feature of *Circle 7* was how it wove gospel, history, and geopolitics into a recognizable national identity.

I imagined what it would be like to receive this message for the first time. I tried in earnest to picture myself as a "Black" man born on a strange continent pulsating with intense immigration and religiosity, as a "negro" just one or two generations removed from slavery. I imagined my parents as southern refugees of white terrorism, myself as a survivor of the 1919 Chicago race riot. I walked around downtown after dinner, imagining it as it was in the Roaring Twenties, the chatter of Italian, Irish, Arabic, and Chinese languages surrounding me.

What would it be like to look into the eyes of these new Americans and know that to varying degrees, they all had more rights than me? I could see now how having a foreign nationality would feel like a superpower.

Ali was extremely controversial within his community. According to reports at the time, he built temples in four states, gained 12,000 followers, and amassed a hoard of cash before his power began to unravel in 1929. One of Ali's closest aides went rogue and split off with several followers, until a team of men killed him in a suspected hit. Detained with others for the murder, Ali was eventually released on bond and died weeks later.

The coroner listed tuberculosis and pulmonary hemorrhage as the cause of Ali's death. But some at his funeral speculated that he'd been murdered in retribution or had succumbed to internal trauma from police brutality.

Rumours aside, the police brutality appears true. The *Chicago Defender*, a historic African American newspaper, confirmed police abuse but also reported the fallen leader had scammed a fortune from his followers and had two wives, one of whom was a minor. These scandals challenged the efforts of acolytes to rebuild the temple, further complicated by fatal skirmishes between factions vying for control of Temple No. 1.

Still, the American prophet's message survived long enough for another Chicago leader to revive it half a century later. Like the prophet and his disciples, Jeff Fort, or Chief Malik, entangled Moorish

Islam in crime and paid the ultimate price. In 1986, the FBI staged a terrorism-for-hire sting that would appeal to Fort's Muslim religion. After catching him on tape speaking jealously of Libya's $5 million loan to the Nation of Islam, the feds sent informants pretending to be weapons dealers representing Moammar Gadhafi to entrap the El Rukn leadership. (Fort is now 34 years into a 168-year sentence. According to one former Rukn and current PhD scholar, Fort leads Friday prison prayers in the Sunni tradition and answers to the name Abdul Malik Ka'bah.)

Were these leaders martyrs or con men? The answer is yes. American institutions have sought to weaken Western Muslim establishments for as long as they've existed. But when those establishments are Afrocentric, those institutions seek to do more than weaken; they seek to destroy. Never was that truer than with the Nation of Islam.

It was founded in 1930 by Wallace Fard Muhammad, a Moorish castaway who claimed to possess Ali's reincarnated spirit before starting anew in Detroit. That's where he established the Nation of Islam's Temple No. 1, and purged his former prophet's mythology of all but a few core qualities, namely Islam, ethnic nationalism, and supreme leadership. The most dramatic ideological difference between Master Fard and Sheik Ali was not that Fard claimed to be God incarnate (though there was that). Rather it was his passionate embrace of African American identity in spite of much evidence that Fard himself was probably a Shiite immigrant from Central Asia.

Fard's run was about as strong and short-lived as Ali's. He mysteriously disappeared in 1934, but first anointed a prophet.

Elijah Muhammad (born Elijah Robert Poole) led the Nation into a new era with some modifications. A soft-spoken yet masterful orator, he made Black supremacy an ideological cornerstone, drawing strong distinctions between Black American Muslims and other Muslims, especially Arabs, whom he classified as white and worthy of suspicion. Muhammad celebrated African American excellence to the point of advocating for racial separation. Under his leadership, the Nation established businesses, a newspaper, and the Muhammad University of

Islam, a chain of K–12 academic Black schools. As a fundraising effort, they invented bean pie, a healthier alternative to soul food that's now imitated and sold by Black grocers across America.

The Nation's opposition to integration made for strange bedfellows. Muhammad infamously invited the leader of the American Nazi Party to address Muslims (it did not go well). According to *The Dead Are Arising: The Life of Malcolm X* by Pulitzer-winning journalist Les Payne and completed by his daughter Tamara Payne after Les's death, Muhammad went as far as sending Malcolm X to negotiate allyship with the Klan. Muhammad reportedly told his top spokesman, "We want what they want."

But Malcolm, University of Islam, and bean pie almost never existed. As soon as Elijah Muhammad took control of the Nation, threats to his life from Muslim adversaries, including his brother, forced him to constantly change location. When he wasn't on the run, he was in and out of prison on sentences arising from civil disobedience. It crushed the movement down to four hundred members. Only after reestablishing headquarters in Chicago in 1932 could Muhammad rebuild the Muslim movement. He was soon heading one of the Western world's fastest-growing religions, with an estimated half a million followers.

"The Honorable Elijah Muhammad gave us six words that sum up all of his teachings," Minister Michael Muhammad told me. "'Accept your own, and be yourself.'"

The minister met me at a Starbucks near the Nation's headquarters (a.k.a. Temple No. 2). I couldn't help but feel giddy connecting with an official member of the Nation of Islam.

Growing up in a town with more churches than traffic lights, the strongest Muslim voices I heard in popular culture were African Americans linked to the organization. In the sixth grade, we had to present a research report on anything of our choosing. My friend picked ghosts. The smart girl, sudden infant death syndrome. I chose Malcolm X (and for it I donned an African kufi I doubt the revolutionary would've appreciated). I was proud to share a faith with esteemed dissidents, artists, and athletes, with Kareem Abdul-Jabbar and Mike Tyson, with

Malcolm and Mumia Abu-Jamal, with Ice Cube and two-thirds of A Tribe Called Quest. No doubt the inspiration I found in these celebrities prolonged my faith by at least a few years. Even now, I feel a twinge of satisfaction whenever Islamic terms sneak into my Spotify, like "My *shahada* is my katana" (Jay Electronica).

I expected Min. Muhammad to show up in the iconic formal attire of male representatives, but in place of a bow tie was a zipped-up Adidas tracksuit. Before we could start, he turned on the voice recorder app on his phone and placed it next to mine. The Nation guards against journalists, preferring instead to get the message out through its own impressive media enterprise and its colossal chairman, Louis Farrakhan. But that's become harder since Big Tech companies started deplatforming Farrakhan on hate speech grounds. I set aside the disturbing anti-Jewish and antigay rhetoric for which the Nation was infamous to allow the middle-aged minister to speak personally to the Nation's values.

Min. Muhammad was late to Elijah Muhammad's message, discovering it in 1982, seven years after the prophet's death. Yet he connected with it for much the same reason that early Muslim converts had five decades prior. The religion, he told me, addressed the unique condition of Black Americans.

"We were locked in a social dilemma that prayer alone will not resolve," he said. "You have to understand that we came here in the hulls of ships from West Africa. Our people that remained on the continent came under the grip of the colonial powers. What makes us unique in America is that slavery stripped us of our language—stripped us of all of the accoutrements of our culture. It robbed us of our cultural history, the integrity of our family lineage. It stripped us back completely, and remade us how the slave masters wanted us to be. The only difference in West Africa is that they remained attached to the land. If you look at Black people anywhere in the world, we struggle with how we see ourselves. We struggle with this concept of classism. This inferiority versus superiority, and this sense of trying to prove that we can be like white people."

Min. Muhammad has deep religious roots. His enslaved ancestors fled West Virginia and began a tradition of establishing Baptist churches throughout South Side Chicago. He was engrossed in books about Black history and world religions. A teenage interest in Islam led him to search for a Muslim community. Despite what seemed like a natural fit, he overlooked the Nation of Islam to instead dabble in a neo-Sufi mosque. The mystical praxis of Islam proliferated across the Western world during the 1970s' alternative religions movement. More a method of worship than denomination, Sufism is probably remembered by how it was (mal)practiced by new age ex-hippies enamoured by the musical liturgy and flamboyant dress of various Sufi orders. Lesser known is its popularity with conscientious Black Americans, a trend that continues to this day.

Michael had never heard of Louis Farrakhan until his last year of high school, which is not all that surprising since the Nation of Islam had been rendered an obscurity after Elijah Muhammad's death.

For all the FBI's efforts to discredit and destroy the movement, the biggest setback for the Nation came from the East. Orthodox preachers of the Muslim revival initially spent little energy on the Nation of Islam, even though the Nation's members comprised the vast majority of Muslim Americans, because they were not regarded as "real" Muslims. The Nation of Islam's heterodoxy, or blasphemy, however you want to look at it, gave them easy cover for dismissing Black converts as illegitimate. They instead focused on purifying suburban Americans of Arab and West Asian descent. It was only after the Nation gained mainstream approval on the heels of Malcolm X that Black Muslims became beneficial to the revival movement's most powerful Sunni organization. The newly formed World Muslim League earned the trust of Malcolm and Elijah Muhammad's seventh child, W. D., who'd become disillusioned with Elijah Muhammad's exploitation and corruption.

After Malcolm broke with the Nation in 1964, the World Muslim League designated him its first US representative, pledging "authorized" teachers for his newly formed Sunni group and over a dozen scholarships for the Islamic University of Madinah. But their partnership was brief: Malcolm was murdered less than a year later. Like

Noble Drew Ali, Malcolm's death was plagued with conspiracy theories that implicated either the police, Elijah Muhammad, or both.

W. D. Mohammed laid a decade of groundwork to succeed his father when he passed. Almost immediately after W. D. assumed leadership, he downgraded his dad from prophethood to a kind of sainthood. Amongst many radical changes, "ministers" became "imams" and the Nation of Islam became the World Community of Islam in the West.

The great "Sunnification" of Black Muslims had begun. But so had the Nation 3.0. Farrakhan, a silver-tongued young minister then named Louis X, pieced it together with scarce loyalists. It took him five years to revive the organization's name, newspaper, and annual convention, but they were still without a headquarters in the early eighties, when seventeen-year-old Michael took notice of the formally dressed apostles and they of him.

A precocious youth involved in Black empowerment groups, Michael was given a copy of Elijah Muhammad's manifesto, *Message to the Blackman in America*, and was invited to Farrakhan's lectures held inside a rotation of venues. "Sometimes it was a storefront," he recalled, "other times it was a church. Several pastors allowed the minister to hold meetings there. The brothers always had an upstanding demeanour and were very warm and receptive."

Min. Muhammad was an early graduate of the new Nation's security force, the Fruit of Islam, and became its first national minister, lecturing at new chapters reopening across the country and offering prison ministry. Throughout his travels, he saw how crack, gangs, police, and prisons had ravaged working-class Blacks. To Michael Muhammad, Farrakhan's unapologetically political nature was a better remedy than W. D.'s gentler preaching of Black power through interfaith and reconciliation dialogues. "No disrespect to W. D.," Muhammad said, "but when he tried to use the Sunni way, it did not have the effect of the way of the Honorable Elijah Muhammad."

In many ways, W. D.'s reformations undermined Black autonomy and came with terrible consequences. "When you're grounded in a school of thought that the best of your faculties and intelligence has made it feel validated through independent and outside study, and then somebody, whom you believe has the same intentions, starts to invalidate it, that causes psychological emotional trauma," he said. "We lost our body of knowledge. Then we tried to embrace what we call 'orthodox Islam,' which was a highly Arabized style of life. We're not in Arabia. We're having a unique experience in America; that's what the Honorable Elijah Muhammad and his teacher understood. We lost our fundamental ideal and all the cultural identity that came with that."

It was impossible to miss the echoes of our earlier conversation about the spiritual devastation precipitated by slavery. Although much of what he described happened before his involvement in the Nation, it was clear that W. D.'s message—that what his father, Elijah Muhammad, had taught was not true Islam—*was, in fact, fiction*—had confused the Nation's followers. Children felt the most whiplash from this crisis of identity, reality, and authority most. (As one former member told me, "I'd seen former Fruit of Islam brothers strung out on crack, gone to jail, Muslim girls 'turned out.'")

The minister was proud to have helped resuscitate the Nation and its values. He smiled recalling high-water marks of their rebuild efforts, like repurchasing the historic Temple No. 2 headquarters (Temple No. 1 is in Detroit), the star-studded grand reopening ceremony, and especially the Million Man March on Washington, DC. The 1995 gathering solidified Farrakhan as a mainstream civil rights activist on par with Jesse Jackson and Al Sharpton. Its success ingratiated Farrakhan with foreign Muslim leaders who'd previously considered him and Nation members "kafir." He received royal invitations to Mecca and reconciled differences with W. D. In fact, as we spoke, Farrakhan was on the final leg of a Ramadan delegation trip to Saudi Arabia.

Between 2000 and 2008, Farrakhan began to integrate Sunni orthodoxy into his sermons and cool his incendiary tone. Part of his transformation came from a health scare with prostate cancer, but another factor was presidential candidate Barack Obama rebuffing Farrakhan's endorsement. During a rededication ceremony for Temple No. 2 held one month before Obama's election, the leader offered a conciliatory message to people of all faiths and races.

This gentler version of Farrakhan behind the podium has not been as effective. The Nation tried to replicate the historic march on its twentieth anniversary but failed to capture the glory. By 2015, Farrakhan had all but suspended his softer side and returned to scapegoating Jewish people more publicly than ever. While social and mainstream media companies have focused on his anti-Jewish rhetoric, Farrakhan's doomsday-mongering, homophobia, and social conservatism have alienated modern Black youth even more.

The group has not commented on its membership numbers in many years. "Anybody who tells you doesn't know, and those who know won't tell you," said Min. Muhammad. A Religion News Services article, "Nation of Islam Is a Shadow of the Group That Muhammad Ali Joined," reported it was thirty thousand, but others estimate it could be one-third of that. By comparison, at least four thousand US citizens wrote themselves into the national census surveys as Moorish Americans between 2011 and 2015. It's safe to guess that many times more Americans worship using Noble Drew Ali's framework, which doesn't mean that Moorish Science is *not* obscure—it is—but we can safely assume the once-glorious Nation of Islam is obscurer.

I threw some membership estimates out at Min. Muhammad, and he threw them back. "A more important number or question to ask is what is the influence of Minister Farrakhan?" he said. "You can have a million or ten million members of your organization but that doesn't mean all ten million are listening." Farrakhan also influences the influencers, so even those not listening still hear his broader message as it's interpreted by public figures like Women's March copresident Tamika Mallory and rappers Jay Electronica, Busta Rhymes, and the late Nipsey Hussle.

For the record, I believe the independent numbers are grossly underestimated. The share metrics on Louis Farrakhan's social media suggest as much. "If you had access to Black social media, you'd see Farrakhan everywhere," said Min. Muhammad. Indeed, on Twitter, where the leader has been left to his devices, hundreds of real people and bona-fide believers retweet his every post, even the most dogmatic. But there's a caveat: most appear to be middle-aged or older.

I ran Michael's comment by a young artist friend who's steeped in "Black Twitter" for a gut check, and the first thing out of her mouth was "Ha!" She couldn't recall Farrakhan's tweets organically appearing in her feed even once.

Nevertheless, stressing Farrakhan's social media reach only served to bring attention to the Nation's lacking influence without him. Across every platform, official accounts for the organization have about as many followers as a moderately successful local musician. Its dependence on a single charismatic leader is made more precarious by Farrakhan's age. You'd never know it from his enviable glow, but the Honourable Minister is nearing ninety. Yet the organization still hasn't signalled a successor, at least not publicly. It's anyone's guess. When cancer forced Farrakhan's only leave of absence, in 2007, he transferred power to an advisory panel rather than appointing a leader from top brass, which includes members of both his family and the late Honorable Elijah Muhammad's.

The clock is running if the Nation hopes to avoid another chaotic leadership transition. Even under the best circumstances, a third re-invention feels inevitable and necessary. Without new members, the Nation will face extinction. But how can it expect to grow when its messages preach things antithetical to millennial and Gen Z values? Civil rights advocate Angela Davis summarized the changing winds best in a 2020 interview. "There are those here in this country who are asking: 'Where is the contemporary Martin Luther King?' 'Where is the new Malcolm X?' 'Where is the next Marcus Garvey?'" she told the *Guardian*. "And, of course, when they think about leaders, they think about Black male charismatic leaders. But the more recent radical organizing among young people, which has been a feminist kind of organizing, has emphasized collective leadership."

I asked the minister how the Nation tried to appeal to Black Lives Matter. "The Nation of Islam has made the Black Lives Matter movement possible," he said. "You have members of the Nation of Islam, at this very moment, in some neighbourhood, engaging drug addicts, people in gang life, people who are the rejects and outcasts of society, and bringing them hope and inspiration, bringing them the light of faith, calling them closer to a relationship with Almighty God." He added, "We must always speak the language of the people, but the message is still the same."

Was it, though? There's no doubt that the confrontational approach of Black Lives Matter owes more to Malcolm than Martin. But its members are also decidedly secular, sex-positive, queer-friendly, intersectional, and antihierarchical, while Nation Muslims are conservative even by the standards of most religious Black folk. It's hard to imagine Gens Y and Z resonating with some of the more colourful aspects of Elijah Muhammad's gospel, such as spaceships currently encircling Earth, preparing for Judgment Day.

I thought Min. Michael oversold Farrakhan's relevance to reach the next generation. At one point, he claimed Farrakhan was "bigger than Colin Kaepernick," which at best sounded out of touch. He also said it was "laughable" that Farrakhan was banned from Facebook as collateral damage when I suggested it was strategic to absolve Facebook of partisanship after it simultaneously kicked off half a dozen other right-wing extremists. "Farrakhan is not the collateral damage. Farrakhan is the target, and they use Alex Jones, and Milos, and the rest of them—that's the collateral damage," he said.

"The Jewish-controlled media has sought to label Minister Farrakhan as an anti-Semite," he continued. "This has been an ongoing process; it just so happens that Facebook was co-created and run by a member of the Jewish community. The United States and the Israeli governments have been pressing him for a number of years to deplatform Minister Farrakhan, and Facebook finally delivered."

And here we are.

Going in, I'd prepared some questions about Farrakhan's anti-Jewish bigotry. I was less prepared to handle it unprompted, and perhaps naive to doubt it would be blatantly espoused by a representative. Later, journalist Sonsyrea Tate, who wrote the memoir *Little X: Growing Up in the Nation of Islam,* would explain to me that the Nation's anti-Jewish beliefs are somewhat of an innovation, though not an aberration. Farrakhan intensified them in the 1980s to curry favour with white evangelicals, similar to Elijah Muhammad ingratiating himself with the Nazi Party. With racial tensions between Blacks and whites easing up through civil rights gains, Farrakhan, in search of a new scapegoat, toned down the white devil rhetoric, and borrowed a classic from the vaults of white Christian supremacy, according to Tate.

I tested the depth of Min. Muhammad's beliefs by raising a few points about Islam, Black power, and the Jewish diaspora. I asked how he squared his antagonism with the fact that the first Muslims studied the Torah and prayed toward Jerusalem. Was the Nation's focus on perceived Jewish "subjugation" not a distraction from battling white supremacy? And how does he reconcile his beliefs with many Ethiopian Jews who've adopted Israel as a homeland?

The minister answered every question in a conclusive manner that revealed Jewish scapegoating was deeply seeded and widely spread in the Nation's clergy. It's one thing to hear casual anti-Jewish remarks in the living room (as I have, more than I wish to admit) but something else entirely to hear it from a Muslim leader, let alone on the record. It left no doubt in my mind that the Nation would not survive the future, at least not as an official entity.

Farrakhan will die. Without a voice of his prowess, the Nation will disperse into breakaway sects. Without a reformist, Black youth will ignore them. In time, they will join the ranks of the Moorish Science Temple.

———

Unless you're familiar with their accoutrements—their colourful headware and bejewelled insignia—Moorish Americans are difficult to identify out in the real world. But they are out there and they are active. US Census records suggest as much, as does a steady trickle of crime stories.

A cursory search of Google News brings up weekly headlines in which self-proclaimed Moors are charged for violating local traffic and property laws in eccentric ways: producing fake Moorish driver's licenses, disobeying eviction notices on convoluted grounds, or attempting to usurp properties using bizarre legalese. As a result, the Southern Poverty Law Center, a US nonprofit that monitors

homegrown extremism, designated Moorish sovereign citizens an extremist group, comparing it to the freeman-on-the-land phenomenon,
a movement of predominantly white libertarians who claim to be sovereign citizens unbound by governmental laws. The most extreme incident, in 2006, involved five quasi-Moors plotting to blow up the Sears
Tower. Like the El Rukn gang, the offshoot group had been lured into
it by the FBI, which seduced them with radical Islamist ideology.

These scandals are the source of much embarrassment on Moorish YouTube, where many adherents have broken down Ali's Divine
Constitution to prove their obligations to US laws. Islamic theology is
also hotly debated. Moorish "Moslems" are divided on the forbidden-
ness of intoxicants and pork, and even the month of Ramadan. Many
celebrate it in October to commemorate the first annual national convention hosted by Noble Drew Ali in Chicago less than a year before
his death. And, of course, nothing is more contested than the legitimacy of one branch over another.

All of this is to say that the spirit of debate is as lively as in any
other religion. When you boil them down, the vast majority of Moors
are very normal and, speaking personally, exceptionally kind people.

Interviewing the Supreme Grand Sheik Kenu Umar Bey opened
a door that I'd been pounding for months. Mentioning his cooperation motivated more invitations to their temples, religious services,
and Sunday schools. One of the oldest branches, led by an octogenar-
ian raised by two of Noble Drew Ali's first acolytes, even invited me
to their ninety-second annual convention later that year. I said I'd do
everything possible to come back for it in September.

It would take a few days to line up the in-person interviews. In the
meantime, it was Eid al-Fitr, and I had nowhere to go. The last time I
celebrated the final day of Ramadan solo was during my first year of
college. It was evidently also my last year as a sincere Muslim. I say
"sincere" not because I had been pure until then. Furthest from it—I'd
just lost my virginity and was feeling pretty good about that. But sitting in that Vancouver mosque, chosen randomly by Google, I think
that really was the last time I felt God in my heart. I officially cut ties
on day one of the next Ramadan. Three hours into my fast, I started

thinking about the emptiness of my loyalty—to what, or whom, I didn't know anymore. I could practically hear the metaphysical rope snap when I finally bit into my lunch.

Since then, I've celebrated it only with my immediate family. I came to appreciate it more in my late twenties and early thirties as my palate for both Lebanese food and family developed. There really is no better feast. Eid al-Fitr, the second holiest day on the Muslim calendar, roughly translates to "feast festival." (And if the people preparing it have been on an intense diet all month, you better believe it's a feast.) It's also the only time of the year that my parents were guaranteed to bring their lineage under one roof. My wife and I started making some room in our budget to buy my nieces and nephews nice presents that complement their personalities; plus, it was a nonthreatening way to try to open them up to new experiences with somewhat suggestive books.

Now that our daughter was out in the world, I knew that I wanted her to cherish Ramadan too. Maybe not fast for the month, though if she comes to that decision herself, I wish her well. But Janae and I read her a picture book about its meaning from time to time, and now that she's talking, my mom's teaching her a song about the month of giving. In fact, while I was in Chicago thinking about where to spend my Eid, my mom had taken Noe to Edmonton's biggest prayer service, held at an elite Islamic school to accommodate the masses. She texted me pictures of Noe all dolled up with a pink do-rag. I really hoped that if our daughter were attending prayer she would look less petrified.

As for my destination for Eid al-Fitr, it would be difficult to find a city in the world with more options. The Ahmadi mufti who is alleged to have introduced Noble Drew Ali to Islam? In 1922, he founded the now eponymous Muhammad Sadiq Mosque, the oldest operating mosque in the United States but one of more than a hundred operating in Chicago. No matter what your Islam is, a Muslim community in this city will accept you for it. There was even a queer-positive congregation holding service at the flex-space it borrows for Friday service.

I considered either of these places, as well as the Nation's headquarters, these days referred to as Maryam Mosque. But since Farrakhan had decided to celebrate Eid at the Great Mosque of Mecca,
I decided I'd use this opportunity to meet the man who might have
been poised to lead the Nation of Islam—not Imam W. D. Mohammed, who died in 2008, but Imam W. D. Mohammed II, who took over
his father's ministry.

———

The physical headquarters of the ministry of Imam W. D. Mohammed wasn't befitting of the prestige that I envisioned. I expected the
great-grandchildren of Elijah Muhammad to worship under a golden
dome at least equal in size to the Nation's flagship temple. Instead, my
Uber driver drove me twenty miles to a stumpy brick building on an
industrial road. I would've asked her to turn back around were it not
for a humble plastic sign reassuring me that I was at the right place.

The Mosque Cares was the fourth and last iteration of the late
Imam W. D. Mohammed's movement. He founded it in 1995 for the
purposes of religious propagation, or *dawah*, and charitable giving.
The Mosque Cares became his primary focus in 2003, after announc-
ing his sudden resignation from the American Muslim Society, which
he'd also been leading. By then, the Muslim Society oversaw more than
a hundred mosques attended by 200,000 Black Americans. Without a
succession plan, the network struggled to restructure and quickly dissolved, leaving a significant portion of the American ummah without
a single unified leadership, as many suspect was his intention. Regardless, he remained their de facto spiritual leader, thanks in part to the
Mosque Cares' prolific production of his books, audio lectures, and the
Muslim Journal newspaper. W. D. was a spiritual leader to non-Muslim
Americans too. Often called "America's imam," he twice recited verses
from the Quran at US presidential inauguration interfaith services.

W. D.'s death a few years later left a massive gap in the canon
of Black American Muslim leaders. W. D. Mohammed II was never
equipped to fill his father's shoes as the Mosque Cares' new chairman, and he must have been sufficiently self-aware of this. Aside from

making "Ministry of Imam W. Deen Mohammed" the charity's official slogan, the forty-year-old entrepreneur enforced copyright of his
father's body of work under a newly formed limited liability company.
"He got everything copyrighted, and you almost had to get permission
to use anything," a Pennsylvania imam told me by phone.

Although the fallout of W. D.'s passing was rough, I was still surprised by the modesty of the Mosque Cares. The website said this was
the place for salat and celebration, and, if I recalled my childhood correctly, there were hundreds of worshippers due anytime. I would say
the building was unequipped to handle heavy traffic, if there was any
traffic whatsoever. Far as I could tell, I was alone yet right on time for
Eid celebrations.

Not that anyone was expecting me.

I had my apprehensions about dropping in on Eid. Even though
I'd grown comfortable walking into mosques unannounced, the last
thing I wanted was to be the centre of anyone's attention on "Muslim Christmas" (as I remembered it). W. D. the Senior rid his father's
movement of race-based theories, but he never ceased being a Black
minister advocating for Black people. He did it through diplomacy at
every level of power, and he did it through sermons, trying to apply
Islamic solutions to the complexities of Black American life. As a ministry, the Mosque Cares, however small, is still a cornerstone of Black
Muslimhood (hence why his intellectual property is so valued). I went
ahead anyway, knowing I'd stand out. As I waited for someone to arrive, two men opened the door from the inside. The brothers were
Black and Latino. "Eid Mubarak," we said to each other. With that, the
Black brother invited me in. I told him about my book as he walked
me into the empty prayer hall. He couldn't be happier that I'd come
all this way to see the mosque. "Just relax," he said, handing me a lyric
sheet of Eid prayers from a stack. Then he left to help set up the buffet.

Tradition dictates that I, as first arrival in the mosque, begin singing "Eid Takbeer" immediately and that everyone who enters thereaf-
ter follows, so that this hypnotic, sixteen-word incantation compounds
and crescendos at the precise moment that worship begins. But I was
way too self-conscious to start incantations by my lonesome. I sat

silently examining the room's marked-up whiteboards and low ceiling tiles and, in spite of all the evidence, was still unconvinced that I'd found the right place.

I spied a portrait of Elijah Muhammad in the corridor. How, I wondered, did self-proclaimed orthodox Muslims reconcile reverence for a heretic, even if his heresy accommodated Black Americans with the best intentions, as Elijah's successor, his son, publicly rationalized? W. D.'s reforms required many historical revisions. He even recast a deceased Pakistani American imam as the true identity of Wallace Fard Muhammad, thus mortalizing the "Master" that his father deified. W. D. also disbanded the sect's paramilitary and army boycott, but he lovingly embraced one thing. Bean pie. Watching my hosts unload boxes of this iconic dessert, I was excited to finally taste this legit Muslim American cuisine immortalized in hip-hop many times over and far more American than apple pie.

Slowly a trickle of worshippers arrived, dressed impeccably in colourful gowns, two-piece suits, and the odd flashy hat. Aside from a few abayas, the dress code was definitely more Sunday best than Friday. I made small talk with the first few arrivals, until a suit-and-tied elderly man initiated the Eid song as he distributed the lyric sheets. As the chorus grew to thirty adults and children, I noticed the Latino brother was gone. Although I stood out even more than feared, I'd been welcomed far better than hoped.

Finally, W. D. II arrived wearing a grey suit. Without a hair below his eyebrows, he was the most cherubic imam I'd ever met. There wasn't much time to speak, so he invited me to feast with them after services. I aligned myself in a neat row, expecting him, as chairman and imam, to lead the occasion. Instead, the dapper senior who made a point of initiating "Eid Takbeer" served as imam.

Imam Agim Muhammed gave me goose bumps with his recitation of al-Fatiha. I'd heard it ten thousand times, but had never heard the Quran's opening salvo sound like blues. Numerous scholars have argued a link between the American music and Islamic hymnody. I was skeptical until hearing Imam Agim bend, blend, and stretch each note as if covering Muddy Waters in a foreign language.

He led us to the last words of worship, "May the peace and mercy of Allah be with you," then pulled himself to his feet with a wide grin. Speaking with a southern flare, he gently chided us for not keeping with Eid tradition, then began his sermon. The topic, he promised, was a sentence in the Quran that would be humanity's salvation. "One sentence, two words, and each one a compound word," he said, building our anticipation. "That word is '*Alhamdu'lillah*.' Praise be to God. The most detrimental thing we do is seek praise for ourselves. But I'm going to give you the medicine. It would cure Donald Trump!"

I laughed aloud, imagining Trump shocking the world by punctuating a tweet with "*Alhamdu'lillah*."

"Here's what you do," Agim continued. "Every time somebody praises you, you say '*Alhamdu'lillah*' and pass it off." The imam pretended to flick praise off his shoulder. "There, you got it off you. That is the cure for the world. When someone wants to praise you, inoculate yourself!"

I felt a big smile creep over my face.

What was happening to me? I'd never enjoyed a khutba in my life, let alone laughed at one intentionally. He made goofy impressions of braggarts and self-deprecating jokes and still connected with the audience. It was damn good advice for anyone of the Instagram age, but even more for a media personality with a weakness for flattery. Funny, my mom constantly impresses upon me *Alhamdu'lillah* whenever I share good news about my work or sport a fresh look. *Praise be to God.* Its utility never occurred to me until now. Would I have made my worst mistakes, done those things that have broken friendships and trusts, if I'd just "innoculated" myself with the occasional *Alhamdu'lillah*? Does one have to believe in a deity, or is it like saying "bless you" after a sneeze? Just one of those good manners that somehow maintains civility.

As the imam said it, "Nothing ever got a human being in trouble but his appetite, and the appetite for praise is the worst one."

But what a curious choice of sermon for Eid al-Fitr. The second imam who gave a sermon waxed about fasting as an intense training regimen akin to any boxer's before fight night. It wasn't as rousing, but it was more pertinent. Why had Agim selected such an evergreen topic as humility for this specific occasion?

I didn't get a chance to ask him at the mosque. Agim was one of the first to leave, and I was occupied with riveting personal stories of Malcolm and Muhammad Ali. But one of the elders connected me with Agim, who welcomed me to his little bungalow. The retired schoolteacher and current Lyft driver was generous with his time and tales. I sat in his living room adorned by his wife's stylish hats on the wall, listening for hours as he reflected on his entire activist career.

He whisked me along the journey of leaving the Jim Crow South; getting fired from Chicago Public Schools for his political views; rallying with the Black Panthers; joining the Nation; and, finally, helping implement Imam W. D. Mohammed's radical reformations—the subtlest but most consequential protest act of his life.

Agim vividly remembers the Saviour's Day convention of 1975 when "Supreme Minister Honourable Wallace D. Mohammed" delivered his first national address. (The late imam changed his first name from Wallace to Warith Deen around the time he renamed the Nation to World Community of Islam in the West and retired the "supreme minister" title.) The annual commemoration of the birth of Wallace Fard—messiah, founder, and namesake of the forty-one-year-old new leader—happened to fall on the day after Elijah Muhammad's death. So, not only was it a national address but a funeral and ordination. One after another, from Muhammad Ali to Louis Farrakhan, key figures came to the stage to pledge fealty to the new chief, who began by saying, "I am too small for all this honour." Though he didn't officiate his revolution for another year, during the newly named "Survival Day," his modest opening hinted at the future.

"The imam taught us against personality worship," said Agim. "That's why you won't find a picture of me and Warith Deen."

Agim obviously took this to heart, but he also recognized the positive power of an ego boost. It can inspire a man just enough to turn his life straight, to resist his oppressors. Confidence, ego, pride, praise—whatever one wishes to call it—it is a prerequisite for fighting the bigger and smaller jihad that push us, our neighbours, and our countries in the right direction. But in large doses, it inflates the worst of us—"blow up our heads so big that it breaks our neck," as Prophet Muhammad is alleged to have said.

Maybe that's why the Prophet democratized the Muslim clergy while stressing their fallibility. If any man can be an imam, and none of us are to be worshipped, then imams are not to be worshipped. It is certainly why W. D. eventually left his Sunni group without a succession plan and was cautious about his own children's Islamic education. W. D. II is imam by title, not by practice. "When he was a little boy, he wanted to be in my class at the University of Islam, but his daddy was sending him to Montessori," said Agim. "I don't boast about it, but he [W. D. II] depends on me a lot."

"Is that why he didn't lead Eid prayers or give one of the khutbas?" I asked.

"Warith Deen Mohammed II is not a dynamic speaker," he said. "But his heart is just like his daddy's."

Many students of W. D. Senior would be insulted by that comparison. A number of imams from the four hundred mosques once under the American Muslim Society banner have cut ties with the ministry, charging its current chairman, W. D. II, with being greedy and opportunistic. The Pennsylvania imam who was frustrated with the ministry's stringent copyright control compared W. D. II to Martin Luther King Jr.'s children. "We didn't really know Dr. King's children until after he died, and the ones that came forward and became prominent had a vested interest in ownership of the legacy."

I must admit my own first impressions of W. D. II were negative. From the get-go, he talked more about business ventures than the Mosque Cares. Our conversation during the Eid feast veered into unsolicited details about his clothing and body cream brand, before railing against members of his own family who've shunned him. I never got to make a second impression of him. His keenness to speak was fleeting.

W. D. II struck me as someone who wished to be freed of his father's and grandfather's legacies but could not bring himself to relinquish its privileges, and was now in over his head. Recent reports of the ministry's tax delinquency suggest as much. His circumstances bring to mind a favourite idiom amongst businesspeople: "Three generations from shirtsleeves to shirtsleeves." The difference is that the second generation, his father, may have purposely set him up to fail.

Many, if not most, religious movements spawn from a struggle for supremacy. Wallace Fard Muhammad founded the Nation of Islam after failing to succeed Noble Drew Ali; the Baha'i faith was founded in exile from Shiite persecution by Persians; Shiites, which translates to "partisans," were founded in a dispute over Prophet Muhammad's succession; and the Prophet, of course, started Islam by preaching a countermovement to Quraysh polytheism. But there often reaches a moment when maintaining a supreme leader becomes unsustainable. That's when power is transferred to the people. Joshua summoned the elders of Israel to share his communion with God. W. D. Mohammed effectively dissolved the American Muslim Society with his unexpected retirement.

In many ways, fewer echelons are a healthy sign for a movement, as it indicates that it's outgrown rigid hierarchy. Catholicism is a wild outlier; most big religions are democratized. Nevertheless, when a movement or ministry meets this moment, it's almost impossible to reverse.

"Warith the Second is doing a good job of holding together what his father left," Agim said, almost reassuringly. "And his father left the ministry in such a way that nobody can get to it. There is no board. There is no membership. When he established it, he said, 'This is my ministry and you can support it if you want to.'" Not *you must* support it, as his father and counterparts going back to Noble Drew Ali mandated. Just as he decentralized the American Muslim Society with his surprise retirement, in 2003, W. D. seemed intent on disempowering his family ministry by leaving it in the hands of a reluctant leader. Even in death, he worked to dispel the cult of personality that could corrupt people.

I returned to Chicago a second time in September to take up the Moorish leader's offer to be a guest at the ninety-second annual Moorish Science Temple of America National Convention. After arriving, I learned there was another, dueling ninety-second annual national convention three miles away. Over the course of both trips, I counted fifteen active temples in metropolitan Chicago and a variety of Moorish Americans. They fell into one of two groups—what are called "civic Moors" and "temple Moors." The civic Moors nitpick about constitutions and declarations and might view temple Moors as too reverential. The temple Moors are into "energies," mysticism, and definitely more into Orientalist fashion. Their prejudices against civic Moors stem from those who take their citizenship to extremes.

Karima Hasan Bey, who cofounded Temple No. 5 of her Moorish Science branch with her husband, told me it was a problem in the Chicago suburb of Gary. "There are a lot of people who are looking for truth," explained the utility company executive. "Unfortunately, you find a lot of misinformation and you have to go through some hoops to get where you really need to be. There are a lot of offshoots that are just so bogus," she said. "You know, the whole driving without a license."

"Are there repercussions?" I asked.

"*Yeah*—you get ticketed. You go to jail. Because it's *against the law* to drive around with your made-up plate and little symbol and say 'I'm sovereign.' There's no sovereignty. The only sovereign person was the prophet."

Between the conventions and other temples I visited, I met dozens of Moorish Americans: teachers and entertainers, nurse practitioners and alternative healers, former marines and paralegals. Only one young man professed any belief in sovereign citizenship. It was more common that members entered the temple through an interest in the idea. Some were "saved" after running into legal trouble as a result of internet indoctrination.

Now, one of these men was poised to become a supreme grand

sheik. Keith Dandridge El would become his branch's ninth supreme leader. His predecessor—a Trump-loving septuagenarian who only stopped calling me a "Roman" to start calling me his "newsman"— was one of the oldest linkages to the first disciples of Noble Drew Ali. Blind and in poor health, he was about to pass the highest seat in Moorish America to this thirty-eight-year-old mechanical engineer from Toledo, Ohio.

Dandridge El's modesty stood out more than his age or distance, or the fact that he lived 250 miles from headquarters. He'd invited me to attend their convention without telling me about his ordination. I found that he bored quickly of my questions about Moorish politicking and constantly circled back to practice and theology. "Our authority states that we can teach the faith of Muhammad," said Dandridge El, who practised Sunnism throughout his late teens and early twenties. "When I began to read the literature of the Moorish Science Temple and the Moorish Qur'an, it really tripped me out how parallel it was to the Qur'an of Mecca."

His belief in Abrahamic prophets and traditional family values did not change when he joined the temple. What did, dramatically, was his sense of national heritage. Sheik Dandridge El was focused on getting the temple organized and mobilized for the 2020 Census, in hopes of representing themselves better as a constituency. His dry pragmatism and team spirit impressed me. For five straight mornings and afternoons, a consortium of early-middle-aged men and women presented on such issues as marriage and burial rites, mental health first aid, positive youth development, and having a deeper respect for womanhood. There was more vigour in this movement than I imagined.

But why?

I understood why Noble Drew Ali's first followers proclaimed their nationality to free themselves from the constraints of 1920s racism. I understood, too, why teenagers in the 1970s thought joining a Moorish gang might free them from poverty. But how could Moorish Science empower them today, in the midst of the biggest civil rights moment in their lifetimes? From what does it free them?

I figured it out after offending conventioneers at the other Moorish gathering. In a private conversation, I said "African Americans." Despite emphatic air quotes, word got out, and I was publicly reprimanded by the supreme grand sheik. "Are you calling us African Americans in this book?" he asked, stamping his finger on my ledger. "Because we're not African Americans. And if you do that, we're not participating."

"You've got to understand," one of the more sympathetic Moors said, "this term—'African American'—is actually a sin for us." The man suggested "Americans of African descent." Fair enough, but I wondered why they didn't see "Moorish American" as tainted, too?

A young father put it to me this way: "I had no idea I was connected to so much grandeur because I was raised with the mentality that 'I'm Black, my history is slavery.'"

Being recognized is very important. "When you're reminded of your illustrious history, you have confidence to speak to anyone of any nationality, and now come to the table of nations to express your culture, and who you are, and that you came with a sense of dignity."

In a world obsessed with colour, I could see what a burden it would be to stake your ancestral heritage on the back of a vague word. We are more the sum of our citizenships and cultures than our complexions. When I call myself "brown," as I sometimes do, what am I communicating besides a vague middle area of racial hierarchy? I call myself "Middle Eastern" too, but that's hardly clearer than "Americans of African descent."

I thought about that clunky suggested term and the pejorative I had uttered, and began to appreciate Moorish nationalism. How would I feel if my primary heritage was reduced to a colour or continent comprising dozens of nations and thousands of ethnicities? "Lebanese" evokes a history, a food, a music. "Arab" evokes a language, an empire, astronomy, and mathematics. "Pan-Africanism" should have the same power for North Americans. But for so many of us, "Africa" does not evoke sophisticated Yoruba kingdoms, ancient universities, and barely a word about the true Moors' glorious history. Too often, it's slavery, mystery, misery.

Noble Drew Ali wrote a semicohesive origin story from which people like himself, the inheritors of deep trauma, could also draw strength and meaning. He did not need a university degree to explain all the negativity associated with Black identity on a subconscious level. Whether he truly believed he could resolve it is irrelevant. The fact is, some Americans have dealt with this trauma by reclaiming Blackness as glorious, but others don't want to validate the Western social construct of race in any way, shape, or form. They'd rather lean on other social constructs, nationalism and imperialism, reclaiming an ancient empire with a set of falsehoods no worse than the myths of scientific racism that enslaved their ancestors.

2

هجرة

Hijrah

(Migration)

I am not speaking for the transient element . . . the man or the woman whose roots are in India and who eventually returns home. I talk for those of us who, by our work and by our sweat and by our blood, have helped build fighting industrial America today.

—*Ibrahim Chaudry, 1945 testimony to the US Committee on Immigration and Naturalization*

The Mecca That Ford Built
Islamic Center of America
(Dearborn, Michigan)

*D*uring a family vacation to Ontario in the 1990s, my parents announced we were taking a day trip to Detroit. This was a big deal for three small-town kids raised on MTV and Nickelodeon. So what if the Motor City was run-down? We were going to the U S of A. We piled into a car and, with high expectations, drove three hours to the Ambassador Bridge. Slowly, the birthplace of such cultural achievements as the automobile, Motown music, and the Insane Clown Posse appeared over the dashboard and then quickly disappeared in the rearview mirror.

"Wait, where are we going?" I asked my dad as he steered onto a freeway exit. I read the direction sign. "What's Dearborn?"

Twenty minutes later, he pulled into the parking lot of a Lebanese bakery. Apparently we'd traveled all that way for baklava.

My parents, guided by an unfamiliar uncle serving as tour guide, then dragged us from shop to shop, gleefully greeting strangers in Arabic. They tried to impress on us the significance of an American city transformed by Middle Easterners. What appeared to them as a mythical place that one must see to believe appeared to me as a mundane suburb. Both are right.

Another twenty-three years passed before I conjured that memory again. It struck me as I approached Dearborn on my own, climbing the same exit in my rental. Crossing Warren and Dix Avenues, I felt as amazed as my parents probably had seeing a stream of Arabic script on regular store buildings. Bilingual signage even spread to Walgreens. I stopped to eat and happened upon a police conference inside the restaurant's banquet room. I spied on the young, dusky officers, each looking as if he could be my relative. I'd never felt like an ethnic majority in this hemisphere before.

If downtown Dearborn were dropped into Lebanon, only the spaciousness and cleanliness would give it away as foreign. About 60 percent of the city's ninety-five thousand residents have Middle Eastern ancestry. More incredible, the demographic proportion is also represented in the highest seats of power. The majority of the city council is Arab American, as is the police chief and district court magistrate.

The Arab American National Museum sits across from City Hall Park. It's an architectural jewel befitting anything in Dubai. From the vantage point of its rooftop, where I stood with Matthew Stiffler, content manager of the museum, I now looked down on this most mundane suburb with wonder.

Dearborn has mystique not just for Arabs and Arab speakers. Since September 11, 2001, racist Americans have also taken an interest in its "peculiarities." Though the museum plan predates 9/11, it wasn't until the aftermath of the tragedy that the community saw the need for it. The attacks motivated them to build it faster, hoping it would humanize Muslims and Middle Easterners for the scared populace. And it did help. Dearborners felt seminormal again.

Then Barack Hussein Obama was elected president. Suddenly thousands of white Americans had PhDs in creeping sharia. Conservative media whipped its audience into a frenzy when development plans for a Muslim community centre in Lower Manhattan were announced—the so-called Ground Zero Mosque. Suddenly the deplorables began making hajj to Dearborn to protest Islam.

"Whenever the anti-Muslim people came to town they'd set up

shop there and scream racist shit pointing to City Hall Park," Stiffler said, "and we would stand here and laugh at them."

It's not that the protesters don't know the difference between Arabs and Islam. Though, speaking as someone who's been asked to "say something in Islam," there were plenty of those people too. They'd tried, and failed, to provoke violence with Quran burnings at the Islamic Center of America, which opened the same year as the museum with a similarly big budget. But having found themselves outnumbered greatly by allies and police, the racists settled on the public plaza across the road from the Arab American Museum.

Close enough, I guess. I doubt many of them visited the museum afterward, which is a shame. Had they come inside, they would have had a most normal experience. The museum's story of Arab Americans begins in the early sixteenth century with Mustafa Azemmouri, better known as Estaban the Moor, an enslaved explorer who left an imprint all over Mesoamerica. The narrative then jumps ahead three centuries to the first wave of Middle Eastern immigrants forming "Little Syrias" in booming cities across North and South America. Three of my great-grandfathers were among the first wave, including Ahmed, my father's namesake, who worked in Henry Ford's original auto plant alongside hundreds of other modern-day Lebanese.

When Ahmed first arrived in America, he landed in Lawrence, Massachusetts. There, two thousand Syrians were packed into poorly ventilated, dark, and diseased tenements within sight of the booming textile mills they served. Destitution must have seemed like fate to him, until Henry Ford announced middle-class wages for Blacks, Jews, Irish, and other "undesirables." Remnants of his colleagues and migrant cohort decorate the permanent gallery, often with comical banality. Looking over a peddler's case, coffeepots, high school jerseys, and war medals on exhibit, I asked Stiffler, "Do you ever feel odd about the fact that you have to reinforce that Arab Americans are just like everyone else?"

"Yes, but it's necessary in a liberal multicultural society," he said. "When you're fighting to humanize your community, sometimes the most basic discourse—'Hey, we drive cars, and go to school, and play football, just like you!'—that's the stuff that reaches our visitors the most. It's the number one way for people to see Arabs as normal people."

It couldn't be more on the nose; there's even a who's who gallery of covert Arabs in NASA, the NFL, and Hollywood. "That one's controversial," admitted Stiffler. "Some scholars who do LGBTQ studies have talked about this gallery as an outing narrative."

Though I wanted to roll my eyes, I knew there was a point buried somewhere inside such virtue signalling. No, Arabs aren't exactly in the closet, but you want to take precautions labelling people Arab. The museum takes a broad definition of an Arab American—those who trace their roots to any of the twenty-two Arab League nations. But not all Arabic-speaking people uniformly agree with this.

Arab, though not a nationality, is better understood as a cultural citizenship with a gradient of shades and ethnic influences. (For example, I've felt more at home in Istanbul than in Dubai on account of my Mediterranean and Ottoman ancestry.) Early twentieth-century lawmakers must have understood as much when they classified Arabs into legal whites and legal nonwhites to determine one's right to citizenship and, vis-à-vis, suburbia. Thus, the Arab roots of Dearborn owe as much to their Syrian Lebanese auto workforce as the workforce's privileged classification, which excluded Gulf and Afro Arabs for decades.

Dearborn's privileged class very much still reflects pre-1952 naturalization laws, but the general population better represents the spectrum of Arab Americans and their many religions. Though less than three-quarters have Middle Eastern ancestry, only 40 percent of the group are Muslim, with the majority being Shiite. The remaining dominant religions are Druze (a mystic Shia offshoot divided on whether to call themselves Muslims) or some variation of Christian. Actually, if you really want to see "Muslim America," drive ten miles east on I-75 to Hamtramck, a smaller suburb that is majority Muslim, though more on account of Bangladeshi and Bosnian than Arab migration.

Nevertheless, when journalists want their American Islam story, they descend on Dearborn, as I did, to note the signage, the minarets, the halal tacos. Hot on their tails, propagandists have pushed lies about "no-go zones" for non-Muslims, or oppositely produce fluff like TLC's

All-American Muslims. The spotlight doesn't just fetishize local Muslims; they work in tandem to divide them between "good" and "bad" based on their varying degrees of patriotism and assimilation. Mostly, though, they make the city synonymous with American Islam.

Academics dubbed it the "Dearborn syndrome": the more Dearborn was name-checked in national media, however positive, the more it was associated with Islamist terrorism. For instance, Dearbornians are second only to New Yorkers in representation in the government's Terrorist Screening Database. Not one resident has been convicted of terrorism, but many have been wrongfully arrested, banned from flying, found their bank accounts frozen, or had their charity shut down. In an extreme case, an imam and others were killed in an FBI raid that to this day has brought no charges, terrorism or otherwise. (It bears noting that the raid victims were Black.)

I spent a week in Dearborn meeting with experts and faith leaders to find out what it's like living inside a national Rorschach test for a religion they may not even practice. How do they manage the push and pull of Western and Eastern opinions? What does it do to an average American suburb, and how would Dearbornian Muslims rather be seen?

September 11 perhaps made Dearborn into a synecdoche for American Islam, but Michiganders have long understood the broader Detroit region as a Muslim powerhouse. One of the first times it was hailed as an "American Mecca" was on the cover of *Detroit* magazine in 1980. The feature story was a profile of Imam Mohamad Jawad Chirri, the Lebanese Shia cleric who published North America's first works of Islamic scholarship and founded the prestigious Islamic Center of America (ICA). An adviser to two US presidents and mentor of Muhammad Ali, Imam Chirri was someone who could call in favours from the king of Jordan and president of Egypt. Someone who might have mediated between President Carter and Ayatollah Ruhollah Khomeini during the 1979 hostage crisis, had Carter taken him up on his offer.

Without a doubt, the imam solidified Muslim Americans' influence in Washington more than anyone else—but more on him later. To understand how a man of his scholarship ended up in Detroit, I had to literally drive past the ICA on Ford Road, on my way to meet Sally Howell, author of *Old Islam in Detroit: Rediscovering the Muslim American Past* and director of the Center for Arab American Studies. We sat in her University of Michigan office decorated with pan-Arabian art and loads of books related to her expertise. The vast majority were published since the centre unceremoniously opened in early 2005. "Suddenly, after 9/11, there was demand for Arab Americanists," said Howell. As the child of a white southern pastor, she has a keen interest in religions.

Professor Howell's book documents how gender, sectarian, and theological issues in modern American mosques took root long before Islam became a focal issue in the West. In her account of historic local congregations, there was one mosque I wanted to visit more than any other. It would be the one my great-grandfather Ahmed probably attended before he returned home to Kab Elias, his village a few miles west of the newly formed Syrian border forged by Europeans. Evidently Henry Ford's middle-class promise evaded him, but it did not evade all Lebanese, specifically those who earned diplomas from Ford English School and who opened their homes to the corporation's "Sociological Department" ensuring that immigrants upheld their American values.

From this cohort came two assemblymen, a Sunni and a Shiite, who'd earned the titles of "shaykh" on the factory floor. In 1920, they collaborated on constructing the first Muslim house of God built for that purpose, mere blocks from the Highland Park Ford Plant. The Moslem Mosque of Highland Park made a splash internationally. News of its announcement attracted gifts from Egyptian and Saudi royalty, and, according to a glowing US newspaper article, "raised Detroit, in their eyes, to the rank of London and Budapest, the only other holy cities in the occident." But the shaykhs made bad decisions early on. They partnered with the Sunni founder's rich older brother who in reality was a sketchy real estate mogul, and an illustrious Indian mufti, who in fact was a travelling Ahmadiyya missionary. The complications that arose stressed sectarian differences that worshippers never knew they had. The Moslem Mosque of Highland barely lived past its first birthday when it was abandoned and then bulldozed by the rich brother out of spite. I'm left only to imagine what it was like inside the mosque.

In its ephemerality, the Moslem Mosque sparked a brief moment in time when Anglo-Protestantism, Muslim migration, and pan-Africanism converged, cross-pollinated, switched tracks, and transformed history. Its founders were like the Rat Pack of American Islam, save for the scandalous older brother, unquestionably the Peter Lawford of the troupe. The Ahmadiyya mufti became the namesake of Chicago's historic Muhammad Sadiq Mosque and may have catalyzed Muslim movements in Black America; the Sunni shaykh went on to found Dearborn Mosque, which now thrives as "Dearborn Masjid" under Yemeni stewardship. The Shiite shaykh's mosque did not survive Imam Jawad Chirri's upstart venture, but it planted its seeds.

"Shaykh Kalil Bazzy was pious," the professor said of the Shiite imam. "He was serious about prayer. But he was a shepherd in the village. He was illiterate when he got to America and taught himself Arabic by reading the Quran." This mattered to Shiites. Although Sunnis will bestow clerical duties on a layman in the absence of someone more qualified, Shiites maintain a complicated canonical structure ruled by grand ayatollahs with varying interpretations; believers choose one to follow. A Shia imam must also be an interlocutor of scholarship, a problem for Bazzy, who, at most, might've been a *hafiz*—one who can recite Quran from memory.

Lebanese Shiites were—and still are back home—a marginalized group predestined for working-class industries. Less incentivized to return to Lebanon, they were more willing than my Sunni great-grandfathers to stick it out in America. "They came here, they got jobs, they got established, and they followed Ford to Dearborn."

Evident in their lower-rung/high-risk factory positions, Syrian Americans didn't receive equal treatment after their national coalition won their legal "white" status in court in 1915. They occupied a middle area in America's racial hierarchy, outnumbering Black employees by ten to one at the Highland Park Plant. But when it came to place of residence, Syrians had the rights and privileges of paler Americans. The suburbs gave their previously abstract whiteness form.

The overwhelmingly Christian lobby that won white classification for Syrians did so by denigrating and distinguishing themselves from darker-skinned Arabs and Muslims. I wondered if local Shiites did the same. Surely the hard-fought battle would leave one of any religion the impression that whiteness was something precarious in need of protection and reinforcement.

"Dearborn itself is filled with an older generation of Arabs who consider (or considered) themselves white and didn't (or don't) have any problem saying so. They are proudly white," said Howell. Some of them may have also harbored anti-Blackness sentiments in line with segregationists, while others collaborated with African Americans on civil rights and labour issues. "But," added Howell, "I'd be stretching to say early Muslims' upward mobility came down to legal and per-ceived whiteness. It was about working-class, immigrant Dearborn, which was also white. They were influenced by their surroundings, which were white."

Their practices, she said, were necessarily adaptive and innovative. This led to some peculiar practices gradually eradicated by postwar Muslim immigrants, including open-casket services, sock hops, and Sunday Sabbath to appease congregants' workaday schedules.

Making it in America has always been a long game, but back then, it took more than patience. Immigration discourse had two sides: melting pot or shut the lid. Cultural pluralism was still a fringe view. Muslims who could thrive in this era were a self-selected bunch willing to assimilate every aspect of life, including their religion. Pan-Islamism was hardly born and the Islamic awakening decades away. Far from seeing eyes, it seemed neither sacrilegious nor difficult to syncretize Islam with American Protestantism.

Imam Jawad Chirri probably felt like he was making alien contact when he arrived from Lebanon in 1948. Pronounced "Shuri"—and definitely not "Cheery"—he was initially repulsed by the innovations that Bazzy approved. Eventually he was swayed by middle-class values.

He assured the upwardly mobile that it's okay to covet social capital and material gains, but prepared them to reach higher for when those yields failed them.

The Islamic Center of America was in part founded on Chirri's certainty that Muslims could cultivate a personal relationship with God. This was downright radical for most Shiites, whose deference and liturgy might be more familiar to Catholics than Sunni Muslims. But Chirri's emphasis on orthodoxy over orthopraxy was necessary to connect with second- and third-generation Americans.

The thought of these old mosques made me nostalgic for an era before me—an era I didn't know previously existed. To me it sounded shrewdly adaptive, even enriching, to embrace new methods of to-getherness. I left Howell's office pondering my conflicted relationship with religion and how my childhood might've panned out differently. If there'd been Christmas activities at my childhood mosque, maybe I would've been more eager to stay and learn. If I'd grown up watching imams preside over interfaith marriages, maybe I wouldn't have felt that Islam conflicted with my values. Would emphasizing belief over practice have stopped me from feeling like I had to choose between them? *Maybe*, but it's likely I'm just bitter about my Christmas-less childhood.

On a gut level, I know that people can't truly separate their rituals from their values. The whole point of the former is to reinforce the latter until they are co-habitual. I also know that transferring culture requires a certain amount of fortification. Christmas at the Mouallems would have probably expedited my apostasy and assimilation, not slowed them. That's probably the case for my daughter, who is more interested in the Elf on the Shelf than the Man in the Sky.

My wife and I encourage Noe to share holidays with her cousins but not creed. We reinforce a respect for personal beliefs, but want her to feel neither pressured to adopt them nor judged if she doesn't. I desperately want Noe to be conscious of her Arab roots without feeling burdened by any cultural baggage. But is that really possible if her parents are ill equipped to foster those feelings at home?

To better understand what it's like to live squeezed within the hyphen of Arab-America, I met the late Imam Mohamad Jawad Chirri's grand-daughter, Rana Abbas Taylor, for lunch at a white tablecloth restaurant. Arriving early, I sipped Turkish tea and read *Arab American News,* a national paper published in Dearborn. It was a bad news week. President Donald Trump proposed revoking green cards and visas for low-income immigrants, even as the United States sold weapons to Saudi Arabia, which was (and still is as of this writing) inflicting war crimes on Yemen, the ancestral nation of many Dearborn Muslims. The cover, though, carried the worst news: After being separated from his wife and children by Trump's travel ban, a distraught Yemeni died by suicide.

It would be hard to find a population more wounded by Trump's disregard for Muslims than that of Dearborn. Over the decades, it's been a lifeline for thousands of Yemenites, Palestinians, and Syrians displaced by war. Sadly, many of their loved ones remained in peril, blocked from entry by Trump's irascible cruelty. A century after US law divided migrant Arabs along colour lines, it was now conflating them along religious lines. The fact that the US Census conflates all Arabs and Middle Easterners as "white," unless otherwise stated, is, at this point, a convenient way of overlooking their unique challenges.

I put away the newspaper when I spotted Rana Taylor enter from the far end of the restaurant. A fashionably dressed professional in her late thirties, it took her a minute or two to make niceties with every-one who knew her. Taylor is director of communications for ACCESS, the largest Arab American nonprofit, which counts the national mu-seum amongst its entities and was currently leading a campaign to get a "MENA" checkbox for Middle Eastern and North African people on the Census. Fielding questions about this, that, and the other are her life.

"Welcome to the jungle," Taylor quipped once she was seated across from me. "Dearborn is like a big town. You only have so many families, and the majority of Lebanese are from Bint Jbeil, a tiny vil-lage in southern Lebanon."

"What's that like?" I asked.

She clenched her teeth and swayed her head. "It has the high points and low points of living in a larger Arab American community," she said. "Your business is not your own. There's a need to keep up appearances, make sure you're representing your family well."

"Because honour," I added.

"And when you're a woman . . ." she trailed off. Ten years ago, Taylor thought she'd left Dearborn for good after suffering sexist backlash from a divorce and from a harassment case brought by Taylor and other female employees against the director of the American-Arab Anti-Discrimination Committee. Though Taylor has returned to metropolitan Detroit, she lives a good twenty miles outside Dearborn city limits. Suffice to say, she has a complicated relationship with her hometown. But like an annoying sibling, she will defend it against bullies.

"People don't see how multilayered Dearborn is," Taylor said over a spread of fattoush salad, lentil soup, and fried haloumi. "You've got your recent immigrants, third- and fourth-generation Arab Americans. Your entrepreneurs, scholars, conservatives, progressives, Arab Americans running for office. The spotlight has been on the city, not so much the people and their influence, which extends far beyond this place."

There's something uniquely, terrifically American about the city that deserves celebrating, but it comes with a burden of responsibility that predates the War on Terror. It's commonly assumed that the "Muslim vote" was energized by President George W. Bush. In fact, it was *presidential candidate* George W. Bush. In the final stretch of his 2000 election, his campaign tried to swing the purple state back into Republican control with Arab and Muslim Americans. They were easily wooed, having been political pariahs for so long due to America's increasing Middle Eastern entanglements. Even Democrats kept them at a distance. Both of Reagan's Democratic opponents rebuffed endorsements and donations from Arab American groups. It had the expected effect of turning the small voting bloc apathetic, until Bush saw their potential.

"Arab Americans have always understood themselves to be the underdog," said Taylor. "It said a lot to the community that a presidential candidate would come to Dearborn specifically to court their vote."

It seemed like a perfect union. Bush's family values, pro-business stance, and religious devotion were qualities perfectly at home with Muslims. Contrary to popular assumption, many of Dearborn's Iraqi and Shia felt Bush Sr. faulted in the Gulf War only by not finishing the job and bringing an end to Saddam Hussein's tyranny. Late in the 2000 presidential election, the Bush campaign invited a coalition of community leaders to Dearborn's Hyatt Regency to make the case for an endorsement. Though he didn't win the county, he secured their support and 70 percent of Muslim voters nationwide, including the majority of Florida's ummah, putting him over the top.

"I remember voting Nader in 2000 and being mad at my parents for voting for Bush," Taylor said with a laugh. "And *then* 9/11 happened, and the world began to shift for us, leaving us to wonder: How valued are we really? It felt like a betrayal with the party."

Taylor felt that betrayal from the inside out. She'd just started her communications job at the Arab-American Anti-Discrimination Committee, fresh out of college, when she entered the office in time to see the second plane crash into the South Tower on TV. As her mind raced with the same questions in every American's mind, her office phone disrupted her thoughts. "It was a Fox News journalist asking for my thoughts on the possibility that it may have been a quote-unquote 'Arab terrorist' behind it. I was still glued to the TV, wondering, 'Are we being attacked on American soil?' and was suddenly forced to put up defences," she said. "We never got to process the attack as Americans."

Thrust into the spotlight, Dearbornians' first instincts were to prove their patriotism. Nary a lawn or store window was without a flag. Mosques welcomed federal law enforcement. Taylor wasn't immune to this collective apologia. In 2008, she took a job with a DC company contracted to provide interpretation and translation services to US soldiers in Iraq. Taylor believed then that she could serve her community better working on the inside, a mistake she'll never make again. "I don't believe in my government the way that I did ten years ago," she said with a strained voice. "None of us ever thought our people—that we would elect . . ."

Taylor swallowed the lump in her throat and dabbed her eyes. She struggled to recall the morning after Trump was elected and that he won it because of Michigan. "While I'd lost faith in my government, I had, up until that point, deeply rooted faith in the people of this country. It was the first time in my life that I felt I wasn't wanted here. It shook me."

Trump's presidency had an unexpected effect on Taylor's Islamic heritage. She'd long stopped practicing her faith and was conflicted about identifying as Muslim. She now covets it not for its spiritualism but its iconoclastic meaning. "I want to get in your face and defy every misconception you have about what a Muslim woman looks like. I want to screw up your worldview," she said.

I related to Taylor completely. Despite lacking Islam's most rudimentary beliefs, I've become protective of my religious roots and feel rebellious when I declare myself Muslim in the face of bigots or zealots. Whether or not you choose to wear your identity, it sometimes wears you and often wears you down. But in the end, a Muslim isn't baptized in the faith. Muslims are those who declare themselves one. That's the egalitarian nature of Islam: you choose what you are, naysayers be damned.

Back on Ford Road, I looked out for the Islamic Center's glimmering dome, twin minarets, and gigantic American flag. It's a $16 million testament to the deep roots and prominence of local Muslims. In addition to the centre's school, lecture hall, and bookstore, there's a miniature museum curated with more portraits of its founder than I could count.

Rebuilt with all the grandiosity of its name in 2005, a little more than a decade after Imam Jawad Chirri died, the ICA remains a stopover for politicians seeking the Muslim vote. It's also a favourite cudgel of trolls seeking to provoke the fabled Muslim rage. "Based on the scale we envisioned, we knew it would be the source of attention both positive and negative," the centre's director, Kassem Allie, told me as we walked the circular corridor before *Salat al-Jumah* (Friday service).

We removed our shoes and placed them on a rack outside the

prayer hall cupped beneath the dome. Sunshine poured through the Turkish windows, and a large gold-plated chandelier inspired by Saudi Arabia's Al-Medina mosque twinkled above me. The sereneness betrayed a stressful morning for Allie, thrust into funeral director mode following the death of a prominent community member the previous night. She was to be buried within twenty-four hours, according to custom. Over a thousand people were expected to arrive immediately after Jumah prayer.

Summoned repeatedly to tend to funeral arrangements, Allie invited me to complete my tour self-guided and then meet him in his office once he felt that he could sit. I spent some of that time chatting with volunteers of a Muslim youth group setting up a voter registration booth for the coming primary election. Hopes were high for one local congressional candidate, Rashida Tlaib, a labour rights lawyer, who would inaugurate her victory with a prescient anti-Trump rallying cry: "Impeach the motherfucker!" (You can get it on a T-shirt now.)

The volunteers were joined by writer and law professor Khaled Beydoun, one of a number of semifamous Arab Americans to come out of Dearborn. He was signing and selling copies of his book, *American Islamophobia: Understanding the Roots and Rise of Fear*, to worshippers who've known him since he was a little boy. The son of a Shia man and a Sunni woman, Beydoun gravitated more to his mother's faith, but he still attended the ICA on occasion. It was vandalized by bigots during his childhood, but after 9/11, Beydoun, then a college freshman, watched it become a target of right-wing extremism. It gave him an up-close view of this uniquely Western hysteria that he would later define as "American Islamophobia."

I asked Beydoun how he felt when the ICA became not just highly politicized but *political*. Its second imam, Sayyid Hassan al-Qazwini, another Muslim celebrity, had the ear of President George W. Bush—literally, in the mosque's museum, there was a picture of Bush kissing the imam's cheek. It was taken after a rally drumming up support for the Iraq War.

"Muslims are citizens. They should be part of this country's halls of power," Beydoun said flatly before easing into his next, more complicated point. "But Muslims must be intelligent about which department or agency they work with. The state has been really clever and strategic in enlisting Muslims in ways that capitalize on their identity to further policies that are disruptive to the communities."

Beydoun witnessed the fault lines within the American experiment *and* within the American ummah experiment that transpired throughout the Iraq War. He saw how the state seized on those divisions to groom informants, push surveillance, and ultimately push their agenda. And he saw Qazwini, his city's most prominent imam, on TV as the face of Muslim American support for the war and administration.

Qazwini was an easy mark for the Bush administration after 9/11. Qazwini's honorific, Sayyid, denotes lineage to Prophet Muhammad, and his grandfather, an esteemed Iraqi ayatollah, was one of many dissidents to disappear during Saddam Hussein's reign. It was obvious to everyone in Dearborn that both Q. and W. had axes to grind. But to everyone watching Qazwini on CNN, he just looked like the face of America's preeminent Islamic centre.

Beydoun does not have many kind things to say about the Obama administration, let alone that of George W. Bush. Yet he was surprisingly forgiving of the imam's transgressions. Qazwini, who recently left to start another megamosque and seminary, was not the only Muslim celebrity at Bush's beck and call. Muslim Americans beyond Dearborn were also swept up in War on Terror propaganda. In fact, Beydoun says it's time the media found itself another so-called American Mecca. "You have different enclaves in New York and cities like Minneapolis, which is home to a huge and concentrated Somali community," he said. "I think it's high time for the media to realize that Dearborn isn't the only American city manifesting the Muslim experience."

I was curious to learn how the ICA was doing under the fascistic new regime without the public face or prowess it had twenty years ago. I finally got a chance to ask Kassem Allie how the centre reconciled with its regrettable past while steering through peak American Islamaphobia. As the Islamic Center of America, it's not enough to only serve its congregants, however many thousands there are; it's expected to also pick up the phone for lecturers, public servants, activists, and, of course, journalists.

Kassem said the centre has backed away from the public square after tiring of the perpetual reactiveness. Every time there's an incident involving Muslims, they're expected to comment. "We're a diverse community that includes Republicans, Democrats, families that have been here for generations, new arrivals, people who practice their faith strictly, and people who don't," said Allie with some frustration. "We have found that the best and most sustainable way of addressing issues and criticisms is to live our faith the way we want to live our faith, as Americans."

He was evading a bit. The centre's most recent political snafu arose from hosting a peace delegation attended by an Israeli military officer. This appalled pro-Palestinian activists and congregants, many of them ordinary people who had lived under Israeli occupation in Lebanon's southern Shiite enclave. The end result was that Allie had to manage a careful apology on behalf of the executive committee.

I pried a little into the board's politics. Most of them are successful Lebanese businessmen, who might have voted Republican in 2016 if the candidate wasn't a lunatic. But Allie deflected any question about the centre's political leanings. He bristled at my use of the terms *progressive* ("How many different definitions are attached to it?" he asked) and *moderate* ("That has connotations that we're 'the good' Muslims, not 'those' Muslims"), and saved the most annoyance for *centrist*. ("It used to mean 'bipartisan'; now it means you want to sit on the fence.")

I sympathized with Allie. Though you'll never hear me whining about "cancel culture," I know exactly what it feels like to get chewed up by your political allies for offending them in bad judgment. Yet if President Trump wanted to step inside the Islamic Center of America, he said, "We would consider it very seriously."

I couldn't believe hospitality was even an option for the godfather of birtherism—a man who launched his political career by repeating "Barrack *Hussein* Obama" over and over again. He followed up with calls for Muslim bans, Muslim registrations, closures of Muslim temples; both Allie and I knew that this was a turning point in American history. That he would even entertain this hypothetical Trump visit indicated the ICA was not ready to part with its founder's vision of the mosque as consulate.

While the centre's civic and social DNA are apparent everywhere, its white Protestant influences are all but gone. Religious services are, by and large, by the book. The changes were not Sayyid Qazwini's, though part of his departure stemmed from the board's lenience on social engagements. The shake-up in religious practice was led by Chirri.

According to Najah Bazzy, a humanitarian and niece of Shaykh Khalil Bazzy, who attended the centre for most of her life, Chirri was a conflicted imam. He struggled with the compromises he made for his congregation. "They had bingo, danced, had Thanksgiving, funerals were open casket!" she told me by phone. (We'd scheduled to meet, but her best friend was the deceased being mourned at the ICA that afternoon.) It might have been a relief for Chirri, then, when the Iranian Islamic Revolution sent shock waves through Dearborn's Shia community.

Ruhollah Khomeini, the most conservative of the "big four" grand ayatollahs, saw the uprising as an opportunity to become the head honcho. Perhaps the Islamic Center mosque would've flown under the radar if Chirri himself wasn't so prominent. "Suddenly, it was like marching orders came from Iran that said, 'Shape up or you're out.' There was no transition time," said Bazzy. Then a young nurse raised on Christmases and Easter egg hunts, she pushed back against the "haram (sin) police" enforcing headscarves at secular events and gender segregation.

Bazzy proudly covers her hair in public today. Obviously, she came to agree with most of the reforms in her mosque. She only wishes they were phased in for those who couldn't adjust as well as her. "Till this day," said Bazzy, "I feel like a generation—thousands—was lost."

Her friend's funeral would be closed casket; the sacred *janazah* prayer, gender segregated. Though small Shia rituals stood out to me, nothing about it would surprise a Shiite from outside Dearborn save for a collection basket sliding across the luxurious carpet.

I popped a few bucks in the basket and handed it to the brother beside me, only a little bemused by this Christian spin on Muslim alms. My attention was focused more on the chasm between males and females together inside the single, open chamber. Once we lined up for salat, you could've held a floor hockey match in the clearing.

I noticed the sparsity of worshippers during the adhan. The megamosque designed for one thousand had about one hundred this day. While it's true that Shiites are more lenient than Sunnis when it comes to attending Friday prayer, based on what I was seeing in the room, they'd need much more in the collection basket to maintain the upkeep on a 92,000-square-foot building.

The centre was supposed to symbolize Islam's place in the West and Dearborn's place in Western Islam. Once the largest mosque west of Africa, it seemed to me now a glorified funeral parlour. Sure enough, as I walked back to my car, the parking lot was quickly filling up with people coming to pay their respects.

The director of the Center for Arab American Studies, Sally Howell, had told me something obvious yet enlightening about American Islam. It's defined by thousands of independent, nonprofit groups—mosques and community centres—which in turn are defined not by religious bureaucrats or mullah elites but by membership. "They're voluntary, so boards of directors have a lot of power. That's a particularly American model," Howell told me. Unlike mosques in stricter Eastern settings, Western mosques, as a matter of law, operate in free-market form without any archdiocese-style structures protecting the establishment from major shake-ups. "Transitions of leadership are just brutal," she added. Brutal, but democratic.

Najah Bazzy echoed this when she pointed me toward a YouTube video of Sayyid al-Qazwini's last sermon at the Islamic Center of America. He had by then rebuilt the jamaat's numbers, evident in a full prayer hall. Compared to the turnout I'd witnessed, I could hardly believe it was the same mosque only a few years ago.

Qazwini's appeal to Western values had refilled the mosque after decades of atrophy, but his relationship with the Lebanese board of directors was strained from the start. It blew up one Friday in 2015 while cameras streamed his sermon, in which he publicly announces his hijrah—referring to the forced migration of persecuted Muslims to Medina.

The mesmerizing video offers a glimpse into the ICA's toxic internal politics. A feud had led to an all-out smear campaign against Qazwini's family and his opponents on the board of directors. As congregants pleaded for him to stay and shouted at each other, Najah Bazzy, Qazwini's close ally, marched from the women's section, through the men, and took the imam's microphone to reprimand their foul behaviour. "We're going to lose the center, we're going to lose our imam, and we're going to lose [another] generation of Muslims?" she asked rhetorically. "Not on my time." She then turned to Qazwini, the imam she helped recruit almost twenty years before. "If you go, we go. If you stay, things must change."

Bazzy did follow Qazwini. But what about the collective "we"— the hundreds of people now missing from the centre's prayer hall? Did they go with Qazwini, too, or did they just stop going, like many a generation before them?

A full year passed until I scheduled a meeting with Imam Qazwini. I timed it for Move, a biennial summit of Arab American art, culture, and activism. Organized by ACCESS in November 2019, the two-day conference launched with a boozy soiree at the Arab American National Museum and ended by giving away five Arab American Book Awards. Over at the ultramodern Henry Hotel, I met the coolest Arab Americans ever—comic book artists, Yemeni craft coffee brewers, and now Congresswoman Rashida Tlaib. One of three panelists discussing intersectional feminism, she told the story of Dearborn's first #MeToo moment, the one in which she, Rana Taylor Abbas, and many other women faced backlash for outing a predator sitting at the top rung of Arab American power.

I was having such a good time that I didn't want to leave for the interviews I'd flown back for. I was tempted to try to reschedule with the illustrious Sayyid. Knowing how busy he keeps at the new Islamic

Institute of America, I sided with better judgment. I drove back onto Ford Road, travelled four miles west of the grand Islamic Center of America, and arrived at a humbler (though definitely not humble) megamosque.

It was converted from a Baptist church in Dearborn Heights, a wealthier suburb gerrymandered as a safe space for whites in the sixties. It still operates that way if you consider fifth-generation Lebanese Americans part of the white race, as the Census does.

Though its dome and banquet hall were still blueprints, the congregation had already accomplished many of their goals. There was a several-hundred-seat lecture hall in addition to its several-hundred-more-seat prayer hall; a state-of-the-art morgue for free funeral services; and a campus seminary of four hundred multigender students attending in-person and online, most working toward a four-year diploma in Islamic theology. This was always Qazwini's dream. He wrote about it over a decade ago in *American Crescent*, his celebrity memoir. I wanted to learn everything I could about his method of training America's next religious leaders.

I checked in at the administration office and asked for the imam.

"Which imam?" the secretary replied.

"Al-Qazwini."

"Which Qazwini? The older or the younger?" Apparently, his eldest son, Ahmed, managed the operation with him.

"The senior Qazwini," I said.

"He's not here yet," she apologized. She summoned a volunteer to give me the full tour. We finished it in the grand prayer hall named after the third infallible imam, Husayn ibn Ali, the Prophet's grandson slaughtered in the Battle of Karbala, the tragedy mourned annually on the Shia holiday Ashura. My young and affable guide, a full-time medical student, asked me if I planned on coming to Friday prayers the next day. I told him yes. "Then you want to get a parking spot quick, because they go fast."

"Brother Omar?" someone called to me. I turned to see Sayyid Hassan al-Qazwini. He wore a neat black turban, a long tunic called a *thobe*, and a brown cape that soared as he approached me with an open palm. Our trim beards bristled together as he pulled me in for a hug. I had already deduced his friendliness from the rose emojis in his text messages, but this was next level. I suspected ulterior motives for it— he wouldn't be the first source to greet me with a hug, or even a kiss if he tried—but the more we spoke, the more I believed his warmth to be genuine.

He didn't hold back about his differences with the ICA. "There was an intellectual incompatibility," he said. "If you dive down, they consider it a Lebanese social club. But if you are the Islamic Center of America, you have to open up to all of America. I wanted to have a place where all Muslims—Sunni, Shia, Arabs, not Arabs, Lebanese, Iraqi—feel welcome." To him, the ICA could've been the Vatican of American Islam. "It's like having the body of a dinosaur but the brain of a bird."

Keeping up the appearance of harmony for so long, he said, had led to an "artificial life." He was too emotionally and psychologically attached to it—an imprisonment, he admitted, that was self-imposed. He said he felt liberated to leave the centre behind, where his "public affairs" duties had kept him from enacting his vision for an English-language seminary. By circumventing Arabic, they've reached Western-born Muslims who might make Islam more accessible for future generations of the English-speaking world.

"Our goal," he said, "is to meet the needs of a growing community in the United States. We have new mosques being established without trained full-time imams. They don't speak the language—by that I mean the intellectual language. Muslims who are born in this country adapt to the American psyche, whether we like it or not. Accepting liberal values, tolerating others, believing that democracy and freedom is embedded within them. Those who come from the Middle East have difficulty understanding that."

The imam can get frank about social issues with his congregants. The most relevant education of this Iranian-educated, Lebanese-trained, American imam might be his bachelor of sociology degree from the University of Michigan. His priorities in America are different than they would be back home. He can't fuss about sectarianism while dealing with America's higher rates of divorce, drug abuse, and parental abandonment. "We owe it to our community."

A knock at the door interrupted our conversation. He answered to an elderly woman who'd scheduled a private meeting with him.

"Please forgive me," he apologized. "I have another appointment." He invited me to continue the interview late that night at his house. "We can order pizza."

I arrived there after dark. The Qazwini family lived in a big house in a suburb west of Dearborn Heights and one degree nicer. Theirs was not the only house without Christmas decorations and an American flag, but it was in the minority.

I knocked and waited. The imam answered the door with a hearty "Salamu alaykum" and pulled me in for another hug. He still looked dressed up in a capeless navy thobe, but his exposed hair, bare feet, and the pizza delivery was an invitation for me to get real with him.

I asked if he regretted befriending President Bush, endorsing him and some of his early policies.

Qazwini said no. "But sometimes," he added, "I think I was pushed beyond my comfort zone. I was surrounded by politicians, and I'm not a politician. I have a mission to build bridges and be a spokesperson for my religion, and so I have to meet with politicians. But in my heart, I'm not one."

He said he never tried to get anything for himself from the Iraq War, though he claimed that he was offered a cabinet position in the country's new government. Minister of religious affairs in Iraq was his or a family member's if he wanted it, according to Qazwini. He said this disturbed him. During his seminary training in Iran, his ethics teacher warned against the trappings of success.

I reminded him of his personal reasons for wanting the removal of Saddam Hussein. He didn't deny it, but he was quick to remind me of Saddam Hussein's body count. Hussein was a political gangster whose brutality only Iraqis, Kurds, and Kuwaitis can truly comprehend. "Yes, I did believe Saddam was a cancer that should be removed," he said, "but not necessarily with the American plan." He said he'd never again lend his voice to another president, Republican or Democrat, except for Bernie Sanders. (The Democratic Party presidential primaries had just begun. Qazwini would, in fact, stump for Sanders during the 2020 primaries, until the progressive Jewish candidate became aware of the imam's "dangerous, hateful" and "toxic" 2015 past statements regarding same-sex marriage and Israel.)

"Did you feel like you had to atone for supporting the war?" I asked.

"No, but I felt like I had to explain myself."

Here's what he says is the true story behind the "kiss." Just days after the United States declared victory in Iraq, Bush, on his way to make his cartoonish "Mission Accomplished" speech on an aircraft carrier, stopped in Dearborn to rally an audience of five hundred Arab and Muslim Americans under a "Renewal in Iraq" banner. His administration invited Qazwini and other community leaders to meet with the president backstage at the Ford Community and Performing Arts Center. Qazwini was the last of the leaders to speak with him; the others had already taken their seats on the rally stage while the crowd chanted, "We love Bush" and "U.S.A."

Qazwini told me he planned to leave immediately after delivering an important message to the president. "I wanted him to know that, now that Saddam is removed, Iraqis will not accept anything less than a democratic government that is truly representative of Iraqis," he told me. Qazwini suspected, correctly as it were, that the United States would hand-pick Iraq's next president from the Shia majority rather than risk the election of an Iranian stooge. He said his piece, it fell on deaf ears, and he was ready to go home. "When we were leaving, I realized all the exits were locked. The only open door was to the rally. And guess what? When I got out there, there was only one seat, left for me, directly behind George W. I was uncomfortable—visibly uncomfortable—sitting behind him."

"This is when the infamous kissing picture was taken?"

"He kissed me!" he said with a laugh.

Tempted as I was to google the picture, show him that the only visibly puckered lips in it are his, I moved on and asked him a question that weighed heavily on his congregation. "Do you feel like you were being used?"

Qazwini thought about this awhile. "Maybe. But I had no way out."

Earlier he'd said that he had no regrets, and I believed that *he* believed this, but I doubted he was fully at peace with his past. "Is there anything you would do differently?" I asked.

"I would do everything the same," he began, "with the exception of not meeting Bush."

"Which meeting?"

"All the meetings. I wasn't the one who convinced him to remove Saddam, but I'm sure it helped convince him."

He'd offered a remarkable confession. According to the imam, "the kiss" photo actually captures their last words, the end of a friendship that began with candidate Bush's courtship in 2000. Subsequent requests from the White House were turned down and unanswered by Qazwini, including a state dinner with President Obama. So, on one hand, Qazwini insisted he'd acted with good judgment, yet if he could change anything, it would be *everything*.

I left his house full on pizza, pondering for the first time an imam's humanity. I had understood them only as influential men preoccupied by scripture, parishioners, and funds. I wondered about the private lives of the other Detroit imams, past and present.

In addition to being preachers, teachers, funeral home directors, youth counsellors, marriage counsellors, and divorce counsellors, they were public figures burdened by interfaith, cultural, and political responsibilities. They were also husbands, parents, patriots, conscientious and fallible people.

These imams didn't always get it right as they tried to explain Islam to confused Americans inside and outside their mosques. How could anyone spread so thinly keep his judgment intact? Regardless, their mistakes were made in good-faith belief in what was best for their fellow Americans.

The medical student volunteering at the Islamic Institute of America was right: the parking does fill up fast on Fridays.

Six or seven hundred worshippers squeezed inside nearly every prayer stall on the blue and gold carpet. Each reached into a basket on the way in, grabbing a chunk of Karbala in the form of a smooth, flat, engraved rock. They placed the pucks on the carpet where their foreheads would touch the floor. I respectfully joined in their Shia tradition, as I squeezed into a patch of carpet under a big chandelier.

The only sign it wasn't purpose-built for Muslims was the qibla's awkward angle, forty-five degrees east of the pulpit, toward an exit. As congregants chatted quietly, I detected generations of American life in their accents. That's who followed Qazwini out the ICA's door—fifth- and sixth-generation Americans, and, quite possibly, the country's oldest continuous Muslim congregation.

The imam entered to a chorus of greetings. His robe flowed like water at his back as he strode to the pulpit to deliver his sermon, first in English, then in Arabic. A woven basket of bills was passed around while the imam beseeched against severing family ties in the face of divorce, inheritance fights, and bad business dealings. It felt relevant to Western life, where the cult of individualism so often complicates Islamic family values.

There's an assumption that Muslim and American values are incompatible, that you can't have one without subverting the other. Muslims in the Eastern Hemisphere are just as likely to believe this as non-Muslims in the West. Everyone else knows it's not true; it's a matter of learning how to make these values click together. The importance of his seminary couldn't be clearer to me now. The homegrown experience and education of his students can prepare a future in which Muslim Americans will feel less tension between their religious and social lives. It occurred to me in that moment that I'd overlooked another Islamic awakening happening before my eyes, not the postcolonial Islamist movement but an American awakening born of another trauma. The Islamic Institute of America showed how far one will go to protect a sacred piece of personal identity.

There's another false assumption, one perpetuated entirely by paranoid Americans: there's something insidious going on inside the mosque next door. True, there's tension aplenty in many mosques small and mega, but they're irrelevant to these deplorables' worst fears. They're clashes over cultural and generational values, gender roles, theological preferences—things that would appear as minutiae to all but the congregation.

After prayer, I lifted myself up, shook a few strangers' hands, grabbed my jacket, and made a dash for the airport. I looped back onto Ford Road one last time. Along the way, I drove past the legendary factory that made Ford king of a whites-only subdivision and quite the social engineer. He built row houses for workers at the bottom of the "white" working class, a place where they could have a stable family life, send their kids to Fordson High, and die peacefully at Henry Ford Hospital.

I really don't know if my great-grandpa could have stomached this Fordlandia. The young man chose to begin his family in Lebanon before Henry Ford could realize his master plans for America. But I'm confident he would be proud of the place that Dearborn has become.

A Tale of Two Mosques
Al Rashid Mosque
(Edmonton, Alberta)

The First Mosque in America
(Ross, North Dakota)

I know that man!"

Seventy-nine-year-old Richard Awid pivoted his walking cane toward the voice. He instantly recognized the gold-trimmed train conductor hat and double-breasted suit. "Bill," said Awid, a big smile under his glasses resting on the tip of his nose. They shook hands outside Fort Edmonton Park, a wormhole through time to the Western frontier. Bill was the living museum's steam train conductor who usually shuttled tourists back and forth between the fur trading era and the Roaring Twenties. However, all that summer the train had been in maintenance, leaving Bill with little to do but hand out walking maps around the entrance, while surrounded by gaggles of kids being advised by chaperones not to harass the goats and turkeys also kept inside.

The two men haven't seen each other since Awid's wife, Soraya Hafez, fell ill in 2015 and he quit volunteering as a historical interpreter to care for her. I knew all about this not only because Richard

Awid and Soraya are my relatives through marriage, but because they're legendary in the local Arab community. Hafez, an Egyptian-born teacher, introduced into Canada's public system a K–12 Arabic bilingual curriculum, which has since expanded to several public schools nationwide. She and Awid also helped get Edmonton's Al Rashid mosque historical designation, making it the country's only Islamic heritage site and launching a fourteen-year effort to save it from the wrecking ball.

I stood by as "Rich" and Bill caught up on changes at the park and their mutual relatives, linked by their shared Ukrainian heritage. The children lined up for tickets would soon learn a great deal about the Alberta capital's Slavic influence from a costumed shop clerk at the Ukrainian Bookstore on 1905 Street, named for the year a train station opened Edmonton up to waves of Eastern Europeans, and whose descendants make up almost a fifth of its 1 million residents today. But back when Awid, a retired teacher, volunteered at the park, he wouldn't have been teaching European settler history in tweed hats and suspenders, like most of the costumed interpreters there. You'd have found him at the Al Rashid Mosque, the first Muslim house of worship built in Canada, and since moved to be carefully preserved on this grassy knoll. It is the last stop of the outdoor museum before the boardwalk curves into a midway—the main attraction for the children racing inside the park. We followed them, entering as we would eventually exit, through the gift shop, past old-timey confection and toys, before the old friends parted ways.

Awid led me to the mosque for a private tour like the ones he used to offer, salary free, for two hundred hours every summer. Along the way, he greeted costumed former colleagues who briefly broke character to make small talk. I recognized them too from a decade prior. My wife put herself through school as a historical interpreter, donning a bustle and gown in the role of "Ms. MacDonald," which isn't far from her Scottish roots. For our first few dates she invited me to after-hours staff parties, infamous for drunken dandies climbing the palisades and couples sneaking off to historical landmarks. (The train—Bill, I'm sorry—was quite popular.) The mosque was perhaps the only place considered off-limits. Al Rashid is widely understood as the park's most culturally sensitive landmark.

Awid and his wife were at the forefront of a contentious campaign to display the mosque in Fort Edmonton. It was moved there from its original site in 1992, but only after three years of politicking and petitioning for its preservation. The museum board fought the inclusion of the mosque based on an arbitrary vision of local history that began in 1846 with the fur trade and ended in 1920 with the metropolitan era. "They weren't open minded enough to realize the value of it, but I've always preached that this is part of Edmonton's history, part of Alberta's history, part of Canada's history," said Awid.

Besides the cane and long shoehorn he used to swat at wasps, Awid was wearing basically the same outfit he'd always worn to teach tourists about Muslim and Arab Canadian history: a plaid shirt and grey cardigan. Visitors to the mosque might have expected to meet a man in gold-threaded robes and turban, but his wardrobe more closely resembled the get-up of Edmonton's first imam, "James," a Lebanese property developer who was elected to lead prayers because few else could recite Quran as well.

"You didn't need a religious person to lead prayer back then. You could nominate someone from the community who was knowledgeable," Awid explained. His own father, Ahmed Awid, was certainly pious enough to qualify to lead prayers, but he wasn't even involved in teaching Awid how to pray. He'd arrived in 1901 from Lebanon's Bekaa Valley. Young Ahmed was running from Ottoman army conscription. His time in Canada was supposed to be temporary, but success as a travelling salesman gave him reason to stay.

Ahmed's story is a common one. By the early 1900s, peddling had become a way of life for Arab bachelors. They usually started in Montreal or New York, working for some warehouse or factory operated by Christian Syrians who had gained mercantile experience back home. Muslims, however, often migrated from rural areas and lacked any of the connections their employers would have made at Sunday mass. "The Christian felt much more comfortable and at home," explained Awid, "whereas the Muslim was more on his own. He becomes the peddler, putting packs on his back, walking around to make a living, moving out westward to small communities that needed stuff."

Their treks ended once they'd earned enough to open a general store in some boomtown. Until then, they relied on the generosity of strangers for a night's rest and reciprocated with fabrics, perfumes, and toys. They also carried lesser-known stock, like chickpeas and sumac, because they were bound to meet Arab farmers across the prairies.

Starting in the 1890s, Syrian–Lebanese took up homesteading to escape factory conditions. The promise of hundreds of acres of land—free, so long as it was cultivated and inhabited within a few years—must have sounded like a dream to my great-great grandpa, Abdul Kareem Mouallem, who ventured off to Saskatchewan with his brother-in-law Dubyan. They were somewhat naive thinking their farming backgrounds would transfer to the unbroken, temperamental land. Abdul Kareem returned to Lebanon after a few years, but Dubyan stayed. He sent for his wife and adult daughter, who worked alongside him. They tied a rope from the sod house to the barn in order to locate their livestock in whiteout conditions. When a blizzard crashed in on his daughter's wedding in January 1930, they made the best of it, stretching festivities on for seven days and nights of dancing and singing until it was safe for guests to return home.

As an Arab Muslim woman, Dubyan's daughter would have fetched quite the dowry. Due to their scarcity, the first Muslim men intermarried. A small Chipewyan Lebanese group emerged in Turtle Mountain, North Dakota, but most, like Awid's father, Ahmed, sought courtship from Eastern Europeans. (English and French women gave the men as little attention as the men gave Indigenous women.) However, as homesteaders arrived in droves, establishing pockets of Arabia amid wheat and mustard fields, mixed families became infrequent. By the 1920s, about three thousand Syrians lived in the Dakotas, of whom one-third were Muslim. They viewed the thousands of kilometres and borders between them almost as they would the next town over in Lebanon's Bekaa Valley. The same Saskatchewan shaykh, an authorized faith leader, oversaw marriages and funerals in Alberta, Wyoming, and the Dakotas.

Despite thousands of Arab farmers, it was the mysterious peddler who'd represent Middle Easterners in white imaginations. He was such an archetype that he appeared in several frontier plays, including *Green Grow the Lilacs* (later *Oklahoma!*, though, by then, the peddler was made a Persian). Newspapers often portrayed the peddler as a sexual menace and trickster, advising Americans to shun him. "Stick to your town and her business people," warned an edition of the Oklahoma *Beaver*, because the peddlers "stick it to you." But for the isolated settlers, the peddler's arrival was a welcome break, an exotic interlude in a monotonous life, and a window to an almost forgotten world.

A modern version of the Lebanese peddler still exists on the prairies. Whenever my dad spotted a utility van parked outside the hockey arena, dressed top to bottom with cannabis flags, Bob Marley beach towels, and other kitsch, he'd pull over to welcome the traveller to town. I might see the van again outside our house, while the driver visited my dad, before it disappeared to the next town, making room for another van outside the rink a few months later. In his admiration of peddlers, Awid reminded me of my father. "They're so creative and so aggressive in wanting to achieve," said Awid, as we turned the corner of 1920 Street.

That ingenuity is one reason Muslims were able to quickly establish themselves across the prairies and construct some of North America's earliest mosques, including Edmonton's Al Rashid in 1938; the Mother Mosque of Cedar Rapids, Iowa, in 1934; and the inaccurately named First Mosque in America in, of all places, a North Dakota hamlet called Ross, in 1929. I knew some of this history already, but this would usually be the moment in the tour when visitors would say, "Seriously? North America's oldest mosques are in the frontier West?"

I may have asked that myself when I first met Awid in 2006, after moving back to Alberta during my peak militant atheism. He'd married into our family and took an interest in my creative pursuits in a way few uncles did. Awid gave me a book he'd written about the first Arabs in Canada, full of distant relatives who extended my Canadian roots by seventy years in an instant. It didn't occur to me that they were actors in an aggressive takeover of treaty territory, accelerants of ethnic cleansing. Rather, in that moment, I felt more connected to my country, and maybe some cognitive dissonance by taking pride in my ancestors for making religious history.

Their legacy, Al Rashid, revealed itself from behind a row of jack pines. Its twin minarets were like arms attached to the wrong body. The single-storey square brick building with arched windows looked more like a Ukrainian Orthodox Church than a mosque, even more so when it was still topped by a purely cosmetic dome, which was lost during a 1947 renovation. The design quirk is often miscredited to its Ukrainian architect's tastes. In fact, the architecture is an eclectic mix of Slavic, Methodist, and Islamic, while the gabled roof is plain practical for five months of winter.

A rope outside the prayer hall stopped Awid and me from entering with our shoes on. I kicked off my sneakers at the heel and he pried his feet from his loafers with his shoehorn. Neither of us bothered to place them on the shelf (tidily, as our fathers taught us). From the looks of it, we might've been the first people all summer to enter the prayer hall, which was more hollow than hallow. The bare white walls framed a room so small it didn't need a structural beam. Only the skillfully crafted *minbar*, an elevated wood pulpit for Friday sermon, drew my attention.

It looked like any small-town mosque across Canada and the United States, though even my childhood mosque in Slave Lake, 250 kilometres north, might've been an upgrade, as it was fully carpeted. Only three of the five large Persian rugs laid across the hardwood floor were original to 1938. "You can tell how people prayed on them from the wear and tear," said Awid. He pointed his foot to a white spot in the rouge damask patterns. "Like right here. The more tear there is, the closer the rug was to the front, but now they're out of order."

Though humble to modern eyes, Al Rashid, meaning "the rightly guided," was an impressive construction at the height of the Great Depression. At $6,000 with land and furnishings ($108,000 today, Canadian dollars) it was a sacrifice in every sense of the word. But the community's spiritual needs were more distressed than its economic realities.

"The mosque was established by local businesspeople who feared they were losing their culture and religion," Awid told me. "Before that, they were gathering at each other's homes to pray and discuss community matters. They had two choices. They could build a secular community centre or they could build a mosque."

"Or they could do both," I said, recalling how after lining up for Eid prayers in my childhood mosque I'd rush downstairs to the social hall, hurrying past trays of meat pies and cheesecake, to be the first in line for Eid money doled out, one five-dollar bill at a time, to each kid by the imam. Awid's mind went back to his childhood too. He remembered the Muslim Ladies Association's Sunday lunches in the mosque's basement attended by the mayor. He listed the delicious Lebanese food they'd sell, some of it provided by his Ukrainian mother. She never formally converted to Islam or learned many Arabic words, but her fried kibbe dumplings were as good as her pierogies.

An informal version of the Ladies Association existed even before the walls of Al Rashid were erected, and the women of the community continued to be important stewards of the mosque and interfaith relations. They were young and energetic homemakers, busied by the caretaking of so many kids. Most men couldn't stick around long after Friday prayers, so it's reasonable to assume it was the women, socializing with sugary sweet tea and bitter coffee, who raised the idea of a formal gathering place. They dedicated themselves to creating an institution that would pass their language and faith to the children running amok in the yard.

Many reasons have been offered for why North America's first minarets would grow in the prairies, thousands of miles from the cities with bigger and better-connected Muslim communities. One theory is the egalitarian nature of Sunni Muslims, whose ambivalence to priesthood made them self-reliant. But why then did it take Toronto's much larger Sunni community until 1969 to open a mosque inside an old church? Regardless, certainly this self-reliance helped, as did the salesmanship and barn-raising spirit cultivated as peddlers and home-steaders. But I believe Muslim women in the frontier West may have been the most essential ingredient.

They'd cultivated more autonomy inside and outside the house. Thinking back to Dubyan's Saskatchewan farm in the 1920s, the stigma of someone seeing his wife and daughter milk cows would have been far too emasculating in Lebanon, even if their work was necessary to pull a profit. But in North America, without a judgmental eye for miles, women became chief partners and often the breadwinners in winter by selling butter and eggs to neighbours.

Outnumbered by Arab men two-to-one, early Muslim women also had more to say about their suitors and could favour open-minded men. One in particular would become a driving force for Al Rashid.

In 1923, my distant relative Ali Hamdon, a successful Alberta businessman, returned to Lebanon for a bride. At seventeen, Hilwie Jomha was half his age. She accepted his hand on a journey that would scare most today, let alone a teenager who'd seldom left her village. From Beirut they sailed to Marseilles, then across the Atlantic and up the Saint Lawrence River to Montreal. There, they boarded a train to Edmonton and rested for a few nights while Ali introduced Hilwie to some of the trappers he dealt with as a fur trader on the northern tip of Alberta—their final destination. To reach it, they took another train to the literal end of the rail—and still required a paddle steamer to send them upriver for two more days before reaching her new home in Fort Chipewyan. There, she learned to speak some Cree and Chipewyan on top of fluent English, and she famously hosted dinners for visiting bush pilots like Wop May, a Canadian flying ace and national hero.

Hilwie brought her gregarious, can-do spirit to Edmonton when she, Ali, and their family eventually moved there for better schools. According to legend, Hilwie and her friends who would form the Muslim Ladies Association approached Mayor John Fry in 1937, asking him to sell them a plot of land for the same price charged to the Jewish community for its synagogue.

"You don't have any money to build a mosque," Fry allegedly said.

"We'll get the money," replied Hilwie.

That the mayor's response wasn't intolerance but reasonable skepticism was telling of how established Muslims were in Edmonton by that point. (It was the Great Depression, after all.) Nevertheless, the mayor agreed to give them the land as long as they raised the money first.

There was only so much the businessmen in Edmonton's Muslim community could give, so Hilwie led the wives up and down the main street, asking shop owners for donations and moral support. Then they had their husbands drive them to Muslim households across the prairies for donations. As my friend Karen Hamdon, Hilwie's granddaughter, had told me, "It was the women who spearheaded the mosque and the men in a supporting role."

This was somewhat controversial. Awid pointed out to me that old articles don't mention Hilwie having any influential role. He didn't doubt that it could have been the tendency of society to overlook women's achievements, nor did he deny that the women were important relationship builders. But he thinks the finances were probably handled by the well-established businessmen. It was a combined effort, he said, that raised more than enough for the mayor to make good on his promise.

The chance to claim the country's first mosque wasn't lost on city government either. Edmonton had the dubious distinction of serving as Canada's Ku Klux Klan headquarters and had earned unwanted attention when the previous mayor gave them his blessing to burn crosses on public property. At Al Rashid's December 1938 opening, with Jewish and Christian faith leaders present, Fry boasted about how rare it was to see many faiths sitting friendly together. "As this couldn't happen in some lands, which you are aware of."

In fact, the founders emigrated from what is now Lebanon, one of the world's most religiously diverse regions, and which hadn't experienced major sectarian clashes in any of their lifetimes. Meanwhile in Canada, the government had implemented racist immigration laws in the 1910s, albeit under categories of continental origin, not a swatch of race-colour definitions like in the United States. "Asiatics" had to prove themselves self-sufficient by having $200 in their possession at the border, compared to $25 to $50 for Europeans or a $500 "head tax" for Chinese Asiatics. When French and British colonizers seized the Levant from the Ottomans, the Syrian Canadian lobby petitioned to have relatives living in those occupied lands recognized as Europeans, but it didn't sway policymakers.

Because of such laws, Canada's Muslim population stagnated until postwar sensitivities gradually brought them to an end. Al Rashid was a beacon to postwar immigrants and to all Muslim Canadians after the Alberta oil boom. Soon the entryway where Awid and I had casually dropped our footwear was overflowing with shoes, washing stations were insufficient, and newcomers kept pointing out that the qibla was off by at least forty-five degrees.

Al Rashid struggled to keep up with its most basic services as Alberta's Muslim population soared to twenty thousand by the 1970s. Amongst the many bright-eyed newcomers was my father, though his memories of the old mosque are ones he'd rather forget. A month after becoming a father, he became a widower: his wife had survived leukemia just long enough to give birth to my sister. It was one of the mosque's last funeral services, in 1979, and the overspill of guests on the sidewalk only underscored the need for a new home.

Fundraising had already begun for its replacement on the city's north side, in a subdivision gaining fame as "Little Lebanon." Worship moved into a temporary space while plans were drawn up for a mosque more impressive than any that then existed in the hemisphere. A $3 million architectural landmark, the white palace was distinguished by high archways and a black dome that could almost swallow the original mosque whole. It opened in 1982, and one of its inaugural guests was boxer Muhammad Ali.

Though this was my first time standing inside the old Al Rashid, I've lost count of how many times I've been to its successor. I didn't anticipate my parents' newfound piety after returning to Alberta from college as a closeted atheist and moving into my parents' McMansion near the palatial mosque. I dreaded my mom's Friday routine of guilt-tripping me to prayer. If nothing else, it was incentive to get a nine-to-five job.

My relationship with Al Rashid is less fraught today as I've come to appreciate its community services. Under the parent name Canadian Islamic Centre, it oversees or financially supports day care, senior services, refugee services, social and senior housing, summer camps and scholarships, banquets, and a film festival called the Mosquers. A public school once housed in the basement has since grown into the largest stand-alone Muslim academy in North America. When a wildfire displaced 100,000 Albertans in 2016, that basement became an emergency shelter. The last time I was there, I spied plans for a $2 million expansion and a room of volunteers making a branded cookbook, antiracism Web series, and a coffee-table book commemorating its eightieth anniversary. There are about twenty mosques in Edmonton today, but only one can carry a person through every aspect of life until death. I know that when my parents pass, it's where their janazah will be held. The same will likely be done for me—something I once assumed would be done against my literal will, but I now desire, if only to offer closure to those who will need it.

Despite its central role in Muslim and immigrant life, the original Little Mosque on the Prairie—as it's been called—barely saw its golden jubilee. It would have toppled before its fiftieth anniversary were it not for the Canadian Council of Muslim Women fighting for its survival against the city, Fort Edmonton Park, Muslims from the business community, and the mosque's own board of directors.

"They couldn't see the value in something old when something new was being constructed," said Awid, as we looked at pictures in a display case of the original mosque in its heyday. It was as if congregants forgot about these memories the moment they set eyes on the bold new plan—and price tag. To save costs, the board agreed to a land swap with the city, accepting a much larger property for the new mosque in exchange for the old property, without considering the fate of the building atop it. When the city ordered its removal to make way for a hospital expansion, Awid tried to mobilize Muslims to rescue and repurpose it as a museum, at a cost of $150,000. But everyone was financially and emotionally tapped out.

In the time between breaking ground and unveiling the new mosque, Alberta entered the worst economic recession in fifty years. Al Rashid had already resorted to sending delegates to beg funding from foreign leaders, who saw no strategic advantage to pouring money into a mosque two thousand miles from Ottawa. The Saudi royals and Emiratis kicked in $30,000, while King Hussein of Jordan offered $100 and some books. Finally, Moammar Gadhafi's World Islamic Call Society underwrote the remaining $1.5 million. The only thing saving the mosque from the wrecking ball was the sluggish economy slowing the city's plans, but when things picked up in the late 1980s, the city informed the community that demolition would begin. By then, Awid's energy was also tapped out.

He opened a creaky door to the office-library. That old-book smell filled my nose as I perused the stacks. Awid pointed to a collection of poetry and history books authored by Lila Fahlman, the woman we are to thank for the mosque still standing and *where* it is standing. "People thought she was crazy," he told me, as he rested on a chair. "They didn't want a woman to have a leadership role and that continues till this day."

Fahlman was a renaissance woman. Born in Swift Current, Saskatchewan, she was the first Canadian woman to hold a doctorate in educational psychology, the first Muslim to serve as a university chaplain in North America, and she established the country's first accredited Islamic school.

Fahlman's ambition was as alien to the renewed community as their orthodoxy was to her. Islamization rapidly transformed the Arab world into a more conservative place than the one her parents remembered. Second-wave immigrants pressured the mosque's board to clamp down on community dinners, Valentine's Day dances, and other social activities overseen by the Ladies Association. When a green curtain suddenly appeared in the prayer hall to separate the genders, Fahlman led a small but futile resistance. So in the late 1980s, when she tried to stop the imminent demolition, she was again met with eye rolls.

Fahlman turned to the Canadian Council of Muslim Women for help. She'd founded the organization after the Al Rashid Ladies Association fizzled out, partly due to members' old age, as well as being worn down by patriarchal encroachments of the previous decades. Although the women's council members were invested in the creation of a new Al Rashid, the original held a special place in their hearts.

It represented not just the legacy of Canadian Islam and the family members who built it but an Islam that was more inclusive of women.

To ensure they could carefully transport the mosque, Fahlman's group formed a fundraising committee, headed by Hilwie Hamdon's granddaughters, to organize charity dinners and request donations, just as their grandmother had fifty years prior. The plan was to display it in Fort Edmonton Park, amid the city's first church and the first premier's house. The museum's historical foundation, however, rejected their proposal in 1989, arguing that it didn't qualify as a heritage building and that including it as such would "open the floodgates."

"The park said the mosque was out of the range of 1846 to 1929, but Edmonton's history should not stop there," said Awid. "There are records of people living here five to ten thousand years." It was hard to believe their rationale when its own bylaws made no mention of this arbitrary rule.

Soraya Hafez was then council president. She led the women's group campaign to challenge the park's white historical narrative and push back against xenophobia. Newspapers ran unfavourable op-eds, including one that called it a "foreign intrusion" and an editorial cartoon titled "Cowboys and Mosques?" Many couldn't fathom, let alone accept, that non-Christians could embody the frontier spirit. Sentiments worsened with the Gulf War, but Hafez and fellow women earned a key ally in the city's only woman mayor, who rallied her colleagues to force the public museum's hand.

After a three-year effort, Canada's oldest mosque was dismantled brick by brick. A heavy-duty moving company removed the roof and lifted the structure off the foundations onto a flatbed truck. They transported it across Edmonton well after midnight so as not to disrupt traffic. A small motorcade of mostly women trailed them, unwilling to rest until the mosque was officially sanctioned history. But the park's board still refused to spend a dime on the project. So the Canadian Council of Muslim Women went back to fundraising, until they could afford to restore the roof and refurbish the interior with original fixtures.

Unfortunately, the park insisted on placing the mosque so that it opened up to the boardwalk, rendering the qibla southwest, in the exact opposite direction of Mecca. But the interior itself has been carefully preserved, looking about the same as it did four decades ago. Except for one thing.

I noticed it as Awid and I were putting on our shoes and about to leave: the velvet green curtain—it was gone. I asked of its whereabouts, but he didn't know. Perhaps it was lost. Perhaps the park dismantled it for political reasons. Perhaps the women's council took it down before it was moved. With the curtain gone, the mosque looked about the same as it did in 1938, before gender segregation. To me its absence was an anachronism, but for old-timers it summoned fading memories of a more liberal and uniquely Canadian Islam. Though its congregation was culturally homogeneous compared to today's Al Rashid, which services Muslims of thirty-plus nationalities, it was in other ways more inclusive, drawing together men and women of various denominations in one prayer hall. A group photo of the founders shows all the women in the downstairs hall wearing their hair openly, with fascinators, skirts, and other styles of the time.

At the risk of perpetuating the good/bad Muslim binary, it's worth comparing mosques of old with the new. Women at the modern Al Rashid enter through a separate entrance to a separate room, where flat-screen TVs broadcast sermons. Hijabs aren't mandatory outside the prayer hall, but they're implicitly suggested with a box of scarves at the entrance. And though the mosque's services are far greater, its focus on social functions and public outreach—all, by the way, managed by one industrious woman program operator—is more of a return to its roots than an evolution of postwar operations. How quickly collective values can change, and change back.

Today, Fort Edmonton Park is a proud steward of this time capsule. Whether through embarrassment or enlightenment, the preservation campaign pushed the museum to be more inclusive of non-European history. When we visited, it was in the midst of constructing the Indigenous Peoples Experience, a $45 million expansion stretching its time frame back thousands of years.

"If it wasn't for the mosque, they would have maintained the status quo," said Awid, using his cane to push down the Velcro straps on his shoes. He heaved himself to his feet and we walked out the open double doors.

Descending the stairs, we crossed paths with a family reading the commemorative plaque by the boardwalk. Awid proceeded to offer them an impromptu history lesson. As they nodded, feigning interest by repeating "Wow" in the dullest tone, I sensed how boring it all was to them.

I suppose their apathy was good news. Canada's Muslim population is proportionally three times larger than that of the United States. Alberta towns of just a few thousand people have mosques, so to remind these kids of local Muslim heritage is to ask them to look out their window. That's not to say exposure makes minorities immune to hate crimes, as anyone from the prairies' many Indigenous communities will tell you, but their visibility and public influence has so far shielded them against the same populist Islamophobic rhetoric spewed out of Quebec, Ottawa, and even regions with near identical history, like North Dakota. The prairie state was once a beacon to Muslim immigrants, has the fourth-highest per capita rate of reported Islamophobic activities in the United States. I went there to find out why their lighthouse went dark.

To find the First Mosque in America, I drove 170 miles northwest of Bismarck to a truck stop in Mountrail County, where the mosque's steward promised to meet me. The highway skirted along glistening lakes and rivers while billboards urged me to "Stop Abortion" and "Meet the Heart of Jesus." It reminded me of the drive to my hometown in northern Alberta.

North Dakota today is decidedly red, white, and Christian. Sixty-three percent of North Dakotans cast their vote for Trump, including Richard Omar, son of Abdallah Omar and Rana Al Kadri. His parents cofounded the original mosque, then called the "Ross Jamea" (jamaat), though it isn't generally considered one of North Dakota's handful of mosques, which are relatively new. The latter group were founded by

South Asian and African immigrants in urban areas, have no connection to the early Muslim farmers. And First Masjid in America itself is more of a memorial than a holy place.

Richard Omar, a retired electrician, entered the truck stop wearing a plaid T-shirt tucked into blue jeans. His tan complexion might stick out were it not already the unofficial last day of an especially hot summer. His wife, children, and grandchildren celebrate Labor Day with an annual rib fest. But plans had fallen through that weekend, so he agreed to spend the day teaching me about the mosque instead. Unlike the other Richard of Fort Edmonton Park, this Richard, now a confirmed Lutheran like his wife, is an odd steward of an Islamic landmark—and he knows it.

It was his cousin, the late Sarah (Omar) Shupe, who designed and funded the reconstruction of the mosque on the footprint of the original, which was torn down in the 1970s. It's impossible to know how Sarah felt about its demolition at the time, but fair to assume it never sat well with her. "She never lost her heritage," said Richard. After 9/11, Sarah, the last Mountrail Muslim who could recite Quran, felt that acknowledging her faith's peaceful legacy was urgent. At ninety years old, she knew that if she didn't do something quickly, no one else would. Sarah quietly spent a modest sum of her savings to build it. "I didn't even know it was going up, till it was going up," said Richard. "Sarah had great intentions but it should've been organized and talked about first." He shook his head solemnly and added, "She never got to see it."

Sarah died less than three months before it opened in 2005. Stewardship first fell to a female relative, Lila (Omar) Thorlakson, perhaps the last practicing Muslim in the area. She looked after it for a decade until her dementia made it difficult to continue. She asked "Cousin Richie" to hold the keys. Born in 1954, Richard isn't old enough to have memories of the mosque as anything but an abandoned building, so he invited his elder cousin, Charles Juma Jr., to help with the tour.

As we waited for Charles, it dawned on me that in both Ross and Edmonton, it was women who ensured the preservation of these monuments to early Muslim life. It brought to mind something Mohamad

Jawad Chirri, Detroit's legendary imam, had once said: "The power of the [mosque] is in the woman's hands." Never had that felt so true than that afternoon as I wondered what Sarah would make of her mosque now.

"There he is," Richard said upon spotting Charles's black truck rolling by. "Drives like an old woman!"

We got in with Charles, who wore a near-identical outfit, plus camouflage hat. "Richie and Charlie" are the last stop for old Islam in Mountrail County, where, according to an academic book, *Prairie Peddlers: The Syrian-Lebanese in North Dakota*, the first Muslim prayer service in the United States took place in 1900 or 1901.

Charles's grandparents, Hassen and Maryam, arrived the following year. They left their daughters with relatives back home, hoping to earn enough in a few years to bring them to America. They made six attempts at putting down roots, first in Detroit, then as peddlers moving together across the Midwest and into Saskatchewan. They decided to follow the influx of Syrians, Swedes, Germans, and Norwegian homesteaders into North Dakota in 1902 and went to work clearing forty acres of land near Ross. Hassen and Maryam were the only married Muslims in the area. A year later, they had cattle, chicken, a horse and plow, and a son—Charles (Sr.), the first Syrian American born in the county.

Raised in isolation, Charles Sr. couldn't speak English when he entered public school. But it wasn't long before relatives started their own farms nearby, and thanks to a steady cross-border exchange with Canada of sons and daughters in marriage, he soon had several cousins to play with. They'd thought free land equalled free money, but Hassen couldn't keep up with the loans for his capital costs. He died unexpectedly in 1917, $7,000 in debt (about $150,000 today, US dollars). At just thirteen years old, Charles Sr. took over the farm and cared for his mom.

The 1920s weren't much kinder, but Ross's Syrian community kept growing. A former Ford Plant worker, Richard's dad gave up their middle-class income to live near family in Ross, where he took up 120 acres. Mountrail's Muslims held informal prayer services at

each other's houses led by the most capable male, until they decided
to build a "Mohammadan church."

This is one of the idiosyncrasies of the OG Dakota Arabs. Even
in the Information Age a century later, Richard and Charles Jr. say
"church" instead of "mosque," "Bible" instead of "Quran," "Assyrian"
instead of "Syrian," and "Syrian" instead of "Arabic." Charles Jr. said he
could once "speak Syrian to beat heck," but now speaks it about as well
as a Dakota tourist in Damascus. Like their prairie patois, the "church"
was distinctly their own. An Arabic-language newspaper in New York
helped raise some funds for it, but the sweat and toil was all theirs.

"The congregation just got together," Charles's father told a historian in the 1960s. "It was all handwork, with horse and scrapers, picks
and shovels, and they started to build it."

The "jamea" was a half-cement basement that protected worshippers from the blistering winds. It was heated with a coal stove and
vented with small square windows. Worshippers arrived in buggies
and wagons, prayer rugs rolled under their arms as they ducked under
the four-foot-tall entrance. They did not build cleansing stations for
wudu (ablution), let alone a social space. Curiously, though, it was furnished with benches, giving it the feel of a church.

Ross is less a town than a jumble of buildings on one side of the
highway. The grain elevators activated memories for Charles Jr., a retired farmer, but they were more to do with his schooldays than his
Muslim upbringing. "Somebody would preach. I suppose they read
it out of the Bible," Charles pondered aloud over the country music
station. He drove thirty miles under the speed limit and turned onto a
dirt road. "About thirty people would come. I remember they used to
get down and pray—what's it called, *sal-way*?"

He means *salat*, or sahlé in Lebanese dialect, the Arabic word for
prayer. As a boy, Charles prayed the same way I did—without a clue
of what he was doing. Through the corner of his eye, he'd imitate the
adults' prostrating and whisper unintelligible things under his breath.
The other thing he remembered was funeral proceedings when a
shaykh would travel 550 kilometres from Swift Current, the community where my great-grandfather tried homesteading and where

Charles Jr.'s mom grew up. Sure enough, it didn't take long to find out we're related through marriage—though our connections are in Calgary, a city his relatives left for during the Dust Bowl years.

The stock market crashed the same year the prayer house opened, in 1929. That, combined with brutal drought, led some homesteaders to abandon their farms and default on their loans. Some Syrians left as single men, went back overseas to marry, and returned when things improved. Others never returned or joined their relatives in western Canadian cities, done with farming once and for all. As Mountrail's Muslim population dwindled, so did the mosque's activities. When the remaining Muslim population did congregate, they prayed for rain.

As Alberta's Muslim population soared, North Dakota's atrophied to near invisibility without new arrivals. It wasn't simply a matter of low immigration, though. Wedded daughters tended to leave home and sons tended to stay, and it became difficult for men in financial trouble to attract Muslim brides. Like Richie and Charlie, other second- and third-generation Syrian men married local Christians. Since spirituality is usually nurtured by mothers, more of their children went to church than mosque. The last Friday prayer was held sometime in the late 1930s or early 1940s.

The building languished in the field for forty years, occasionally used for funeral services whenever an old-timer was buried in the adjacent Assyrian Moslem Cemetery. Bullet holes in the door (displayed at the Arab American National Museum) suggest it was used as target practice. It fell into disrepair, and the cemetery committee agreed to tear it down in 1975. But its indentations remained in the ground, and it was on a part of the Ross mosque's original footprint that the replica was built in 2005—though "replica" is a loose interpretation.

"Memorial" or "fancy shed" might be a better descriptor for the structure that randomly appeared on the dirt road ahead of us. Charles stopped at the entrance so Richard could unlock a chain around a creaky old farm gate. A crescent and star hung over his head in the steel archway. Charles drove in and parked outside the mosque, a perfect cinder-block square—about sixteen-by-sixteen feet—clad with stone veneer. There was a small copper-coloured dome on the metal roof siding. What it lacked in size it made up for in minarets: five black spires reached fifteen feet to Allah. An outdoor plaque dedicated the site to Sarah Shupe.

As we walked to the green double doors, Richard suddenly exclaimed, "What the heck?" He crouched and pushed a finger into a dent in the metal door.

"Looks like a gunshot," said Charles, sounding chilled.

Unlike seventy years ago, anyone shooting at the mosque now would have to know what it represented. But after closer inspection, Richard and Charles concluded it was probably a rock ricocheting off a lawnmower blade. Their reaction was telling, though.

"I'm amazed that it's still standing with, you know, stuff going on with the Muslims," said Richard, puffing a cigarette. "I've been afraid for this thing because—well, just look at our president saying no Muslims allowed in the United States. I thought 'This is not going to last,' but so far it has."

Now seemed like as good a time as any to ask about their politics, though I had a general idea. Trump's call for a Muslim ban had made them unwitting representatives of the phantom Muslim community for other journalists. Both men condemned the Muslim ban in past newspaper interviews or in interviews with other reporters yet agreed with halting refugees. It struck me as odd, considering Richard's dad and Charles's grandpa were essentially Syrian refugees fleeing wars they wanted no part in.

Two years into Trump's tenure, both had had a change of heart. "Fine, so long as they come legally," said Richard, whose defense of Trump's "good intentions" sounded tinged with shame to me.

We put politics aside and entered. Richard, lit cigarette in hand, propped the door open with a rock. Ignoring sacred etiquette, we didn't remove our shoes but were careful not to step on the stack of individual prayer rugs in the centre of the concrete floor. (One was just a bath towel.) Where a pulpit might be was a framed memorial to their parents and the mosque's other dozen founders. Richard knocked cobwebs off ceiling beams with a broom, while I scanned the memorial for familiar surnames.

The mosque was not a very good representation of the original, but photos of Richard's and Charles's deceased ancestors took them back to the old days. Charles stood with one foot to the wall, swaying as names like "Ali" and "Osman" flew off his tongue. "Oh yaa! I'll be darned," Richard said every time Charles jogged his memory. This was followed by his fleeting desire to know what happened to them. Only some of them were buried in the local Muslim cemetery.

When we left, Richard locked the door behind us. The incessant wind threatened to blow off my hat as we crossed the field to the rows of gravestones shaded by pines. A number of them honoured World War I and II vets, and a surprising number of burials were from the last fifteen years, including a Ghanaian oil worker who died in a nearby highway collision. Richard didn't know any of them, but he was the cemetery's lone caretaker, keeping records of available grave sites in a manila envelope.

As Richard stood over his parents' ornate gravestones side-by-side, I asked him if he wanted to be buried with them. "I don't know," he replied. "I'm Christian now, because of my wife. So when I pass away, it'll be up to the kids."

I asked Charles the same question as he rested on a bench. He hesitated for a while. "Eventually, if they don't get somebody to take care of this, it's going to be a forest out here," he said. "I want to be buried somewhere that I know people will look after." He and his wife had already bought lots in the next town over.

Driving back to Bismarck later that day, I thought about how it was always my mom who dragged me to mosque, all while my dad waited for me in the car. The role of women in fostering Islam at home is widely acknowledged, but as mosques became male domains, the important role women had in them has been minimized or forgotten. I thought about how the Dakotas might have turned out differently had there been more people like Sarah and Lila, ensuring an appreciation of Islamic history. Instead, Dakotans put more effort into passing legislation for "protection from foreign laws" founded on bogus fears of sharia. In 2012, South Dakota's governor signed the first of its kind in the United States, while North Dakota's house of representatives waited until Trump was in office to table its bill (the state senate killed it weeks later). This might explain the conspiracy of silence following a rash of anti-Muslim arsons, assaults, and harassment in North Dakota—or, as a particularly glib Grand Forks city councillor described them, "the cost of doing business" for refugees.

I couldn't imagine my elected officials pandering to racists so nakedly, responding to hate crimes so crassly, or stoking them after an attack. Even my premier, Jason Kenney, a right-wing Catholic ideologue who frequently stoked anti-Muslim hysteria as Canada's former immigration minister, was sure to weed out those who did the same before his provincial election. He'd seen how poorly anti-Muslim rhetoric had served his federal Conservative Party in the 2015 election, when they dog-whistled too loudly and lost their nine-year reign in the backlash. Yet the majority of North Dakotan voters were, if not rooting for Trump's incendiary anti-Muslim policies, at least tolerant of them.

When I've seen Islamophobia flare up in Alberta, non-Muslims tend to rally around victims even before other Muslims. In 2015, vandals smashed the windows of a small-town mosque on the Alberta-Saskatchewan border and spray-painted "Go Home" on the building. By midafternoon, residents had replaced the windows, repainted the walls, and decorated the exterior with signs like "You Are Home" and "Love Your Neighbour." I would suspect the same happens across most of Canada, even if animosity toward immigrants and Muslims has risen. Though enthusiasm for multiculturalism wanes and grows, it's still one of the few distinct features of Canadian identity. That in itself is worth protecting, even if it's just a matter of keeping up appearances.

Still, Canada hasn't been collectively traumatized by Islamist terrorism on the same level as Europe and the United States. What few and comparatively minor attacks that have occurred have, for the most part, spared Alberta. I've often wondered if all that goodwill, weighed in the balance, would fall under the slightest pressure from a few bad actors. That is the true test of a multicultural society and hardly a month after returning home to Edmonton, it was tested.

The first sign that something wasn't right came around 8:45 p.m. on a Saturday in September. Police checkpoints were set up in every direction around my house. I live in a gentrifying neighbourhood where a drug bust isn't out of the ordinary, but this was unheard of. As I rode my bike to a party downtown, there was hardly an intersection without flashing lights. My wife, working the night shift at the hospital, texted me once I was home. "Crazy stuff happening downtown," she wrote. "I heard a guy killed a police officer right by our house."

In fact, the officer survived what was soon deemed to be a terrorist attack. On traffic duty for a football game, he fended off the attacker, who rammed him with a car before stabbing him repeatedly in an attempt to steal his gun. The officer then rose to his feet and, remarkably, gave chase. The suspect got away. When the accused—a thirty-year-old Somali Canadian refugee once investigated for espousing extremism—was discovered driving a rental truck at a checkpoint, he made a dash for downtown. He was captured alive, without a single shot fired, but not before he had driven over four pedestrians on the city's main drag, only a few blocks from my engagement.

But in the early Sunday morning hours following the attack, nobody knew much about anything and were prone to getting things wrong. An image from a video journalist, who zoomed into the open door of the suspect's vehicle, captured what looked a lot like an Islamic State flag. I saw the still shot on Twitter, where some people debated whether to jump to conclusions and others mocked them for not doing so. In bed, I thought about 9/11, how it felt watching the plane slice into the South Tower, and the sense that what was unfolding was world changing but still distant. The unthinkable had moved closer and closer. Now it was three blocks from my house, where my wife catches a bus to work.

I didn't get much sleep. A Facebook friend posted that their relative was one of the victims and in the ICU. She asked that we pray for her, for all the victims, for the police, for the man responsible, and for his family. The clock radio clicked on at 8:00 a.m., playing clips of the police chief confirming the ISIS flag and calling it an "act of terrorism."

Online and in broadcasters' voices, it sounded like a meteor had struck Edmonton. On social media, people spoke of Canadians "reeling" and described a dark energy forming over the city. But I saw no such thing on my way to the scene of the stabbing. The streets were filled with traffic, the sidewalks with strollers and pedestrians. I got coffee from a convenience store and asked the clerk about the incident. The first thing he wanted to talk about was the response of the intrepid police. They had succeeded in their first manhunt for a Muslim extremist on the loose. They chased him through a crowd, and the incident had resulted in no deaths (so far). This could've been so much worse, we agreed.

The clerk was also Somali Canadian, a community that for years has struggled with losing young men to gang violence and radicalism. Many of them lived in our neighbourhood and attended the mosque beside the crime scene. A very visible and integral part of local life, they would—with this incident—be under even greater scrutiny. But if this worried the clerk, he kept it to himself.

By the time I arrived at the second crime scene, the rental truck—which had crashed on its side and had its windshield smashed so the police could use a Taser on the attacker—was already gone. The only sign of the event were small strips of caution tape flailing in the breeze and a two-person news crew trying to stay warm before the next live segment.

Around the corner, I ran into friends on their way to get pancakes and spotted bridal wear models posing for a fashion photographer. Inside a busy café, little girls coloured in books, and people chatted about whether a new Korean restaurant actually served intestines. The only source of fear was a scary clown taunting teenagers waiting to enter a Halloween haunted house on the downtown strip.

I caught word of an anti-extremism rally at city hall. From time to time, the anti-Muslim group Soldiers of Odin would publicly organize, but this was put together by a Muslim group of antiracists. I arrived and saw the mayor, Alberta premier, and faith leaders waiting

on the stage before hundreds of people imbued with unusually positive spirits.

Many of the faces onstage and in the crowd were brown, bearded,
or wrapped in headscarves—everything average Canadians are encouraged to fear. A Middle Eastern boy in a costume police hat held
a piece of paper flapping in the wind. It read: "We are Muslims, not
ISIS." He seemed to have a better grip on reality than the middle-aged
white couple on the opposite side of the rally, twenty feet behind the
nearest vigil-goer, whose placard read: "No Shariah [sic] in Canada."
Their sign was not meant to be an observation, but it read like one.

One of the first speakers was an imam from Al Rashid Mosque.
Speaking with the fervour of a fatwa decree, he addressed any radicals
in his community: "We will call you out—we have no place for you
in this society!" He was followed by a member of Parliament, Amar-
jeet Sohi, himself once tortured and imprisoned in India on wrongful
charges of terrorism. "That act of terror had a purpose. That purpose
was to instill fear. That purpose was to divide us. But that purpose has
failed miserably," he said.

The most heartening words came from Mayor Don Iveson, who
spoke in a way that simultaneously comforted and strengthened the
community: "We have all been tested by this act. But we have already
shown, and continue to show, where we stand tonight. We stand together. All faiths. All cultures." His only fear, he said, was that a refugee child would go to school on Monday, scared. "If we find it within
ourselves to care for that child in the coming days, the coming months,
the coming years, that person will be able to look back on this moment
and will have felt included, supported as part of our community." The
usually subdued mayor then repeatedly shouted, "We will not be divided!" The crowd erupted in cheers and joined in his refrain. I turned
to the lonely racists. They looked confused, even disappointed. Where
was the resistance to an ever-present jihadi threat?

If this can happen in Edmonton, it can happen anywhere, and the
city's sudden adjustment to this fact is indeed remarkable. The city's
reaction looked like resilience to me, but to others, it will understand-
ably look like complacency. I imagine the crowd would have been

larger and the grief more pronounced had there been a death toll, but in no scenario could I picture a widespread anti-Muslim backlash.

I was at once proud of and surprised by my city. No doubt Edmonton is now the liberal bastion of Alberta, the Austin of the so-called Texas of the North, but it wasn't just progressiveness at play. Their measured response represented their comfort with fellow Muslims. Their great-grandparents may have been acquainted with Muslim mink farmers and fur traders, their grandparents with Muslim accountants, and their parents with Muslim lawyers. All four generations have probably had a Muslim barber at least once in their lives.

But even if their roots in the boom-and-bust city were short, their children at least would know Alberta's Islamic history from a field trip to Fort Edmonton Park. Some wouldn't even have to leave class to be exposed to that history; three public schools were recently named after Hilwie Hamdon, Dr. Lila Fahlman, and Soraya Hafez.

At the time of their efforts, these women couldn't fathom a time when a third of Canadians would consider Muslims to be fundamentally incompatible with Western life, let alone an existential threat. They simply wanted to protect their heritage. They did not understand that by keeping history out of the dustbin, they were helping inoculate future generations from hatred.

Good Uncle/Bad Uncle

Islamic Society of Greater Houston

(Houston, Texas)

*O*n the afternoon of January 20, 2019, the same date that every US president since Franklin Roosevelt has taken the oath of office, the Islamic Society of Greater Houston was also swearing in a new president. During the previous fall election leading up to inauguration day, fifteen local Muslims campaigned for a handful of voluntary board positions, including five aldermen-of-sorts overseeing twenty-two religious centres split into regional zones.

With three thousand votes at stake, the 2018 referendum was the largest and dirtiest yet. Some candidates spent $5,000 to $10,000 on campaigns and formed unofficial political parties, according to the outgoing president. Fake social media accounts spread while others attempted to counter disinformation. A progressive candidate hoping to become the first woman on the traditional Islamic advisory group, Majlis-e-Shura, or Shura Council, was accused by her male opponent of soliciting gender-based votes. Her entire coalition was shut out after being accused of a Watergate-like scheme to improperly obtain membership data.

I flew to Houston to attend the inauguration day ceremony at River Oaks Islamic Center, the first building in the society's network of twenty mosques and medical centres. Opened in 1969, River Oaks is not the society's most beautiful venue, but it is its administrative headquarters. More important, it's the most convenient. It sits inside the Loop, a ring road delineating the megacity's rapid sprawl, which began in the 1970s in no small part because of Asian immigration.

Houston's urban development and Muslim population have ballooned in tandem with the Islamic Center's board of directors. Evidently, so has the number of well-heeled immigrants aspiring to hold one of its volunteer positions. Though some of Metro Houston's 160,000 Muslims lament its boys' club environment, with all the disagreements and crosstalk of uncles gathered around the TV, few find fault with what the uncles have accomplished in America's fourth-largest city. They've imported a South Asian philosophy of the mosque as core service, ensuring that all its programs—from funeral services and financial assistance to Urdu and Arabic schools—are as accessible in one suburb as the next.

Back in Pakistan, where the majority have roots, these responsibilities fell under the Islamic Republic's Ministry of Religious Affairs. Now they're the responsibilities of average Americans volunteering for the Islamic Society of Greater Houston. But it's not too complicated an endeavour for the community's professional class to combine American civics and "Robert's Rules" with the traditional Islamic Shura Council.

The referendum, though, more resembles US general elections, and, like them, it is not for the faint of heart. If nothing else, it disproves anyone still arguing that Islam and Western democracy are fundamentally incompatible.

Trying to book interviews with the society's executive team felt like chasing an exclusive with politicians. After months of unanswered emails and voice mails, I booked a flight for inauguration day. But, alas, a flight delay made me hours too late.

From the outside, River Oaks is a bright neoclassical-modernist mash-up with a Spanish colonial touch. I pulled into the parking lot as attendees pulled out. I roamed the corridors, following chatter until I found the event space situated between a canteen and prayer hall. A few stragglers ate cake while volunteers stacked the chairs. By luck, one of them was an office employee. A young, second-generation woman of South Asian ancestry, she was thrilled by my interest in the organization. Although the entire council and executive team had left, she took my phone number and agreed to coordinate with me the next morning.

With little else to do until then, I bought biryani from the canteen, joined a small sunset prayer, then drove twenty miles to the southwestern corner of Greater Houston, arriving in time for night prayer at the society's crown jewel. Sitting at the end of a dark, pastoral road, the palatial Maryam Islamic Center is as beautiful as any in Mumbai. Bricks along a grand bridgeway were painted to match its bronze dome. You'd never guess that it began as a double-wide trailer four decades ago, back when the suburb of Sugar Land was emerging as a tech hub.

The prayer hall boasted a luxurious carpet, quality wood finishes, and a big touchscreen to make donations or buy a membership card. There was one lightly partitioned women's section and another behind one-way glass for more conservative members. So as far as I could tell, it was just me, a middle-aged muezzin calling prayer into a microphone at exactly 6:59 p.m., and an elderly man seated in a chair at the very back. Feeling a bit silly, I stepped forward and prayed *Isha* beside the man who called the nighttime prayer. He didn't seem to mind the breach of protocol.

"You're not from here," he said, shaking my hand afterward. "I mean, I haven't seen you here before."

I told him about my business and struggles thus far. "I hoped I'd find some contacts here but . . ." I trailed off. "Where is everyone?"

He told me not to worry. To adjust for commuting times from corporate offices, Isha services were regularly delayed thirty minutes. He just liked to maintain tradition. "After that we shut our doors around eight thirty," he added.

"Why's that?"

"Security," he said very casually. "I don't know if you followed the news, but there was a fire at one of our mosques."

I had followed the news, and it wasn't just an ordinary fire, nor was it the one mosque terrorized in recent years. Fifteen miles from here, a doctor was shot on his way to early-morning prayer. At another mosque farther east, an arson attempt. The week I arrived, a mosque was riddled with bullets by a nighttime drive-by shooter. A week later, another drive-by targeted the home of one of its congregants. On numerous occasions, ACT for America, an anti-Muslim extremist group claiming to have nearly a thousand chapters and eight hundred thousand members, mobilized gun nuts to "protest" outside mosques with machine guns and army fatigues.

The Islamic Society tried to keep doors unlocked, in keeping with the spirit of traditional mosques, but could no longer ignore the dangers when their families felt endangered. Luckily, the size, means, and willpower of their vast membership allowed them to respond with impressive speed. The society hired a sheriff's department and security firm to audit and help implement recommendations for each mosque. Emergency exits and elaborate camera systems are now standard precautions. The Sugar Land branch also hired a night guard and ramped up its outreach.

"We usually make some type of appreciation day," the man explained. "We used to distribute flowers to make sure they know we are nice people—we are not here to harm you."

"To who?" I asked.

"To non-Muslims."

"You hand out flowers to random people on the street?"

"Yes," he said, like, *duh*. He did not seem to mind doing that at all and was quick to emphasize how protected he'd felt by his non-Muslim neighbours, as if it was a triumph of interfaith solidarity. And maybe it was. Still, it sounded tragic to me. No religious community should need the police and comfort of their neighbours to feel safe, but especially one as accomplished as American South Asians—Muslims who made modern space travel possible, engineered the structural systems of skyscrapers, and invented chemotherapy for brain tumors.

I say this fully aware that the model minority concept is problematic, to say the least. It promotes assimilation over multiculturalism and devalues the contributions of less educated and less privileged minorities. Most of all, it enforces a caste system of "good Muslims" and "bad Muslims," that is, those who are laudably educated, affluent, patriotic, and submissive, and those who are not.

Yet to the Muslim kid lingering inside me, it meant something to be a model minority. It meant my parents had the status to feel secure with themselves and their decision to move across the world. It also meant feeling pressure to live up to their expectations. So in imagining my potential, I looked up to the achievements of South Asian Muslims, who, at least in my young mind, were the upper-middle-class professionals who'd worked many times harder and who became the things my parents wished I'd become. What's more, South Asian Muslims did it in one generation.

Until half a century ago, it was nearly impossible for brown people to immigrate to North America, save for a few thousand South Asian peasants and seamen who migrated before World War I. Legally "black" and barred from citizenship, they were sometimes accused of carrying diseases and practicing dark magic. In rare instances, they were victims of lynchings.

The Immigration and Nationality Act of 1965 changed US policy to favour the world's brightest minds in order to help implement Medicare and beat the Commies. Over the next three decades, about 3 million people emigrated from countries with significant Muslim populations, resulting in a form of social engineering. The trope of Asian kids being naturally gifted at math and spelling bees is the outcome of being raised among—and compared to—brilliant counterparts within an intensified version of the American dream. With its STEM universities and petroleum industry, Houston was a magnet for advanced degrees. Consequently, the metro area has large concentrations of South Asians, and in 2010 it surpassed metro New York as America's most ethnically diverse population.

The Isha worshippers started arriving at Maryam Islamic Center about a quarter past seven. At first a trickle, then a leak. They made small talk, prayed, and then caught up some more. By the time I left, it was 8:15 p.m. Some teenagers stuck around to play basketball in the attached court, but soon the custodian arrived and locked the doors behind him.

Even if there wasn't a sign on the door, I probably could've guessed which was for the office of the Council on American-Islamic Relations (CAIR). Only an organization as vilified as CAIR would need to install automatic-locking doors and security cameras. I rang the only doorbell inside the office corridor and waited.

A bubbly young woman, Sobia Siddiqui, then spokesperson for the Houston chapter, answered. Beneath a black hijab tightly folded over the nub of her chin, she wore a cheeky T-shirt with the silhouette of a man in five different prostration positions, emulating the evolutionary march of progress.

There was a time when I would have scoffed at her shirt's jab at evolutionary science. I used to bristle at anything that contradicted pure atheism, and no doubt would have lumped her in my "bad Muslim" category. Just over a decade ago, I was the type of guy to ensure my opinions were known by sticking a "Darwin fish" emblem on my car and naming an adopted kitten after the godfather of evolutionary science. Darwin is now an elderly crank picking fights with other neighbourhood cats, but, thankfully, I've evolved to appreciate Siddiqui's fashion on its comedic merits.

I quickly realized that Siddiqui defaulted on humour and was able to laugh at the darkest parts of Muslim American life, perhaps as a coping mechanism. She'd graciously agreed to drive me around Houston for an afternoon and help me map out the city's South Asian universe from the perspective of a second-generation American. But first we talked about the civil rights group itself.

We sat in a boardroom with the official CAIR backdrop flanked by Texas and American flags (a permanent setup for press conferences whenever allegations of discrimination make headlines) and were joined by staff attorney Arsalan Safiullah, her only other coworker, while the chapter searched for a new director. CAIR has the international image of a big lobby group, but that's somewhat of an illusion, resulting from being the only mainstream voice box on Islamophobia and, consequently, brutalized for it. Publicly, it helps protect the national image of Muslim Americans, and, in my hosts' opinions, offers itself to racists as a punching bag so that a random hijabi on the street isn't the target.

The guts of its operation, though, is legal consultation. Few are privy to its day-to-day work of showing Muslim Americans where their constitutional rights begin and end. For example, Safiullah recently advised parents of a teenage boy whose school demanded he shave his beard for graduation. Safiullah told the parents he could probably help protect their son on religious grounds, but probably couldn't prove the school's racist motives should it escalate to legal action. It didn't, and the kid rocked a sick beard at graduation.

Another legal education effort involves facilitating "know your rights" workshops at mosques. It's especially important for immigrants to know they're not obligated to invite the FBI into their home if they come knocking—and, for God's sake, stop serving them tea! "That's what gets them in trouble every time," said Siddiqui. "Here's the tea, here's some snacks, let me tell you about all my houses overseas."

"Or they basically try to explain what Islam is," said Safiullah.

"Trying to give *dawah*," Siddiqui added, using the Islamic term for religious propagation, "while they're the ones being surveilled."

"Like, 'If I can convince this person of what Islam is truly about, they would lay off.'"

Second-generation South Asians like them adopted a defensive nature, but the immigrant mentality and hospitality is such that if they don't feel like they have anything to hide, then what's the harm? "It's a very difficult thing to understand for people," said Safiullah. "Maybe they were ruled by the British for so long, then other corrupt regimes, but, to them, it's *the government*, it's *the state*." In some of their clients' minds, noncooperation could get you hooked up to a car battery.

I left the office a little later with Siddiqui. She cleaned out her front seat and comfortably entered the roles of local ambassador, tour guide, and pilot. "Houston is known for having the most aggressive drivers," she said. "I am one of them. If I start yelling in Urdu, it's not at you. Everyone on the road is an uncle."

I wasn't sure what she meant until, seconds later, she honked at a careless driver, and sighed, "Oh, uncle," while shaking her head disapprovingly.

We'd barely crossed the first intersection when the fullness of Houston's diversity started to reveal itself in taco trucks, Afghani restaurants, and Vietnamese-owned wholesalers. "They stock up on a butt-tonne of hijabs every Ramadan," she boasted. "And they appeal to you with a 'buy five, get one free' discount—hell yeah!" Siddiqui drove in and out of mundane plazas that comprised the regrettably named Mahatma Gandhi District (most purveyors are Pakistani), pointing out a Bollywood record store, a Bombay sweetshop, and a sari emporium, as well as a sanctuary for undocumented people.

"So this was my childhood growing up," she said about Hillcroft. The southwest Houston neighbourhood was practically inner city compared to where many of her peers and cousins grew up. Her parents belonged to the second wave of South Asian immigrants from the 1980s and 1990s. Often arriving on family-class visas, they ascended to the suburbs by driving taxis for Americans, widening their culinary palates, and selling them beer at one in the morning. That American pop culture derived Indian stereotypes from this cohort, giving us *The Simpsons'* Apu Nahasapeemapetilon, instead of their predecessors, which gave us five Nobel Prize winners, reveals just how little the human capital of immigrants meant to the masses.

Siddiqui's upbringing matched that of her wealthier peers in some respects. For instance, everyone went to weekend school and was subject to three categories of questions: How's your schooling?; What are your career plans?; and When are you getting married/having kids? But in bigger and more lasting ways, Siddiqui's world was very different.

Her father and uncles had sweat their way into managerial positions of several gas stations within the same franchise. "We're glad we got to see our parents kind of scruff it out and *we* had to scruff it out. It wasn't just about academia for us. It was, 'Sometimes you have to get your hands dirty—and that's okay too. But that doesn't mean you let go of school.' This combination of values allowed for us to get in tune with who we are." But on September 11, 2001, nine-year-old Sobia learned the limits of pure scruff. "Within a month, all three of them lost their jobs for one reason or another."

The Siddiqui family couldn't really prove it was racially or religiously motivated, and they did not want to "rock the boat." After all, Balbir Singh Sodhi, the first fatal victim of a post-9/11 hate crime, was an Arizona gas station owner-attendant. His killer, a white ex-con on a retaliatory shooting spree, also targeted, and missed, a Lebanese gas clerk and his own Afghani rental tenants. Sodhi, singled out for his beard and turban, was Sikh, not Muslim, but as Safiullah had put it to me earlier that day, "Most of our discrimination is not based on religion. It's based on being *perceived* as a Muslim."

Siddiqui's parents' resistance to legal retaliation wasn't only fear driven. "They still feel like guests in this nation," she said. This extreme form of accomodation is unacceptable to her generation. "We grew up with the American attitude to be more rebellious."

At twenty-seven, Siddiqui and I were six years apart but it might as well be a full generation. My adolescence was defined by the bleakness of the Bush years. Her cohort came of age with a hopeful Black president and personalized social media. The first time she saw a commercial for CAIR, in high school, she thought to herself, "It would be a dream to work there." When Sobia finally got the job after a few years as an Islamic school teacher, her mom freaked out over safety concerns. She still does whenever CAIR workers wind up in the news, but Sobia was beginning to convert her mother to activism's dark arts.

"I took her to her first protest last year," Sobia said, turning onto an exit ramp. "She was very passionate about the Rohingya and wanted to know what she could do about their suffering. I said, 'Well, we can take very limited action here, but you can join me at a protest. She came out very scared, asking, 'Is there security. Are you safe? Should I put on a *duppata* [makeshift headscarf], so you're not the only hijabi they see?' I said, 'No, relax.' We got there and as soon as people started chanting, my mom was getting into it. She left exhilarated, like, 'We should be coming to these all the time!'"

Siddiqui laughed. "*Totally, Mom.*"

We stopped at a Pakistani sweetshop. Loud Quran recitation played on the overhead speakers as we ordered two boxes of milky doughnut balls, syrupy dumplings, and crispy jalebi rings. I figured we'd sit at a table to enjoy them, but Siddiqui had more to show me. Back in the car, I was appointed "food DJ," tasked with passing desserts to her free and increasingly sticky hand. "We call this eating 'jungly,'" she said. "It means wild, like, completely uncivilized."

She drove us around Lakes on Eldridge, an unincorporated area with pretty town houses off to one side, refugee residences off to another, and, in between, a dollar cinema she'd patronized since childhood. "No matter how rich you are, you're always going to want a dollar movie." Siddiqui loves her hometown's down-to-earthness. In fact, she was in the process of trying to get married, meaning she'd become a client of the infamous South Asian romance bureaucracy (think *Indian Matchmaker* on Netflix), and her top prerequisite? Staying in Houston. "Literally," she said, "I have listed on my profile that 'I'm not leaving the greatest city.'"

"What makes it the greatest city?" I asked.

"The diversity, the friendliness, it's how at home and relaxed you feel. Everyone's so busy in their own lives they don't really care to mess with yours. That's why, when we have Islamophobic incidents, it's not normally in the heart of Houston." In fact, the CAIR chapters for Dallas and San Antonio, both significantly smaller cities, manage many more discrimination and potential hate crime cases than Houston does, a fact that Siddiqui attributes to her hometown's diversity. She's found that local authorities, in both the police department and city hall, have to answer to minority constituents and are more accommodating than the Austin and DC legislators pushing anticonstitutional "anti-sharia" bills for no set purpose other than showmanship.

I did not expect Siddiqui to be a walking advertisement for the city. Neither did I expect her to be a fan of recreational shooting ranges.

But her capacity for understanding and forgiveness surprised me most. Siddiqui wasn't an apologist for racists. But she wasn't an "all-or-nothing" progressive warrior either. For instance, she censured the "nutter-butters" standing outside mosques with their assault rifles without attacking the open-carry laws that legalized it. She also sympathized with a dwindling Christian congregation who'd protested the opening of a mosque inside their recently shuttered church, thinking it was somewhat insensitive of the Muslim organization to have moved in so soon after the church was evicted because it could no longer pay its bills.

Siddiqui's big heart even led her to make an unlikely friend: a teen mother whose boyfriend celebrated President Trump's signing of Executive Order 13769 (a.k.a. the Muslim ban) by torching the only mosque in Victoria, a town west of Houston. What's worse, he lit the fire while she was in the hospital giving birth to their second child, then texted her pictures for bragging rights, which ultimately led to his conviction and twenty-four-year sentence. Nevertheless, the arsonist's girlfriend defended him, believing what she needed to believe and saying what she needed to say, to protect herself against devastating shame. As heinous details emerged about how he abandoned her in labour at 2:00 a.m., Siddiqui felt the young woman suffered more than anyone else in that room.

Siddiqui was surprised to see her at the grand reopening for the mosque and spoke to the young woman empathetically, the way she did with parents of Muslim extremists on rare occasions. Gradually she opened up to Siddiqui about her ex's past abuse. The young woman had begun psychology courses in college and felt strongly that he met the criteria of a high-functioning sociopath. Siddiqui and the Victoria Muslims became some of the strongest supporters of the young mom, who in turn comforted Siddiqui when the community's trauma brought her to tears.

Political scientists looking at how Siddiqui handled a once-hostile person might call this a matter of "strategic incrementalism" versus "absolutism." But, really, it was just patience. Similarly, CAIR staged a comeback in the Trump era largely because it was patient with media bias and public misperception. Despite relentless efforts to shut them up and shut them down, the civil rights group managed to mainstream itself. It now gets more airtime in media, and generally for the right reasons.

Siddiqui embodies that patience, but more than that, she has a formidable sense of fairness. I admired the way she talked about people, Muslims or not, and that she rarely categorized them as good or bad, allies or adversaries. She treated them like the uncles she honked at on the street or bickered with at home—equally frustrating and endearing. She resisted rhetorical generalizations about conservative voters, seeing such judgments as no less prejudiced than those to which Muslims are routinely subjected. Save for the rare sociopath who would terrorize others for kicks, everyone was good, but nobody was good all the time.

Siddiqui also helped me appreciate how varied the experiences are amongst Muslim immigrants and their children. Siddiqui and I both grew up in immigrant households transitioning from working to middle class. We also came of age in a post-9/11 Western world. Yet neither my rural Alberta community nor I faced anything close to what Siddiqui's highly racialized community endured in spite of their collective wealth and influence. Nobody tried to run my parents out of business or force us to choose between justice and peace. If we were called "Paki," as we sometimes were, the sheer stupidity, if not irony, blunted the insult before it could pierce us.

We were safeguarded by our lighter skin. Capital "B" Brown kids, however, had to cultivate thicker brown skin and try harder, *much* harder, to gain acceptance as "good Muslims."

The story of how Mohammed Nasrullah helped astronauts drink recycled urine would not be an appropriate conversation at any other dinner table, but it's a standard topic at Muslims of NASA, a lunch meet-up organized by the mechanical engineer and others working in and around the Johnson Space Center. "They can only extract about sixty-five to seventy-five percent of the water. The astronaut's pee goes into a tank. The rest is a highly toxic, gooey substance. The astronauts can't even touch it with their bare hands because it's so corrosive. They have to put it into these disposable bags," said Nasrullah, who looked dressed for work despite recently retiring from Boeing's space exploration unit.

"I have a question about the perspiration your system collects," I said, aware that whatever came out of my mouth next was guaranteed to be the stupidest question ever asked at Muslims of NASA. "Like, do they actually have to squeegee it off their bodies?"

"No, no, no, no, no," said Nasrullah. "Perspiration is collected from the atmosphere."

Condensation. *Of course.* Graded on this curve, my IQ ranked closer to the tabbouleh on the table than the people sitting around it.

Of the five scientists present, Nasrullah wasn't alone in having worked on this water system project, which began in 1979 and has since made modern space exploration possible. When it costs NASA $80,000 to cargo a gallon of water, celestial human travel depends on their ingenuity. In the brief time that I got to know the Muslims of NASA, I was struck by the similarities of their pasts. Either they immigrated to the United States during the same twenty-year period, or their parents had, and, regardless of ancestry, nearly all came from privileged homes.

Back in Hyderabad, Nasrullah's parents kept the kind of rigorous routine that breeds a Texas scientist, a California finance manager, and an Australian doctor. Their children went to an English immersion school, then hurried home for Urdu and Quran classes from back-to-back tutors. His father was a mathematician; his mother, less a homemaker than a home manager with six servants under her direction. Before he set off to study at the University of Oklahoma in 1974, she taught him two final lessons: how to boil an egg and how to make tea.

Nasrullah's immigrant class is sometimes referred to as the "Post-65" Americans. From the perspective of the nations from which they came, the US Immigration and Nationality Act of 1965 marks a devastating brain drain, but from a US perspective, it initiated a scientific golden age. As the United States begins mending the damage of

Trump's travel ban on seven predominantly Muslim nations (a list that Pakistan narrowly escaped), it's worth reminding ourselves that the Post-65 were ushered to help make America great again.

Spread throughout offices in Clear Lake—Houston's aerospace district—the Muslims of NASA meet every second Wednesday of the month at the same Palestinian restaurant. Normally more people are present, but their NASA counterparts stayed home, enjoying an unexpected vacation thanks to another government shutdown in Congress. At the heart of the previous shutdown, in January 2018, was the deportation of so-called Dreamers, mostly Latin American children unlawfully brought to America; only eleven months later, the impasse was funding for the Mexican border wall. Opposition to the Muslim ban was never strong enough to end nonessential government services. But all are derived from the same white supremacy underpinning Republican foreign policy.

"Was it a delicate time to be a Muslim government employee?" I asked.

"What is the importance of this question?" said one attendee with pronounced disdain.

His prickliness surprised me. This man, the only medical doctor at the meeting, happened to be the founding president of CAIR Houston, which locals formed in the aftermath of 9/11. Along with board members like Nasrullah, he must have endured the council's embattled years—a period defined by false accusations of funding terrorism. (It was so bad that Canada's national chapter dissolved and reinvented itself under a new name.) Although its reputation has improved, the council was demonized on a semiregular basis by President Trump. My point being: If anyone at that table should have understood the premise of my question, it was this guy—CAIR Houston's inaugural president.

But apparently not.

"If the Muslim does not show his identity as a Muslim, he's just a worker. What is the issue?" he grilled me.

There might not be one, I said, but given overlap between aeronautic and military technology, was there an issue? (My actual response was too convoluted and stammered to quote verbatim.) In their unrelenting creativity, Islamophobes have gone after NASA before, during the Obama administration, when a directive encouraging more outreach between NASA and the Muslim world became fodder for right-wing media. Now they have a commander in chief who has said, "Islam hates us," not to mention Texas senator Ted Cruz, one of the Senate's loudest proponents of patrolling Muslim neighbourhoods. Was it far-fetched to think institutional bigotry could trickle down on them through state departments?

"Let me tell you my experience," Nasrullah interjected. "We used to get together in a conference room to pray. It became so well known in my group that people around me and my secretary would remind me: 'Mohammed, it's your prayer time. Go pray, and pray for us.'" Muslim employees held Jumah prayers in a conference room, taking turns delivering sermons, until they started renting a prayer space, or *musalla*, inside a strip mall across the street from NASA Space Center. For as long as Nasrullah could remember, colleagues were nothing but accommodating so long as it didn't interfere with the quality of their work.

There was no reason not to believe this rosy picture. North America's technical workforce is one of the most diverse and educated there is, and you don't get to the moon dismissing people over petty differences. It takes a culture of extreme cohesion and single-minded goal setting. And even if a colleague did harbour some racism, it's doubtful he'd ever apply his ugly stereotypes to the "good Muslims" among him.

As for the humble NASA musalla, it's now Clear Lake Islamic Center, a mosque independent of the Islamic Society of Greater Houston (and its politicking), but similar in its broadness. Nasrullah invited me there to meet more Muslims of NASA during night prayers. I arrived at a gorgeous Spanish colonial building sharing parking, garbage bins, and babysitting services with the Unitarian Church next door. There was a Lone Star on the street-side signage, a Persian star above the door between two towering minarets, and the interior was decorated with Islamic Chinese calligraphy and tasteful artwork donated by the Muslim Girl Scouts of Texas Troop. A lounge area had table tennis and billiard tables. And the only room that smelled like feet was an indoor playground.

The floor plan was about as well designed as you'd expect from a community potent with engineers, though I still accidentally walked into the women's section despite many arrows and signs. I finally reached the men's prayer hall furnished with ergonomic cushions and window-side barstools for pre- and postprayer chitchat. It was the mosque version of the model minority.

Some version of the western perceived good Muslim/bad Muslim binary has existed for centuries. But the modern definition, coined by political scientist Mahmood Mamdani to criticize the War on Terror, categorizes the "good" as moderate Muslims who submit to or collaborate with imperial powers, adopt their culture, and testify loyalty to western values; and the "bad" Muslims as those who are dissenting and deeply pious. Of course, most orthodox Muslim leaders would flip these definitions, but, by the standards of the former, the Clear Lake jamaat might fit on the left side of the forward slash.

The imam that evening was a zen-like man with a long grey beard and fixed smile. He remained sitting after prayer to offer a short sermon about the sacred meaning of the word *Al-Rahman*, one of God's ninety-nine attributes. "It means the most merciful," he said without flourish or fervour, then tried to tally up how many times a Muslim might say the word in a single day. "Four times per *rakat* [a round of prayer], sixteen times per prayer [salat], five prayers a day . . ." He requested some help from the congregation and estimated it to be between eighty and a hundred depending on the individual's prayer regime. "Sometimes we get so carried away with the sharia that we forget the essence. We forget that mercy is established within these laws of Islam." The imam, making individual eye contact throughout his sermon, urged us to maximize our patience and tolerance, not to misrepresent the faith with harshness, and to prove wrong those who present it with "ugliness."

"For those who've studied law, you know it's a dry subject, and it makes you feel like you're void of spirit and soul," he added. "The rules of Islam and the knowledge of Islam are tough enough for any person, so don't make it more difficult. Present it upon others in a way that is more appealing, more welcoming, and has a more merciful side."

It was inspiring advice that should be heard by many—the deeply religious, free speech absolutists, collections agents, and so on. But his message also burdens Muslims to prove their beneficence, not the other way around. It struck me as an old-fashioned thought process, one my aunties and uncles would embrace but that my cousins would scold. I certainly have wanted to push back when up against it myself.

I recalled an encounter I had with a well-known Jewish doctor and philanthropist at an Edmonton literary event a decade ago. The man straight-up asked me why Muslims don't ever seem to speak out against terrorism. I should have said that it's neither mine nor any practicing Muslim's responsibility to do public relations for a billion autonomous individuals with whom we may share little in common. Instead, I told him that Muslims *do* condemn terrorism, loudly and publicly, through group and individual efforts, but media ignore it. Both answers are true, but the first one was what he needed to hear.

We met again several years later at another event, where I hosted a Mizrahi Jewish author and asked her questions about Israeli identity politics explored throughout her memoir. As soon as she left to sign books, the good doctor accosted me. "How come you never have anything good to say about Israel?" he began. "Is it because you're prejudiced?"

It was clear to me then that no matter how much one tries to be a "good Muslim," you're always a step away from being a bad one. This time I embraced his preconceived notions of me. I called him a "motherfucker" and tore into him until the fear in his face became too pitiful to bear. The good imam's lesson to be more appealing, welcoming, and merciful notwithstanding, it felt good to be bad.

———

Throughout my stay in Houston, I asked locals to share their opinions about the massively influential nonprofit Islamic Society of Greater Houston.

Most agreed the society deserved credit for fundraising, developing, and overseeing beautiful Islamic centres with essential services. The Islamic Society of Greater Houston must care for a rapidly growing community in a city that itself rapidly grows. Despite the wealth, prestige, and specialized degrees accumulated by Houston's Muslims, population growth is driven more by family immigration than employment and education. The original Post-65 immigration class represented the professional class, but the siblings, parents, and fiancées who followed them often start with low-paying service jobs. And that trend is evolving again, as the last decade has brought more refugees than ever before, notwithstanding the Trump years. In a state like Texas, where small government is good government, delivering basic services to newcomers often falls to nonprofits.

But if local Muslims had issues with the society, it was regarding the governance board's cringe-worthy politicking. It was a boys' club, said a writer who'd volunteered with the organization before. A Latino imam credited an unsatisfying tenure at an Islamic Society of Greater Houston mosque as a motivating factor to create IslamInSpanish, the only religious centre of its kind in the United States. It was abundantly clear that for all the painstaking efforts the society made to present itself to the outside community as the good Muslims, many within its own community saw it as patriarchal and exclusive.

This was on display when I had my first conversation with an executive after months of trying. My contact at the Islamic Society welcomed me with a big smile and strong handshake. She summoned her boss, executive director Humayun Mahmood, an avuncular late-middle-aged man with a scraggly chin-strap beard. The guy who'd blown me off for the past three months suddenly had the talkative energy of an uncle happy to run into you at Jumah. We shot the shit for thirty minutes, discussing Islamic pluralism and the silliness of the term "Muslim community" in spite of it comprising so many disparate cultures and philosophies.

Suddenly chums, we constructed a working theory for why South Asian Americans' political energy was comparably dynamic. I suggested the Arab tradition of monarchs and tribal chiefs had much to do with my people's notoriety for political apathy, and Humayan agreed.

However, he attributed their low voter turnout to their suppression under dictatorships. As Mahmood saw it, Pakistanis' experiences with resisting the British Raj injected civics into their bloodstream. "Elections, democracies, they love it—they love to run in politics," he said. "They'll sit here in a board meeting and fight each other like politicians." Sure, it can be annoying, but it was a vital part of the process. "Living in America, you can't have a one-man show or even a two-man show." Nevertheless, the scale and political complexities of its nongovernmental election risk overshadowing what's at stake for the organization.

Mahmood slid the Islamic Society's district map across the table. He traced each of the five zones with his finger as he listed the various positions required to make every mosque as equitable as the next. You can't organize that many overachievers without inviting ego to the table. Whether or not the system can work better, it works—so well, in fact, that Islamic networks in other American cities use it as a model.

I had further questions about how the Islamic Society functions, bureaucratically and politically, to which Mahmood said, "Talk to the president. I am not a spokesperson."

I returned to the society's offices the next afternoon to meet the new commander in chief, president Sohail Syed, in the boardroom with Mahmood. I began with some personal questions.

Syed immigrated to the United States in 1985 and plowed through an undergraduate degree in finance at the University of Illinois. He worked in Rhode Island for a decade before setting out on one last migration journey. In search of a city with adequate Muslim services for his growing family, he toured eight cities in five states. "What I saw in Houston was a thriving Muslim community," he told me. Syed found that Houston's several Islamic schools benefited from a libertarian education policy, which gave religious schools more latitude and autonomy over their course material. "We were really impressed with the curriculum and the whole infrastructure."

Most impressive were its mosques, not just in abundance (estimates today run from one hundred to over two hundred) but the high degree of organization, thanks to the nonprofit board that he would eventually head, as well as the efforts of Pakistani Americans. They're remarkable for their ability to establish mosques in their community, he told me. It's often the first thing they do, even if it means renting time in a community hall every Friday. In fact, Syed established a weekly prayer in Cypress, one of Houston's largest suburbs, shortly after arriving in 1999.

Three months later, the congregation had grown to fifty and become a parking nuisance, leading them to lease a larger space, until running into growth-related traffic woes once again. Syed scoured Cypress for an affordable piece of land that eliminated the only major obstacle to being a good, God-fearing Muslim in H-Town. Fifteen families chipped in half a million dollars to build a new mosque. Through partnership with the Islamic Society, they accessed a roster of full-time imams and dozens of preapproved Friday lecturers.

Syed did not want to own up to the Islamic Society's warts to me. He denied the party politics and flashy campaigns for which the organization's elections have become infamous. He tiptoed around the absence of women from the electoral process. So be it. I'm not his constituent. He only needs to answer to them and their needs.

Whatever improvements the nonprofit stood to make, nobody could deny the potential good of one as robust as this. It gave local Sunnis buying power and brand trust. Its zakat committee operated like a reliable social services office; the sermon committee, like a casting agency for keen, albeit exclusively male, public speakers. And its ulama committee helped worshippers navigate complex religious scholarship and even request the occasional fatwa in order to address modern challenges.

The day before Syed took his oath of office, a community member made a peculiar request on behalf of a hospitalized family member. Their sibling was grieving his amputated leg. "He wanted us, the ISGH, to take the leg and use our funeral services to bury it," said Syed with an unpreventable laugh. "That was a first for me, and I had not even started my job as president." After a few calls, though, Syed was guided to send someone to the hospital to pick up the leg and give it a proper burial. The amputee was comforted to know that someone washed and wrapped his limb in clean cloth and offered a modest blessing before placing it in the earth. If that's not good constituent service, I don't know what is.

Becoming a model minority doesn't have to make one more submissive. For many immigrants and people of colour, it's no different from being a model citizen. It's a genuine attempt to be an active, productive, and engaged member of society, working toward their own definition of the American dream.

I left H-town realizing that I'd arrived with many prejudices. For one, I presumed red state Muslims endured constant hostility, which just wasn't true, at least not in Houston. As Sobia had put it to me, "Southern hospitality and Muslim hospitality really go hand in hand."

The community socioeconomics were also far more complicated than I'd thought, as were their respectability politics. Meeting South Asian Muslims in Texas proved the problematic nature of the "good Muslim/bad Muslim" binary, whether defined by religious leaders, community members, secularists, or pop culture. Embracing Western notions of an equal society, assimilating to workplaces, and meriting elite jobs doesn't make one "good" any more than praying five times daily. Every Muslim has their own conception of good and bad believers, and so it should be. Nor should the self-defined "good Muslim" have to consider his or her broader audience. But there's also nothing inherently wrong with trying to be a good one if it makes one more self-reliant, compassionate, and tolerant.

3

وسط
Wasat
(Moderation)

If he orders us to veil, we veil,
and if he now demands that we
unveil, we unveil, and if he wishes
us to be educated, we are educated. Is he well intentioned in all
he asks of us and on our behalf,
or does he wish us ill?

—*Malak Hifni Nasif, Egyptian
feminist and writer (1886–1918)*

In the Shadow of
a Walking Imam

The Ismaili Centre

(Toronto, Ontario)

*I*n February 2014, Aga Khan IV addressed the Canadian Parliament to announce plans for the Global Centre for Pluralism. It was a natural fit for many reasons. For one, the billionaire philanthropist has always been a special friend to Canada. He was a pallbearer at Prime Minister Pierre Trudeau's funeral and one of the first foreigners to receive honorary Canadian citizenship.

A more obvious reason to build it in Ottawa was Canada's constitution; it was the world's first to enshrine everyone's right to practise the cultures of their national or ethnic origins (within reason). Even politicians like Stephen Harper, a staunch conservative who launched his political career on a campaign to ban turbans in the Royal Canadian Mounted Police, must pay fealty to pluralistic values if they want to succeed on the national stage.

Harper's government was so eager to lay claim to the Centre for Pluralism that it offered to house it inside the former national war museum. But there's probably another reason for this: Harper's decade-long reign as prime minister was marred by xenophobia targeting Muslims. What better way to prove that he is a friend to Islam than to partner with Prophet Muhammad's most famous descendant?

Though this would need explaining for general audiences.

The Aga Khan Development Network reaches so far around the globe that one can be forgiven for thinking he is a brand, not a man. In some respects, they'd be right. Born Karim Al Husseini, he was appointed the title (Persian for "chief commander") following the death of his grandfather, Aga Khan III. The other titles he carries—"Prince," "Shah," "His Highness"—suggest he might rule an obscure monarchy. Adding to his ambiguity, IV is a white Swiss with British, Persian, and Karachi ancestry. If the Aga Khan is known to people at all, it's for his charity, lucrative racehorses, and playboy father (a.k.a. Rita Hayworth's third husband). But to a tiny but influential Shia subsect known as Nizari Ismailis, he's the forty-ninth divine leader of a Muslim papacy called the Imamat—an authorized representative of God.

I streamed the imam's official address and the announcement at home. Ottawa celebrated with a red-carpet ceremony, during which Harper announced the Global Centre for Pluralism and pledged more development partnerships between the philanthropic arm of the Imamat and the government of Canada.

I could practically feel backs straightening in Canada's literal seats of power as the genteel European began his speech with an Arabic prayer. He briefly related the uniqueness of the Nizari Ismailis as the only Muslim community led by a "living hereditary imam in direct descent from the Prophet." I imagined non-Ismaili Muslims watching, scoffing at their screens.

Even among those more "open-minded" Muslims who don't consider Ismailis heretics, Aga Khan's jet-setting lifestyle and coziness with imperialists is hard to swallow. He seems concocted from European imaginations of what a proper Muslim leader should be, kind of like white Jesus.

I count myself among his admirers. The Aga Khan's reverence for democracy, tolerance, and pluralism seems like an antidote for many ills of modern society. Lavishness aside, he's probably more charitable, and more inclusive with his charity, than any Muslim leader in recent memory. While Aga Khan III focused on bringing social reforms to followers, most notably the advancement of Ismaili women, IV made secular humanitarianism his mission. Since being anointed Aga Khan at age twenty, he has established hundreds of clinics, campuses, and social programs in the world's most impoverished places; opened independent newsrooms in dicey locales; and expanded his grandfather's feminist cause beyond their sect. He even funded a multimillion-dollar botanical garden with Islamic architecture outside Edmonton, about forty kilometres from my home. The number of lives he's indirectly improved through the Development Network is incalculable. What gives me pause is the way he placates the powerful and panders to them to advance his causes.

Ottawa's partnership with the Aga Khan overlapped with a historic refugee crisis and a dark chapter for Canadian foreign policy. Once a model of compassion, the government had begun reducing health coverage for asylum seekers while imposing a process of "extreme vetting" on desperate Syrians applying for refuge. In the three years between the civil war outbreak and the Global Centre for Pluralism announcement, Canada only accepted two hundred Syrians, mostly non-Muslims. Harper rationalized the restrictions as terror-related security concerns. In fact, it fit perfectly within his party's preelection campaign to activate the base with anti-Muslim dog whistling, which would soon crescendo with the "Barbaric Cultural Practices Hotline."

I didn't expect Aga Khan IV to mention or even hint that Canadian refugee rights were backsliding during his hour-long speech, but I did expect him to acknowledge the worst refugee crisis since World War II. He did not. He instead spoke about Islam and Canada's shared values of inclusiveness, higher learning, and meritocracy.

His silence was strange considering the 300,000 Ismailis endangered by the Syrian civil war and targeted by ISIS. Stranger still, Aga Khan IV is hugely responsible for transforming Canada's refugee laws. In 1972, the Ismaili leader used his close ties with Pierre Trudeau to rescue a significant chunk of Asian Ugandans from Idi Amin Dada's violent revolution. After the dictator's populist nationalism vowed to expel the non-Black population, the Aga Khan urged his friend,

Canada's prime minister, to swiftly give the refugees security in Canada. Trudeau's government followed through by stripping down the barriers designed to disadvantage immigrants of colour (or privilege white immigrants, however you'd rather see it).

The imam's diplomatic efforts helped produce Canada's first wave of Muslim immigrants—eight thousand brown and mostly Ismaili refugees who paved the way for hundreds of thousands more people displaced by war and persecution.

I met with an Ismaili acquaintance to learn more about how his community shaped and was shaped by Canada. Azim Jeraj welcomed me at his acreage home looking primped as usual. His loud, fitted shirt and designer glasses competed for my attention with impressive artwork throughout his home. I passed up a glass of wine for a fragrant tea instead.

Jeraj was among the first cohort of Canadian refugees from Uganda. He and his wife, Shenaz, embody a common image of North American Ismailis as prosperous, educated, and ostensibly secular high-achievers. They give their time to a variety of organizations but none more than those linked to the Ismaili Imamat. They are absolute pillars of their community, having served at Edmonton's Ismaili mosques (called *jamatkhana*), the Ismaili Council for Canada headquartered in Toronto, and the Aga Khan Foundation Canada in Ottawa. Jeraj and Shenaz began negotiations between the University of Alberta and the Aga Khan Development Network in Geneva on the $25 million botanical garden.

I've befriended a number of Ismailis in my artsy/liberal/media bubble—campaign managers, radio hosts, queer activists—but I didn't know much about their history until Jeraj invited me to a dinner party a few years ago. We sat at an end of the table discussing theology while everyone tuned us out. Afterward, he invited me into his office to view a hand-painted antique Quran that he procured almost by accident.

Jeraj's openness contradicted all the stereotypes I'd known and accepted about the Nizari Ismaili, namely, that they are an exclusive and secretive bunch. There's some truth in that accusation (even Jeraj admits so), but it's not for the absurdly devilish reasons claimed by fundamentalist Muslim quacks. "Ismailis have had a history of persecution for a long time," he explained. "We're *the* 'heretics.'"

It was not always so. The Ismaili caliphate known as the Fatimid dynasty governed swaths of North Africa, the Levant, and Italy for two and a half centuries. During that time, it established Cairo as a cultural capital and two of the oldest known universities, including the prestigious Al-Azhar. Ruling by minority, the Arab Ismaili imams tolerated other religions, but failure to convert the Sunni Berbers majority left them vulnerable to conquest in 1171.

The Imamat was reestablished as a nexus of heavily fortified city-states in Persian territory, but was forced into hiding after Genghis Khan called for their extermination with these words: "None of that people should be spared, not even the babe in its cradle." "About one hundred thousand Ismailis were wiped out. And that is when *taqiyyah* in the Ismaili community starts to happen," said Jeraj.

The term he used, *taqiyyah,* is an Islamic concept that sanctions concealment of one's faith for self-preservation. It has been recently pulled out of obscurity by Islamophobes to accuse people of being Muslims in disguise. To cite an example from my in-box, "I think you['re] maybe just using *taqiyya* to push Islam in a fuzzy, warm, 'nothing-to-see-here' kind of way." Historically though, taqiyyah was almost exclusively used to shield Muslims from other Muslims. It's how Ismailis survived for centuries. They performed the dominant sect, while privately giving allegiance to an Imamat, who somehow secretly disseminated *firman* (in the Imamat's context, something between royal decree and fatwa) to people living continents apart, until the forty-sixth imam, Aga Khan I, pulled them out of the shadows in 1835.

Most of the world's 13 million Ismailis live evenly across half a dozen West, Central, and South Asian countries, but most of Canada's diaspora descended from Indian labourers in British-occupied Africa. Many Asians in Southeast Africa were indentured, and like their Caribbean counterparts, they were more privileged than Blacks. As Britain's holdings in Africa moved toward independence in the 1960s, Britain ensured Asians controlled the bureaucracy tasked with carrying out the transition.

If their ascension to elite positions didn't fuel anti-Asian populism, it certainly couldn't protect Asians from hostility. European- and Asian-dominated industries were nationalized under the second, socialist government. Many Ismailis were initially hopeful when General Idi Amin Dada usurped the presidency in 1971. "One of the first things Idi Amin promised was giving the businesses back to people," recalled Jeraj, whose family owned a tea factory. "Everybody was happy that we wouldn't have to write a cheque to the government."

Amin followed through on his promise. Then he did a complete one-eighty on August 4, 1972, by ordering all noncitizens to leave the country. They had ninety days, after which their properties and businesses would become expropriated for his supporters. Jeraj's family was not worried: "Everyone knew there would be a time when the noncitizens would be asked to leave." A significant Indian population decided to keep their British nationality, but most Ismailis gave it up after independence to become citizens of Uganda. This was on the advice of Aga Khan IV, who'd invested heavily in the region, establishing media, colleges, banks, and the public corporation Jubilee Insurance. He'd encouraged Ismailis to make their East African nations their homelands in a firman. His wisdom had seemed to pan out. "They were very prosperous years for us, while in the UK there were race riots," said Jeraj.

But only a week after Amin's ultimatum to noncitizens, he expanded the expulsion to all "coloured people," meaning non-Blacks. "We thought, *This can't be real*," said Jeraj, who assumed it was just bluster from a strongman populist. (Sound familiar?) "You can't kick citizens out of their own country. Surely the international community will not stand by and allow this," recalled Jeraj. "Around day forty, we saw a newspaper ad from the American embassy pledging visas to one hundred doctors and their families. There was a real panic after that."

Yet diplomats operated as if there was no potential for genocide. Jeraj remembers the absurdity of Kampala embassies maintaining their regular Monday to Friday hours: 9:00 a.m. to 3:00 p.m., with a ninety-minute lunch break. Even the UK—the nation responsible for colonizing Uganda, populating it with Indians, and elevating them to power—resisted resettling those who lacked British citizenship, about thirty thousand in all.

Given the apathy, Jeraj's family didn't fully believe a speaker at their jamatkhana when he told congregants to prepare for a move to Canada. But what sounded like rumour was in fact a tip from His Holiness himself.

Aga Khan IV visited Ottawa in late September to discuss the total number of Asians that Canada would accept. His arrival coincided with game eight of the Canada versus Russia hockey Summit Series, which may explain why Prime Minister Trudeau sent the assistant deputy minister, James Cross, to the lunch meeting instead. Official documents confirm that the Canadian diplomat was getting up-to-date scores from the kitchen staff, via the maître d', using discreet hand signals. Legend has it that he unwittingly set the number of Ismaili refugees when he flashed six fingers, confirming the score, to the maître d' standing behind the Aga Khan, which the imam apparently saw and misinterpreted to mean six thousand. (An additional two thousand were welcomed the next year.)

If the story sounds dubious, just imagine how unbelievable the offer sounded to Ismailis. Canada didn't even have a consulate office in Kampala. But when one popped up in an empty office on Embassy Row, Jeraj's community started to believe it. "The Canadians put an ad in the paper saying the consulate will be open at six a.m.," he recalled. "'Of course,' all of us said, 'it's a typo.' They meant nine. But sure enough, they opened their doors at six fifteen. They even had chairs for us to sit outside." Not even the British and Indian embassies—which by far had the longest queues—provided seating.

Jeraj, the eldest son, accompanied his father there. They waited to be called from a line of over two thousand applicants. He felt his heart sink as a tank convoy rolled down Embassy Row. One by one, the embassies locked their doors, leaving hundreds of people panicked in the streets. Jeraj and his father prepared to run for their lives when a young Canadian diplomat pulled them and about fifty others inside the consulate. "The tank stopped there and turned its gun barrel toward us, and the diplomat just kept saying, 'Don't worry, you're on Canadian soil. No harm will come to you.'" They locked eyes with soldiers pointing their barrels at the broad glass door. After what seemed like eternity, the soldiers finally turned away, laughing.

"At that moment, my father said, 'Any place that treats us with this much dignity is worth moving to. We're going to Canada,'" recalled Jeraj. Their family held their hopes and breath all the way to the airport, through a gamut of harassment and assault at every checkpoint, until the plane took off. Only then did they exhale.

The Ismaili Canadian population grew following other East African expulsions and persecutions. A study of Ismaili refugees found that less than 5 percent of those who received public assistance still required it one year later. Their unemployment rate was also well below the national average. By 1978, they'd established an impressive network of jamatkhanas stretching from Vancouver to Montreal.

During a country-wide tour, Aga Khan issued a new firman for the Afro-Asian diaspora: "I would like my spiritual children to think of Canada as their homeland. Make it your homeland, work for your homeland, defend your homeland, and from here in the future assist the jamats who are less fortunate than yourselves. Think of the people in other parts of the world who can benefit from your knowledge, from your experience, but above all establish this as your home, as your permanent home."

Have they ever.

Nearly one in ten Canadian Muslims are Nizari Ismailis, which is stunning in its own right. On the public stage, their representation is larger still. Ismailis anchor the news, lead telecom giants, and serve as big-city mayors. In Parliament, they've been elected across the political spectrum. In culture, they've won premier art and literature prizes. In general, Ismaili Canadians are famous for their volunteerism.

In 2017, the Ismaili Council for Canada celebrated the country's 150th birthday with a pledge of 1 million hours of community service by its members. They smashed their goal in six months. Ismailis obviously took the 1978 firman to heart, but Jeraj said the ethos of volunteerism exists worldwide. It's fostered at the jamatkhana in children as young as five, who wear "junior volunteer" uniforms as they usher guests and clean the temple, and it's nurtured further through Aga Khan Development Network volunteerism. "We believe that if you want influence in the community, you have to participate; otherwise someone else will decide for you."

The individual and collective achievements of Ismailis no doubt help improve public perceptions of Muslims as a whole. But they're also used to vilify Muslims in Canada and abroad. It's a common tactic of Far Right and neoconservative figures to highlight the minority group's accomplishments before critiquing the other 99 percent. (To quote an article by Ezra Levant, Canada's third-rate Tucker Carlson, "I'm glad Canada took in Ismailis, who are secular, educated, integrated in the wider community and grateful to have been rescued." He soon added, "There are so many rapes by Muslim cab drivers in Halifax, police have stopped describing the suspects.")

Even qualifying them as "Ismaili Muslim" has the effect of sorting the good ones from the bad. Some high-placed members, such as Alykhan Velshi, Stephen Harper's former head of strategy, fuel these divisions by distinguishing their Muslimness as Ismaili. Other noteworthy members, like Calgary mayor Naheed Nenshi and celebrity science journalist Latif Nasser, avoid qualifying their Muslimness as "Ismaili," partly to demonstrate solidarity with victims of Islamophobia. As Nasser explained to me, "It feels good to say, 'I stand with this broader group, I am one of them; if you consider me, consider them.'" The mayor also raised this point to me, and added, "Ismailis have historically been persecuted by the greater ummah, but if we can have Muslims take pride in the achievement of Ismaili Muslims that does a little bit of good towards unification of the ummah, which I also think is a good thing."

Ismailis are sometimes called the "Jews of Muslims" for their business prowess. "Those comments are supposed to be compliments, but they're insulting," said Jeraj. "They're trying to divide us and put us in different boxes, but I don't want to be there. I belong in more than one box."

One doesn't need to make overt comparisons between Ismaili and non-Ismaili Muslims to play wedge politics. The Nizari refugees were outliers. Most arrived with wealth, English fluency, and high school diplomas, to say nothing of their political influence via the Aga Khan. Celebrating their accomplishments without context raises the expectations for other newcomers to impossible standards.

A huge perk of being Ismaili is access to its global network of members. There are eighty jamatkhanas in Canada—all organized by the Ismaili Council for Canada, an extension of the Imamat—where a tightly knit social culture nurtures material opportunities on top of spiritual well-being. "Success both in your worldly life as well as your spiritual life is extremely important," explained Jeraj. "You do not give up one for the other. That is the advice from the imams. That both lives matter." While Aga Khan III morally sanctioned the pursuit of material pursuits, his grandson, IV, made it a tenet of life.

Due to the democratic nature of Sunni jurisprudence, orthodox Muslims may struggle to agree on how to interpret scripture for modern life. Mainstream Shia receive slightly more direction from a number of ayatollahs qualified to determine sharia for their followers. But Ismailis are of the view that the Quran is a living document demanding updated clarity by one leader. It's one benefit of having a so-called walking imam. There are downsides too.

Once they receive a moral directive from the Aga Khan in the form of a firman, the pressure on individuals to "reform," or rather assimilate, is immense. Jeraj's grandmother told him she felt ashamed and exposed after Aga Khan III introduced feminist reformations against veiling and strict modest dress. Achieving material success is a more recent version of this peer pressure, as it fosters what one ex-Ismaili described to me as a "culture of elitism." The Imamat is using firman as a tool to purify Muslims of what it sees as antiquated habits.

For this non-Ismaili writer, the downside of a walking imam is his obfuscation. I hoped to access a jamatkhana to complete this narrative portrait of mosques across the Americas. Any of Edmonton's three would do, but I'd even fly out to Toronto, where the Ismaili Centre, a mega-jamatkhana, if ever there was one, hosts scheduled tours as part of an ambassadorial mandate. My attempts to access executive council members of the Ismaili Council for Canada in Toronto were repeatedly ignored.

Jeraj said he'd consider the possibility of asking members of his Edmonton mosque to welcome me *after* prayers; joining them during prayer, however, was rejected outright. "It's only for people who have given their allegiance to the imam," he said.

"Do you think that they could make an exception for journalistic or literary purposes?" I asked, pandering to his bibliophilia. We sat on the board of a literary festival together, plus his home teemed with Islamic books in every room, including taboo titles banned by some governments. If nothing else, I hoped my request could appeal to cultural values of pluralism and a free press.

But no. It all came back to the culture of secrecy fostered after the Mongol pogroms of the mid-thirteenth century. "Opening any jamaat anywhere in the world is still a little scary," said Jeraj. "We're not afraid in the Western world, but can somebody in other parts of the world demand that you open your jamatkhana as well?"

This storied persecution cultivated a reasonable suspicion that permeates their religious life. Unlike Ahmadi and Tablighi, Ismailis don't do *dawah* in the traditional sense of propagating their faith. Becoming Ismaili is nothing like taking shahada. "It's a difficult process," said Jeraj. "We have huge challenges with intermarriages—not that we oppose them." Spouses are discouraged from converting unless spiritually sincere, as was the case with Rita Hayworth, but this inevitably poses huge challenges.

Their persecution has also bred a false sense of victimhood. It has taken on a mythic power in Ismaili consciousness, a sort of pacifist extension of the traditional Shia martyrdom complex. True, it's not been long since Sunni extremists massacred Ismaili pilgrims in Pakistan or since Saudi Arabia's government mass incarcerated Ismaili citizens, but the same is true of many religious minorities who don't guard their beliefs, including, and especially, Ahmadi Muslims.

The fact is, North American and European Ismailis are privileged, and those abroad are increasingly protected by the Aga Khan's political clout. It left me wondering whom or what His Holiness was actually protecting with his micromanagement of the broader Ismaili image. Is it really the most vulnerable of his followers, or is it the Aga Khan himself?

————

After interviewing Jeraj, I tried once more to access the Imamat's Canadian leadership. I requested an interview with the national president. I respected their restrictions on worship attendance, but asked for a private visit to the tourist-friendly Ismaili Centre in Toronto. I also asked to meet the flagship temple's *mukhi* and *kamadia*, a traditionally husband-and-wife duo elected to lead communal prayer. I made this request first by telephone, then in writing, at the instruction of a regional representative friendly to my cause. A conference call with Ismaili Centre staff in Toronto followed. I hesitantly provided them with a chapter-by-chapter synopsis of this book. I then endured a months-long communications gauntlet, only to receive a firm denial.

The more I pushed for access to the Aga Khan's national leadership, the more I sensed that the victimhood narrative was used to shield him from moral scrutiny on one of the most important social issues of our time: gay rights. They voiced concerns with my interest in profiling a queer-friendly Toronto mosque later in this book. It didn't matter that the premise of my project was demonstrating Islamic pluralism or that this chapter on Ismaili Muslims was separated from the other on the queer Muslim movement. Even if they were at opposite ends of this book, I was told there was a risk of being associated with the Toronto mosque, which could endanger vulnerable Ismailis across the globe.

To hammer the point, one of the Ismaili representatives (though not an official spokesperson) relayed an anecdote they'd heard about an unauthorized Ismaili float at the Toronto Pride Parade that supposedly incited anti-Ismaili violence in Pakistan. It was easy enough to verify the first part of this claim—photos were circulated online by a group called Ismaili Queers—but my attempt to verify the claimed attack came up short. I contacted Rahim Thawer, the LGBTQ group's founder, who was unaware of the claim that his organization had unwittingly incited violence or that the photos had gone viral. Far as we could tell, they hadn't. The whole thing was a fabrication.

The Ismaili's public relations team had weaponized its historic victimhood using ugly contemporary tropes of Muslim extremists overreacting to offensive images. The horrific violence provoked in 2005 by the infamous cartoons of Prophet Muhammad in a Danish newspaper and again in 2015 at *Charlie Hebdo* offices in France are difficult subjects for me personally and professionally. I was deeply insulted by the suggestion that my good-faith reporting could spill innocent blood.

The fear of anti-Ismaili backlash suggests the Aga Khan's caution protects Ismailis in ultraconservative countries. More likely it's for fear of losing the allegiance of those Ismailis, who make up the vast majority of the sect, and consequently the Aga Khan's legitimacy in many Muslim-majority nations.

I felt a righteous duty to force open the door that they'd all but told me not to look behind. To help me understand why homosexuality is such a thorny issue for His Holiness, progressive activists from the Ismaili community pointed me toward the story of Andrew Ali Aga Khan Embiricos, Aga Khan IV's nephew and grandson of Hayworth, who died of an apparent suicide in 2011. The young socialite had scandalized the family name when it was discovered he'd performed in gay porn. His sexuality and battles with HIV and drugs are talking points for Muslim elites who wish to undermine the Imamat's legitimacy. Andrew is a useful trope for their anti-Western, anti-Ismaili propaganda.

But it's not just mullahs trying to force Aga Khan IV into a conversation about homosexuals in the community; liberal Ismailis are doing it too. As they see it, the imam's refusal to take an official position in support of same-sex marriage and LGBTQ rights undermines his commitment to modernism and social justice.

I wanted to explore this more with Thawer, who leads another LGBTQ group, Salaam Canada, in addition to Ismaili Queers. As luck would have it, Salaam organized a cross-country meet-up, which included a stop at an Edmonton board game café. Thawer is a fashionable and upbeat social worker in his early thirties. He'd never met most of the people attending the social event, yet could keep the conversation going for hours, jumping from one topic to another, smiling the whole way through. We broke away from the fun to speak privately about his community's sensitivities around homosexuality.

About the claims that his group unwittingly endangered Ismailis in fundamentalist regions, Thawer was more disturbed by the rationale than the falsities. "I wouldn't tell women in one part of the world not to fight for their rights for fear of women being denigrated in another part of the world," he said. "It doesn't make sense to me."

He didn't doubt the sincerity of the institutional staff who felt protective of their coreligionists in Kyrgyzstan, Tajikistan, and Pakistan in particular. It's common for privileged Ismailis to volunteer in developing countries and forge genuine connections with locals. But he also felt a bureaucratic culture had permeated his coreligionists. "Ismailis are very cautious and politically minded," he explained.

The community members he knows don't have a problem with his work per se, but they sometimes email Salaam Canada or Ismaili Queers to question why he uses "Muslim" or "Ismaili" as labels in his LGBTQ advocacy. "They ask, 'Why do these have to inform each other?'" said Thawer. "It's a mix of blatant homophobia and transphobia, but also the good Muslim/bad Muslim divide."

Ismaili Muslims are happy to speak about their achievements, personally and collectively, and about Islam in general, but they often resist discussing personal beliefs. The institution's insistence on speaking in a singular strategized voice has led believers, especially the influential, to overconsider their audiences.

Thawer can empathize with their self-consciousness. Once a loudmouth atheist and fan of Sam Harris, just like I had been, he's wrestled with the internal machinations many racialized people feel trying to represent themselves to the white majority. Those preoccupations are multiplied for Ismailis. "They're regularly thinking about how they look to other Muslims because we are often looked at as 'not real' or 'too progressive.'"

Despite his frustrations with Ismailism, Thawer has deep affection for his community and their values. The promotion of pluralism, solidarity, volunteerism, and helping the disenfranchised inspired him to become a social worker. It was hard for him to appreciate these things in university, afraid of coming out lest his sexuality find its way back to Toronto through the whisper network, as it eventually did. He feared it would scandalize his family, but in the end, the morality stood up. With his community supporting him, Thawer released his resentment and self-hate and gradually reclaimed his Ismaili Muslim identity on his own terms.

Aga Khan IV has not yet issued a firman to unequivocally accept homosexuality, but it's already sanctioned in the Western liberal values that he espouses. There are openly gay Ismaili Muslims in the public eye, same-sex married couples who feel comfortable attending jamatkhana together, and LGBTQ advocates who've also served in secular roles in the institutions. In 2017, the Aga Khan Museum, an extravagant Islamic art gallery adjacent to the Ismaili Centre in Toronto, installed a rainbow sculpture for Pride Month. Thawer understood it to be a gesture of acceptance, but he wished it was explicit. "We know that homophobia and transphobia kill people, that silence leads to depression, anxiety, suicide, failed marriages, domestic violence."

The purpose of a walking imam is to help Muslims reconcile modernity with ancient wisdom, to clear the fog between this life and the next. Previous Aga Khans defied Muslim orthodoxy with firman in support of more simplified worship, women's rights, religious tolerance, and "cosmopolitan ethics." Some Ismailis have interpreted the last as code for acceptance of homosexuality, but is it enough? For those who take the Imamat's firman to heart, his evasion may leave them in the dark, questioning their own sense of morality.

To me, it's part of the Aga Khan's moral ambiguity, no different from how he rationalized building the Global Centre for Pluralism with a Canadian government backsliding on the very principle of his prestige project. Did he partner with the Harper government despite his personal disapproval of the Conservative Party's discrimination against Muslim immigrants and refugees, or did the Aga Khan approve of these policies in spite of his own message? I also wonder if the coded language the Aga Khan uses to condone homosexuality is designed to placate conservative factions of Ismailism or whether it's to placate influential Western liberals.

———

Aga Khan IV likes to say that his authority is religious only. "It is not a political role," he once said. "I do not govern any land." It's an absurd claim given that his grandfather served as the president of the League of Nations, and his great-grandfather Aga Khan II, served on the British Crown's Bombay government, to say nothing of the highly political affairs of their predecessors, going back to Shia Islam's founding fathers. But even by IV's own dubious metric—that one must govern land to be a political leader—does he not effectively govern the many Aga Khan Development Network and Ismaili Centre buildings spread across the world? His prolific reach through these entities is no doubt owed more to his political prowess than religious authority.

The volume of Aga Khan projects is staggering, and judging from the striking modernist beauty of the Aga Khan Museum and Ismaili Centre buildings, so is their collective value. I visited them during a work trip to Toronto in February 2019, using my press credentials to book an interview with the museum's director and my cell phone to book a spot on the centre's public tours. Despite sharing land together, the museum and centre live separately under the Aga Khan's secular and religious entities, which is why I could access one communications office without the other's knowledge.

There are six Ismaili Centres in the world. They're as much temples as international embassies by virtue of the national council offices and public outreach mandates. The Imamat wished to reclaim the Ismaili narrative after centuries of silence allowed Muslim detractors and Western Orientalists to redefine Ismailism in history books. (For example, *hashashin,* the Persian root of *assassin*, was a pejorative term for the Nizari Muslims. When medieval historians glamorize Genghis Khan's conquest of the Assassins, they are in fact glamorizing an Ismaili holocaust.) The Imamat wishes to reclaim the Ismaili narrative on its own terms. The first two Ismaili Centres opened in 1985, in London and Vancouver, followed by Lisbon, Dubai, and Toronto.

Another is underway in Houston. While the Texas design hasn't been released as of this writing, it will be hard for it to outdo Toronto's centre: a white stone building curling around an eight-sided crystalline dome, as if hugging a massive jewel excavated from the snow.

It was certainly the most beautiful house of worship—any worship—that I'd ever seen. I kept turning back to photograph it as I crossed the plaza on my way to the Aga Khan Museum, where I was scheduled to first meet CEO and director Henry Kim.

In comparison, the brutalism-meets-futurism museum looks like a galactic prison. But inside, its glass ceiling and courtyard walls transform it into a lantern. "His Highness is very concerned with the principle behind lights," said Kim, who is originally from London, where the museum was proposed in the early 2000s. After years of running into bureaucratic hurdles, the Aga Khan decided to move it to Toronto in 2010. He followed that announcement with news of the complementary Ismaili Centre.

As a gallery of Islamic arts, past and present, the museum serves a greater purpose. The world needs an urgent reminder of the religion's record of harmony, diversity, and cultural cross-pollination, evident in such exhibits as a medieval Nativity painting with Arabic inscriptions. Exhibits largely collected from Africa, Persia, and Arabia during Islam's Golden Age prove the faith's adaptability. Altogether they defy Orientalists who've erased Muslim contributions to science and philosophy and Occidentalists who've erased Hindu and Christian contributions to Muslim societies.

"His Highness talks about a 'clash of ignorance' because there's such fundamental misunderstandings about Islam in the West today," said Kim. "A museum like this can help with that narrative insofar that we can actually showcase not only the diversity of Muslims and the beauty of the book that's contained within Islam, but that for fourteen hundred years, Islam was not living in a vacuum." He gestured me toward a glass case to view his favourite piece in the museum: a gold plate with two movable inner discs. It looked like the inside of a luxury watch.

"What is it?" I asked.

"An astrolabe." Kim explained how it triangulates one's ground po-sition on Earth using the stars overhead, like an ancient GPS. "What's incredible is, it comes from fourteenth-century Spain. And when you look at the inscriptions, you'll see that the stars are identified in both Latin and Arabic. It's a bilingual translation."

I leaned forward and squinted at the inscriptions.

"What you're seeing here are two different cultures, or two dif-ferent religions," he continued. "Culturally, the Spanish Muslims and Spanish Christians are very similar. They're living side by side, inter-changeably using an object such as this. In addition to those markings, someone scratched in the transliteration into Hebrew. It's very faint; you can't see it from this far away."

Canadians and Americans often tout their country's multicultur-alism as unique, but here was proof of it thriving nearly a millennium ago. Christians and Jews played important roles in Moorish society. Ancient caliphate capitals such as Cairo, Timbuktu, and Baghdad em-bodied pluralistic attitudes that many people today wrongly believe are antithetical to Islam.

"If you're looking for evidence of coexistence, these objects tell you that story," said Kim.

But, I asked, was this message about Muslim and non-Muslim co-existence undermined by the Aga Khan's insistence on slapping the family name across the museum? If this noble and peace-promoting story is so urgent, why not communicate that in the name? Surely, the "Museum of Islamic Civilization," or something like it, would express these values better than his family's vaguely monarchic title. It would probably help with poor attendance too; the museum had thirty thou-sand visitors in its opening year, compared to six hundred thousand visitors to Toronto's quirky shoe museum.

Kim admitted the name is a challenge. "We have to get people be-yond the conception of 'this might be a museum about the Aga Khan.' But when you look at the Aga Khan's projects throughout the world, it's never about him or his family. It's about what they do."

It was a nice but unconvincing sentiment. Similarly, the Aga Khan

Garden in Edmonton, which was billed as an "Islamic garden," opened without any Arabic script or Islamic message at all. There are Moghul-inspired features, but the most prominent symbol is that of the official Aga Khan star sculpted into fountains. This self-aggrandizement reveals the imam's tendency to put brand recognition above outcome, and prestige above purpose.

I thanked Kim for the interview and guidance and left for my appointment at the Ismaili Centre, where I was welcomed by an elderly volunteer. I stowed my belongings and signed a waiver stating strict rules against audio and video recordings, leaving me to narrate my visit from memory, photos, and phone notes. (I'll also respect the volunteer's privacy by changing his name to Zahid, meaning "devotee.")

Zahid runs an engineering consultancy but closes shop every week to guide visitors. He led me from room to room, each sunlit by gorgeous glass ceilings, even on that dead-of-winter day. Light, Zahid explained, summons the role of the divine creator. This wasn't allegorical; Ismailism vows that each Abrahamic prophet possessed a cosmic light—the first flash of "let there be light" fame. Whereas most Shiites believe this light ceded with the twelfth imam, Ismailis, who split after the supreme leader, still see it glow in the forty-ninth imam.

As we approached the last leg of the tour, the mosque (or jamat-khana) itself, I noticed there weren't washing stations for ablutions. Zahid explained that wudu is no longer compulsory; worship rituals have been updated to account for modern plumbing and air-conditioning. "The world has advanced," he said. Similarly, there was no need for women to cover their hair before entering the prayer space. Removal of shoes, however, remained compulsory.

The prayer hall was vast and ostentatious. The geometric patterns across the panel walls, the *mihrab* (a semicircular niche from which imams lead prayer), and carpet at first dazzled and then dizzied me. Light crashed through a patterned glass ceiling, casting octagonal symbols onto a rug with an identical pattern. For a brief and beautiful moment every day, light and Earth align perfectly.

"How do you indicate where people stand for prayer?" I asked, noting there were no linear lines. They pray in a seated position, Zahid explained, as an expression of humility and submission before God. He redirected my attention to the quiet of the room. He explained that heating and ventilation technology in the floor acts as a vacuum, allowing fifteen hundred people every Friday to meditate in absolute silence.

I could tell Zahid found my line of questioning curious. Most visitors come for the architectural and design features, the world-class pan-Islamic art. I was awestruck by it all, but I was also there to understand religious Ismaili's scriptural interpretations. So I decided to get a single random Ismaili's opinion on a most sensitive issue: "Do Ismailis believe the Quran supports queer lifestyles and the inclusion of gay people in holy activities?" I asked.

Zahid didn't clamp up or bristle at my question. He held it in his head a moment, considered closely, and then offered his personal opinion. Belief, he said, is only a very small show of the Muslim faith. The bigger part is one's actions and how they interact with creation. "You have to be like God. God is compassionate. God is nice," he said. And then my septuagenarian guide said something kind of radical, almost as an afterthought. It was something to the effect of the Quran being a reflection not of God but of ourselves. "You read it depending on your own internal structure," I recall him saying, "and you take from it *what you feel is right*." The way he emphasized *you* and *your* didn't sound like how people generally speak in second-person tense. It sounded like he was speaking directly to me—*what I feel is right*. I'm quite sure Zahid thought I was a Muslim struggling with my sexuality, but I also felt that he was connecting me to my, well, religious heritage. Maybe better to say my faith, if you'll allow me to call it that—not *faith* in the traditional definition of a structured belief system, but faith as a feeling one has in life to always work out for the best. Faith in people to do the right thing. Faith in myself and my abilities. Faith that everything has meaning. Islam poured the foundations of this faith, and though the structure wobbles and shifts, those faiths have rarely failed me.

I liked the idea of religiousness as more of a feeling. The Abrahamic faiths prescribe too much to their charters. It is why esoteric branches have evolved from all of them. Ismailism is but one response.

At its heart is a personal search for God. And if you feel Its warm light within you, then does it matter what some behatted religious monarch thinks? Even the Aga Khan, I'm sure, would agree it doesn't.

I decided not to prod Zahid's theology further and turned my curiosity to our material surroundings. There were portraits of Prince Shah Karim Al Husseini on opposite sides of the mihrab. One was recent, the other taken in 1957, when he was a twentysomething Harvard sophomore unexpectedly called up by the Imamat to succeed his grandfather. He looks positively nervous in his three-piece suit, like a boy being told he's the man of the house now. In fact, he was. His father, Prince Aly Khan, was the next in line until Aga Khan III posthumously announced the imamship would skip a generation. Announced in his will, it was widely understood as a rebuke of his son's superficial lifestyle.

It read like a firman. "Ever since the time of my ancestor Ali, the first Imam, a period of thirteen hundred years, it has always been the tradition of our family that each Imam chooses his successor at his absolute and unfettered discretion from amongst any of his descendants," he wrote. "I am convinced that it is in the best interest of the Shia Ismaili Muslim Community that I should be succeeded by a young man who has been brought up and developed during recent years and in the midst of the new age and who brings a new outlook on life to his office as Imam."

Looking at that young man grinning nervously in the photo, it's hard to believe that he could be up for the job. And yet he's been of more consequence to the world than his grandfather and many predecessors, and more positive for the world today than most religious and state leaders.

His playboy father, his tragic nephew, and other family scandals are sometimes trotted out by mainstream Muslims as cautionary tales of Westernism gone wild. They're often overlooking the ways that Western liberalism and Islam can adapt to each other, especially when carrying out humanitarian missions, as the North American Ismaili Muslims and their imam have proved.

I turned around and looked at the other framed portrait hanging on the opposite wall. In this, IV looked as pompous as anyone would in an ornate, personalized robe and big hat. But it wasn't anything people had to look at. Both portraits were small and carefully placed to fall out of view when one turns to face Mecca. If nothing else, it was a concession from the imam himself that there are some things in life better known by turning to God.

The Most Villainous of All Screen Villains

IMAN Cultural Center

(Los Angeles, California)

Zigzagging my way through US Customs in the Calgary airport, I studied the agents carefully. I hoped for the jovial young Latino or chatty white woman, who looked like they might grant me a hassle-free trip to Los Angeles, and not the dour guy who looked deprived of sleep and, probably, childhood birthday parties.

I didn't used to be a nervous traveller, but starting around 2014, when Westerners of my sex, age, and heritage started flocking to the Islamic State, random searches got a lot less random for me. True, I'd never been dragged off a plane, denied a connection, strip-searched (like my friend's mother), or detained (save for once in Israel). But increased secondary screenings—those once-novel interviews, swabbings, pat-downs, bag searches—gave me a glimpse of the phenomenon known as "flying while Muslim," or better yet, "flying while looking Muslim."

With my luck, I got the whammy. "What's the purpose of your trip?" asked the surly agent, analyzing every passport stamp with extra attention, especially Iraqi Kurdistan.

"Work," I replied.

"What do you do?"

"I'm a writer."

"What does that mean? You're doing *stories*?" he said, his pitch rising as he looked at me for the first time. The chip on his shoulder could fill a cargo jet.

I was going to LA during Nowruz, the Persian New Year festival, to investigate why more Iranian Americans are reclaiming Muslim culture after decades of suppression. But I wasn't about to share that with a US border guard when the Trump administration was rattling sabers at Tehran.

"I'm writing an article about a famous actor," I said.

This was my second reason for travelling to LA, so I wasn't lying. Well, maybe just the "famous" part. My subject had been dead for fifty years and even the handful of B-movie nerds who'd be familiar with Frank Lackteen would not call him a celebrity. But I was assigned to profile the late actor for *The Ringer*, a sports and pop culture website, and had an appointment that afternoon to view his records at the Academy of Motion Picture Arts and Sciences archives in Beverly Hills.

I predicted the agent would now ask about my story, as this is usually how I disarm authorities, with some novel trivia to take home to their family. Not so. "How are they paying you?" he asked.

I could feel him homing in on some unbeknownst breach.

"US dollars?"

"Yes—" *aaaand* that's the answer that got me detained long enough to miss my flight.

An hour later, I was released, never to learn why I was held back for questioning. The airline refused to rebook me, and I paid three times more for the only available flight that day. The hot towels and legroom in business class were no consolation for how violated I'd felt. I could've lied for expediency, but my honesty had cost my family a thousand dollars and a research day. I rebooked my library appointment and spent the layover poring over the dozens of personal records and clippings I'd collected since learning I had a distant relative in the movies.

Two years back, my dad needed to show me something on his iPad, eager as ever since he'd learned how to use it. He'd come across a post in his hometown's Facebook group about a local boy done good. I grew accustomed to elders obsessively outing Hollywood's secret Lebanese—Shakira, Salma Hayek, Vince Vaughn, Farrah Fawcett—so I prepared for some marginalia about an actor's great-grandfather. Instead, I fell down my own genealogy rabbit hole. Born Mohammed Hassan Yachteen in 1897, Lackteen (as he was later known) was a grandson of my great-great-great-grandparents. He lived in Kab Elias until he was seven or eight, when his family immigrated to Lawrence, Massachusetts, and sent him to work in perilous textile factories instead of school. They resided in a diseased Syrian ghetto, possibly taking in my great-grandfather when he arrived in the 1910s, before they all moved to Detroit.

Lackteen caught the acting bug when a director discovered his face in a crowd. "Basilisk," "wolfish," "hungry," and "cadaverous looking" were some Hollywood labels used to describe him. After six years of working on and off between Detroit car factories and New York studios, he moved to Hollywood and quickly gained fame as "the most villainous of all screen villains." Audiences loved to hate Lackteen, and Lackteen loved to be hated. He bragged about his mug well past his prime, a self-styled character actor boasting about how it earned him over five hundred parts alongside Mary Pickford and other silent film icons. I was less intrigued with the quantity of his credits than their names: Chinese Heavy, Malay George, Pawnee Killer, Pablo, Shamba. From the silent era into the talkies and through the technicolour and TV ages, Lackteen was typecast as foreigner more than as villain, though usually both. His versatile complexion even fooled those who'd misreported him as Persian, Turkish, Russian, and Italian.

Since learning about Lackteen, I've tried to understand how he reconciled with participating in the vilification of minorities and whether he was aware that he'd helped shape Islamophobic tropes still present in Hollywood today. Had he ever addressed racism in his roles or Hollywood publicly? I'd only found clippings in which he'd boasted about being fluent in Arabic and claimed to be a trained Oriental rug maker groomed for the family trade, which was a lie; we were farmers and merchants. I hoped a visit to the library would give me insight into his conscience. But it would have to wait a couple days.

I landed at LAX hours late and drove straight to the Iranian-American Muslim Association of North America (IMAN), on the edge of downtown. Despite a quarter million Angelinos claiming Iranian descent, IMAN was the only Iranian Muslim mosque I found. It surprised me, considering most Western mosques are founded, if not controlled, on ethnic lines. As I dug deeper, I found several secular or nationalist community centres and various institutions serving Jewish, Armenian, or Baha'i Iranians. To find out why Muslim Iranians weren't similarly organized, I contacted IMAN's founder, Sadegh Namazikhah, who invited me to interview him during the community centre's Nowruz Eve party.

IMAN's vast courtyard was filled with food trucks, upbeat music, and bonfires. The middle-aged man outside IMAN's entrance gate took a long, hard look at my camera bag and notebook and said, "Ticket." I didn't have one. I tried explaining that I was personally invited by Dr. Namazikhah, but Persian (or Farsi) surnames do not trip off my tongue. "I'm interviewing Dr. Nam . . . Zik—Dr. 'N' is expecting me," I said.

I followed the guard's gaze to the LAPD officers keeping a lookout from the street. The guard turned back to me and looked me straight in the eye. "Who are you?"

I hesitated. "Omar" is an unfriendly name to some Shiites. Ever since 635 C.E., when Omar ibn al-Khattab usurped the caliphate from Ali ibn Abi Talib, the first of twelve divine imams in Twelver Shia theology, the name has gained about as much popularity as "Adolf" has for Europeans.

"Omar Mouallem. I'm from Canada," I said. "Look, Dr. N is waiting for me in his office. I just talked to him on the phone."

"Buy a ticket," he said, waving me to the side.

"Can I show you some emails so I can prove I'm telling you the truth?"

He looked past me and waved the next guests forward. Clearly this was not my day.

I walked to the counter, bought one ticket, and handed it to the stern guard. He stepped aside, allowing me to cross the courtyard and enter the main building. I eventually found Dr. Namazikhah, an endodontist and University of Southern California professor, nibbling medjool dates in a boardroom with two uniformed LAPD. I sat under a map of Iran and listened as they reflected on past outreach successes with the Muslim community. I started to wonder what "success" meant if four squad cars were required to protect the community centre.

Officer Alexander, a Black man in his thirties, noticed my scribbling pen and turned to me. "Nobody's causing trouble per se," he explained. "It's more preventative, to make the community feel safe. Right now, they need a little *extra*, especially in light of everything going on in other parts of the world."

Was he referring to the heinous Christchurch massacre that had occurred earlier that week, or was he talking about the United States as well? The Far Right terrorist's assault had a particularly American flavour to it, as did his view of Muslims as powerful and predisposed to conquering, and if American Islamophobia had a patient zero, it was the Iranian community. It was Washington's and US media's handling of the 1979 Iran hostage crisis that made Muslims into an existential threat, so much so that American "patriots," wound up by *Nightline*'s slick daily coverage, took out their rage on Iranian immigrants, many themselves victims of the Ayatollah Khomeini.

America's first anti-Islamophobia groups grew from that streak of hate crimes, but they've never been able to stem the tide after every domestic incident involving Muslims. Since the 2015 San Bernardino massacre carried out by a radicalized Muslim couple, hate crimes in the state have surged. California leads the country in reported discrimination against Muslims. (Most such crimes across the United States go unreported, according to CAIR, which publishes the data annually, so the high reporting number in California might actually speak to the state's anti-racist values.)

Namazikhah finished his meeting with the police, and I asked him for his thoughts on the extra protection. "Unfortunately, racism is growing, but the sickness is not limited to any religion or group," the doctor told me. Despite the staggering death toll and evil of the Christchurch massacre, Namazikhah thought it no more tragic than the Pittsburgh synagogue shooting months earlier, or the Wisconsin Gurdwara killings in 2012.

Maybe so, but the days of media and politicians openly fanning anti-Jewish and anti-Sikh rhetoric peaked a long time ago. Not so anti-Muslim hysteria. The Christchurch shooter himself wrote that he chose Muslim victims not because *he* hated them but because they were the easiest targets to rally white power: "They are the most despised group of invaders in the West, attacking them receives the greatest level of support." But Namazikhah, a soft-spoken sexagenarian with wispy white hair, feels Muslims have more allies now than a generation ago.

When he arrived from Tehran to study at the University of Southern California in June 1978, six months into the Iranian Revolution, Iranians represented the biggest demographic of US international students, and Southern California became a hub for them because its climate and landscape are so similar. First-wave Iranians were well-regarded and increasingly representative of LA's highly paid professions and business owners. But there was friction between those who opposed the shah's corrupt consolidation of power and those who opposed the rebellion for the sake of secular modernism. The royalists grew ever larger after Ayatollah Khomeini took control, and the former quieted down for their own safety after revolutionaries took American hostages.

Namazikhah fell into neither camp. He just focused on completing his medical education, somewhat protected by anti-Iranian racism in his ivory tower, while ignoring what can only be described as Islamophobia within his own community. Backlash to the US embassy siege and fifteen-month crisis did not unite Iranians abroad. As Iran gradually eclipsed the USSR as foreign enemy number one, the diaspora disassociated from their nationality, rebranding themselves "Persians," and from each other. Even today, community events like Chaharshanbe Suri, or Nowruz Eve celebrations, attract distinct ethnic and religious groups, but for a long time, few came out as practicing Muslims.

"Iranians are a diverse group, and a lot are antireligion. They created that environment themselves. They had conflict with that government, but they thought their conflict should be with [Islam] instead of the government," he told me between starts and stops along a walkabout of the IMAN community center. The conversation moved like an LA traffic jam, as he paused to shake one extended hand after another. Ambling through corridors decorated with old furniture, Namazikhah did his best to juggle his obligations politely, introducing his friends to me not by name but by profession: *"He's an art professor. This is his daughter—she's a dentist. This man taught acting at University of Tehran—he was on a very famous soap opera in the seventies."*

That these folk would even openly support an Iranian Muslim association was remarkable. "IMAN gave these people confidence in their religion," Namazikhah said, once we got back on track.

Namazikhah didn't carry the same baggage as the second wave of immigrants. He had more in common with the third wave, a significantly larger group of apolitical refugees of a savage eight-year war with Iraq. This wave was more economically mixed, majority Muslim, and desperate for spiritual nourishment. But unlike Namazikhah's experience, they arrived to a cultural infrastructure that included private schools, business associations, and ornate community halls for those famously lavish Persian weddings. It was impressive, if not socially competitive in the way they were used to, and sharply non-Islamic.

Refugees of the revolution kept a certain distance from refugees of the war, who bore many of the markers that Westernized Iranians despised, like beards, headscarves, and a conspicuous aversion to wearing ties. To anyone traumatized by the regime it was natural to wonder: *Why did they hold on to the revolution's false promise for so long?* Similarly, many newcomers found the absence of Islamic activity in

"Tehrangeles" suspect. "Iranian Jewish, Iranian Christian, Iranian Baha'i all had their centres, and it was embarrassing that the Iranian Muslims didn't have theirs," said Namazikhah.

The closest thing to a Muslim congregation were poetry groups that tried to fill the spiritual vacuum with Rumi, often glossing over the Sufi scholar's allegorical references to the Quran and hadith. These gatherings were a foreign concept to him, but they were vaguely reminiscent of Thursday night *dua*, a more relaxed tradition of singing a supplication, followed by an informal khutba and communal dinner. "The Thursday gathering was dictated by Imam Ali for the beginning of the Muslim weekend," explained Namazikhah. Partly because of Iranians' rich poetic traditions, as well as their professional workday schedules, many Twelver Shiite prefer Friday eve to Friday prayer. Whereas Sunni doctrine obligates able-bodied men to attend Salat al-Jumah, a lineage of Shiite muftis ended the mandate after the twelfth divine imam "vanished" (his return marks the end of days). "I do Friday prayer by myself because my mosque is too far from my office," he said.

He realized the limits of solitary prayer when his ten-year-old daughter, Sepideh, was diagnosed with a brain tumour. In the midst of a spiritual crisis, he opened his spacious Woodland Hills home for Thursday dua. Two worshippers grew to two hundred spread across several rooms and yards. They considered establishing a mosque but concluded it wasn't worth the trouble. "There were a lot of reservations among the people," he said. "They were afraid."

They had every reason. Persian American media have outed alleged traitors and spies for less than building a mosque. For example, a restaurateur who joined a Persian cultural centre's board was accused of using his kebab shop and grocery store as a money-laundering front for the regime. But the voices of their critics fell into the background when Sepideh reached end-of-life care in 1989. It dawned on Namazikhah that even with hundreds of thousands of Iranians and Muslims in LA, there wasn't one Islamic centre available for her memorial services, which would be in the Shia tradition of gathering on the seventh and fortieth days after burial. "We had to do it in the church," he said.

The ordeal exposed a need. Others who'd struggled to bury their dead pooled their finances together, and over seven years their vision grew from a Shia funeral parlour into a robust community centre. Even so, many Iranians today still don't enter it until their own funeral. (One American-born academic, who was raised on Rumi poems instead of the Quran, told me that holding services at IMAN for his deceased uncles symbolically honoured their heritage.) Yet the essential service didn't quell rumours that IMAN was a secret arm of the Iranian government.

"I had a lot of problems with Iranians when I wanted to build this; they claimed we are affiliated with the government," Namazikhah said, as he guided me from room to room. "It's cooled down since, but one night, some people fired a gun at my son's bedroom—thank God we weren't there. Another time I was walking, and they threw eggs at me. There were times in the middle of the night, at four a.m., when they called to say, 'We are going to throw a bomb in your garden. Get your family out of the house.'" The doctor recalled these so cavalierly that I doubted my hearing. "Someone shot at your son's bedroom?"

"I was on the main floor with my son. It was about eleven thirty at night. We heard explosions, and we called the police and they found two bullets in his bedroom."

The police presence made more sense to me now. I told him it sounded like a most extreme case of Islamophobia—literally, an irrational fear that a Muslim community centre could be a Trojan horse for espionage—but in this case perpetrated by members of a community that's often a target of Islamophobia itself. The doctor protested my assumption. He said it was *not* anti-Muslim but antiregime. His loudest critic, in fact, was a Muslim Persian-language radio personality who demanded Namazikhah pledge allegiance to the shah, decades after the monarch's death. "That's the biggest problem we have in the community. If you are not pro-monarchy, you are with the Iranian government. If you're not for the Iranian government, you're for the monarchy."

Still, I couldn't avoid noticing his centre's many overtures to Iranian monarchists. Throughout the tour, he emphasized the day care, lecture hall, and robust library of Persian literature and noted all the activities inside, like Farsi school and, yes, Rumi classes (with the poet's Islamic references intact). But the prayer hall—the actual mosque— was an afterthought in his tour and in the building's design. Under low-ceiling office tiles, it looked like something between a staff lounge and cafeteria. Burgundy velvet couch cushions leaned against the wall for back support, while bistro tables offered a place for women in loose headscarves, or none at all, to quietly chat. There was no partition between genders, and women far outnumbered men.

Namazikhah ushered me outside, eager to show off IMAN's architecture. Comprising thousands of blue tiles, the exterior was fashioned after a shrine in Shiraz, Iran, right down to the Islamic calligraphy dancing across the layered archway. A plaque tucked to the side of the entrance quoted a Persian Sufi philosopher: *Anyone who comes to this house, give him food and do not ask about his faith. Because, as he merits a life next to the exalted God, no doubt he deserves a meal on my table.*

Namazikhah's peaceful agenda couldn't be clearer. "We have two buildings. This one is Iranian architecture *after* Islam. He then gestured across the courtyard toward a bleached white community centre rattling with music. "And that one is before Islam." The Achaemenid-style pyramids across its parapet recalled the limestone ruins of the first Persian Empire that's most revered (and mourned) by the secular diaspora. To them it evoked Cyrus the Great's conquest of Babylonia, religious toleration, and emancipation of Jews. "This is a culture centre, not a mosque," he said with finality.

By the looks of the crowd, IMAN's careful calculations had paid off. But the real proof of Namazikhah's wish to destigmatize Islam amongst Iranians is on holy days. On the twenty-seventh night of Ramadan, fifteen hundred people worship in this courtyard, and even more come out for the annual coed prayer led by a woman from the Women's Mosque of America. Namazikhah went on to explain that now, the disapproval is more likely to come from conservative Muslims who call IMAN too liberal. "I say, religious people can go to any mosque they want, but we opened this place to bring people from the nightclub *to* the mosque."

Namazikhah, summoned to break up an argument, soon disappeared into the crowd. After fifteen minutes, I figured he wasn't coming back and made my way to the bonfire to scratch fire-jumping off my list of Nowruz experiences. Jumping over flames is a purification ritual done on Chaharshanbe Suri. Right before the leap, I am to address the fire, saying in Persian, "My yellowness (paleness) becomes yours; your redness (health) becomes mine." Flames shot up to my knees as I jumped, and in the literal heat of the moment, I forgot the phrase entirely and instead yelped *"Woo!"*

I spent the rest of the night enjoying piping-hot tea and spinach stew with a hospitable table of flashy young adults, who, for all I know, could've been the cast of *Shahs of Sunset*. Perhaps because they were born into better finances and were distanced from the revolution by a generation, they saw no need for the survival instincts that might've prevented their immigrant parents and grandparents from proclaiming Muslimness.

But as I exchanged airport detention stories with a young man who spent half a day with Israeli customs, I got the sense that their attendance was about more than just comfort with Iran's Islamic heritage or their own. Regardless of how observant they were, by choosing to celebrate here over any number of secular venues, they were reclaiming a part of their identity that they were taught was shameful—first by mainstream Americans, then by their elders. It was a small act of defiance.

———

Buoyed by the IMAN community's hospitality, I spent the next day on Westwood Boulevard, a.k.a. "Tehrangeles," where I met Zahra Noorbakhsh, a subversive comedian, satirist, and actor. Born and bred in Danville, a white Oakland suburb, Noorbakhsh was not much more familiar than I was with Westwood, the commercial centre of Iranian American life—or at least the bougie side that's clustered in Beverly Hills. (Most of the middle-class majority live in Orange County.) But the traffic from her house delayed our meeting past one o'clock, when the Persian antique shops, bookstores, and carpet dealerships started closing up.

It was officially Nowruz and for most Iranians, that means spending the day with family and a telephone at the ready. At the precise moment of the spring equinox—1:28:27 a.m. in Tehran, 1:58:27 p.m. in Tehrangeles—they proceed to call a litany of relatives spread across time zones, and feasting until night. Without family in town, Noorbakhsh agreed to spend her Nowruz with me. She arrived in a colourful scarf and leather jacket better suited for San Francisco.

"I avoided this town for ten years," said Noorbakhsh, as we strolled the avenue, past Nowruz-themed banners on lampposts. "We're in the city where probably one in every two women has a nose job. Sometimes Iranians will look at my face, and they will judge me based on the fact that I haven't had one. It's like a sign of lacking affluence and commitment to fit in."

Our plan was to meet over plentiful kebabs, followed by saffron and rose ice cream, but Noorbakhsh wanted a goldfish to place on her *haft-sin* at home, a festival table not unlike a Christmas tree. "You decorate it with seven things that start with the letter *sin*," she explained as we strolled the avenue. *Sin* is equivalent to the English letter *S*, but goldfish is *maheeyeh kayrmaise* in Persian.

"What's up with that?" I asked.

Noorbakhsh shrugged. Like most of the 300 million other people celebrating Nowruz, she didn't always know the whys behind the hows. "Nowruz is the one holiday all Iranians can unite around because it's not religiously specific," she said. True, I thought, but it's got its own political baggage, apparent in the traditional "sacred text" chosen for the haft-sin, which in America is often a collection of poetry rather than a Quran.

I asked Noorbakhsh what it was like to perform for Iranian crowds. She doesn't hide the fact that she's a queer, pork-eating, alcohol-drinking, white atheist–marrying kind of gal, but that's the least controversial part of her set. It's not her being a "bad" Muslim that usually offends Iranians; it's her being Muslim. "I've gotten a lot of pushback from the community for identifying so prominently as Muslim." She launched into an accented impression of a community elder: "Why do you identify as Muslim when most of us are not Muslim? Oh, and in your set, do more jokes about your family. Your dad is really funny and, you know, you're very tall, you should lose some weight, dress differently. Don't talk about politics," she said, then returned to her Californian accent. "It's about respectability politics, a big thing in the Persian community."

I couldn't help notice how she used "Iranian" and "Persian" interchangeably. Persian is a language, a culture, a criminally underrated cuisine. But it's an anachronistic label for a multiethnic community, half of whom aren't Persian at all. Intentionally or not, she explained, self-identifying as "Persian" is one of the semantic shields Iranians have used for protection from racists. Another is claiming Caucasian ancestry from a sliver of northern Iranian terrain in the Caucasus Mountains, and stressing the etymology of Iran ("Aryan") to anyone who doubts their whiteness. If that fails, then break the emergency glass case and wield your overbearing patriotism.

Speaking rapidly, she imitated how that might go: "Yes, I'm Iranian. Is this a headscarf? I wear this for my religion. Why? Because I like it as a tradition I grew up with. Isn't it important, though, that we all be able to dress the way that we want? Isn't that what makes this country great?" Her comically sized grin disappeared like a blown-out candle flame. "Iranians are masters of deescalation."

Once when Noorbakhsh was small, a man accosted her mother, who wore a headscarf, in a supermarket aisle. "Why do you hate America?" he ranted. Noorbakhsh ran toward him brandishing a Lucky Charms box. "Please, please, please, tell my mother to buy me Lucky Charms!" she said. "She's not from here. She doesn't understand every kid eats them."

The man went from angry to confused to amused. "You don't need more sugar. Listen to your mother," he said before leaving them alone. That's when Noorbakhsh had an epiphany: "I learned I could be the funny, amiable kid—a foil to my mom."

But when I met with Noorbakhsh, she wasn't sure comedy could

challenge Islamophobia anymore. Like many other radicalized com-
ics who performed after 9/11, she used humour and laughter to humanize Muslims to Middle America. But more recently, her approach
had become confrontational. As she wrote in a *New York Times* op-ed,
"The primary role of political humour today shouldn't be to alleviate
tensions or smooth out differences. It should be to heighten them and
illuminate for everyone what is a moment of crisis."

Noorbakhsh spied a row of fishbowls displayed in the window of
a Persian grocer. She snatched up one of the last bowls and got in the
checkout line, where she tapped an old man on the shoulder. "Excuse
me. Do you know what the fish is about?"

"It's a symbol of life," he said matter-of-factly.

She turned to me grinning, satisfied. After her symbols of life were
bagged up, we left the store and headed to a cozy restaurant in Persian
Square to ring in the new year. With a minute to Nowruz, we joined
a middle-aged couple watching Tehran countdown celebrations live
on a phone. "Eid-e Shoma Mubarak!" they exclaimed after the countdown, and I, of course, fumbled my response. "He's Canadian," Noorbakhsh said apologetically.

We continued our conversation over a platter of food and saffron
ice cream at a trendy Persian dessert shop. I asked Noorbakhsh about
On Behalf of All Muslims, her comedic monologue about the ups and
downs of being a Muslim woman in America, which she was midway done rehearsing. She wasn't sure how it would go over with Iranians, as she sensed a new kind of tension when she performed for
them. They seemed less willing to laugh at political humour, even
lighthearted stuff. She'd heard reports of state surveillance of Orange
County's predominantly Muslim Persians and others' bank accounts
being wrongfully frozen or closed. Iranian Americans are especially
wary of journalists, she warned.

"Why?"

"You'll get reporters asking you to divulge your life story, and you
don't know if they're real," she said. "I verify them on Twitter." But
even legitimate reporters have given Iranians cause to keep their guard
up. When President Bush arbitrarily named Iran as one-third of the

"axis of evil," reporters willfully ignored the fact that both the Iranian and Iraqi governments were sworn enemies of al-Qaeda (and each other). It didn't seem to matter to journalists that Shiites are far more likely to be victims of Islamist terrorism than perpetrators of it, or that Iran's Revolutionary Guards helped overthrow the Taliban in the first weeks of the Afghanistan War. Instead, the independent press imitated Iranian state media whenever it lends a megaphone to demonize Washington, or perhaps American journalists imitated their predecessors during the hostage crisis.

"Do you think it was worse for Iranians in the early eighties?" I asked.

Noorbakhsh's face scrunched with slight annoyance. "Yes and no, and part of me questions the utility of your question," she said. "What are we trying to assess when we say, 'Is it worse or better'? Is it less of an issue if people are dealing with racism more acutely? The more I learn about United States history, the more I realize we've always been racist. I think it's just different racism now, not better or worse." Daily crimes against Black Americans might not be "acceptable" to polite society but they are still "normative," she explained.

Likewise, anti-Muslim discrimination has taken many forms over the centuries, going back to Orientalism. Through literature, paintings, and historical revision this seventeenth-century movement portrayed the Occident as civilized and congenial and the Orient as a lawless, erotic, and mystical land, at once alluring and treacherous. This idea helped cement who was white, who wasn't, and what being one or the other truly meant.

The librarian handed me a thin manila folder, looking somewhat apologetic when I opened it and found four sheets of paper. These were all the clippings they'd collected on Lackteen: a wedding announcement, a death announcement, and a couple of newspaper reviews. There were also headshots in leather-bound talent directories, a retrospective titled "Mysterious Villain," and a small mention in a 1920s chapbook written by a close friend who, by his own admittance, struggled to get a read on Lackteen. In total, about fifteen pages. But I'd expected as much when I left Canada prepared to comb through the production files on every title in his filmography, especially the silent pictures lost to time, hence two file boxes with my name on them behind the reference desk. I spent most of the next two days piecing together his conscience from a thousand fragments.

Judging from the synopses and production files of his earliest films, Lackteen's ambiguous foreignness was perfectly timed for the height of reactionary nativism. It wasn't just movies like *The Birth of a Nation* feeding off segregationists; World War I roused a series of government-sanctioned "preparedness" pictures intended to warn Americans of their foreign adversaries. Lackteen helped vaudeville's ugliest tropes transition to the silver screen, even working in *The Yellow Menace*. A notorious serial hailed for its insight into the "cunning, scheming character of the plotting Oriental," the movie helped boost support for the 1917 Asiatic Barred Zone Act that effectively cut him and a quarter-million Asian immigrants off from their families. In return, Lackteen got three weeks' pay and a good deal of encouragement.

Lackteen spent the next decade portraying bad hombres—as a certain president might call them—and other ethnic miscreants, like a witch doctor, opium smuggler, and a "half-breed" so vile that one reviewer wrote, "You wish some bullet would lay him low." He mastered the gaze and poise of a baddie who intimidates with chilling self-possession. As a film historian put it: "His pantomime was subdued and quite restrained, giving an audience the feeling that he wasn't really acting at all but that the evil which seemed to exude from his pores was indeed very natural."

There was much Lackteen could conceal from 1920s audiences— his guttural, stilted English, his lack of education, the fact that behind the scenes, complex scripts rendered him "nervous and confused"— but his threatening face was not one of them. So he leaned into his sinister persona and the security it afforded him. His family followed him to LA, and he continued living two separate lives—movie star on

set, immigrant son at home. Frank probably helped care for his father until his death in 1927. The next year, the thirty-year-old thespian,
newly married to a white American woman and at the peak of his
fame, finally applied for American citizenship. He proudly declared
his occupation as "picture actor" and forever renounced "the present
sovereignty in Syria and the Lebanon [sic]."

His application was rejected. Lackteen was served a second, third,
and fourth blow in 1930. His wife divorced him in the same year that
movies transitioned to sound and the Motion Picture Production Code
(now the MPAA) ushered in moral guidelines restricting most of what
made his movies so titillating.

For Lackteen and the handful of minorities whose repertoires relied on the fear, or fetishizing, of foreigners, overcoming thick accents
was only the beginning. In addition to a ban on interracial romances,
the code included this clause: "The history, institutions, prominent
people and citizenry of all nations shall be represented fairly." Intended
to prevent further boycotts and trade embargoes from embassies and
ethnic lobbies, it effectively gave Lackteen's livelihood over to white
actors playing white Americans.

Luckily for him, the MPAA didn't police Middle Eastern and North
African portrayals to the same degree as others. As imbecile Blacks,
shyster Jews, diseased Chinese, and boozy Irish faded from the screen,
Lackteen fell back on subhuman brown people, making a living off the
same stereotypes that might've gotten in the way of his citizenship—
and still plague Muslims today.

Ironically, he'd landed only one of these parts before the code
came into effect, despite Hollywood's early cashing in on Orientalism. Inspired by a loose and lewd translation of *One Thousand and One
Nights* (or *Arabian Nights*), *The Sheik* and *The Thief of Baghdad* were
the Marvel movie blockbusters of the early 1920s. But by the time
Lackteen's career was on the up, Orientalism was on the out. Though
a passing fad, these movies popularized the lecherous Muslim trope,
and bonded the image of the barbaric, retrogressive desert in American imaginations. The MPAA's ambivalence toward offending these

nationalities, who lacked pressure groups, buying power, and sovereign embassies, allowed them to endure as long as Hollywood's creatives played along.

Lackteen began to Orientalize himself by donning fezzes, turbans, and head robes, and he sprinkled Arabic throughout his lines regardless of whether he played an Arab camel driver, Pashtun peasant, or Iranian dignitary. He worked steadily for another three decades, approaching his craft with the pliability of a low-paid immigrant, even after finally gaining citizenship in 1941. Forever convinced his face—not race—was his greatest asset, Lackteen maintained his emaciated look with extreme dieting. "The irony of it all is that I'm a good cook, specializing in rich pastries," he told a gossip writer on the set of *King of the Khyber Rifles* in 1952. "If I eat my cooking, my hollows fill up and I look like a thousand other out-of-work actors."

When audiences grew bored of colonial adventures and mummy flicks, Lackteen fell back on feathers and beaded headbands, doing the odd $100 walk-on in B Westerns. He died in 1968, struggling to pay rent on his one-bedroom Hollywood apartment. Because of what Lackteen represented, few in civil-rights-era America paid tribute or even noticed his passing. He did not become the subject of books or receive a posthumous Walk of Fame star like other colour barrier–breaking actors. His death didn't garner anything like the retrospectives that followed his immigrant contemporaries' deaths. His four-sentence obit in the *Hollywood Reporter* made no mention of his ancestry, race-bending qualities, or race at all. But it was sure about one thing: he was a great villain.

No doubt, had Lackteen been an actor decades later, he would've been gainfully employed. The success of *Nightline* and CNN, which premiered with heavy Iran coverage in 1980, taught Hollywood producers how much money could be made scaring the bejesus out of people with Islamic fundamentalists. The image of Muslim terrorists was so mentally embedded that screenwriters could pass them off as frivolous plot devices—an easy way to get Doc and Marty to the past, fleeing fanatical Libyans in the first minutes of *Back to the Future*, or to get another roundhouse kick out of Chuck Norris. Lackteen died unaware that his villainous beginnings foretold the next fifty years of Muslim and Middle Eastern misrepresentation.

But would he have cared?

I left the library with a bundle of photocopies but no more insight into his conscience than when I arrived. Several of his contemporaries and costars, like Anna May Wong, became outspoken critics of movie racism, but if Lackteen felt similarly conflicted, he kept it to himself. His greatest ambition, he told a reporter, was to live tax free, earn a lot, give more, and "make mankind happy." His people-pleasing benevolence reminded me of how my older relatives are often quick to mirror their surroundings and slow to complain about unfair Canadians. In fact, he sounded a lot like my dad in a 1987 article about our restaurant's grand opening: "I hope to serve the town and the community my best. I came to the town so that it will have a nice place for people to eat," my dad told the reporter, adding that he enjoyed cooking for people and working with others. Either that was a different dad from the one I witnessed barking orders in the kitchen, and who only seemed relaxed when he counted the register at the end of the night, or my dad was saying what people wanted to hear so we could have the life he imagined for us.

Was Lackteen just another immigrant in survival mode? I couldn't blame him for it, especially considering his impoverished beginnings. Still, I understood the power of having a media platform. That he never used it to correct misconceptions of his people or any marginalized group he exploited, that he only perpetuated them, left me disappointed with my genealogical discovery.

I thought I might understand my ancestor better if I met with an empathetic actor. Maz Jobrani launched his career on negative Muslim stereotypes and, in fact, had received one of those fabled Chuck Norris roundhouse kicks in *The President's Man: A Line in the Sand*. That was the movie that opened his eyes to these stories' harms. He played a maniacal Afghani nuclear scientist, one of his first jobs and one he dreaded after being forced to wear a humiliating costume. "I said, 'Afghans in America don't wear turbans,' and the costume designer says,

'Well, the producer wants a turban,'" recalled the actor-comic, sitting outside a café on the southern fringe of Hollywood, occasionally stopping to greet a fellow actor or selfie-seeking fan. "It was an awakening moment for me. I said, 'I don't want to do these parts anymore.'"

The September 11 attacks and Afghanistan War did nothing to stall the TV movie's release in January 2002. The backlash to 9/11 took Jobrani back to his childhood in California, an Iranian newcomer during the earliest days of the revolution and hostage crisis. "Back then they'd call you 'fucking Iranian,'" said Jobrani, whose family was, at best, disaffected Muslims. "That's when the whole 'you're a terrorist,' 'you're a towel head,' 'camel jockey'—all those things came to front and centre." I'm barely old enough to remember those antiquated slurs, but I did. They'd been hurled at me once or twice in the schoolyard.

"When the hostage crisis happened," he continued, "people called my Arab friends 'fucking Iranian.' That had a lot to do with the negative depiction of Muslims in the West. If you look at Steven Seagal and Chuck Norris movies, there's no distinction between Lebanese, or Saudi, or Libyan, or Persian, or Iranian, or Iraqi. We're all the same. We all have the furrowed brows. We're all trying to take over America, capture the blond woman, and blow something up."

Jobrani, who titled his memoir *I'm Not a Terrorist, But I've Played One on TV*, could've followed in Frank Lackteen's footsteps had he not quit auditioning for anything stoking Islamophobia. But he said, it's only because he's built a successful comedy career as the "Persian Eddie Murphy" that he can say no to racist gigs.

In 2005, he launched the Axis of Evil comedy tour with Arab comedians to enormous success and found his niche with immigrant audiences. I asked him how white audience members respond to his work. "I've had people reach out to say, 'Hey, I've never seen you guys laugh. It's so good to see you guys laugh,'" he replied, baffled by his own words. "Like, wow, they hadn't thought about that before—people of Middle Eastern descent laughing."

I asked Jobrani if he regretted the stereotypical and demeaning parts of his filmography.

"No," he said. Without those early roles, he wouldn't have had an acting career or a comedy career. That's all that was available to actors of colour at the turn of the twenty-first century, but, he said, things were changing. "A lot of us are pushing for that positive depiction now." TV had a critically acclaimed comedy about an Arab-American Muslim family (*Ramy*), a Muslim woman superhero (*Legends of Tomorrow*), and a hijabi surgeon (*Grey's Anatomy*). The highest-grossing rom-com of 2017, *The Big Sick*, was about a Muslim-ish Pakistani man and white woman—a pairing that would have been unthinkable not just in Frank Lackteen's time but during my childhood.

Los Angeles got me thinking about the ways Hollywood shaped my young mind. Growing up with two working parents, my guardianship was regularly outsourced to a giant satellite dish siphoning American channels for the many TVs in our home. I rarely saw myself reflected on the screen, so even a glimpse of a Muslim in movies and music videos enthralled me.

The first film that made an impact was *Not Without My Daughter*, a 1991 melodrama about a sweet American woman trapped in post-revolution Iran by her abusive husband and his fanatical family. I was six when I saw it, and I doubt my folks ever explained differences between Arab and Persian culture, let alone the geopolitics at play in this film. My only takeaway was that Muslims were scary and mean.

The second was Disney's *Aladdin*, 1992's top-grossing movie and the first film I can recall my family watching in a movie theatre. Finally, they'd made a Disney movie about *us*. I remember leaving the theatre jazzed, pleased to recognize familiar words and subtle nods to our heritage. And then my teenage sister brought up a line from the musical's opening song: *I come from a land from a far-away place . . . Where they cut off your ear if they don't like your face. It's barbaric, but hey, it's home.*

"We don't do *that*," she said, with an uncomfortable laugh.

My sister pointed out other things that bothered her, like the conflation of Indian imagery and the exaggerated Semitic features, to the point of grotesque. Yet we were still proud to be seen.

The third movie was *Malcolm X*. To hear a star like Denzel

Washington call himself Muslim, to see him pray like me and circle the Kaaba in white robes like my grandparents had the year before, inspired me to take my faith seriously, to fast my first few Ramadan days, and unapologetically decline Christian traditions. But looking back now at *Malcolm X*, I see how Denzel portrayed what cultural historian Maytha Alhassen calls "the Black redeemer" and how Spike Lee's script downplayed Sunni-Arab supremacy that divided Black Muslims after Malcolm's conversion to "true Islam." Though *Malcolm X* was crafted to instill Black pride, it inspired a moment of Muslim pride in my generation, and, in so doing, mended the damage done to Muslim public image more than any other movie. But it couldn't counter the century of films prior, nor the blockbusters that followed.

I thought about the long-term effects of negative movie stereotypes as I recalled something I'd overheard that week in a Venice Beach dive bar. An inebriated man was questioning the veracity of the Christchurch massacre. Somehow he'd stomached watching the carnage, recorded in first-person-shooter style by the killer himself, and concluded that it was all a hoax—no more real than watching Samuel L. Jackson mow down wild-eyed Yemenis in the first minutes of *The Rules of Engagement*. Clearly, any improvements in media portrayals were too late or too outnumbered for him to see Muslims as actual human beings.

One of my last interviews was with Justin Mashouf, the director of two very touching movies about Muslims, including *Warring Factions*, a documentary about the Iran-US cold war told through the eyes of Iranian break-dancers like himself. Mashouf also saw *Malcolm X* as an impressionable fourth grader. But unlike me, he wasn't exposed to Islam at home, in Tucson, Arizona, with a German Irish mother and secular Persian father. Through X and hip-hop, Mashouf started identifying as Muslim, sipping droplets of the faith from popular culture until attending his first dua at an apartment. Hearing these spellbinding hymns, particularly Dua Kamayl, a supplication for hubris, unlocked a world he felt had been hidden away from him. He leaned into Shiism, while slipping further from Persian traditions like Nowruz.

Mashouf continued attending Thursday dua, first as a passive listener, then as the reciter's understudy, and finally as lead reciter for Yaseen Educational Institute. He invited me to experience dua with his prayer circle on a Thursday night in West LA. I declined at first, opting instead to attend dua at IMAN, but the doors were locked when I arrived. Prayer had been cancelled to extend Nowruz celebrations another day, one of the reasons IMAN's conservative critics now accuse it of being too liberal and ethnocentric. With that, I took Mashouf up on his invitation.

Inside a neighbourhood rec centre, Mashouf busily created a prayer hall from limited supplies. He placed a speaker on an area rug and shook my hand. "I have to be straightforward," I said. "I have no familiarity with these prayers."

"No problem," said Mashouf, handing me a pamphlet to follow along. I unfolded it. Over two hundred lines and three columns— Arabic, English translation and transliteration—spread across six pages. *Al-Fatiha* this was not. I glanced at Mashouf, his European and Central Asian genes balanced by bright blue eyes, golden brown hair, fair skin, and thick brows. He gestured at a row of chairs. "Seat, floor, whatever you like."

I poured myself tea, grabbed a biscuit, and sat alone on the rug. Three women and two older men arrived in time for Mashouf to make the call to prayer against a faint sound of yelping and clapping from Russian dance lessons down the hall.

Mashouf shut the lights and crouched in the corner of the room, below a green Islamic tapestry over a whiteboard. Serenely lit by a desk lamp, he sang into a microphone. His voice was at once exquisite and haunting. He sang for nearly thirty minutes, pausing for a few sips of water. Occasionally he broke from Arabic to offer a line or two in English: "I have wronged myself, and I have been audacious in my ignorance"; and "O Allah! You know my secrets. Do not hasten to punish me for what I have done in private"; and "I am your weak, lowly, base, wretched, and miserable slave." The potency of guilt in the lyrics startled me. It felt like a collective criminal confession. What effect would reading this week after week have on one's ego? While it must require a good amount of confidence to bear his soul like this, it must also demand striking humility to cast oneself this way.

The dua ended with Mashouf repeating "Y'Rubby, Y'Rubby"—"My Lord, My Lord"—softly into the microphone, while gatherers whispered it to themselves. As he lay the mic aside, the other men and I scooted toward him, joined hands in a circle, and bowed. The women did the same. Halfway through the prayer Dua Wahda ("Supplication for Unity"), a young African American tiptoed into the room. Without skipping a beat, Ebraheem Fontaine took my hand and joined the chorus. I pitched in on the parts I knew, "La ilaha illa Allah" (There is no god but God), feeling none of its meaning but all of its intended humility. By spring of that year, I'd participated in communal prayers across five disparate regions, with Arab Shias, heterodox African American Muslims, and an array of Sunnis, but this was the closest I'd come to feeling divine.

As quickly as it began, it ended. Fontaine flicked the light switch and greetings and snacking immediately ensued.

"What a turnout," Mashouf joked, trying to maintain a sense of humour but clearly embarrassed by post-Nowruz attendance. "I'm going to pass it over to Brother Ebraheem to offer a khutba to our sold-out crowd."

Fontaine pulled a chair to the front of the room and delivered a thorough sermon about a Quranic verse. It was all too intellectual and high-minded for me, and I could tell from the quiet chitchat behind us that others felt the same. Fontaine wrapped up, and the lights went out again. Justin took the microphone and recited a prayer "for the oppressed, those who have lost their lives in New Zealand, and especially our awaited imam." Finally, we broke for dinner at around 11:00 p.m.

I sat on the rug with Fontaine and the other gentlemen, recent Iranian immigrants with limited English. Mashouf served us warm plates of biryani, meaty herb stew, and fresh loquats. He told me about Yaseen's origins in UCLA, where it was founded in 1998 by a predominantly Iranian student group more interested in celebrating their faith with other Shiites than forming another cultural association. "It's the story of a lot of Islamic centers. People started to feel that they didn't have a space in other masjids. The lectures and a lot of the programs weren't even in English," he said. While he acknowledged that English lyrics dilute the dua's spiritual essence, he believed the translations made it more personal for English speakers like ourselves. "That's the beauty of our dua tradition," added Fontaine. It's *mustahabb*—a highly recommended act that doesn't have its own particular form, unlike our daily prayers, which you can remix a little bit, but for the most part, it's fixed."

Mashouf placed his plate beside mine and sat crossed-legged. He came across as naturally humble, but from earlier conversations I knew this wasn't always true. His arrogant younger self constantly butted heads with his right-leaning father over religion and politics, especially during the Iraq invasion. I asked him what it meant to him personally to recite this one long, heavy supplication over one thousand nights of his life.

"It's like a recharge," he said. "Because throughout the week, I can slip in different directions, maybe shameful things I said or rude ways I acted with people, without catching it until later. Thursday nights are a way for me to be in penitence for those moments and a reminder to myself of *why* I can still act better."

I was beginning to understand how central this once-hidden-away faith was to him. Though he speaks Persian with his wife and children and started celebrating Nowruz with his in-laws, he said "Muslim" was his prominent identity, more so than Iranian, multiracial, American, or B-boy. "How have your parents taken this?" I asked.

"My mom always saw it as a positive thing because she's a practicing Protestant who goes to church every Sunday. With my dad being so secular, she was pretty thankful."

"And your dad?"

"Very apprehensive about the whole situation," he said. "He was like, 'You're kind of regressing. It's a bit of a backward situation you're getting yourself into.' But one night, I came home for dinner and over-heard him talking about me on the phone in Farsi. He was like, 'Justin speaks Arabic. He can read, write, understand the Quran, he's really good.' He was talking me up, like, 'This is dope!' So it's complicated, I would say."

In the second quarter of his life, Mashouf was beginning to understand how culture, creed, and family cohere. In 2018, he made a pilgrimage to Najaf, Iraq, the Shia capital city, to visit Imam Ali's burial site. Through his father-in-law's connections, Grand Ayatollah Ali al-Sistani granted him a private meeting. "It's like meeting the Dalai Lama," he explained to me. "It's not uncommon for groups of ten to fifteen people to sit with him to ask questions, especially when they are coming from Western countries, as there is a lack of legal experts, *mujahideen*, living in the West."

I pictured Mashouf as he was now, in stylish joggers and bomber jacket, entering the home of one of the world's most revered religious figures. Mashouf had so many questions for the ayatollah, but only one mattered. Earlier that week, he and his wife learned they were pregnant with their second child, so he asked, "How do I instill the love of Islam and the Prophet and his family in my children?"

"Religion is not necessarily the answer here," he recalled the aya-tollah replying. "Make your kid aware of their own Iranian heritage. They need to know who you are, where you came from, because when they lose that connection, they can get very confused."

His answer reminded Mashouf of a hadith from Imam Ali: *Who-soever knows himself, knows his lord*. I nodded silently, letting Imam Ali's words sink in. Mashouf's journey was the inverse of mine. While drift-ing away from religion in my teens and twenties, I gradually embraced my Arab heritage more. But abandoning the former may have left a hole in my self-knowledge.

I saw in Mashouf something I'd only recently come to understand about myself: for better or worse, I am also preoccupied with a nag-ging sense of not leading a good enough life. Though our conclusions about how to go about self-improvement were different, both were rooted in the same confusion over what a Muslim should be.

America's unique brand of Islamophobia teaches us that Muslim piety equals savagery. The narrative was shaped during the hostage crisis and refined for many years before we were even aware of it. The difference is that Mashouf rejected the message and internalized his faith, while I internalized the message and rejected my faith.

Until my trip to LA, I always thought of my atheism as a rebellious act. After seeing how Justin Mashouf and Zahra Noorbakhsh reclaimed their faith on their own terms, I wondered: Were they the rebels, and I the conformist? By tuning out my family's Islamic traditions and teachings, I'd left it to media and pop culture to dictate a fundamental part of my heritage. I'd only come to appreciate those roots in my thirties, after accepting that Islam will always be a part of me, even if I didn't practice it.

But what if I did practice it? Although prayer could only be a perfunctory routine at this point in my life, I wondered if it could still serve a purpose. Maybe it's like hitting the gym: Would prayer tone my ego and strengthen my kindness even if my devotion remained directionless? Would I even have the right to call myself a Muslim? I know secular Jews and cultural Christians—hell, I'm probably one in essence. But who's ever heard of an atheist Muslim?

Say Their Names
Grande Mosquée de Québec
(Quebec City, Quebec)

*A*long the busy Chemin Sainte-Foy in Quebec City stood an unusual-looking mosque. Converted from a Desjardins Bank, the Centre Culturel Islamique de Québec still looked like a bank, with rows of blackened glass panes and a barricaded drive-through. Its only crescent and minaret were two clip-art graphics flanking the society's name on a fibreglass sign obscured by trees. You could hardly blame random motorists who used to pull over to the Quebec City Grande Mosque hoping to withdraw money. But since January 29, 2017, no one makes that mistake.

On that date, a right-wing terrorist ambushed it after night prayers. He opened fire on forty-one men and children, killing six, injuring nineteen, and traumatizing an entire community. This boxy red building is now imprinted on every local's mind.

On an overcast day in August 2018, I stood beneath the mosque's sign, more befitting of a tailor than a temple, wondering how early was too early for afternoon prayers. The men's entrance door was locked, as expected. Earlier that Monday I met with a survivor, Aymen Derbali, who advised me that I'd have to wait for him or somebody else with a fob to open the door for me.

A red light on the access pad glowed at me, confirming it was locked. I peered at nothing through opaque windows, scanned a parking lot empty but for my car, and headed to a bustling Parisian-style café across the street for coffee. I took my cup for a walk around the neighbourhood, looking back at the Islamic centre with some incredulity. I couldn't get over how unremarkable it was, not just for a place burdened with immense tragedy but for any holy place. I'd seen little storefront mosques sandwiched between tattoo and adult toy shops with more prominent displays of religion on their green awnings than this. And yet this quiet, nondescript building had provoked a string of attacks before culminating in ultraviolence.

Police had been called to the mosque at least seven times before January 29, 2017, and they've been called since: once after the outside was vandalized with excrement and another time when the board president's car was set ablaze. Other attacks have continued too. The same radio shock jocks who condemned the mosque as a menace to Québécois values still vilify it. The same government that pandered to social hysteria, resolving to ban women in niqabs from receiving public services, continued its anti-Muslim policies. All this hatred built on a lie that Muslims cannot or will not integrate into society. In reality, if you factor out first-generation immigrants, Muslims' views on gender equality and LGBTQ rights are in line with the general population's, and Muslims—especially Quebec's—are much more patriotic. At least, they were when surveyed in 2016 by Environics.

The bloodshed at two Christchurch mosques shocked New Zealand into adopting more restrictive policies on guns and hate speech (not to mention giving permanent visas to about 200 survivors and family members). But Quebec's soul searching quickly ran its course and things have gotten worse for Muslims there. Anti-Muslim hate crime rates have more than doubled city- and province-wide. Two-fifths of Quebecers polled in 2017 and 2019 sincerely believe Canadian Muslims adhere not to constitutional law but sharia, one-third would support a ban on Muslim immigrants, and more than half confess to having very negative views of Islam—though it's hardly a confession.

Hostility toward religion is one of the bipartisan values Quebecers share. Islam, argued the new premier, François Legault (who revived failed legislation to prohibit religious emblems from the walls of public spaces and bodies of public servants), threatens their hard-earned secular society. This too is a lie, and one that was in plain sight of me as I circled the block, wasting time before Asr.

Directly across the mosque's driveway stands a historically significant French colonial cathedral that the province has gone through great pains to restore and maintain. Itself a beleaguered holy place, several fires over the centuries have reduced the Notre-Dame-de-Foy to an ornate stone facade and partial bell tower. I entered an open archway into the burned-out cathedral, its three remaining walls built by the Jesuits who founded the old town on swaths of New France given by the French Crown to the Roman Catholic Church. Some of the ordained missionaries, famous for their militaristic spirit and willingness to kill and die in the name of the papacy (not unlike jihadists), are buried in a well-kept cemetery abutting the cathedral.

Less care has been shown to the Muslim community. For almost twenty years, the Centre Culturel Islamique de Québec had tried to purchase land for a cemetery to perform Islamic funeral rites, like resting the body directly into the ground without a casket. Its efforts constantly came up against resistance. It hoped that would change in the aftermath of January 29, but rezoning approval for the land it secured was voted down by a narrow margin in a public referendum. The city council did eventually step up and sell the centre a prezoned land parcel near Université Laval, where thousands of French-speaking Muslim immigrants started their new lives in Canada. And yet when several of these men were murdered, the victim's families couldn't lay them to rest as hoped.

The victims, all African immigrants, didn't *leave* home in search of a better life, as the cliché goes. They were pushed from their homes toward the West to enrich the progeny of the same imperialists who set their displacement, and need for asylum, in motion. Algeria. Guinea. Morocco. Tunisia. The homelands of all six victims of January 29 had been devastated by French colonialism and set up to fail when France gave them independence in name only, as it continued to dominate their resource wealth.

I walked between the rows of cross-engraved tombstones, beneath trimmed tree branches and traipsing squirrels, toward a pavilion. A life-sized Jesus loomed inside, crucified but sheltered. From my vantage point, the Grande Mosque across the road somehow looked even less grand. As neighbours, the mosque and cathedral reveal the cultural blind spots and the selective memory that holds one religion as intrinsic and another as interloper.

Premier Legault admitted as much. A week after winning the election, thanks in no small part to his hard line on religious emblems, Legault said his government had no intention of removing an eighty-year-old crucifix from the National Assembly. "We have to understand our past," he said. Yet when asked whether he supported the idea of making January 29 an official day against Islamophobia, as suggested by the National Council of Canadian Muslims and other Islamic organizations, Legault denied Islamophobia is a problem. He later walked back his denial, but not to the point of supporting a day of remembrance.

Legault's landslide victory was two months away when I arrived in Quebec City in August 2018, but even before the writ officially dropped, Muslim women had reported a surge of harassment. Seeking the opinion of an average Muslim woman who gets unwanted attention for her hijab, the mosque's English spokesman put me in touch with his wife. She asked to go by "Yasmin," fearing harassment.

"The insults in the street are more frequent," the Tunisian-born mother told me in a phone call. Usually one or two slurs are hurled at Yasmin per year, but she'd heard as many in the lead-up to the election. "If Legault wins, it's going to be a mess. When people like that win they give others the courage to insult, as if they know the government has their back." (Indeed, harassment spiked. Her friend had eggs thrown at her twice by the same neighbour. The police did nothing, citing no evidence.)

At times, it sounded to me as if Yasmin lived in another country. I was born and raised in Alberta, the conservative heartland, sometimes called "Canada's Bible Belt," amongst people who, according to polls, harbour comparable xenophobic sentiments. But violently acting out on anti-Muslim prejudices is a rarity, and I can comfortably and thankfully say none of my hijabi family have reported anything as hurtful as what Yasmin described. "Is harassment really that rampant?" I asked.

Without missing a beat, she gave me five recent examples of strangers insulting her at clothing stores, Tim Hortons, and traffic lights, where one man told her to "go back to *Musulmanie*" (the French equivalent of "Muslimistan"). Before he peeled off, she told him, "I wish, but it doesn't exist. If you could show me on a map, I'll go."

Yasmin has a good sense of humour, but it was harder for her to be lighthearted about career discrimination. Like most of Quebec City's Muslim immigrants, she arrived on a student visa. She earned a marketing degree at Université Laval, but despite that, and being fluent in three languages, nobody would hire her. She considered returning to school to become a psychologist. "Then I said to myself, 'Oh, the hijab is never going to work. Nobody's going to want to see me. Nobody's going to trust me.'" Yasmin permanently shelved her ambitions after the birth of her special-needs daughter, who requires her full attention. "There are lots of times where I think, 'What could I have done?'"

Quebec Muslim women frequently report workplace discrimination. A business professor told me that several of his students stopped wearing veils after graduation; another public servant said that her employer would ask her to sit out of meetings with clients, for the good of the team. Were Yasmin to remove her headscarf, employers wouldn't tell her apart from a fifth-generation Québécois; her mother is white American.

That these women feel they must choose between their appearances and careers is all the more ironic given that feminist values are central to Quebec's *laïcité*, the French concept of secular statehood that broke the Roman Catholic Church's shackles fifty years ago and propelled

Canada's most traditional province into modernity. This period is known as the Quiet Revolution.

It's not surprising that a society fearful of religion would have strong roots in it. Jesuits founded schools and colleges, including Laval's antecedent, Collège des Jésuites, while Catholic nuns controlled the educational and hospital systems, in addition to most welfare institutions on which the poor, hungry, orphaned, and abandoned relied. Montreal was dominated by the British business class, but the rest of Quebec was under the thumb of the Roman Catholic Church, enforcing a traditional culture that was way out of step with society.

More than 150 years after the French Revolution began to implement laïcité principles into law, Québécois still lived like citizens of New France. The power of the clergy wasn't enshrined in Quebec law, but it didn't have to be in order for the church to control the education, health, and charitable institutions. It merely had to exploit the autonomy given to Francophone Canada, enshrined in the Constitution Act of 1867, to dominate private and public life. Resentment of the church boiled over after World War II and mass communications opened Quebec to outside influence. The quasi-Catholic government could never the survive the women's and civil rights movements accelerating across North America. Still, few expected Catholic influence to blow up the way it has.

Quebec has the lowest marriage rates and highest abortion rates of any other state or province in North America. Five hundred churches have closed in the past two decades, many of them historical. It's incumbent on municipalities to rescue them from dilapidation, an effort supported by most Quebecers since, paradoxically, the vast majority still identify as Catholic.

As the *Economist* has pointed out, the culture's combined "glorious past and secular present" resembles life in historically Catholic European countries. "Quebecers recall the Italians in their residual attachment to Catholic labels and symbols and cheerful indifference to Catholic morals. The resentment felt by many French Canadians over the church's perceived abuse of power would also be familiar to many in Spain." But Quebecers' closest relatives are the Irish, whose rapid turn from conservatism to modernism and whose fervent rejection of religious authority has left little room for moderation.

Quebecers pride themselves on social mores that are closer to European than North American. Perhaps that's why its style of Islamophobia is also more European, stigmatizing Muslims not as fifth columnists undermining society on behalf of a foreign enemy, as they're often portrayed in the United States, but as uncivilized intruders set to overtake society by migration and birth rates.

This is science fiction. The birth rates of second-generation Muslims are roughly equal to that of the general population. More important, Quebec is already impossibly and stubbornly white.

On paper, Quebec's immigrant and minority population isn't significantly less than the rest of Canada's until you factor out Montreal and its suburbs. Then you're left with a population that's 96 percent white—even in the capital, Quebec City. If multiculturalism, that wobbly foundation for Canadian identity, has proven anything, it's that exposure to foreign cultures breeds tolerance. Since multiculturalism was adopted as policy in the 1970s, negative stereotypes of immigrants—whether as criminals, unassimilable, or a drain on society—have plummeted everywhere except in Quebec.

So long as the minorities you're brushing shoulders against are middle class, as most immigrants either arrive as or inevitably become, you're likely to favour most immigration. But to brush shoulders, restrictions must be lifted. Consumed by protecting the French language that replaced Catholicism as a rallying identity, Quebec hasn't relinquished control of its borders to Ottawa. In fact, it has gained more control over policies that could alter its culture and language, and by virtue of these its ethnic makeup.

After the Charter of the French Language went into effect in 1977, the once-insular province, desperate for labour, opened up to the rest of the world and extended scholarships across the French-speaking nations. Since few European French would move to Canada, and few sub-Saharan Africans could afford it, North Africans helped Quebec realize its vision of secular nationhood.

But Quebec seems about as comfortable with non-Christian

immigrants as it is with Canadian confederation. It's as evident now as it was in the 1920s, when Jewish children were barred from schools, or in 1995, when Quebec's secessionist premier blamed "ethnic votes" for losing an independence referendum by a tiny margin. Since then, each new government has resolved to protect social cohesion in a post-Catholic society, first through language, then immigration, and, after those proved inadequate, through its provincial constitution.

Quebec's great white whale grew not from post-9/11 panic but from a rash of "reasonable accommodation" cases in the mid-2000s. These stories about what cultural baggage was or was not acceptable in public almost always had a Muslim immigrant at the centre. Often the subjects were children traumatized by public humiliation, such as an eleven-year-old girl ejected from a soccer game for her refusal to remove her hijab. To temper public discontent (and in a vie to hold power), the Quebec Liberal government commissioned a study that proved nearly every case of reasonable accommodation was misconstrued by media.

The hope was that Quebecers would see their findings as proof of false alarms and begin to appreciate that each example involved immigrants trying to participate in society, not eschew it. But it backfired. The study's dominance in public discourse gave social license to discriminate with honour, to villify in the name of protecting Quebec's values.

That's when Yasmin felt the air change. When she arrived in Canada from Tunisia in 2001, the xenophobia was standard—a lack of interest in her heritage from classmates, strangers doubting her command of French. With each new headline about disorder-making Muslims, she'd witness more racism, though rarely directed at her. "I don't look Muslim," she said. Not until she wore a hijab in 2012 did she get the dirty looks, the slurs, and the overall message that she was not welcome.

"There's fear behind these hostilities," she said. "I can feel it. They're so afraid of losing their own culture and identity, which is already a little rocky and unstable." Yasmin surprised me with her empathy. She understood and accepted Quebecers' sour experience with the church. She only wished they reciprocated her curiosity. "They don't know our history. They don't know what happened. I didn't live in a country where you could be free, religiously."

From the 1980s onward, few Tunisians dared to don headscarves under a brutal dictatorship. As was the case in Algeria, overt Muslim practices could have you suspected of being with the Islamist opposition, arrested, charged with terrorism, imprisoned, or disappeared. Jews and Christians went to their temples freely, but not the Muslim majority. "They were scared to show any sign of religion," said Yasmin. "I've known people personally who went to jail for many years just because they were accused of being extremist, even though all they did was go to the mosque often. Women who kept wearing a hijab in Tunisia would be forced to take it off in the street or dragged into a police station and forced to remove it."

Even after living in Canada for a decade, she didn't feel secure enough to wear hijabs. Not until Tunisians overthrew president Zine El Abidine Ben Ali and launched the Arab Spring in 2011 did Yasmin wear a headscarf, only to face another intimidation campaign under her new government in Canada.

Bill 21, the Quebec National Assembly's fourth attempt at restricting religious minorities' rights, does so, ironically, by amending Canada's Charter of Rights and Freedoms. The bill bans religious symbols on public servants and mandates that women must reveal their faces to receive public services—everything from taking a driver's license photo to riding public transit. It passed in summer 2019 and was immediately challenged in separate civil action suits, including one mostly comprising Muslim schoolteachers. A 2021 decision upheld the law, despite acknowledging its negative effects on women in the public sector ("a cruel consequence that dehumanizes those who are targeted," by the Superior Court judge's own admission).

The leaders of Canada's four main political parties have been conspicuously quiet on this issue. Not one vowed to challenge the law during the 2019 federal election. Even the New Democrats' Jagmeet Singh, who wears a turban for religious reasons and made antiracism central to his leadership campaign, accepted the advice of his French caucus not to intervene. His hypocritical pandering would be laugh-able if it wasn't so frightening.

——————

At about a quarter to five, I returned to the Grande Mosque and ap-proached a man flashing his keycard by the men's entrance. "Salamu alaykum," I greeted with a hearty accent. "I'm here to pray Asr," I said. He sized me up and held the door for me, then hurriedly snatched a brown robe off a wall hook on his way downstairs for wudu. He was the imam.

The mosque was even humbler on the inside. Above me, ceiling tiles inherited from the bank; below me, a striped rug devoid of any design or embroidery. Prayers were led not from a framed mihrab, but an individual prayer rug front and centre. The only artwork was a can-vas scribbled with children's condolences and architectural drawings of a more attractive mosque tacked to the bulletin board. These reno-vations were still tentative when I visited, and would not be approved and completed for another two years.

I felt the eyes of onlookers behind and around me as men entered the prayer hall, as I examined the drawings near the arched entrance-ways. Upon closer look, I realized the contemporary whitewashed building surrounded by ghostly figures in white robes was meant to be the one I was standing inside. A stone-clad Grande Mosque befit-ting of its name with bold Islamic accents, classical arabesque designs, a tapered minaret, and bold Islamic features.

The imam returned donning his robe. He placed his keys and cell phone next to the prayer rug and began to lead prayers for thirty men and children on the main floor and possibly a few women upstairs, who entered from a separate door on the other side of the building. Together we made up about a row and a half, while the gaggle of chil-dren ran amok.

I'd expected this moment to be somber. I'd anticipated the heavy emotions that would tumble off the survivors' shoulders onto mine and the agony I might absorb when my head touched the rug. As we prostrated, though, I couldn't help but crack a smile. While toddlers jangled their fathers' keys and slightly bigger kids practiced their ABCs *en français,* another boy had recently discovered the infinite joy of blowing *toots* into your palm.

I tried to return to a meditation state before the end of salat. Hands on my knees, I silently repeated the only prayer I knew, and raised my right index finger which signifies oneness with God and the oneness *of* God, until the imam broke his silence with the last words of salat: "May the peace and mercy of Allah be with you." I repeated it in Arabic, addressing it first to the brother on my right and then the brother on my left, who was immediately pounced on by his daughter before he could rise to his feet. He flipped her over his shoulder and tickled her, her giggles erupting along with the buzz of banter and small talk as everyone shook hands and exchanged niceties: "Mashallah, mashallah."

I scanned the prayer hall for any of the three members I'd expected to see, though the only person who'd recognize me was Aymen Derbali, and he was nowhere to be seen. It would have been hard to miss him in his motorized wheelchair. I glanced at my phone and saw his apologetic text: "Unfortunately, my brother, I'm not able to go to the mosque because I have to guard my daughter."

By "guard" Derbali meant supervise, a task complicated by his new body, in a new home, and the unreasonable tendencies of a two-year-old. During our interview earlier that day, little Maryem's voice echoed across the bungalow, amplified by its vastness and sparsity. Unable to get around their previous fourth-storey apartment, the father of three had lived at a rehabilitation centre, prolonging their family's eighteen-month separation, until nearly five thousand strangers pitched in for a disabled-accessible home with extra space for the growing family. The Derbalis moved into the ranch-style house a month prior, but he'd been discharged only days before. It hadn't been "home" for a week, and its quirks were only beginning to show.

Aymen repeatedly tried to calm Maryem with his soft-spoken words while I attempted the "box of chocolates method," but all we could do to dim her screaming was close the French doors. Maryem continued to howl for attention, but it was difficult to come by as her mother Nedra struggled with upkeep and her father shared his life story with me.

We can start his story in January 2001, on the day he arrived at Laval from Tunisia, or go back a little further to that coffee shop on the Mediterranean coast, where Derbali's friend urged him to pursue his MBA in Canada instead of France, as planned. We could begin with his childhood amid a destabilizing nation or his birthday amid a hopeful economic boom. Or we can begin in 1881 with the French invasion of Tunisia—a tiny wedge of the Maghreb, "the place of sunsets"— that introduced the common language of another colonized land that would siphon the brightest minds of the Maghreb a century later.

But I'll dare to go back another four centuries, to 1492, the year the Spanish court upended the Maghreb with Moorish refugees and the Americas with "discovery." It may appear tangential, but the conquest of Granada, the last holdout of Muslim-ruled Europe, set in motion the white Christian supremacist theology that centuries later resulted in a mass shooting that paralyzed Derbali from the chest down.

That deep-rooted racism was exactly what Derbali hoped to avoid when he applied to Laval University against his father's wishes for him to study closer to home. Derbali didn't know much about Canadian society, but he knew what to expect as a North African in France: shunned, stigmatized, and vilified for living segregated lives.

"Have you changed your opinion of Canada as a tolerant society?" I asked.

Derbali delicately lifted a water bottle from his wheelchair tray with his thumb through an attached rubber band, sucked on the nozzle, and slowly set it back in the cup holder. Looking at me through glasses midway down his nose, he explained, "This attack could happen anywhere in the world. It could happen in France, it could happen in Tunisia. There's no safe place in the world." The difference, Derbali said, was that *only* in Canada would there be so much national solidarity against racism.

Since the attack, the now unemployed IT specialist rediscovered his purpose in anti-hate advocacy. He's a frequent guest speaker in college classrooms to discuss the nature of hate crimes and sometimes debates the differences between free speech and hate speech. But the most satisfying work is at high school conferences, or wherever he finds a Muslim audience that he can encourage to take up civic participation. "If we want to protect our children from hate crimes," he said softly, "we have to be engaged in society. You have to forget about the idea of Muslim services. We have to be a more active community."

Derbali then requested we pause a few minutes so he could get his *dhuhur* prayer in before the afternoon window closed on it. He did not excuse himself from the room or unravel a prayer rug. He stayed within three feet of me and adjusted his motorized wheelchair ten degrees to his right with his toggle. Paralyzed from the chest down, Derbali used the strength of his shoulders to lift his hands as close to his ears as he could get them, beckoned God with "Allahu akbar," and let them drop onto his stomach.

I watched him improvise the prescribed movements of rakat: stand, bow, stand, prostrate, sit, prostrate, stand again. He may have felt these motions in his muscles, as he hunched his neck instead of bending forward, and the faintest pressure on his fingers as he spread his hands a few inches apart, in place of pressing them onto a rug. He raised his right index finger slowly, declaring his oneness with God, and the oneness *of* God, exactly as he had tens of thousands of times in his forty-two years.

Watching a man worship like this, upright and face forward, felt too sacred and intimate. Part of me was unnerved by literally coming face-to-face with the religion I'd abandoned. Another part felt like I'd intruded on his private conversation with God. Most of all, I didn't believe I'd earned the privilege of seeing a grown man's naked vulnerability, his ego laid bare before me. But I'd misread the moment as a feeble struggle instead of an act of defiance.

Derbali suffered such brain damage in the shooting that doctors induced a coma, during which they gave Nedra the option of removing him from life support. She refused and stuck by his side daily until visiting hours ended at midnight. When he awoke two months later, witnesses filled in the details of that horrible night. Once he could speak again, one of his first requests was to attend worship at the Grande Mosque. "In order to pass through this tragedy, I have to face it another time," he said.

He would have to wait another seven months. He arrived at the mosque with the help of friends who assisted him through the doors. Gliding through the prayer hall, he was overwhelmed by his brothers' greetings. He noticed the new emergency exit doors and other changes.

To mitigate posttraumatic triggers, trauma scene specialists suggested they repaint the interior walls a new colour and replace the decor. They'd also recommended changing the green and pink carpet too, but the board had just gone through the trouble of installing them. They instead opted to cut out the damaged sections, patch up the bullet holes and rigorously shampoo the blood spots. Some stains were too stubborn, including the faintest blotches reminding Derbali of the exact place he nearly died. His eyes filled with tears as he remembered the first pops of gunfire and the screams that followed.

Respecting the Don't Name Them media initiative that denies mass shooters the notoriety they seek, I won't print the murderer's name. I will, however, attempt a portrait of him to understand, to the extent one can, the indoctrination that turns a frail, nerdy boy into a hateful killer.

Bullied for many of his years, his low self-esteem got in the way of talking to girls or building strong friendships. He kept his pastimes quiet, if not solitary, developing talents as a pianist, a chess player, and a marksman in army cadets. He failed to launch despite his talents, especially when compared to his twin brother. At age twenty-seven, the would-be killer had dropped out of a political science degree at Laval without telling his parents, whose judgment worried him constantly. He had a drinking problem that had interfered with his call centre job, ironically for a blood bank. He felt most comfortable on Facebook, trolling feminist and refugee groups online, proudly donning a MAGA hat in his profile picture.

Isolated, lonely, and lacking ambition, his fragile masculinity was highly susceptible to extremism. But while his tragic actions were extreme, his political views were mainstream. In the month leading up to the attack, he checked the feeds of conservative commentator Ben Shapiro ninety-three times, Fox News host Tucker Carlson forty-seven times, and provocateur Ann Coulter nineteen times. He also followed neo-Nazi figures but paid secular attention to mainstream American conservatism.

His American bent is all the more curious since Quebec's French media is crowded with Islamophobic voices. The hosts on *radio-poubelle* ("trash radio"), Quebec's uniquely corrosive brand of conservative talk shows, battle for advertisers by testing the limits of free speech. Hosts are known to debase feminists, gays, Indigenous peoples, welfare recipients, and especially religious minorities. Their popularity exploded with the reasonable accommodations debate and opened airwaves to public fury that streamed back to outraged listeners in a toxic feedback loop. It created an environment in which it's acceptable to ponder whether the purchase of halal meats finances terrorism or whether assimilated Muslims pretended to integrate in order to "strike at the opportune moment." The vitriol targeted the Centre Culturel Islamique de Québec specifically, falsely linking it to the Muslim Brotherhood. When a severed pig's head, gift-wrapped in cellophane and with a greeting card, was left on its doorstep, a notorious radio personality laughed it off as a prank.

It's unclear to what extent the shooter followed radio-poubelle, but his information about the Grande Mosque certainly didn't come from American commentators. The Quebec media diet is significantly more homogeneous than the rest of Canada's, and it's reasonable to believe his hatred and fear of the mosque was directly shaped by its most Islamophobic personalities.

But the content that sent him over the edge, or so he'd tell police, was a tweet from Canada's prime minister, posted alongside a photo of him hugging a Syrian boy at an airport:

> To those fleeing persecution, terror & war, Canadians will welcome you, regardless of your faith. Diversity is our strength #WelcomeToCanada—@justintrudeau

The tweet, sent in light of Trump's first attempt at a Muslim ban the previous day, supposedly implied to the shooter that Canada would accept every Muslim en route to America who would inevitably "kill my parents" and stage an Islamic takeover—"like [in] Europe." It's difficult to take his confession seriously. He'd studiously researched mass shootings all month and throughout the investigation veered between cold-blooded murderer and hapless delusional. One minute he regretted not killing more people, the next he had remorse.

The night of the shooting, he finished dinner at his parents' and bid them goodbye on his way to the shooting range, taking with him a handgun, a semiautomatic in a guitar case, and twenty-nine magazines: a typical sight in their household. But he soon called home to tell his mom the range was closed on Sundays, a pretext to hear her voice for potentially one last time.

This is the detail that stops me from writing him off as a monster. I sincerely believe he must have felt something human bubbling inside him when he made that call. He knew how mass shootings typically ended for the shooter. Maybe he had a brief consideration for what that would do to his loving parents. Maybe he thought that his mother's intuition could sense his plans, that she might say the right words to lure him back. However limited his conscience, he did possess one. Tragically, like so many other extremists, it was distorted by hate and invasive voices motivated by profit, which convinced this vulnerable young man that there was more virtue in martyrdom than peace.

———

About fifteen minutes before the killer fired at them, his first two victims, Mamadou Tanou Barry and Ibrahima Barry, stood shoulder to shoulder in prayer. They'd come to the mosque together after paying respects to their friend, who'd just lost his father. The Barrys, though unrelated, were inseparable. Both civil servants, both fathers of young children, they were close in age and lived in the same apartment building a few kilometres from the mosque, often carpooling together to prayer. Since meeting in Quebec City, they were more like brothers than friends. They'd leaned on each other many times: when Ibrahima's wife's health started declining, when Mamadou's father died and it became incumbent on him to support his extended family. And they leaned on each other one last time as they walked to their cars in the dark after Isha prayer.

They saw the shooter's rifle pointed at them in the parking lot. They slipped on the ice trying to back away. As Mamadou and Ibrahima scrambled to get away in the snow, the shooter pulled the trigger. The semiautomatic .223-caliber rifle jammed. Nothing fired. They may have felt the slightest relief until he fished that handgun from his pocket. He shot Mamadou and Ibrahima in the snow, walked up to their bodies, and shot them each once more.

To some of the thirty-nine men and children inside the prayer hall, milling about and socializing after salat, those first pops sounded like someone was throwing rocks at the windows. Because that happened before, the mosque had bulked up security, including installing doors programmed to automatically unlock fifteen minutes before prayer and lock fifteen minutes after. But fifteen minutes had not yet passed.

For those pulling on their shoes by the front door, the sight of the two men bleeding on the pavement left little confusion. As they registered the killer standing over the Barrys, some dashed downstairs to the cleaning stations, others into the prayer hall, not realizing they'd trapped themselves. Fathers and uncles hurried to scoop up the children sitting near the archway. One child sporadically ran across the carpet while the shooter emptied the magazine into the prayer hall. The shooter took cover behind the archway, reloading as if he were under attack. Over the next ninety seconds, he'd continue acting like someone in combat—charging in and out of the prayer hall, running between archways, reloading five times.

Aymen Derbali hid behind structural pillars, along with pharmacist Aboubaker Thabti, a Tunisian Canadian. He came to Canada to study and decided to stay. Thabti was famous for his work ethic. He slept little, working two jobs day and night, except on Sundays. With his one night off per week, the forty-four-year-old husband and father of two enjoyed attending prayer and staying to catch up with friends.

Another victim was IT consultant Abdelkrim Hassane. The Algerian immigrant had just returned to his job with the provincial government after three months of parental leave. He was an ever sensitive and doting father. His eldest children would wait for him to come home all night, refusing to sleep until his warmth returned to comfort them. It never did.

Most who huddled in an open storage room right of the mihrab survived, but the alcove couldn't shelter everyone. A bullet entered Khaled Belkacemi, killing one of Quebec's most renowned food scientists. Khaled's life had revolved around academia. He arrived from Algeria in the 1980s with a bachelor's in chemical engineering, earned a PhD from Sherbrooke University, became a researcher emeritus at Laval University, and worked to advance food and health safety for his adopted country.

It became clear the assailant would not run out of ammunition soon. Azzeddine Soufiane tried to band together men to fight back. Soufiane was like a godfather to the whole community. The Moroccan had come to Canada years earlier to study geology, but he'd found more success as Quebec City's first halal butcher. Business at his shop grew steadily along with the community, and he served as a touch point for newcomers still learning to navigate the city and country. The fifty-seven-year-old father of three never missed an opportunity to help guide newcomers to the right services. He became one of Aymen's closest friends, as the pair socialized and worked together on a charity they cofounded for Palestinian orphans.

Soufiane would be hailed a hero after that night. Unable to recruit others, he alone tackled the killer, pinning him against the wall. The assailant rapidly shot at Soufiane, sending him back toward a pillar, where he collapsed by Derbali's legs.

The image of his dying friend is one of the last things Aymen recalled from that night. The rest he'd recall from surveillance tapes played at the trial for the man who paralyzed him. When Derbali saw the gunman make a run for the alcove, he pounced on him, tackling the killer three times and taking seven bullets in the process, including the one still in his spinal cord.

The shooter tried to end Derbali's life and faith simultaneously, but only ended up intensifying his resolve for both. Derbali still tries to make it to the mosque for daily prayers. However, what was once a five-minute drive from home is now a half-hour bus commute. It's just not possible anymore. "When I start to think about not being about to pray like the others," he told me, "I just think I'm miraculous to be alive. I accept this destiny."

After sunset prayer, a barefoot man approached me and shook my hand. He wore prescription sunglasses above his white beard and introduced himself as Mohamed Labidi.

Labidi was the mosque's president until the summer of 2017, when a neighbour torched his car with a Molotov cocktail. Though he didn't resign immediately, not even after becoming the target of another conspiracy theory spread by one shock jock who suggested the mosque's president may have set the fire himself. Only after Labidi's family asked him to resign did he let his term lapse. Much to his family's chagrin, though, Labidi still acted as a spokesman for the mosque, refusing to acquiesce to those who want to silence him.

Labidi's English was limited and so was his time. He invited along Zied Kallel, Yasmin's husband. On our way to the office upstairs, we stopped on the landing to admire a painting of two hands, open in prayer, scrawled with hopeful messages in three languages at a Montreal vigil. "We get lots of people saying very sincere and positive messages, that's for sure," said Kallel.

There'd been more scrutiny of radio-poubelle too, especially after the trash radio's patron saint "King" André Arthur went on a nine-minute screed detailing health code violations at the late Azeddinne Soufiane's butcher shop. (However, that wasn't why the station eventually fired Arthur; it was slurring gays that did him in.) While local media have toned down creeping sharia panic, Kallel said another narrative was afoot. "What we're hearing is, 'You're exaggerating and trying to play the victim.'" Echoing Premier Legault's refusal to make January 29 a day against Islamophobia, nearly half of Quebecers still deny Islamophobia is a problem. How can they address a problem that people don't believe exists?

In an administrative office, where a monitor displayed a rotation of at least a dozen security camera angles, Labidi and Kallel recalled that first board meeting held after the shooting. About fifty members gathered in the women's section upstairs, the small carpeted section filled with grieving families, survivors recovering from injuries and trauma, and a general mix of stress, fear, and hyperalertness. They wanted solutions. Windowless walls to shut out the sunlight. Light switches every few feet for an emergency blackout. Billiard balls they could throw at an assailant in lieu of gun restrictions. A survivor with posttraumatic stress disorder volunteered to monitor the camera feeds twenty-four hours a day from his apartment down the street, and everyone agreed to instruct their children never to open the doors to the outside themselves.

While the vast majority of the congregation favoured permanently locked doors, some felt the barriers were not Islamic. Mosques are supposed to welcome worshippers at all hours, and many hoped they'd left such restrictions behind in their oppressive homelands. Kallel understood their points, but, he said, mosques in the Muslim world have one purpose, whereas mosques in the West have many that are central to immigrant communities. The cultural centre ran a Sunday school, Arabic class, nursery, and family activity centre inside the Grande Mosque, inflaming the fears of parents especially. Locking the doors around the clock simply wasn't feasible.

Some members would rather forgo the planned renovations entirely, worrying that the attractive architecture—especially the minaret—could provoke further attacks and undermine the very measures that prompted the redesign, which had been approved by the board of directors months before the massacre, primarily to enhance security.

"It's not easy to say who is right and who is wrong," said Kallel, who, like his wife, is in the latter camp that wishes to be discreet. "One point feels like this is symbolic: 'We can do something architecturally beautiful to present the mosque as part of Quebec culture, and why should we hide something that symbolizes us beautifully?' The other group says, 'We don't need it to pray and the extreme right wing will take it as an opportunity to say we're imposing our religion on people.'"

I'd seen mosques with private security, night patrol, bulletproof glass, coded keypads, and thick binders containing security firm audits. Each such mosque I'd seen struggled to balance openness and safety, not to mention its bottom line. At $300,000, the Grande Mosque's security investment was the highest I'd seen—and that was budgeted *before* the tragedy.

The rest of the project would expand and beautify the mosque for a growing population, though they didn't expect to raise the full $1 million so soon. "It's sad to say but we are famous because of what happened," said Kallel, craning his head toward the monitor to inspect a passerby. "The problem isn't with the money; it's with the planning."

Labidi, who has lived in Quebec much longer, reminisced about the Muslim community's early days. Back in 1990, it took two years to raise a tenth as much for the mosque's first iteration near Laval University. "It was very tough, because most of the people were students," he said.

Quebec City's Muslim community grew from its student population, largely due to North African scholarships and international partnerships. The students were highly skilled like Houston's Muslims but financially insecure, like early Syrian–Lebanese. By 2005, Quebec City's few hundred Muslims ballooned to several thousand, and though Labidi's counterparts were established, the majority were in the same place as the founders were when they arrived. It took another three years just to raise the down payment for the old Desjardins Bank. Now Quebec City's Muslim population is estimated to be seven thousand, many of them refugees. The Grande Mosque had struggled to keep up with the growth, hence the renovation plans to expand the space for over one thousand worshippers.

Kallel sympathized with the financial needs of young, immigrant communities like his own, but the hyperfocus in the community on work and family had other downsides, namely a lack of civic participation. The minimum services provided by the mosque were already more than they could handle, and there was plenty more he wanted to do. That included responding to every letter of support and help offered by allies worldwide—and the hate mail too.

"I started talking to the racists very calmly, and you see that it can change their behaviour," Kallel said. "I don't think they're bad people. They're just ignorant and brainwashed. To them, every Muslim is a potential terrorist. But the problem is we, as a community, aren't doing enough to give them the real picture of Islam and Muslims."

Kallel continued, growing ever more passionate and idealistic. "We should make our own community radio. Our own talk show. We should have debates. We should do artistic works. Community works. At the end of every winter, we should clean up the streets and wear shirts that say, 'I'm Muslim.' But it's not happening because we have a community that—probably out of fear and lack of motivation—is not involved."

Noble as they were, his ideas smacked of respectability politics. Nobody should have to condemn terrorists, let alone prove they're not one, to comfort the ignorant. It's not like the Canadian Cadet Organizations had to issue a press release condemning the shooter.

Kallel agreed with me, but he felt it was on Muslims to change the narrative. "The racist people really see us as different kinds of human beings. I'm not sure what they have in mind when my wife and I go home, like everything is black and we have torture rooms," he joked. "They need to know that we have jokes, and we laugh, and we don't just think about prayer. That we make mistakes."

His last point might as well have been a mea culpa for his own complicity a decade prior. Back when he was doing his MBA at Laval, Kallel and other members of a Muslim students' association failed to control radical voices in the group. In Friday sermons, the group's president—an energetic, attention-loving Salafist from Morocco—advocated stoning and whipping violators of sharia and decried democracy as incompatible with Islam. "The students themselves, ninety percent wanted to pray and return to their studies," said Kallel. But when media caught wind of the sermons, everything got blown out of proportion.

I asked Kallel about his hopes for the future. More than the mosque's expansion, renovation, or advocacy, he wanted people to remember the date: January 29, 2017. It wasn't just non-Muslims who'd proven it forgettable. At an Ontario Muslim conference, Kallel surveyed attendees with a simple question: "What does January 29 represent to you?" Two-thirds chose the option "regular day."

"We cannot just wipe off everything and turn the page," said Kallel. "You have to have something symbolic."

"What do you have in mind?" I asked.

Kallel led me back downstairs. I thought he was going to show me the canvas tenderly decorated by children, but then he started reenacting the shooting itself. Unnerved and startled, I followed him between the archways as he aimed his outstretched arm into the sunlit empty prayer hall like a gun, mimicking the barrage of bullets—"tuk, tuk, tuk, tuk, tuk, tuk." He imitated the kickback after each shot and pretended to reload around the corner wall. Kallel wasn't present during the shooting, but he'd committed the surveillance tape to memory.

"There was an old guy, about seventy, he was in the restroom. He heard someone shooting," Kallel said, leading me to the door at the end of the hall. "As soon as he tried to open the door"—Kallel pushed it open and immediately slammed it shut—"he was facing [the shooter]. He went back in and closed the door. [The shooter] shot at him right here." Kallel pushed his finger through a nickel-sized hole in the door. He twisted the knob and showed me the exit hole on the opposite wall.

Kallel continued narrating the tragedy, leading me from one scar to another—in the roof above the alcove, by the baseboards of the back wall, in a section of the rug they forgot to replace. Kallel lifted the children's painting off the glass wall, revealing a web of cracks around a bullet hole. Downstairs, rolled-up patches of green and pink rug marked with bullet holes and the blood of his friends collected dust. Kallel felt they should be up in a museum or displayed somewhere as a reminder that "we lost brothers who were simply worshipping."

In fact, the city had been planning such a thing: a memorial park near the mosque with the victims' names engraved on a jet-black monument. But Kallel wished for people who visit the mosque ("us and our children") to be reminded of the shooting every time they stepped inside. "This is part of the collective memory of the community members, who have an obligation not to forget, to not turn the page.

"You know this famous church out here?" he asked, pointing out the window toward the heritage site. Just as the cathedral was maintained as a reminder of its Jesuit roots and its role in the Seven Years' War, Kallel wanted the tragic artifacts from the mosque to stand as reminders of the worst mass murder in a Canadian place of worship.

He brought me back over to the architecture renderings of "Phase 2" on the wall. "When we came up with the architecture, they made the minaret look like the tower on the church." I leaned in and noticed for the first time that the steel spires in the renovation plans were fashioned after the neighbouring bell tower. Though he'd rather the mosque keep a low profile, he did like the symbolic harmony of the towers.

Staring into the Grande Mosque's future, I saw something more than a good-hearted gesture. To me, it marked Christendom's monopolized power over the past and the power that now everyone *could* have over the future. Quebec was built by Catholics who believed their sovereignty hinged on their ability to outbreed the English, restricting reproductive control until their agenda backfired in a revolt. But in its essence, white Catholic supremacy remains strong and will remain so unless Quebecers are exposed to other cultures in their everyday lives.

The Grande Mosque, through its reimagined presence, both as a landmark and social organization, can help demystify Islam and, more importantly, normalize different people. It needs to be noticed before it can be unnoticed, even by drivers zipping past with no other interest than getting to and from work or maybe to do some banking.

Whether passersby or memorial park visitors will remember the names of January 29's victims is another question. Ibrahima Barry. Mamadou Tanou Barry. Khaled Belkacemi. Aboubaker Thabti. Abdelkrim Hassane. Azzedine Soufiane. Even after trying to honour their lives and prying into their deaths, I still have to look up their names, while the shooter's name, hard as I've tried to forget it, comes to mind without effort. It's a natural function of the human mind, I suppose, to favour the storage of threatening information. But it's a defect of the soul to do nothing with it.

The name Alexandre Bissonnette—maybe we *should* say it too—didn't only have to signify carnage. The name could have been remembered for the changes that leaders made to try to prevent a repeat massacre. But that wasn't the outcome. Nothing changed either after a man of nearly the same age killed fifty-one Muslims in Christchurch, New Zealand, using a gun painted with the dedication "For Alexandre Bissonnette."

In 2021, the government of Canada, under intense public pressure, finally designated January 29 a National Day of Remembrance and Action Against Islamophobia. But it still hasn't taken any meaningful steps to challenge Quebec's legislative attacks on Muslim people or support the litigant challengers. If heinous attacks on Muslims in sacred prayer can't convince Western leaders that Islamophobia kills, then I'm resigned to believe nothing will.

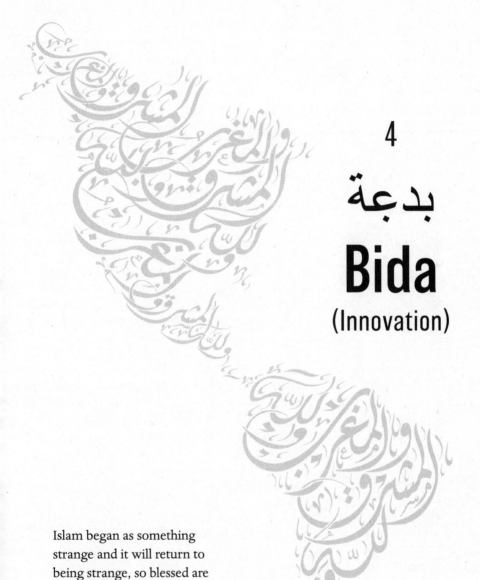

4

بدعة

Bida

(Innovation)

Islam began as something
strange and it will return to
being strange, so blessed are
the strangers.

—*Hadith (Sahih Muslim), c. 850*

Expelled
Comunidad Musulmana Ahmadiyya
(San Cristóbal de las Casas, Mexico)

*E*ven from the view of a gas station parking lot, the city of San Cristóbal de las Casas is gorgeous. Perched atop a plateau in the dead center of the Chiapas Highlands, the Mayan power capital is surrounded by forested hill peaks resembling the heads of prostrating green-haired giants. I snapped a few pictures to boast about on Instagram while I waited with my translator for our interview subject to arrive.

"I can't believe you get to live here," I told Flor, who flashed a knowing smile. Over the course of her young life, the small city has transformed from an asylum for persecuted Protestant Indigenous people to a magnet for Marxist revolutionaries to what it is today: a hippie paradise popular with artists and seekers. A young and tattooed designer from Guadalajara, Flor knows San Cristóbal only in its modern form, but Anastasio Gomez Gomez, the Tzotzil Mayan man we had prepared to meet, has lived at the cross section of the city's three dramatic stages.

Gomez was born the rebellious grandson of an influential evangelical preacher. At thirteen, he was recruited by the Zapatista Army of National Liberation to help seize control of half of Chiapas State in 1994. At fifteen, he became Ibrahim Chechev, the promising protégé of a European Sufi, and helped the guru convert hundreds of Tzotzil and Tzeltal Maya to Islam. Today, at thirty-eight, he's better known as Imam Ibrahim, a key figure in the Ahmadiyya Muslim community of Latin America. He heads a small Ahmadi parish consisting almost entirely of his relatives.

The imam arrived in a sedan wearing all-black everything—slacks, shirt, and sweater vest. He unlocked the doors for us. No need for introductions. We'd met over breakfast to discuss the logistics of joining him on a mission to Guatemala, combining proselytizing and medical relief aid for an Ahmadiyya-affiliated nongovernmental organization (NGO). We planned to shadow the imam, camping overnight in mosques and Maya households, but, unfortunately, the charity changed his schedule before we'd finished eating.

I was disappointed, but the postponement gave me more time to spend with a Muslim community that has fascinated people since the mid-1990s. What made the Maya Muslims of San Cristóbal so compelling wasn't just their indigeneity and rapid growth, but their visibility in a region of one of the world's most Catholic nations.

Ibrahim gave us a driving tour of the city's other mosques before making his way toward his own on the northern fringes. Before Ibrahim was born, the mosque was his father's evangelical church. It sits halfway between the city core and the squatter settlements of the *expuldo*—comprising Ibrahim's clan and other Maya expelled from their Chamula villages by Catholic chieftains and mobs.

Check-stop police pulled him over as we approached. They may have mistook the foreigner in Ibrahim's back seat for a kidnapping victim. A cop walked straight to my open window and shook my hand. I smiled as Ibrahim explained my presence with one of the glossy brochures he offers on missions. The officer, who had surely encountered his share of religious revivalists here, let us go with a smile.

We passed one more mosque before approaching his former house of God, the Sufi mosque that converted the expuldos to Islam, and from which they were later expelled. Mezquita Imam Malik—a

Spanish colonial palace funded by the United Arab Emirates—was half-hidden behind an imposing white wall.

The mosque that Ibrahim led, Comunidad Musulmana Ahmadiyya—a stumpy box pressed between cinder-block shanties—stood directly across the street like David in Goliath's shadow. I collected burrs on my socks as I crossed a ditch to photograph both buildings. "This is just provisional," Ibrahim said about his mosque. I looked up at the vinyl sign stretched across the peach-coloured wall. I recognized the words in Arabic calligraphy (*There is no god but God*), but would have to google the Spanish phrase later. It read, "Love for all, hatred for none." It's an Ahmadiyya refrain to counter their persecutors.

Ibrahim knocked on a steel door. His brother Marcos answered and let us into a courtyard. A clothesline hung along a sunny wall. Stacked seating, toys, and a small aviary were tucked away neatly. Marcos's wife greeted us and returned to sweeping the painted floor. Two open doors led to Chechev family homes, a third to a shared washroom, another to a chicken coop, and the last to the prayer room.

We sat on a layer of carpets, beneath a tin roof that startles whenever a wind-swept rock lands with a loud pop. As I scanned the spare hall, Ibrahim noticed my eyes set on an old black-and-white portrait. It stood on an office desk in the corner, a South Asian man staring from beneath a humble turban. "That's the founder of the Ahmadiyya community," he said. "Mirza Ghulam Ahmad."

"Do followers believe he is a prophet?" I asked, feeling out Ibrahim's views. Ahmadiyya are split between purists who view the Indian founder to be, as he claimed, both a prophet and the Mahdi (Messiah) who will reappear at the end of times, and the reformists who revere him only as Mahdi.

"Just as Jesus brought back the teachings of Moses, Mirza brings back the teachings of Prophet Muhammad," said Ibrahim. "So, for us, he is a prophet and a messiah, but not a prophet of law because he does not bring any new teaching with reference to the Prophet Muhammad."

"Was it difficult to adjust from Christianity without sacrificing either family or Indigenous heritage?" I asked, noting that pork and *pox*, a ceremonial spirit, are staples of Maya diet. Ibrahim said no. His family's strict Protestantism forbade swine and alcohol. What's more, he said, Islam reconnected him spiritually with his grandfather, Miguel Gómez Hernández, a venerable pastor known only from legend.

A decade after his expulsion from Chamula, Miguel's congregation had grown to hundreds of families. Ibrahim was a baby in 1981 when Catholic zealots hunted down his grandfather in San Cristóbal, kidnapped him in broad daylight, and dragged him to Chamula's town square. They gave pastor Miguel the choice of renouncing Protestantism or death. "They began to torture him with an icepick," said Ibrahim, recounting news reports. "Then they scalped him alive, took out his eye, his tongue, and practically skinned him until he bled to death." Ibrahim's father, Manuel, was amongst the group that found Miguel's body glowing bright green in the woods as fireflies feasted on his remains.

Then the trauma feasted on Manuel. He tried, for over a decade, to continue Miguel's legacy amid their suffering. After wearing through Seventh Day Adventists, Sabbaticals, and Jehovah's Witnesses, Manuel succumbed to a personal tyrannical Christianity that justified his alcoholic rages.

In 1995, a tall, white Sufi imam mysteriously arrived in Chiapas with a few European and Mexican acolytes. They set up their mission inside a bakery and began requesting meetings with Tzotzil and Tzeltal patriarchs. Ibrahim's father reluctantly accepted an invitation to Eid al-Fitr celebrations, bringing along everyone in his family, except for Ibrahim, now fifteen, who'd been kicked out of the house. Young Ibrahim, or "Tacho" as he was known amongst family and Zapatista fighters, had adopted a revolutionary's distaste for his father's hypocrisies.

Manuel went to the location, finding neither feast nor festival. The Sufis explained that a lunar sighting had postponed Eid by one day, which only angered him. The Sufis sent apologies and repeated invitations to make up for the offence. Finally, to get them off his back, Manuel sent his rebellious son to meet the Muslims—payback for wasting his time.

"The only thing I knew about Muslims was what I saw in the news about the Gulf War, but I didn't associate it with what was about to happen," reflected Ibrahim, sitting beside Marcos cross-legged on a green prayer rug serving as qibla. The teenager was first to the bakery, followed by a *chilango* (slang for Mexico City resident). The chilango convert led him a couple of doors down to the home of their "sidi," an obscure Andalusian feudal title similar to "my lord."

Muhammad Nafia led a dozen men in Sufi chants. An imposing Spaniard with a light beard and eyes, he radiated the power of his title.

Ibrahim did not understand a word of their prayer, but it moved him. Before he could ask any questions, though, Nafia ordered one of the dutiful Mexicans to take the boy out for cookies at the bakery. He was about to start a sermon, and he did not want non-Muslims present.

Ibrahim was allowed to return that evening for dinner, where he was told that Nafia's home, a house of joy, would welcome him and his family anytime they liked. Ibrahim continued coming for prayers, and after two months he was knowledgeable enough to pray alone at home. As his brother Marcos described it, "We started to think he was crazy. We didn't understand what he was saying." They thought it was devil worship until the changes in Ibrahim's personality started to show. He became courteous, compassionate, and forgiving.

His father was critically ill with internal infections. Convinced he would die soon, he demanded Ibrahim explain his transformation. As he confessed his new faith, Manuel began to weep. He begged Ibrahim to forgive his abuses and vowed to become a Muslim if he survived.

If his recollection sounds grandiose, even embellished, understand the family sincerely believed Ibrahim, the youngest of five children, was predestined as a spiritual leader. "He was six months old when my grandfather told him, 'You are going to take what I have, you are going to be one of those who guide people,' " Marcos recalled about his baby brother. "My grandfather gave him that gift two hours before he was killed." So you begin to understand why Manuel soon recovered, accepted his son's invitation to Islam, and changed his name to Muhammad.

As Nafia had predicted and hoped, the conversion of the late Miguel Gómez Hernández's family brought waves of new believers—so many, in fact, that Nafia's people organized a public event in which two to three hundred Indigenous took shahada over a weekend. Ibrahim assisted Nafia, translating for Tzotzil speakers like his father. By the end of the millennium, there were some seven hundred Muslims in San Cristóbal, comparable to the ummah of Mexico City, at fifty times the size.

There had been a Latin American conversion movement bubbling for some time. Beginning in the eighties, an organized movement of urban Mexican nationals began to profess Islam. Trading on anti-imperialist resentment, they drew followers with an imagined nostalgia for Moorish Andalusia. For white Hispanics, it offered pride and rebellion—a way to embrace their history while skirting the Catholic agenda. But what's the appeal for the Indigenous Mexicans wearing the scars of European colonialism?

"Islam has many benefits," said Ibrahim. "The true jihad, within yourself, is not being selfish and forgiving those who offend you." From his perspective, the Christian elite had exploited Maya desperation, fracturing families and leaving communities to feud. "There are no secrets between brothers. You cannot talk behind your brother's back or ignore him for more than a few days." Ibrahim is closer now to his father than ever before, and his father has atoned for his sins. "The difference between Christianity and Islam, Islam really fosters brotherhood," added Ibrahim. What's more, he said Islam mitigated obesity, substance abuse, extramarital affairs, and single parenthood in his community.

I could see how sharia—enshrined, divine, nonnegotiable laws— benefitted a marginalized and racialized group disproportionately plagued by social ills. Like many African American Muslims, Maya found stability, dignity, and wholesomeness in the Quran. Though they didn't share the romanticism of Blacks or Hispanics, and for the most part had never heard of Muhammad before embracing his prophethood, Maya saw Islam as a homecoming of sorts: reversion, not conversion. The concept of *fitra*, or natural disposition, professes that all humans are born Muslim. So goes the hadith: "No child is born except on *al-fitra* (Islam) and then his parents make him Jewish, Christian, or Magian (Zoroastrian)." It's meant as forgiveness, not condemnation, of past beliefs.

I couldn't help but see the undertones of religious colonization that severs people from their roots, leaving behind a legacy of confusion and misery. At the same time, if faith of any kind makes one happier today than yesterday, who am I to condescend with my critical social theories?

Since the evangelical movement of the 1960s, the Maya have been known to experiment with Christian denominations. ("They change religions like socks," goes the joke.) But mass conversion to Islam alarmed observers immediately. Government agents began to spy on the community and attempted to deport Nafia and his disciples. Driven into hiding, the Chechevs donated the dormant church as a temporary *musalla* until things cooled down. The Spaniards eventually got visas and brought their families. With growth, they expanded the mission's enterprises to include a pizzeria, natural health clinic, and woodshop, which together supported an Islamic school offering quality bilingual education. A young Spanish teacher, the daughter of Nafia's second-in-command, married Ibrahim, further entwining East and West.

Many accounts of the San Cristóbal Muslims story end there. An ethnographic curiosity: the Maya who read Arabic and pray to Allah. An oft-recycled quote that Ibrahim, then twenty-one, once gave to a US reporter sums it up: "Five hundred years ago, they came to destroy us; five hundred years later, other Spaniards came to return a knowledge that was taken away from us."

But of course, the story does not end there. It cannot, evident in the houses of worship facing off across the street; evident in the other mosques scattered about the city; evident in the dozens of ex-Muslim

Maya who regard their conversion as a curious phase, or something much worse.

Wherever there is a Muslim community, there is a difference of opinion, practice, and beliefs. While Islam has the power to heal wounds and bring people together, it can also do the opposite.

To understand the speed at which the Maya both embraced and then rejected Islam, we must understand Nafia's roots, and to understand his roots, we must briefly go to Granada, the heart of Muslim Andalusia, as I did three months later in summer 2019.

The excursion was born of happenstance. Close friends of mine planned a destination wedding in Spain. Janae and I eagerly handed Noe off to our parents and left for a week in the province of Barcelona and two days in Granada before heading home. I made loose plans to drop by the mosque belonging to the Murabitun World Movement, where Nafia's Muslim education began, but otherwise kept our getaway leisurely.

There was plenty to learn about Muslim Spain by being tourists. I immediately noticed the city's official logo featured "Granada" written in Arabic-inspired script. We did the majority of our eating and dining in an impressive souk run by North African migrants, and our walking-tour guide was quick to note the most subtle Moorish architecture and Arabic instruments in flamenco music. Despite the region's Muslim roots, most of the modern Islamo-Arab culture emerged in the past fifteen years. The "halal tourism" boom sparked fascination for southern Europe's last emirate, turning this small city into a premier destination. Unsurprisingly, the palace of Andalusia's last and mightiest emirate, Alhambra, or "The Red One" in Arabic, is now Spain's top historic tourist attraction. Alhambra's architectural splendor spared it from destruction in 1492 after Christian conquerors seized the region's last Muslim holdout. Just about every other historic Muslim symbol was forcibly removed or converted, much like the Moors themselves, but Alhambra preserved Spain's Islamic DNA long enough to be resuscitated centuries later.

In the end, I didn't have to seek out the Murabitun mosque, known as Mestizo Mayor Granada (the Great Mosque of Granada). It was in many ways the most prominent Islamic symbol in the city. I stumbled on it on our way back from watching the sunset from atop Albacín, a historic district directly across the valley from Alhambra. While most tourists returned to their hotels and downtown amenities, I noticed a trickle of Middle Eastern people, presumably tourists, walk toward a white tower: the Great Mosque's minaret.

I asked Janae for twenty minutes to "work." She ordered dinner at a Moroccan bistro outside the mosque while I went inside, seeking permission first from a man guarding the gate entrance (code word: "Salamu alaykum"). A group of British European women donning bright turbans drank tea in the tiled courtyard while their fair-skinned children had their run of the garden. The interior looked expensive and even newer than it actually was.

Designed in luxurious Moorish style, the Great Mosque opened in 2003 after more decades of opposition. Locals fought every piece of the development, right down to the minaret, even though Saint Nicolás's steeple, a minaret until 1492, stood metres away. "The people have hate in their blood because of the history of Al-Andalus," explained a Muslim congregant whom I interviewed by phone back in Canada. (The person requested anonymity to speak freely about Muhammad Nafia, the Murabitun movement, and its controversial founder, so I'll refer to them by the unisex name Nour.)

Nour moved to Granada in the late 1970s with their partner and a handful of young couples seeking spiritual enlightenment. They left everything behind in their village to join a new Sufi movement led by an eccentric Scotsman named Abdalqadir as-Sufi al-Murabit. In his former life, the emir/shaykh was Ian Dallas, an actor-writer who worked with Federico Fellini and claimed to have inspired Eric Clapton's song "Layla."

There is no better exemplar of the 1960s Muslim hippie movement than Abdalqadir. A radical intellectual of the psychedelic era, he discovered Islam while in North Africa, a saga recounted in his semiautobiographical novel *The Book of Strangers*. He founded his first community in London in 1972, a Darqawi brotherhood frequented by rock stars until the community started taking on "cult-like qualities," according to a published interview with Ian Whiteman of the band Mighty Baby.

An agitator, Abdalqadir supplemented the faith with anarcho-communist politics and gold-based economics. The Islamic elements adhered to three Sufi orders, including Qadiriyya, the predominant tradition of ancient Moors, whose exile in 1492 proliferated Qadiriyya in North Africa. Abdalqadir's movement was also heavily influenced by his personal interpretations of sharia. Chief amongst them was that every Muslim community must be governed by an emir and that every Muslim subject must pay the emir allegiance and tax—what he said were the Islamic concepts *bayat* and *zakat*.

As shaykh and emir, the last European emirate held a special place in his heart. He relocated his mission, officially now the Murabitun World Movement, to Granada in 1978 after the death of President Francisco Franco and Spanish dictatorship. "Franco just died, and there was a newfound freedom," recalled Nour. "Spain was just bubbling; it was effervescent."

Against the backdrop of social liberation and new age seeking, Abdalqadir attracted people like Nour—young artisans, musicians, and alternative thinkers who travelled across Spain and Europe to study at his feet. "We were searchers. I didn't understand a word of it, but I felt empowered by it. But when I look back at our lives, we kind of were in a sect." Nour said the Murabitun ("protectors of the fortress") was too insular in those early days. Many followers "forgot how to go back into the world."

Nour has mixed feelings about Abdalqadir. He could be harsh and controlling. Some members felt forced to choose him over their families. But he also gave them Islam, what Nour called the greatest gift of their life. Nour's feelings about Muhammad Nafia are less complicated. "I always had had problems with Nafia. He was always someone who wanted power, a wannabe emir. I always found him impossible." Nafia, known in the late 1970s as Aureliano Pérez Yruela, rose in Abdalqadir's ranks as one of his most vocal defenders and proselytizers.

He absorbed the ideological mash-up of Sunni theology, Sufi mysticism, and radical anticapitalism and may have believed that he would succeed Abdalqadir as the Granadan emir.

The possibility came earlier than Nafia expected, when Abdalqadir decided to move headquarters to the place of his birth, the Scottish Highlands. But Abdalqadir did not give the Granadan reins to Nafia. Instead, he offered Nafia the opportunity to establish a mission abroad. By 1994, the Murabitun World Movement had spread across the world to several nations, but Mexico, the largest Spanish-speaking country in the world, was not one of them.

It seemed like a no-brainer, but Nafia had underestimated the grip Catholicism had on Mexicans and overestimated their romance for Moorish Spain. Nafia, the newly fashioned *sidi*, had few subjects after a year of preaching in Mexico City. Struggling to reach chilangos in the fast-paced capital, he began fixating on the southern border state of Chiapas, where a leftist uprising broke out in defence of Indigenous rights. The Zapatista Army of National Liberation—the insurgent movement that Ibrahim Chechev assisted at thirteen—excited the politically oriented preacher, as did the Zapatista's mysterious and masked leader, Subcomandante Marcos.

Sidi Nafia and his few acolytes entered Chiapas by disguising themselves as journalists. Once they were through, Nafia attempted to pass a letter to Subcomandante Marcos. More manifesto than message, it read:

> Do you agree that the main demands of the Mexican people are: land, housing, work, food, health, education, culture, information, independence, democracy, freedom, justice and peace? . . . Economically, the State must be dismantled by rejecting the payment of any tax and ceasing to use the fictitious and imposed currency to subdue the population. . . . The struggle for the freedom of all people must be under the flag of a transformative Islam, following the message revealed and brought to us by Muhammad the last of the prophets, the liberator of humanity.

Nafia promised the Zapatista a series of "guilds" to spur productivity and economic liberation. It's not a stretch to assume Nafia hoped to achieve the Murabutin dream through the Zapatista's gains, though Nafia emphatically denied this to reporters (back when he gave interviews). Regardless, the Murabutin utopia never stood a chance in Chiapas—or the Highlands, for that matter.

Abdalqadir as-Sufi al-Murabit's homecoming fell apart following damning exposés in the British press. He instead relocated to Cape Town, South Africa, where he remains. Ninety-one years old at the time of publication, Abdalqadir has been inactive for a few years, though he spent the latter part of his life denouncing some of his foundational beliefs and distancing himself from the Murabutin, even scrubbing "al-Murabit" ("the Soldier") from his name. As for his protégé in Chiapas, Muhammad Nafia was just getting started.

After refocusing his mission on ex-Catholic Maya and making unbelievable gains with the expuldo of San Cristóbal de las Casas, he eventually recast himself as "emir" and began to micromanage the behaviour of his hundreds of followers. No longer satisfied with their allegiance to him or Islam, he forbade them from working for any business that was not part of the community's "guilds." He banned the peso from their hands, enforcing a gold-minted currency that he created himself. According to Ibrahim, he forbade them from watching television and using pharmaceutical medicine.

Then Nafia went further: he controlled their diet, forbidding them to eat tortillas and beans (what he called "monkey's food"), and then their mother tongue—speaking Tzotzil around him was banned. "It all went to his head," said Nour, who was knowledgeable of Nafia's Western endeavours and close to some of his victims. It was clear to them that Nafia had gone beyond the duties of emir or shaykh; he'd reenacted La Conquista. Nafia became a modern-day conquistador "civilizing" Indigenous Americans as divine duty.

———

I'd tried repeatedly for a face-to-face interview with Nafia. Two hired researchers delivered my request to people in his inner circle, but they respectfully declined, citing sensational and dubious works of previous journalists. Indeed, there's some excoriating and dubious reporting about Nafia in the Spanish press, but more on account of his politics, not his peculiar gnosticism.

During my trip to San Cristóbal in March 2019, I met with activist journalist Gaspar Morquecho, an early observer of the Muslim revival in Chiapas. The author of *Bajo la bandera del Islam* (*Under the Flag of Islam*) would engage with me only on the condition that I have a Spanish translator present, not because he isn't fluent in English but that English is the language of modern imperialists. He also insisted that Flor and I meet on the fly in the downtown public square before taking us to a tucked-away tea shop. He sat facing the entrance out of precaution and turned his back toward it only once in order to grab a decorative book off a wall shelf.

I had asked why Maya in the area were more amenable to Nafia than other demographics he targeted, Indigenous or not. "This is the whole version of the story about Catholic and non-Catholic Christians' oppression in Chamula and the highlands of Chiapas," he said, calmly steeping his tea while I flipped the pages. He added, "The prologue is mine."

To summarize the whole story: The Chamula people were governed by a consortium of political chiefs, called *caciques*, to which powerful corporations and churches paid fealty in order to access the lands and minds of villagers. "The children were not receiving an education, so the parents changed their religions to free themselves from the oppression of the caciques, to break with the system."

Morquecho was friends with Ibrahim Chechev's family. He'd reported on his grandfather's murder in 1981 and witnessed Muhammad Chechev's religious fluidity up close. Gaspar had a bad feeling about Nafia almost as soon as the emir ingratiated himself with Indigenous leaders. Nafia convinced them that their sect, the Murabitun World Movement, was pure Islam—that is, Islam as it should be practised globally.

While Morquecho noted impressive intermarriage between the Spanish and Chamula, he also observed a vertical power gradient with

the emir above European expats, above chilangos and mestizo converts, above Spanish-speaking Maya, above non-fluent Maya—usually
their elders—at the bottom. "There were the racist and discriminatory
practices," said Morquecho, who claimed he once caught Nafia in public reading a book titled *Cómo fue la Conquista de México* (*The Conquest of
Mexico*). "He had Indians in front of him and he wanted to know how
they were conquered," he said, laughing at the ham-fisted symbolism.

The true scale of Nafia's cruelty was hidden from Morquecho
and other non-Muslims. As Ibrahim had explained to me earlier, Nafia
presented a different face outside the mosque. "You couldn't cough
or sneeze or you'd be thrown out for interrupting prayer, but people
who'd only met him a couple of times would not believe he was capable of doing that," Ibrahim had told me.

Nafia's group got a lot of bad press during the early Zapatista
movement, but that changed after 9/11, when the Mexican government began harassing and monitoring Muslim citizens. The press had
the best intentions when they began to counter anti-Muslim propaganda, but they may have overcorrected. San Cristóbal Muslims were
instead naively portrayed as a harmonious bonding of East and West.
Pious yet liberal, socialist yet industrious, they were an idyllic colonial
fantasy.

Tablighi missionaries were intrigued. A Sunni mission contacted
Ibrahim's cousin, Yahia Chechev, requesting an introduction to the
mythic preacher who'd achieved unimaginable conversions. Nafia was
rude and dismissive to them, greatly humiliating Yahia in front of his
new friends. It was the last straw for Yahia. On top of the abuse he
suffered along with everyone else, he felt Nafia had undervalued his
immediate family in comparison to Ibrahim's. Yahia, his family, and
a few others formed their own mosque with support from Sunnis in
Mexico City.

Nafia clamped down with his usual mix of hot and cold. He enticed
some members to stay by promising to take them on a hajj pilgrimage;
in 2001, he secured money from a Dubai prince to take them.

Extraordinary doesn't even begin to describe what it would have
been like for Indigenous who'd never left Chiapas before. "For them

it was reaching the Land of God, where the floors are golden, an encounter with the Muslim world, of such magnitude that not even the Virgin of Guadalupe could achieve," said Morquecho.

At the cave of Hira, where Muhammad is believed to have received his first revelation from the angel Gabriel, Nafia asked them to sit at his feet. According to Ibrahim, Nafia said the following: "I want you to swear to me that, in front of me or not, you will not speak Tzotzil, and you will stop eating beans and tortilla because they are a fool's food with no nutrients. I want you to promise me here in this sacred place that you will be loyal to me." One of the young men began to weep, knowing he would no longer be able to communicate with elders who spoke only Tzotzil. To make matters worse, Nafia enforced isolation from non-Muslims, including Yahia's parish, who were now unbelievers in the emir's eyes.

In demanding they choose religion over family, Nafia had revived the traumas of their Catholic excommunication. Things began to crack after that, and piece by piece the parish broke away, leaving him with even fewer followers than he'd arrived with in 1995. "He can't manage to fill one row in the 'Great Mosque' with people," said Gaspar. At least, that's what Gaspar has been told by ex-members. He has not stepped inside Mezquita Imam Malik since it opened in 2017, as Nafia's group has become even more secluded.

———

I went to see the Mezquita Imam Malik for myself the following afternoon, fully prepared to be turned away at its arched solid wood doors. A cab driver dropped me off in the parking lot in time for Asr, the afternoon prayer. Even half-obscured by an imposing wall, it was an extraordinary structure.

I did not have to wait there for long. A white, bearded man with light eyes arrived to unlock the entrance. I said salamu alaykum and he replied in a Spanish European accent, *"Wa alaykumu salam"* (and peace be upon you). I introduced myself as a Canadian journalist who'd come for prayer. It was about all the English he understood, but all he needed to welcome me through the barrier.

The mosque was stunning inside and out. Bright Moroccan tiles covered the lower half exterior, each row topped with the words "Only God is victorious" in Arabic. Through one of many Moorish archways, he led me to a marbled washing station that could accommodate twenty at one time. But in the prayer hall itself, it was us and another man; neither of them was Nafia. Standing beneath an opulent bronze chandelier, I felt as if I'd been given after-hours access to a museum.

The man who welcomed me threw on a tasseled white robe hanging inside the gold mihrab. The other guy, a chilango named Ahmad, and I stood one row behind the imam. As the imam sang scripture in a loud, melodic voice, Ahmad belted *Allahu akbar* back in a flourished falsetto. Their voices echoed and intertwined like an eerie choir. After prayer, they sat cross-legged to sing a Sufi dua into their open palms together. I participated insofar as I could cup my hands and wash them over my face when the dua ended.

We remained in a seated triangle and chatted, with Ahmad translating in imperfect English. I kept my questions simple and unobtrusive, allowing them to speak to me as they would a layman. They told me that the mosque was generously financed by the Dubai royal family and that its founder, Muhammad Nafia, didn't spend much time in San Cristóbal anymore, as he travelled often (presumably to replenish his parish). Thus, the imam in front of me was also the acting emir.

I asked why they needed an emir in the first place. Shouldn't a lead imam suffice? Ahmad said it was more complicated since the group collectively owns businesses and properties. "There has to be an authority. One person has to have the voice, the authority, otherwise people will go . . ." He paused, reaching for the right terminology.

"In all different directions?" I asked.

"Exactly," said Ahmad, apologizing for his limited English—and his limited time. He had to return to running their homeopathy clinic, but I could join him for a cup of tea there if I wanted to learn more.

We listened to Spanish covers of Motown songs on the drive to the apothecary. Ahmad told me about becoming Muslim three decades ago, prior to Nafia's arrival. He'd taken shahada to marry a woman from a Muslim family but had become more pious than she'd signed up for. After the divorce, he went on a religious sojourn to Granada, where he first met Nafia. They stayed in touch. Years later, in Mexico City, Ahmad helped Nafia establish the first Murabitun mission, though they don't really call it "Murabitun" anymore. (The name was phased out with Abdalqadir as-Sufi's own late-stage mellowing.)

At the apothecary Ahmad slipped on a white coat and served me sweetened maté tea. We spoke for another hour, breaking occasionally so he could serve a customer. I also met Nafia's son-in-law, who worked alongside Ahmad, and Nafia's daughter, a warm and friendly English teacher. During our conversation, Ahmad spoke about Shaykh Nafia with reverence. He fawned over Nafia's willingness to create an ummah from nothing—to "make something very special for the Zapatista"— and praised the shaykh's persistence in the face of rejection.

But Ahmad also spoke highly of Indigenous Mexicans, highlighting the similarities between ancient Muslim and Maya cultures: eating communally off a floor mat, gendered segregation, and polygamy. In his romanticized notion of Maya—tinged with noble savage tropes as it was—the Chamula had warded off the effects of Christianity better than majority Mexicans. "We think the Indian people are very special people," he said. "The Spanish rulers corrupted them, made them lose their connection with God." He blamed the conquistadors for the pork in Maya diets, which is technically true, as well as pox liquor, which is certainly not—it's an ancient ceremonial tradition.

"Is there anything in their diets, other than pox and pork, that is haram?" I asked, testing the claims made to me by Ibrahim and other Indigenous excommunicates. Ahmad said no. Tortillas, beans, corn: nothing was wrong with these staples.

Was he lying, or simply unaware of Nafia's repressive tactics? Ibrahim told me that Nafia had two faces—one inside the mosque, one outside. But what if he had a third one that he only showed Maya members, such as he did in the Cave of Hira. Hierarchies, of course, are typical of cult leaders. Favouritism and division are their weapons of control.

I enjoyed the company of Nafia's family and acolytes. They were hospitable, polite, humble, sincere. Who am I to judge them for believing that they were the benevolent ones? Brainwashed or not, being in a religious or other minority group often convinces one to believe their presence in the West can help undo white Christian oppression.

I've fallen into this line of thinking. For most of my life, I believed that my immigrant Muslim community bore less responsibility for Indigenous injustice than our settler predecessors. After all, our history is also one of European colonialism, of strategic divisions and disempowerment, of self-hate and self-preservation. But overcommitting to this self-victimhood—this relativist fallacy that the success of non-Christian immigrants somehow benefits all minorities—is to blindly follow the cult of multiculturalism. It ignores the fact that we too are agents of genocide. We reaped our benefits from stolen land.

Nafia's circle would have you believe that capitalism and Christianity are inherently disenfranchising systems. But that alone isn't why Indigenous Mexican communities have startling levels of illiteracy, malnourishment, and maternal and infant mortality. Indigenous Americans were violently severed from their roots and left with the trauma of their brutalized ancestors. Can any imported religion, economic, or political system ever repair that?

Perhaps Islam offers an incremental, sometimes even radical, improvement to their quality of life. Ibrahim claimed as much to me earlier that week, noting how the Quran's promotion of fidelity, abstinence, and the nuclear family naturally treated common social ills. Gaspar also wrote in his book, *Under the Flag of Islam*, that Muslim Maya women "noted the feeling of protection provided by the headscarves, a more harmonious family life, mainly due to the prohibition of alcohol, a better economic situation."

But Islam also distances Indigenous Americans further from heritage. It simply cannot replace it, regardless of their vague similarities. Heritage is self-knowledge, and self-knowledge is the most profound source of self-worth. The best method of empowerment is recognizing and resuscitating what's been lost: culture, language, religion, land, self-determination. That is the foundation of the Jewish state, isn't it? Putting aside how that recognition has been abused in Israel, it is doubtless the most successful cultural revival in modern history—a revival widely supported by the white Western world. The racist double standard needs no explaining.

"Looking back at it now, do you think you were in a cult?" This was not an easy question to ask Ibrahim. It was even harder for him to answer.

Ibrahim leaned back in his chair and looked toward the shortbread cookies on his dining table. He sat with it awhile in the two-storey shanty he nailed together with the help of his father, brothers, and sons. His dutiful twelve-year-old, Omar, sat beside him quietly, looking as though he too was considering the question. It was one that the Chechev clan surely must have all asked themselves many times before, but maybe never aloud, as uttering the question was an answer in itself.

"*Si*," Ibrahim said. "Nafia had it in mind that he could experiment on new people, Indigenous people, with a distinct religion and new customs, as if he was making a 'superman.' We participated in everything that Nafia proposed," Ibrahim had told me. "We could not choose or think whether to do it or not. Nafia ordered everything that had to be done—even renting a house to live with another family—and we had to abide by those orders without question."

The emir would allegedly coerce members by citing the first half of the Verse of Obedience from the Quran: "Obey Allah and obey the Messenger and those in authority among you." (The second half reads: "Should you disagree on anything, then refer it to Allah and His Messenger . . . This is the best and fairest resolution.")

The teachings didn't always make sense to Ibrahim, who could not distinguish between the Islamic and the arbitrary, but they'd healed his father, their relationship, and elevated their family again. At least, they had once before. Nafia's fatwa on the Tzotzil language effectively meant Ibrahim could no longer speak with his parents.

Muhammad Chechev insisted on speaking Tzotzil. That, or his inability to speak anything else, grated on Ibrahim. He blamed his father for their estrangement. "I remember saying to my dad, 'I can't talk to you because you're indigenous and I'm Muslim, so disappear from my sight,'" Ibrahim recalled with palpable shame. "I broke off my relationship *with my father.* Nafia had shaped me as he wanted."

"Why did you stay?" I asked.

Leaving was difficult for many reasons. For one, he grew up believing he was the prodigal son on account of his grandfather's prophecy before dying. Breaking with Nafia after vouching for him to elders was an admission of his failure to live up to his predestined greatness. He also feared being shunned like Yahia's loyalists after their break. Most of all, he was afraid of what it would do to his marriage.

In 2001, Ibrahim married a Spanish immigrant named Yanna, the daughter of Nafia's top aide, whom he'd been in love with since adolescence. In 2007, her mother left the cult and returned to Spain, maintaining minimal contact with Yanna. If Ibrahim left too, would Yanna have to choose between her father or her husband? If she divorced Ibrahim, would Nafia allow his children to have a relationship with their father? If she stayed, would their children have a relationship with their grandparents?

"It was total slavery," said Ibrahim. His faith in God waned. He blamed himself for bringing Nafia into his family's lives and locking Yanna into an impossible situation. "I owe everything to her for supporting me," he said. "She was like my doctor, my psychologist."

Yanna convinced him to seek out Islam for himself in Granada. Yanna accompanied him there and set him up with family before Ibrahim set out on his own to tour mosques across Spain, North Africa, and the Middle East. The abundance of Sufi orders and Muslim traditions stunned him. None were perfect, but he'd learned that it is best to collect the positive to bring home to San Cristóbal, where he made his break with Nafia official. His family became expuldo yet again, but this time it was by choice.

Ibrahim's and his brothers' families joined Yahia's parish. They raised funds to construct their own mosque in this shantytown founded by the Zapatista rebels. A Muslim architect in the capital volunteered to design it. Named Al Kausar, "the Place of Abundance," it's undoubtedly one of the sturdiest buildings around. But of course it did not end well.

The Sunni financiers, said Ibrahim, had fundamentalist leanings that he found arrogant, sexist, and oppressive, while his personal convictions increasingly moved toward the liberal traditions of the Ahmadi order. Ibrahim had become close with the Guatemala Ahmadiyya office after it had invited him to give a sermon about Islam in Latin America. He began to host Ahmadi missionaries in San Cristóbal, but their doctrine rankled his orthodox relatives. Unlike Ismailis, who as a rule maintain exclusivity, Ahmadiyya take an opposite approach of active recruitment. Dawah, the call for others to embrace Islam, is a central tenet of the Ahmadiyya and the primary source of its growth in the Western world. Evidently it's also the reason Ahmadis face more violence and slander than possibly any other Muslim group.

After the fourth invitation to Al Kausar Friday prayer, Yahia allegedly snapped at Ibrahim and his guests. He told them that "the mosque was for Salafis, Sunnis, Sufis, but not Ahmadiyya. *Find another mosque.*" According to Ibrahim, Yahia had humiliated them just as Nafia had humiliated his orthodox Sunni guests years prior. (Yahia initially agreed to participate in this book, but multiple attempts at following up in person and later by phone failed. I never got his side of the story.)

"I was so angry I could hit him," said Ibrahim, continuing his story. "But the Ahmadi imam calmed us down and said our religion is to unite and forgive people, not to confront. If Allah wills it, we will have a new mosque." The Ahmadi imam thanked the congregation for letting them pray in their mosque and left. Ibrahim followed, and so did his brothers and parents eventually. Expelled for a third time, they set about turning their father's former church into a holy place again.

I asked Ibrahim why the family rift continued to fester if Islam's greatest virtue, in his view, was unconditional forgiveness. On one hand, he told me, "Islam calls for forgiving those who offend you. It's what keeps families together. You can get angry but you have to forgive your brothers and your people." On the other hand, he said, "The other community of Muslims don't consider us real Muslims. They say we pray to India, not to Mecca, and they think we have a different Quran."

Things were improving naturally, Ibrahim reassured me. The previous Ramadan, Yahia attended a party outside their Ahmadiyya mosque. They chatted awhile, but Yahia never entered the prayer hall. Mutual acceptance was still a distance away.

Ibrahim said he doesn't have any resentment, but his resistance to Yahia suggested otherwise. While I'm not one to judge a family feud—I've seen my share—a difference of opinion over the identity of the messiah seemed too insignificant to warrant a five-year rift. After all they'd been through together, it saddened me that religion, once again, had become a force of division.

Friday prayer attendance at the Ahmadiyya mosque was small. Ibrahim arrived with Yanna and their children. His brothers and their families attended too, though of course they live on the compound. And Ibrahim's parents were there also. A few other relatives were present, though obviously not his cousin, Imam Yahia. Salat al-Jumah was a family affair in every sense of the term, but it was still more people than who gathered at Mezquita Imam Malik, one of the Americas' most luxurious mosques, at least judging from the empty parking lot across the road.

Ibrahim entered the pink prayer hall wearing a suit and brown beret. He carried a book titled *Salat* under his armpit and flashed a smile at Yanna, sitting directly behind me wearing a bonnet and light scarf. Everyone was dressed their best, just as they would at any sabbath, regardless of the day of the week. Kids were everywhere, small ones goofing around and throwing tantrums and exceptionally well-behaved ones who knew instinctively that a temple is sacred.

I stood beside Omar, who appeared wise beyond his years. I wonder if Muhammad, Ibrahim's dad, ever looks at Omar and sees flickers of his prodigal son? Though early in his sixties, he carried himself with frailty and the solemnity of a grand elder. Despite all the vices he'd used to try to heal his trauma—despite the temper, drinking, and abusive behaviour—Muhammad was always a man in search of the Creator. He must surely have an eye for any sign of It in someone.

Ibrahim's son and I stood out amongst the congregation. We were the only two males over 5'3" and lighter in our complexion. We were two Omars born into an alien world, a place where the customs of our homes do not always match those in the rest of society. We stood shoulder to shoulder and prostrated in concert. What nobody else knew was that the Junior Omar (and not his dad) was leading the Senior Omar in prayer.

Even after praying in at least two dozen mosques all over the hemisphere, I'd still not memorized anything past the Fatiha or the meaning of the opening verse. I don't know if that's also true of Ibrahim's son—he seemed intelligent enough to have at least looked up the words he says five or more times a day in a Spanish translation book—but I was quite confident that there were others just like me, speaking to God in ways we still don't fully understand.

I talked to the other Omar briefly after prayer. We sat around a long communal table that had been set up for lunch, though occasionally he would leave to help prepare the fragrant meat stew brewing in a gigantic firepot. His freckles blared in the sun.

"What's it like for you growing up a Muslim in a Christian community?" I asked him.

Omar giggled and admitted it's a little strange. "When they ask, 'Why are you Muslim?' I say, 'I was born this way,'" he said with a shrug. Islam makes him feel a little bit special, just as it did with me at his age.

"Does it remind you of your Spanish heritage, from Europe?"

"Not really," he said. The romance of Andalusia was meaningless to him. His religious pride comes from personal conviction. I admired him for that, given the fragility of my own spiritual certainties. *Is there a God? Probably not, but who could be so sure. Nothing can come of nothing, but the fact that there is something instead of nothing? That's something. Is something a God? Who could be sure when all we know as humans is a droplet of the known universe. But, damn, is it ever neat to be alive enough to love.*

That, in a nutshell, is the depth of my faith, and such "convictions" are nowhere near as resilient as his must be.

Ibrahim's brother and nephew began to serve lunch. They started with the elderly and worked themselves around the table by age. Flor advised me to put away my notebook out of respect for the sabbath meal. I was more than happy to. The cabbage and meat stew looked delicious. I polished off my bowl with fresh tortillas stacked across the table—"monkey's food"—feeling the warmth of this family's hospitality. By the end of my trip, I felt much more like a guest of the family than a researcher, and I was even a little relieved that our original plans to go to Guatemala fell through. This was kind of what I needed after fifteen straight days of travel and missing a quarter of Noe's first eighteen months of life. I wanted to run back to her every time I saw Ibrahim twirl his second littlest by the hands and hum a little song to her.

I sat in the centre seat between the men and women. Once the plates were cleared, I talked to Yanna beside me, getting into some heavy stuff while an infant tried wiggling free of her arms.

Yanna didn't realize how controlling Nafia really was until marrying into Ibrahim's family. She was too adventurous to see the problems or understand why it was such a scandal when she "ran off" with Ibrahim for a day trip through the countryside on horseback. Her parents were strongly against the marriage. Nafia helped arrange it. He must have thought himself such a generous and great man too when he apparently took Ibrahim aside on the week of their wedding and told the groom that he would soon marry another wife.

Nafia's enticement of polygamy never sat well with her either. She thinks her father's "request" for a second wife destroyed her parents' marriage. Since she and her father, presumably sitting one hundred metres away in the other mosque, still don't speak, the twenty people around the table are what's left of her family in Mexico.

Although Nafia was directly responsible for so much damage to her family, his worst cruelty was inflicted on children. Even before Yanna was a teacher, she noticed that her children and her in-laws' children were getting different qualities of education at the Muslim school that Nafia directed. "The non-Indigenous"—and by that, Yanna means her own children—"were very advanced." She apparently asked Nafia about the disparity. "He said that they had to prioritize the children with the most potential." She was horrified.

Yanna told me that being disowned helped her appreciate the experience of the expuldo, having to create a whole new life because of powerlessness. And yet she feels the freest she's ever been. "The Ahmadi respect the level of compromise you need to accept Islam," she told me with some translation help from Flor. "You can learn it at your own pace," she added. By that, I think she meant that you are allowed to interpret God's message for yourself.

I'm not sure if Yanna would call herself a feminist—the question was too trite for asking—but her values obviously were. Something she loves about being with Ahmadiyya is that as a woman, you are expected to participate in religious and public life. Yanna sits on a women's council that organizes and provides community work in Spanish Latin America. The Ahmadi order might be a better fit for her in-laws too. Maya women are accustomed to being income drivers with their crafts. Now, free of Nafia, they can pursue their own family income again.

I looked at Ibrahim and his father at the head of the table. With English and Spanish fluttering all around Muhammad, the old man mostly kept to himself while Ibrahim talked to male relatives. Every once in a while, though, Muhammad had something to say. When he did, Ibrahim always stopped his other conversation to hear his father speak. Often he shared that message.

Seeing them together reminded me of being with my father. Growing up, I knew we were similar in our stubbornness. He must have recognized this too, because he seemed to give me more independence than my older siblings. But he also disciplined me more than my siblings, though never because of our religious differences. It always came about from a failure of judgment and character.

I think the same was true of the Chechevs. Ibrahim says religion got between him and his father the first time, when Ibrahim was a skeptical teen done with his father's serialized Christian messages, and the second time, when Muhammad was done with the cult. But, really, it was about each other's judgment and character. Muhammad had become a drunk wife abuser; Ibrahim had adopted a false father and had transferred Nafia's tyranny onto the man who raised him.

These are not about differences in belief; they're short-circuits in the souls of otherwise good men. But looking at them now, I found it hard to imagine peace was ever lost between father and son or would ever be lost again.

I checked up on Ibrahim a little less than a year later, just before the COVID-19 outbreak. Unaware of what was ahead, our conversation turned to reconciliation with the other half of his clan. He and Yahia were working on it. They'd already begun sharing meals together as a family again. What could be better than that? Reuniting the mosques seemed trivial in comparison.

Even if you can't see the family lore sparkling inside Ibrahim, it's obvious that he's an exceptional leader. He acted as if he was in charge of people's comfort, not the other way around. His soft confidence and firm kindness made him trustworthy.

Although I never met Nafia, I doubted he was as gifted a leader. He was persuasive, of course, though how much of that was class privilege? Regardless, he has barely held on to anyone he persuaded. Anyone can be a shaykh or call themselves emir. It takes a talent for diplomacy to be a true leader. It takes tolerance and solicitude.

12

Northern Calling
The Midnight Sun Mosque
(Inuvik, Northwest Territories)

*S*mack dab between the Arctic Circle and Arctic Ocean, the town of Inuvik is both new and ancient. Inuit survived on the coastline's massive game and fish since the eleventh century, but Inuvik as a municipality is sixty years old. Before it was a boomtown, it was a Government of Canada project, an administrative centre for Inuvialuit people to replace the previous centre that was terribly prone to floods and erosion. Comprising several Inuit, the Inuvialuit society had been neglected for centuries until the abundant discoveries of oil and gas.

Now thanks to arctic air travel, the boomtown is also a tourist town. People come from all over just to drive across the 200 kilometre ice highway to Tuktoyaktuk (which everyone agrees to just call "Tuk"), but typically stop within 50 kilometres of the town to take a selfie posing next to the ARCTIC OCEAN sign. And that is exactly how I stumbled onto the mosque on the edge of the Earth. It's probably one of the only mosques that's famous enough to get listed as a destination in a hotel pamphlet, yet I had never heard of the Midnight Sun Mosque.

It was this happy accident, and the following two days, that propelled me to write this book. I arrived in April 2017, after enduring
the most intense twelve months of my life. It all happened so fast:
Janae and I bought a house, Trump won his nomination, I separated
from Janae, Trump won the election, Janae and I reconciled with each
other, the Quebec Mosque City shooting happened, and our daughter
was conceived. These were simultaneously the happiest and scariest
days of my life, and all that nervous energy demanded a purpose.

I knew I wanted to help normalize Muslim people in the Christian
world, to show that they are no better or worse than everyone else,
but equally accountable and influential. I just hadn't figured out the
approach. You could say, I was looking for God—not searching, more
like waiting for a signal in the new normal. I continued on with the
routines of freelance writing, a life that basically looks the same every
day until something exciting lands in your email.

We didn't know Janae was pregnant when a luxury car magazine
asked me to take the road trip of a lifetime. We just found out a few
days before I set off to join a caravan of former racers and European
auto journalists. I landed in Inuvik with two days to prepare for our
1,300-kilometre trip from Tuktoyaktuk, Northwest Territories, to
Whitehorse, Yukon. With ice driving season about to close and the
paved replacement road to Tuk almost completed, we'd be amongst
the last humans on Earth to drive the famous road. Certainly, we'd be
the last to drive doughnuts over in Mercedes-Benz SUVs.

The assignment was, as the people say, "problematic." Most travel
writing *is* to some degree, but this one was glaring. Yet it's very hard
not to side with your privileges, especially when they're extraordinary,
and I would say that frolicking around the world, not in comfort but
excess, is an extraordinary privilege.

The trip went sideways almost immediately. White-out conditions
closed the Dempster Highway to the south until further notice. Ironically, the winter roads were mint, so we could get to Tuk, just not
Whitehorse in order to fly home. We spent our extra time in the islet
villages, while our handler figured out how to get everyone home.

As I had come from Edmonton, the "Gateway to the North," my

plans were the least complicated, so I wasn't so concerned. Stuck in one of the iciest towns on the planet, I zipped up my parka and ventured out of the hotel with a guidebook, and that's where I saw this:

> Among other things, Inuvik is home to the world's northernmost mosque. The Midnight Sun Mosque, affectionately called the Little Mosque on the Tundra, was built in Winnipeg before setting off on its 4,000 km journey to Inuvik in August 2010.

I had a vague recollection of the Midnight Sun Mosque's journey. A CBC radio program kept up with the temple's transport from Winnipeg, calling on all *ye* true Canadians to cheer an emblem of multiculturalism across land and water. Contrasted with the ferocious "Ground Zero mosque" coverage down south, the "Little Mosque on the Tundra" story fell into a journalism subgenre known as "meanwhile in Canada."

I remembered just enough to recognize its name in print. I made my way there gradually, stopping into businesses to fill my belly, buy some gifts, and, I hoped, learn more about who lives in Inuvik.

With a population of 3,200, Inuvik is only slightly bigger than my hometown High Prairie, but it was vastly more diverse. Oil and gas, and now tourism, drove a surprising number of immigrants to the edge of the Arctic. The staff of a Chinese diner included a Filipina hostess, Sudanese deliveryman, Chinese and Indigenous cooks, and a Palestinian server named Moe. I asked Moe about the mosque when he took my order. Moe had lived there for less than a year, so he didn't know much about it, only that it was there for him on Fridays and holidays. When he returned with my food, I invited him to sit with me. "How long have you lived in Canada?" I asked.

"Eight years but mostly in Edmonton," said Moe, sliding in and out of Arabic and English, or "speaking Arabisi," as we say.

"How did you end up so far north?"

Moe grew up in one of Lebanon's many refugee communities and had never gone far until his aunty sponsored him. She lived in Edmonton with her adult children, but her husband, Tayssir Kadri, lived mostly in Inuvik to run their family business—the Chinese restaurant. "Uncle Tayssir's lived here a long time," Moe said. Determined not to live anywhere colder than Edmonton, Moe initially resisted any opportunities to work alongside his uncle. But Alberta was a constant struggle for a man lacking in both education and skills. "I arrived eight months ago."

"So how are you finding Inuvik?" I asked.

"The people here are the best," he said enthusiastically. "In Edmonton, I couldn't order a coffee at Tim Hortons. If I got one word wrong, they would act like they don't know what I'm talking about. I came to Inuvik and learned all my English, a little bit every day, by talking with people here." It was the first time Moe felt that Canadians had taken interest in him.

Moe continued to sing the praises of northern Indigenous but quickly fell into some uncomfortable stereotypes. "Their hearts are great, like the people back home, but then they drink too much and swear at me." He shook his head reflectively, still in awe of his surroundings. "I studied native people at school in Lebanon"—he abruptly clapped the tabletop—"and now I'm here!"

I cringed, but kept my thoughts to myself. I resisted the urge to educate our newcomer on Canadian history and political correctness because I'd heard worse from well-intended relatives who've lived in Canada much longer than Moe. Working on my parents' understanding of systemic Canadian oppression has been a twenty-year project.

I doubt the lessons on the "natives" that they and Moe studied in Lebanon included modules on residential schools, the Indian Act, and the Sixties Scoop, a forced mass transfer of twenty thousand Indigenous children from their homes to adoptive white parents. If they did, then their upward mobility as immigrants has convinced them that such wounds are curable with grit. Despite coming from homelands shocked by violence and colonialism, they simply don't have a reference for genocide and intergenerational trauma of this scale.

Truthfully, my frame of reference is even further removed from that of my elders. In terms of the obstacles they faced with money, language, and racism, they have more in common with Canada's

Indigenous people than second-generation Canadians like me. Here in the Arctic, I wondered if the two groups, immigrants and Inuvialuit, had even more similarities in the resourcefulness required to thrive here.

Successful immigrants are supposed to symbolize our fair and just society, but there's an undeniable unfairness in their prosperity. It's true that they sacrifice much to reap stability and peace from the Arctic. However, these benefits are not always afforded to northern Indigenous people. That's very apparent in the Arctic communities marred by staggering rates of unemployment and suicide, sexual assault, and hunger. Infrastructure we "southerners" take for granted is underdeveloped and sometimes nonexistent for northerners. Even after the paved highway to Tuk is completed, thousands of other northerners will still have to rely on air travel to come and go.

After my encounter with Moe, I was more interested in the interfaith relations between Arctic Indigenous and immigrants. I stopped inside a home-based crafts shop. Mavis Jacobson, an Inuk local, runs it out of her living room with her son. Moose hide aroma filled the home. Glass cabinets displayed seal hats, beaded clothes, stone carvings, and sunglasses carved from whale bone, everything made by First Nations and Inuit. Jacobson grew up in Tuk, where her father worked as a bear monitor—protecting oil workers from Earth's largest land carnivore with a shotgun. She moved to Inuvik when she was twelve, compelled to continue her education at a residential school, one of the last to close (it has since been demolished).

Jacobson recalled her childhood in Tuk, where a favourite pastime was looking for artifacts. She still makes regular trips home to see her many family members, though they find themselves visiting Inuvik more out of necessity, and at a great cost. The end of the Tuktoyaktuk Winter Road was to be celebrated, not mourned. "It's going to be awesome for them. And for us, to visit more."

I told Jacobson I was curious about the mosque and the Muslim presence in general. She described the Muslims as the embodiment of the town spirit. "Last year, before school started, they gave every kid in

Inuvik a backpack. If there's a death, you see them sending someone
to give their condolences and ask if there's anything they can do. They
have a food bank that's open to everyone. I see them deliver food to
elders at their homes for free if they can't come to the food bank themselves. They went to Tuk a couple months ago with a big van and gave
food out to whoever needed it."

She said a Sudanese man named Abdalla looks after it. A cab company owner and driver, he's lived there for nearly as long as the Palestinian family. He's someone she trusts to help desperate elders who
need a lift but can't pay for it until pension day.

"Is he the one who built the mosque?" I asked.

Jacobson attended the mosque's grand opening community feast
and prayer, but far as she could tell, an entire community was behind it.

Moe's and Abdalla's families might actually be the first Muslims to
set roots in the tundra, arriving in the late 1980s and early 1990s. The
community ballooned soon after, largely because of their invitations
to friends and family from afar. But while the local immigrant community was the first to prosper and organize well enough to construct
a traditional mosque in the Far North, they're by no means the first
Muslims familiar with the Arctic. Beginning in the early 1900s, a network of Lebanese peddlers ventured into the Canadian territories on
river floats, selling their wares to Indigenous communities as they
drifted along. The traders learned how to communicate and navigate
from the local Indigenous populations, flying under the radar of the
Big Five companies that divvied up and monopolized the North.

White settler traders big and small villainized the foreign interlop-
ers. In *Memoirs of an Arctic Arab: The Story of a Free-Trader in Northern
Canada*, Bedouin Ferran, a legendary trader-turned-postman-turned-
lawmaker, better known as Peter Baker, recounted how competitors
and police called any Arab-owned store a "Jew store" and warned trappers from trading with them. "In those days, when anybody was called
a Jew, it meant 'outcast and despised,' because a Jew was a 'Christ-
killer.' I was called that most often," wrote Baker.

Baker became Canada's first Muslim elected to public office when he won a seat in the Northwest Territories' legislative assembly in 1964. He never married, never had children, and apparently enjoyed bachelorhood to the fullest until developing snow-blindness in his eighties. But Baker is the exception. Trading was a job, not a career, for most Arab bachelors in the Far North. Their goal was purely extraction. They wanted to succeed just enough to eventually be bought out by Hudson's Bay Company and forced into non-competitive contracts. With enough luck and grit, they could afford to open a brick-and-mortar store in warmer climes and begin their search for a bride.

It's still difficult to convince Muslim immigrant women to live with their husbands up North. What's changed is the economic prosperity of Arctic cities. Thanks to a diversity of rock and mineral mining projects, Inuvik jobs are often more stable, secure, and better paying than their southern city equivalents. One need not have a trade ticket or specialized skill to enjoy the gains of northern mining and construction booms. For the humble taxi driver or restaurateur, backbones of a much larger transient workforce, there's little incentive to leave, even if their partners live below the 60th parallel. In fact, the Arctic's living costs mean it's often cheaper to shelter and feed family far away to the south while they work in the north.

In just over a decade, the Muslim population grew from about ten to one hundred, mostly men. They include Sudanese, Somali, and Egyptians, virtually all of them displaced by war zones, despots, and failed states. Such national turmoil no doubt made the Arctic seem more hospitable and maybe equipped them with the survival instincts required of foreigners to endure nearly six months of straight darkness and snowstorms that routinely disable infrastructure. But it would be years before they could justify the funds, time, and energy it takes to build an Islamic centre.

For a few of the boom years, Inuvik's growing Muslim population held Friday prayers at the Igloo Church—literally, a Catholic church designed to resemble an igloo, ice bricks and all. As more Muslims settled in town, they pooled their funds to buy a trailer, not unlike the mosque of my childhood but in a mobile park. A simple crescent moon was painted above the entrance.

The informal Islamic centre wasn't designed for more than worship. Prayer rows were demarcated on a plain carpet with masking tape. Men took turns leading prayers and giving Jumah sermons. But the hall always filled to the shoe rack with worshippers.

An Egyptian imam visited the Inuvik congregation in 2008. Impressed by their industriousness, he encouraged the community to formalize a nonprofit society in order to build a mosque. Abdalla Mustafa Mohamed, the Sudanese cab driver mentioned earlier, led the effort from his own pocket, purchasing a double lot in town.

Land is relatively cheap in the hinterlands, but the costs of materials and labour are astronomical. A one-storey building with the most basic features would run them over half a million dollars. These immigrant families had found stability and success in the Arctic, but they were still working class. In addition, most pay two mortgages or rents in Canada—one for themselves and another for family members residing in the South. The Muslim Association of Inuvik, the charity they formed for the new mosque, would need outside funds. A community member reached out to a Saudi businessman in Winnipeg for help.

I called Hussain Guisti months after my Inuvik assignment. I learned that his Saudi heritage isn't what made him the perfect guy for the job. He'd built a little yellow mosque in Thompson, Manitoba, 800 kilometres north of Winnipeg, where he and his wife lived during her medical fellowship. The local construction costs were also extremely high, but Hussain found a cost-effective way to do it. He had it built in Winnipeg, then transported on the back of a truck. Inuvik Muslims wanted to know if the same could be done but for the 3,500 kilometres they needed—the same distance between Mecca and Rome.

"I'd never heard of Inuvik in my life," Guisti told me by phone. "I took out the map and said, 'Oh my goodness. This is a chance to make Muslim history.' I didn't care if I had to put the mosque on my shoulders and carry it up there myself. I was going to pull it off."

Guisti sincerely believed the call from Inuvik was a chance to fulfill an Islamic prophecy. He recited the hadith to me in English: "This

[the Prophet's] message will reach an area where nights overtake day."
He explained, "Nobody knew what this message meant, but now we
do. It's Inuvik. It's the only town that has a mosque where you have
thirty days of complete darkness and fifty-six of complete light. For
the non-Muslim world, it was the world's most northern mosque. For
the Muslim world, it's finally prophesying the Prophet's saying."

Actually, it's not the world's northernmost mosque. Both Hussain and the Inuvik tourist brochure are wrong. Much older and lavish mosques in Norilsk, Siberia, share that title. But a bigger issue is his
translation of a rather obscure hadith. More accurately it reads, "This
matter will reach what the night and day reach"—basically everywhere.

But I don't raise these points to nitpick. Rather, they reveal the
mindset of a man who was born in Mecca during the Islamic awakening. He revered Muslim commanders of the once-great empires and
accepted any hardships as God's will. His father died during his teens,
and Guisti, a trained physician, has not been able to work as a doctor
since arriving in Manitoba. "I believe there's a reason Allah didn't let
me practice," said Guisti, who ran a jumpy castle enterprise in Winnipeg. As he patiently waited for his true purpose to reveal itself, the Inuvik mosque wasn't just a project or prophecy; it was personal destiny.

Zubaidah Tallab Foundation, the charity Guisti had formed in
Thompson, took on fundraising efforts for Inuvik's mosque, but he
had three conditions. The mosque would welcome Muslims of all denominations, but communal worship itself would be in accordance
with Sunni tradition. The second condition was that Guisti's job would
be done the day the mosque opened. The Inuvik Muslim Association
would have to sustain operations afterward. The third was more of
a personal request: Guisti wanted to call the inaugural prayer. They
made a deal.

Funding and building the Midnight Sun Mosque in Winnipeg
was relatively simple, but transportation was a logistical nightmare.
The tail end of the highway to Inuvik was a bumpy dirt road with
four bridges far too narrow for the thirty-foot-wide, ten-tonne load.
It would have to travel the last 1,500 kilometres by barge, northwest
through the Mackenzie River to Inuvik. There were only three such

shipments per year, between May and September. But an unusually dry summer receded the Mackenzie coast, bumping up the last departure by three weeks. Builders were still hammering when the moving crew arrived for it in September 2010.

On the day it was supposed to arrive at the barge, the mosque was still 1,000 kilometres away. It got held up north of Edmonton for nearly three days due to Labour Day weekend traffic; the highway authority blocked it until the holiday was over. They hit another snag soon after resuming their journey. While trying to needle the very wide load through a creek bridge, the mosque started tipping sideways over the bridge. They stopped in time to save it, but now the mosque was buckled between the rails. A bulldozer came to its rescue. The barge company waited four extra days for the Midnight Sun to reach the shipyard, greeted by a crowd of locals who'd followed its journey on the news. A bigger crowd welcomed it on the Inuvik coast ten days later.

But there remained lots of work and nobody to do it. The few handymen amongst the congregation volunteered, though none had the slightest notion of how to build a dome or minbar. Enter Fathallah Farjat, a custom cabinet maker living in Hamilton, Ontario.

If there was any one man who built the Midnight Sun Mosque, it was Farjat. In his previous life, he'd renovated mosques in Jenin, Palestine, where he grew up in a refugee camp. He arrived in Canada in 2005. Despite living and working illegally (his asylum case was rejected), Farjat found great success as a carpenter. He was searching for a way to repay his good fortune when news of the Midnight Sun Mosque caught his attention.

Guisti paid for his flight to the North and Abdalla put him up in a room, but Farjat received no salary for the six weeks that he framed, drywalled, installed carpets and doors, built out a kitchen, and went to work on a pulpit and dome of his design. When someone floated the possibility of a minaret to him, "he didn't say, 'I've never done that before,'" Guisti recalled. "He said, 'No problem.'"

Forty days later, the Midnight Sun opened its doors to the whole town. Guisti's hands shook as he lifted them to his ears during the inaugural prayer. He sobbed through the first words of the call to prayer: *Allahu akbar, God is great.* His tears continued through its last words—*There is no god but God*—through the rest of the prayer and the next forty minutes. "It was an out-of-body experience," he recalled. "I felt like my feet weren't on the ground—the most powerful feeling of achievement I've ever had or will ever have."

The Midnight Sun might not be the world's northernmost masjid, as he initially believed, but in terms of distance from Mecca and accessibility, it's truly the *masjid al-aqsa* of the twenty-first century—that is, "the farthest mosque." It was not a conquest like its Jerusalem forebearer, but the Midnight Sun took on a similar mythic quality. It also inspired northern ummah to forge closer bonds with their non-Muslim hosts.

Back in Inuvik during my April 2017 assignment, I spotted the minaret on Wolverine Road. At thirty feet, it towered in the pigeon-blue sky, topped by a sickle-shaped moon that could eclipse the sun were the sun not so impossibly high. It had a green dome, though most of it was covered in snow. The mosque was small in size and ambitious in design, but the detached black trailer at the back of its parking lot stood out the most. A vinyl sign above the steel door read "Arctic Food Bank: A Muslim Welfare Centre Project."

The mosque's door was locked. Luckily, a taxi pulled in and out stepped a Sudanese man wearing an expedition jacket, polarized sunglasses, and sleek Bluetooth headset. He introduced himself as Abdul Azim Ahmed and asked if I'd come for midday prayers. I admitted to having no sense of the time anymore. He welcomed me inside anyway.

The Muslim community had taken great care to make the humble mosque evoke the feeling of one back home. The interior was decorated with a striped carpet, Islamic art, and abundant books. The mihrab was curved into the wall and furnished with a well-crafted pulpit.

I peered through a window into the enclosed women's section to discover it had apparently been transformed into a young man's apartment. He lay on a pile of pillows and blankets, wearing wool socks on his outstretched feet and a knit toque on his head as he aimlessly scrolled the internet on his phone. As I entered, he sat up and shook my hand from his spot on the floor.

"Brother Jabriel," said Abdul Azim, "this is Brother Omar from Edmonton."

The three of us sat on the floor and talked. Jabriel, a twenty-three-year-old Somali Canadian, had arrived from Vancouver a few days earlier, looking for work. "I met this woman in B.C. She said she would get me a job at a mining camp in the Beaufort Delta," he said, referring to the broader Inuvik region. Jabriel was vague on the woman's identity, just as he was on the details of his plan. After spending almost two thousand dollars on a flight to Paulatuk airport, 400 kilometres northeast, Jabriel learned that position had been filled by the woman's relative. "She said, 'Go to Inuvik. You'll find a job there.'"

Jabriel barely had enough for the forty-five-minute flight, let alone a hotel priced for corporate rates and peak tourist season. As he walked from hotel to hotel, the minaret caught his attention. "I was surprised to see the mosque here," he said. "I came right away. I came in to pray, and I was just, like, home."

"And you're living at the mosque?"

"I don't have anywhere to stay," he said. "I'm going to start working tomorrow, maybe, at this store downtown. Many of the Muslims work there. They said they needed some kitchen help, making sandwiches and stuff. It's minimum wage, but it's still more than I was making in Vancouver. If I start tomorrow, inshallah, they'll move me into a room at one of their houses."

"I know it's only been a few days, but how are you finding Inuvik so far?" I asked.

"It's cold," he said flatly, "but I'm mostly dealing with my patience, holding on to hope for as long as I can. Everything will hopefully fall into place."

"Inshallah," I said, trying to inflect the tone my mom uses when she's being hopeful, not dismissive. "Do you think you'll stay long?"

"If it's good. And I'm going to move my family here and we'll all work together—inshallah, inshallah." Jabriel couldn't help but get ahead of himself with optimism. His mom and sister were in Vancouver, his brother with a family of his own in Ottawa, all struggling to make ends meet. "I dream of uniting with my siblings together in some sort of business."

"Would they really want to live here?"

"Well," he said, laughing, "summer's coming in—so it's a good time to trap them."

I turned my attention to Abdul Azim. Both Jabriel and I had lots of questions for our Muslim elder about life near the northern pole. How does one schedule the five daily prayers when dawn, midday, afternoon, sunset, and night are compressed to a few hours? How does one fast from sunrise to sunset when the sun neither rises nor sets? The latter became a moral predicament for the community in 2014 when the Islamic lunar calendar set Ramadan at the height of summer. The Assembly of Muslim Jurists of America, a moderate body of qualified Islamic scholars catering to the specific needs of Western Muslims, had already issued a fatwa permitting them to fast and pray on the Meccan clock when day and night are indistinguishable, but old-timers, who'd been going by Edmonton time for many years, thought it was a cop-out. Of course, some of the newest members of the community, which had doubled in size within a few years, thought Edmonton time was weak. They were prepared to abstain from food and water for the full twenty-two hours of daylight.

The individual practices of those fasting until 7:00 p.m., 10:00 p.m., and 2:30 a.m. made it difficult to bring them together—the very thing Ramadan was designed to do. "We asked a scholar for help," said Abdul Azim. "They gave us the option to choose, go by the nearest big city with a sunset (Edmonton) or follow Mecca time. We got together at the mosque and decided to follow the time of Saudi Arabia. Now we break fast even before my wife and daughter in Alberta."

"Sounds like a bit of a cheat," I said, recalling my last fasting attempt, on the first day of Ramadan 2005, which I surrendered at Wendy's before noon.

"I think I'm going to do Ramadan up here," joked Jabriel.

There was one other quirk at the northern mosque, one too subtle for me to see: the qibla did not face east like every other Western mosque I'd ever visited or would soon visit. Rather, it pointed due north, over the Pole, the shortest path to Mecca.

Hussain Guisti had set out to make Islamic history, and in a small but not insignificant way he did. When Prophet Muhammad redirected the qibla from Jerusalem, he never fathomed a civilization on the other side of the Earth, let alone one that would return his message to Mecca across the northern axis. There was no precedent for the Midnight Sun's advancement. No hadith or fatwa. It was adapted on the suggestion of an engineer in the Inuvik Muslim group. In other words, it came about by *ijtihad*—independent jurisdiction—and it has set a template for thousands of other worshippers above the 60th parallel.

From Fairbanks, Alaska, to Iqaluit, Nunavut, seven new mosques opened in a decade. Because the jamaat are too small and multicultural for segmentation, the mosques cater to everyone with English sermons. Culture also affects the architecture. For instance, South Asian Muslims, who are most prominent in Iqaluit, have more liberal views on women's roles in the community and thus designed the women's section of their mosque to be larger, run side by side with the men's. It can offend immigrants unaccustomed to women coming to worship, let alone standing in their sight line. But if anything, these multiethnic, multidenominational temples only emphasize how small their differences really are.

Abdul Azim's phone suddenly belted out a digital adhan. He excused himself, making no assumption that we'd join him. He returned to his spot on the floor next to Jabriel ten minutes later, still in his heavy outerwear. "I don't think you're getting to Whitehorse," he told me. "Sometimes the roads are closed for two days."

I was fine with that. I wanted to get to know my hosts better. I asked Abdul Azim about the logistics of supporting a family in Calgary, securing Arab and African staple foods, and the exorbitant cost of living. I might have watched the light in Jabriel's eyes extinguish as our host explained that virtually everything is imported but fish and game meat. The cost of a gallon of milk is $11—more when fuel prices spike, he told us. "That's why we started the food bank."

"I noticed!" I said. "Am I able to see it?"

"You'll have to call Brother Abdalla. He has the keys."

This marked the third mention of the same Sudanese cab driver in one day. Obviously Abdalla Mustafa Mohamed was legendary up here.

I'd soon learn that he arrived in Edmonton in 1989 with a degree in English from the University of Khartoum in Sudan. He applied successfully to the University of Alberta for a master's in linguistics, and then took a job in Inuvik to earn money for tuition. Abdalla never returned. In 1994, he established a pirate ambulance business, since no emergency medical services existed within 800 kilometres. He soon realized the lack of another essential service: taxis. He attracted a network of fellow Sudanese immigrants who now dominate the taxi business, making up a small majority of Inuvik's Muslims.

Abdul Azim called Abdalla on his Bluetooth. "He's already on his way," he said, tapping his earpiece to hang up. Not five minutes later, I heard the snow crunch under tires directly outside the window. A man with hair white as the landscape entered the prayer hall with a hearty "Salamu alaykum." I got up to shake his hand, pulled on my parka, and followed him to the trailer.

Abdalla coordinates with the Muslim Welfare Centre in Scarborough, Ontario, to ship $35,000 in groceries, clothes, and household items three times per year. Locals can pick up supplies once every two weeks, as needed, so long as they're registered. About seven hundred families are registered to benefit from the bank, some driving two hours each way to feed their families. At any given time, one-quarter to one-third of the immediate area's residents rely on the Muslim Welfare Centre's charity.

"We get minimal donations here," said Abdalla, searching for his keys. "People, they try, but there are two types here: the local who doesn't have anything to give or the people who come to work and, soon as they land, realize the cost of living is so high."

"And this is the town's first food bank?" I asked, finding it hard to believe. The closest comparable one, he said, was a one-woman operation, a Good Samaritan who collected and distributed canned foods from a shed, charging $10 per ration to keep it running.

Abdalla pushed open the door, revealing shelves across every wall stacked with groceries, winter gear, and cooking supplies. "We give sugar, we give rice, we give boxes of KD [Kraft Dinner]." He pointed at the bulk inventory items running the length of each shelf, neatly placed like a grocer hyperspecialized in a dozen products. There were three types of soup and one type of oil, flour, and high-temperature pasteurization milk. "And on top of that," he said, opening a deep freezer in the centre of the room, "chicken."

I peeked inside at mounds of vacuum-sealed poultry stickered with a halal label. Around Ramadan, the freezers fill with plentiful *qurbani* meat—lamb, goat, and beef that Muslims who can afford it are obligated to sacrifice and distribute to the needy during Eid al-Adha. Only one time did my father and his friends actually attempt this, each chasing a scrappy lamb around the backyard with a blade while the farmer who supplied them watched horrified. My mom worried I'd have nightmares forever, but luckily, I was too young to form such a traumatic memory. Now my parents do as most other Western Muslims: they pay a couple of hundred bucks to a butcher—maybe the same butcher in Edmonton supplying Inuvik's needy.

When the Arctic Food Bank opened in 2015, hunters offered their oversupply of game meat, but the food bank supplies only halal food. "Whenever we find a hunter, we support them with a nominal fee, for their gas and work, to get caribou, moose, reindeer," Abdalla explained. "We just ask them, don't kill the animal with the shot—face it to the qibla, cut the two jugular veins, and say, 'In the name of Allah.' That's all." Inuit hunters have their own sacrificial practices, so it's rare that someone takes them up on the offer. Still, they never turn down fresh trout and pike from local fishermen in summer.

I wondered if the food bank had other intentions. Was it also a proselytizing tool, like any number of Christian missions in sub-Saharan Africa? Orthodox Islam teaches that dawah is obligatory. While there are different interpretations of dawah, the most common, to invite non-Muslims to learn the Quran's teachings, seemed to me highly inappropriate given our surroundings.

Abdalla and I stood one mile from the former site of Grollier Hall, a residential school where Roman Catholic teachers traumatized generations of Inuvialuit and Gwich'in Dene. They snatched children from their families, cultures, and beliefs. They sometimes taped their mouths shut for speaking in their mother tongues and sexually exploited them at will. Proselytizing any foreign religion, regardless how congenially, could not make up for the scars left by another of the world's major religions.

Abdalla assured me that preaching Islam was not the Inuvik Muslim Association's kind of dawah. Rather, they teach Islam by trying to be model citizens. "Our motto here is just giving back to community, whether as Muslim or as immigrant," he said. "We are saying we are part of the Canadian Muslims, we have a masjid—*alhamdu'lillah*—we are here, we have a food bank, this is who we are."

An Inuk converted after marrying a Somali widower who'd lost his family in war; they now live in Yellowknife with seven children of their own. There was another young Indigenous man who also took shahada. He came for a few Friday prayers, but hadn't been back for some years. Abdalla still saw him around town and at the food bank, where he collected his biweekly needs. The young man understood he was always welcome at the mosque again, but Abdalla never pushed it. Whatever his needs are, they are bigger than faith.

There were Muslims who objected to the food bank, Abdalla said. They had a bootstrap mentality and believed the free supplies would "spoil" the needy, allowing them to waste more money on drinking and gambling. Abdalla strongly disagreed. "Most of the social problems you see in poor communities, whether alcoholism, addiction, it's presented as a symptom of a larger problem," he said. "Lack of education, lack of opportunity, and these are the same things you'd see in a third-world country. In Sudan, it's the same."

Abdalla closed up the freezers and locked the door behind us. He offered to drive me back to my hotel in his taxi. "It must have surprised you to see some of the same social problems you'd left behind in Sudan," I said once he pulled out of the driveway.

"That's true; it was a little overwhelming at first," he admitted. Abdalla never imagined Canadians living in similar conditions,

sometimes without clean water or toilets, and he never imagined residential schools. He got a dose of reality with his first job in Inuvik:
as a teacher's aide at Grollier Hall seven years before it was closed
and eventually demolished. The school had long rooted out its abusers
and Roman Catholic administration, operating as a standard public
school. But the effects were clear to him whenever he ventured into
town. "The image you have as someone from the Third World, you
think Canada is paradise until you come and face reality. You don't
think there's discrimination, neglected people, people who can't read
and write. You won't envision it. You won't comprehend it, until you
realize, well, they are just a normal human being, and there's a lot of
things that happened in their life."

By allowing himself to be absorbed into Indigenous, and not settler Canada, and by becoming a vital member of it, Abdalla had earned
both the Inuit's knowledge and welcome. I asked if that's why he's so
charitable. But Abdalla said his motivations were far more pragmatic.

"To reach the afterlife," he said, "charity—*sadaqah*—is one thing
that Allah—*subhanahu wa ta'ala* [the most glorified, the most high]—
recommended to us. Not to pray, not to fast, but charity." In Arabic, he
quoted a chapter from the Quran that translates to, "Whatever good
you give, shall be rendered back to you, and you shall not be dealt with
unjustly."

"So that's number one," he continued. "Number two, we are here
in the community, and I don't think we are just here to work as a taxi
driver and leave. This is our legacy, our *dïn* [creed]. This is who we
are, and if we are able to do anything for anyone at any point in time,
we should not hesitate, especially if, like Allah said, it will benefit the
community. That's all what it is. If you treat people well, they treat
you well. If you make charity, you won't have enemies."

There was a third, final reason. Abdalla just wanted to give back
to the land that gave him the only thing he's ever wanted: peace. "Life
is easy here."

Abdalla had word-for-word repeated something I'd heard my parents say many times: *Life is easy here.* It is the purest form of acknowledging your privilege, words wrung from a former life way beyond

here. It is *easy* to exist *here* on a Christian continent, where you may be a stranger to most, including your children, and constantly feel misunderstood. But Abdalla seemed to mean it in a different way. It was more personally pronounced, that *his* Canadian life is easy, but life is not easy for every Canadian.

I thanked him for the ride and returned to my hotel room. The next morning, I checked in at the single-terminal airport and dragged my carry-on to a chair. Jabriel sat across from me, wearing the same sweatpants and black shirt from the previous day.

"You changed your mind?" I asked.

"I don't think I can stay here," he said.

I don't know where he found the money for a ticket to fly back to his family on short notice. The question was too personal to ask at the time, but maybe he would share in correspondence. Unfortunately, he never replied to my emails, and his phone line was soon disconnected. I couldn't track him down anywhere online. So I'm left to guess.

From the moment Jabriel saw the minaret, the brothers had looked after him like an old friend. They did whatever they could to make him feel at home, even if it meant sending him away. While that's not a generosity I'd expect any jamaat to offer an anonymous wayward youth, it seemed completely feasible of this one jamaat that relies so heavily on a true brotherhood—that is, actually treating the "brother" next to you like a brother.

Until my northern excursion, I'd never thought much about the people who built mosques. Who were they, and what was their signal to create a new holy place? I know now that some were driven by necessity, others by glory or spite. Some felt like they didn't have a choice.

Their only uniformity was a desire to feel at home. It was not always the case that they did. Over the next two or so years, as I set out researching this book and visiting extraordinary mosques and communities all over the Americas, I couldn't help but wonder what my place in all of this was. To my surprise, I did find a mosque that accepted me and my beliefs as they are.

13

Who Is Muslim?
El-Tawhid Juma Circle Unity Mosque
(Turtle Island)

The last thing I expected to see at Friday prayer was a bowl of packaged condoms. "Are you here for Unity Mosque?" the secretary asked. "It's in the boardroom down the hall."

Of the dozens of jamaat that I'd met since 2017, none were as adaptive, alternative, and radically inclusive as el-Tawhid Juma Circle, better known as Unity Mosque. The prayer hall is discreet and nomadic, roving between borrowed spaces to protect its many lesbian, gay, transgendered, two-spirited, and nonbinary worshippers—hence, why we had met inside a community centre in downtown Toronto. Other times they meet in high-rise offices, churches, conference halls, and living rooms, and sometimes it's all of those simultaneously.

More meme than mosque, Juma Circle groups organize in ten North American cities and inside bedrooms worldwide via Facebook Live. These Muslims in the Netherlands and Pakistan, the Middle East and the West Coast, set their clocks to Toronto time, prostrating in all directions toward the same speck of Earth.

Some of the traditions will appear foreign to them, but that's true for everyone entering the prayer space for the first time. It's a mix of so many different traditions—including Indigenous—that together can challenge anyone's comfort zone. *Would it also challenge mine?* I wondered as I turned away from the bowl of condoms toward the prayer space.

Often called the "gay mosque," members prefer "inclusive mosque." You do not have to be queer or Muslim to join a Juma Circle, but you do have to prove yourself an ally to an exclusive Facebook group with two thousand members.

Unity Mosque's cofounder, El-Farouk Khaki, pointed me toward this private group before I could obtain the secret address. To access the group, I answered a questionnaire about my opinions on three major issues:

Am I comfortable with the notion of women or nonheterosexual people leading my prayer? Yes.

Am I comfortable praying with mixed genders, denominations, and people who do not necessarily identify as Muslims? Definitely, yes.

What's my opinion on Black Lives Matter, environmental stewardship, and Indigenous self-determination movements?

I filled it out and applied, thinking that I may have finally met my people. But when I started to read members' comments and look at their photos, I had good reason to question that assumption. The most engaged members revealed themselves to be refugees, immigrants, and outcasts—people who may not actually prefer the Unity Mosque but who need it for safety and well-being.

Stepping inside the mosque on that Friday in late February, I had a feeling I'd be the most privileged person in the jamaat, which really is not that unusual for a Canadian-born, middle-class, straight, and straight-passing male. Unless I met another able-bodied straight dude, who was also one shade lighter than caramel and an inch taller than Tom Cruz, I would probably be *that dude*. I'd likely take up more space regardless, because Imam Khaki had permitted me to document the circle and interview willing members.

The first person I met had been in Canada barely one month. A young Swahili-speaking man, it was his first time attending, so we were equally confused about how the boardroom would transform into a musalla. There were no prayer rugs, and not all the tables and chairs had been folded away. With great difficultly, he asked me if I knew what to do.

"It's my first time too," I said.

He seemed nervous for a host of reasons, not the least of which might be his knowledge of what would happen to him if he were ever "found out" in his homeland. He'd left a country where police routinely entrap gay men with online sting operations.

One of the next people I met was a victim of those sting arrests, but in another country entirely. The Egyptian refugee claimant, who asked to go by "Ali," told me that the undercover cop was surprised to realize that Ali was not a cruiser looking for sex. "I just want to marry someone who practices their religion—fasts, prays, and at the same time is LGBTQ," said Ali, who spoke and carried himself like a gentleman.

The cop took pity on him. He advised Ali to deactivate and delete the dating app and hide any trace of him using it. Ali didn't listen because he wasn't committing a definable crime. There was no exchange of request for sex, let alone money. "I'm very proud of my religion as a Muslim, and I'd like to get married—it's my right."

Evidently it was not his right. The second time Ali was entrapped, police publicly arrested and jailed him for a night of insults and beatings. His parents still don't know the real reason he's six thousand miles away in Toronto. He won't tell them until his asylum case has been officially approved.

Ali was a returning member. He and the first few regulars gave direction for assembling the prayer space. We cleared aside tables and chairs to make room for a patchwork of yoga mats. Once our shoes were off, we overlaid the mats with an array of fabrics and prayer rugs, with one somewhat ornate rug as qibla for the imam.

Imam Khaki entered with a box of Timbits ("doughnut holes," for the un-Canadian). He unwrapped a purple scarf from around his neck and removed his reflective sunglasses quickly, like a *Miami Vice* character but brown and flamboyant. He tossed aside his green beret and attached a sequined West African–style kufi. He piled his winter gear on a table with the rest of ours and announced with a mouth full of doughnut, "Let's get settled here."

He set up the webcam while worshippers filled mugs of tea and brought them along to the floor. "Sit in a circle," said the imam. "That's you, Omar." I looked up from my ledger as I scribbled notes. The congregation was sitting around me—*the dude* literally at the centre of the room. Everyone had a good laugh as I scooted backward until the circle closed.

Finally, Imam Khaki could begin. "This is a sacred space, please refrain from using profanity. It's also a safe space," he said. We were to be mindful of the comfort of fellow worshippers and the community centre lending its boardroom.

He then read aloud the Unity Mosque's religious code of conduct. "Islam is *not* and has *never* been a monolith," he began. "Speak of your understanding of Islam without telling somebody else they are wrong. *Our* community is not monolithic."

He advised all to speak in terms of "my Islam," encouraged us to speak of God with a feminine pronoun to overcorrect an eternity of masculinizing our Creator, and discouraged us from using the word "Lord" (too feudalistic). On dress code: modesty is in the eye of the beholder. If you don't like what you see—too much or too little—refer to the Quran with instruction to "lower your gaze." Finally, he prepared us to accept the traditions of the people volunteering to call the prayer, lead it, or lecture afterward. "Don't be shocked or terrified by what you hear," he said.

Khaki happened to be in charge of this Friday sermon. He initiated it with an acknowledgment unlike any other I'd heard before:

I begin by acknowledging that Allah created humanity in and of this earth as our khalifa, and that the land that we are on has been inhabited continuously for over fifteen thousand years. To end systemic and institutional violence we must centre the narratives of Indigenous people in our struggles for dignity and justice. Those of us who are not indigenous to Turtle Island, especially those of us who are settlers or settler descent, directly benefit from occupation, colonization, and genocide of Indigenous people's land.

He acknowledged how kidnapping, forced and indentured labour, slavery, and occupation of Indigenous people everywhere benefited settlers. And beyond recognizing the traditional stewardship of the region's six First Nations, he acknowledged it is also the home of the red tail hawk, the grey squirrel, the red fox, "lots of raccoons," white-tailed deer, bats, and "many insects and other species," and paid respects to First Nation elders who might be present metaphysically or otherwise. Winding down, he added: "Let's remember that we are guests on this land. And we need to be better guests."

Sometimes, the imam invites a First Nation elder to smudge the room and offer the acknowledgment. Regardless, this was the first time I'd heard one from a non-Indigenous person that sounded heartfelt and teachable.

Khaki, I quickly realized, took time to educate worshippers as few other faith leaders do. He dedicated his Black History Month khutba to the debt that's owed to Black Muslims. His speech began with a brief history of Islam in the Americas. He noted how a few "enumerated" Europeans made it into the Canadian encyclopedia as the country's "first Muslims," instead of any one of the many anonymous Muslim Africans who'd probably crossed the same port centuries earlier. Bringing us to the present day, Khaki quoted from Malcolm X's biography with as much zeal as he quoted the Quran. He finished and cleared the qibla rug to make space for a Black woman to lead us in prayer. Her words were familiar yet foreign in their femininity.

There was something delightfully new and fringe about this gathering. We were twenty-seven people standing equally like the teeth of a comb. On my right, a Jewish man, on my left a woman muezzin, and behind me a South Asian mother and son, and an elderly white woman who could have been with Code Pink. Khaki stood at the back, giving a hearty *takbeer* each time our imam said God is Great.

Praying alongside these strangers felt like bearing witness to a new branch of Islam, or maybe an ancient version of it. We were brought together by eccentric reformists, outcasts of various tribes forced to negotiate with each other's differences, ignorance, and experiences before we could unify around a notion of equity.

———

"Inclusive Islam," as Khaki and his peers call it, has no distinguished leader or written philosophy, but it's evolving into a definable practice called the "Inclusive Mosque Initiative." It was coined by a feminist collective headquartered in London and made into ritual by mosques like Unity. However, my introduction to the initiative began at home in September 2017.

Junaid Jahangir, a professor at MacEwan University in Edmonton, was organizing a symposium for LGBTQ Muslims called Allah Loves Us All. I was as surprised as anyone else to read about it in a newspaper, though I was familiar with Jahangir. Aside from being an economics professor, he's a prominent gay Muslim, a prolific essayist, and an accomplished lay theologian. His analysis of the Quran and hadith for homosexual contexts made him a target of hate mail from extremist Muslims long before the conference was announced. The newspaper coverage had introduced him to a new kind of threat: Far Right racists. "They make for strange bedfellows," he told me as we sat in his office. "They're thinking in the binary. We're thinking in the intersection that you get to decide *who you are* and define *yourself.* Nobody gets to decide that for you."

Jahangir invited me to his office to parse scripture for any clear condemnation of homosexuality. "I'm an orthodox Sunni Muslim. We try to remain as close to the text as possible," he said, opening select verses of Quran.com into new and specifically sequenced tabs. Indeed, his scholarship covers ancient jurisprudence on many intimate acts, including marrying *jinn*. I skimmed *Islamic Law and Muslim Same-Sex Unions*, an academic book he coauthored with Hussein Abdullatif, an Alabama pediatrician. They may be lay theologians, but so were many influential Muslim scholars.

Jahangir was raised by Pakistani expats in Dubai. He devoured the Quran after his father taught him how to read it in classical Arabic. On the road to his economics PhD, he took elective courses on Muslim theology and served as a research assistant to an Islamic scholar. Though he writes for mainstream audiences from time to time, his scientific audience, he hopes, are textualists like him.

He's the first to admit that he doesn't have an answer for "everyone in the LGBTQ2S+ acronym." He finds many Gen Z perspectives to be genuinely incomprehensible. Muslim identity may be nonbinary, but gender identity is not according to traditional sources. "If you look at the Islamic texts, it's very binary," he said. "There is a male and a female, a father, a mother. Distinct roles and sacredness to these roles."

Jahangir praised young Muslim activists who promote same-sex rights and groups like Juma Circle creating safe and sacred spaces, but he felt serious and comprehensive analysis is lacking from the movement. It's one big reason why he believes that leaders of the inclusive movement are rarely offered to sit at the table with Muslim institutions. The Islamic Society of North America, a staid but still influential organization founded in 1963, publicly supports the rights of LGBTQ workers but has stopped short of fully accepting LGBTQ worshippers. Not until 2016 had the more progressive civil liberty groups CAIR and the National Council of Canadian Muslims begun condemning anti-gay bigotry, ever strategically, without explicitly calling for religious inclusion.

Jahangir's own efforts to engage with institutions have been ignored. Yet these are exactly the types of legacy institutions he hoped he'd reach with the Allah Loves Us All symposium. The Muslim Women's Council was the only one to accept his invitation to send one delegate.

"Why do you care so much about the interpretation of ancient texts?" I asked. "You're a modern gay man. Why does fifteen-hundred-year-old jurisprudence matter so much to you?"

Jahangir spun around in my direction and spoke with sincerity rare of academics. "We all search for identity in our life," he said. "'Who am I? What's my culture? Where do I come from?' For many of us, our identities are rooted in religion. For me, as a young boy growing up in the Middle East, these texts would appeal to me on an emotional level." Jahangir recalled the story of the Prophet's companions going hungry for days at a time to feed the resting traveller. "These texts affect you here," he said, patting his heart. "My values of patience, forgiveness, being the bigger person, they come from *that*. These texts become a part of you."

I heard my own thoughts in Jahangir's words. What brought me to his office were similar questions about my culture and origins, and a hope that I could reconcile my core scientific beliefs with Muslim parables I've always cherished and Muslim values that have shaped me.

Jahangir reverted to professor mode once scriptures were ready for dissection. It was important to start with the various jurisprudence, he said, and work backward through the Prophet's sayings and, finally, the Quran. He established that he would interpret in the Hanafi tradition, one of the four schools of thought, or *fiqh*, because it's most common and "more reason based." Afterward, he tossed out four books of hadith that he considered unreliable, which left us with two collections of sayings, *Sahih al-Bukhari* and *Sahih Muslim*. "These are the gold standard of hadith," he said.

Jahangir warned me that he was about to get sexually explicit with me. He now had my full and undivided attention.

He delved into Arabic semantics of vaginal and anal penetration; pedophilia and hebephilia; consensual adultery and non. Jahangir made an interesting case for why some Muslim cultures have precedent of male-to-male sex (though not always between two adults), and why, in some societies, homosexuality was an open secret. Jafar al-Sadiq, the sixth Shia imam, viewed homosexuality as a medical condition that could be cured with a severed camel's hump. What is clear is that early Hanafi jurists did *not* prescribe death for homosexuality.

"Do you know of any hadith that clearly accepts homosexual behaviour?" I asked.

"No."

"So either homosexuality is unmentioned, or it's mentioned *and* condemned."

"Yes. Our point of view is that the Prophet never addressed the issue."

"What does the Quran say?"

"The Quran is silent."

That was news to me. The Quran's version of Sodom and Gomorrah are similar to the Old Testament's, save for Prophet Lot (or "Lut") being an incestuous drunk. The important lesson from both is God's executive decision to smite the heathens for their indecent sexual acts. God's judgment, in verse 7:81, reads: "Indeed, you approach men with desire, instead of women. Rather, you are a transgressing people."

"This is the verse that a fifteen-year-old boy would be referred to by his imam if he had questions about his sexuality," said Jahangir.

"That doesn't sound very silent," I said.

"Only if you are cherry-picking."

Read as a whole chapter with contextual interpretation, Jahangir believed that the issue with the Sodomites was not that they were "men who have sex with men" but "men who have sex with men without any legal responsibilities." In other words, it would be different if they approached men, instead of women, with a legal contract for consensual intimacy.

"I don't think you can say that the Quran is silent," I persisted. "I think it's accurate that *some* people interpret the Quran to have no mention of homosexuality, positive or negative, and some people interpret this story—however vague—as explicit proof of condemnation." Jahangir was encyclopedic and earnest, but I had to wonder if he was cherry-picking from the exegesis himself in order to live with being a gay Muslim. "What do you say to people who accuse you of—forgive me for the analogy—trying to fit a square peg in a round hole?"

"We are all struggling with interpretation and the tradition," Jahangir said. "A secular person will say this is stupid. But to the faithful, the Quran is a dialogue. This is us wrestling with the dialogue, and we are not letting go." There has never been one way to read scripture—that's his point. He wants religious leaders to acknowledge the ambiguity. Reasonable doubt, he hoped, can open their hearts and minds and allow spiritual compassion to fill the voids.

"But mere doubt is not enough," he added. "Mainstream Muslims have no incentive to address this issue properly unless social changes demand a fresh look at the issue. Problem is, many LGBTQ activists speak the language of 'critical race/queer theory' and mainstream Muslims speak the language of Islamic fiqh. So there is no conversation."

Everything went smoothly at Allah Loves Us All, the symposium Jahangir organized in September 2017, despite anonymous haters who threatened some disruption by tearing down event posters. Its scholarly founder was somewhat of an outlier amongst speakers, who focused more on cultural histories, and especially attendees, who were mostly loud-and-liberal or out-and-proud activists, plus a couple (female) delegates of well-established Muslim organizations.

I witnessed a few hijabi students of MacEwan University wandering into the talks, presumably between classes. They left partway through, looking neither visibly offended nor inspired. The majority of millennial Muslim Americans accept homosexuality as normal, according to Pew Research Center. At 60 percent, their views are somewhat more conservative than their non-Muslim peers, but in line with the general public and twice that of white evangelical Christians.

If the symposium had a rock star, it was Imam Daayiee Abdullah. The sixty-three-year-old African American faith leader was a large, friendly figure. He shared his personal story during a panel titled "Islam and LGBTQ+ Muslims," recalling how he came out as gay following the 1969 Stonewall uprising in Greenwich Village, fifteen years before taking shahada.

Although he knew many Nation of Islam Muslims in his native Detroit, Imam Abdullah discovered the faith in China, where he studied at Beijing University in 1984. He continued Arabic and Islamic studies at prestigious universities in Saudi Arabia and the United States until 2003, when he was expelled from the Graduate School of Islamic Social Sciences in Virginia. The institution learned he was gay after he presided over *janazah* of a man who succumbed to AIDs-related illness. The funeral and expulsion motivated him to become the first openly gay imam in the United States, pushing for grassroots reform through such causes as the Light of Reform Mosque in DC, which closed after four years due to a lack of resources.

At the time of the symposium, Imam Abdullah was building the Mecca Institute, an online Islamic seminary. He hoped it would help address the absence of locally trained imams in the English-speaking world. We discussed it over the phone months later, in 2018. "Most imams are brought from 'the old country' and they cannot deal with what it means to be a Muslim in America," Abdullah explained. It is one of the biggest hindrances to religious reform. So far, only a handful of students were enrolled in one of its diploma programs.

Despite low-enrolment (and cyberattacks disrupting their studies), the Mecca Institute credo is a blueprint of tomorrow's American Islam. Research shows that American Muslims young or old, naturalized or natural born, are twice as likely to support LGBTQ rights as they were a decade ago. Widespread acceptance amongst Muslim organizations is slow but inevitable. When it finally reaches the senior levels of Islamic centres, it won't be because of the efforts of researchers like Jahangir or imams like Abdullah or his protégés. Rather it will be because of the teachers, social workers, and parents who hold sway over the congregation. The leaders are merely catching up to them.

"America is developing its own Islam, so there will be, in time, a form of American Islam, just as there is in China and Southeast Asia," he said. American Islam—or Islams—had been developing into a unique form for much of the past century. The process wasn't stopped by the Islamic awakening and hegemony of postwar immigrants, but it was slowed and sometimes reversed.

We may be reaching an end to this fifty-year detour in the Information Age. But what if this were not the evolution of a regional Islam but the beginnings of a new global movement? Imam Abdullah believes that as developing nations become more modernized and globalized, Western Islam can guide the so-called Muslim world through their social revolutions.

Could American Islam—or inclusive Islam—really be packaged and propagated like Salafism was throughout the late twentieth century? It's hard to imagine this considering the nativist direction societies seem to be moving in. Regardless, if inclusive Islam is to ever cohere into a standardized practice, the movement's leading voices will have to sort out some striking differences of opinion. There are experimentalists like El-Farouk Khaki and textualists like Jahangir, and they do not always agree about conduct in sacred places or even the importance of sacred places.

When I interviewed Jahangir, he expressed his frustration with organizing queer-friendly worship at his home, which was often overtaken by critical theory. "I have a hard time jelling with people more interested in discussing social justice than Islamic scripture," said Jahangir, who is in his midforties. He was most bothered by the way discreet communal prayers "extended the closet," perpetuating homophobic stigma.

Imam Abdullah also admitted some frustration with the congregation of his former mosque. To him, such activist rhetoric "sounded like they wanted to have a parade in the mosque." A masjid, he said, is for prayer, funeral services, and marriages. "It's not to have a drag show."

Attendees of Juma Circles in Toronto, Atlanta, and other cities shouldn't expect RuPaul to offer the next khutba. However, Khaki and his cofounders do embrace the politics of decolonization, and were in the process of solidifying these values within an official document to guide Juma Circle chapters.

With or without this, inclusive Islam is becoming a coherent movement via the mission statement of the Inclusive Mosque Initiative. Founded in 2012 and led by a set of ethnically and theologically diverse women, the initiative also operates like a "nomadic" mosque wherever its chapters coordinate. In addition, it looks for precedent in modern Muslim communities to build up a body of work based on what's happening in Juma Circle and a growing number of inclusive congregations in Chicago, Berlin, Copenhagen, Zurich, Kashmir, Pakistan, and Malaysia.

"I did not initiate the inclusive-mosque initiative, but I am very blessed to be a part of it and a representative of it," said Imam amina wadud, an African American woman famous for leading Friday prayers and giving khutbas to mixed-gender congregations. wadud, who prefers her name in lowercase to imitate Arabic grammar, spoke with me by phone in 2018, midway between my attendance at Allah Loves Us All in Edmonton and the Unity Mosque in Toronto. She believed Islam has always been more about discussion than edict, so any attempt to standardize and fix any Muslim movement was inherently problematic.

A scholar and author of two books on women's perspectives and reform, wadud believed that the idea of a "permanent fixed Islam" was a barrier to embracing one's own soul because it forces Muslims to measure themselves against the monolith. What's more, it's an impossibility. "You have to accept challenges, and challenges to a faith can be catastrophic to people," said the imam. "They 'leave Islam' in their frustrations or seek knowledge of other ways of being Muslim."

Indeed, every mosque I'd visited on my journey started in somebody's home or field or boardroom. Along the way, they adjusted their Islam to the needs of the people, and those mosques that did not adjust to the changes spawned new congregations, which in turn brought new Muslims into the fold. Friction, not conventionalism, grows a faith community.

Just as there's no such thing as a "proper" Muslim, there is no such thing as a "proper" mosque. "The Prophet said that the whole of the

Earth is a masjid. Wherever you are, you can and should perform the daily salat, anywhere," she said. "If you construct a place that is inclusive, people will inhabit it."

I'd always thought of a mosque as a physical place with a set of rules and traditions. But this project has taught me that a mosque is more of a forum than an institution, and more—much more—about the congregation than the space they occupy. None were more emblematic of the metaphysical masjid than Unity Mosque.

Returning the story to my trip to Toronto, I appreciated Unity Mosque's disregard for norms. Even calling itself a mosque—that is, not a musalla or another downgrading term—challenged orthodoxy. The word demands legitimacy in spite of heterodoxy.

Juma Circle is a reason that Ali, the asylum seeker I met in Toronto, moved to Canada. As the Egyptian government cracked down on LGBTQ people, he messaged inclusive mosques around the world to suss out those cities' social services for gay Muslims. He visited one in Europe, experiencing something he described as in between a dream and a miracle. The only problem? The gay Muslim community was too small.

Canada was the last country on his list when he connected with Khaki through the Unity Mosque Facebook page. Himself a Tanzanian-born refugee and an immigration lawyer by profession, Khaki told Ali about Toronto's formidable infrastructure for LGBTQ Muslims. "He explained that here there is a freedom, you can express yourself, live your life. That there are a lot of LGBTQ Muslims," Ali told me.

Juma Circle seemed like the icing on the cake. But Ali was taken aback by the service once he finally saw it. "It was very weird for me, like a wonderland, not just because of the sexual orientation of members but the inclusion of women, and some women are covered, and some are not, and all people are welcomed—Jewish, Shiite, nonbelievers. Anyone can attend," he said. He admitted that he struggled to accept Juma Circle as legitimate salat. "It's a wonderful tolerance, of course, but worship or Friday prayer is supposed to belong to

Muslims. Frankly speaking, it didn't feel like a real Friday prayer. It felt like a meeting or gathering. I could accept it, obviously—I'm very tolerant—but it's not normal and I didn't feel comfortable."

I understood the sources of his discomfort once I'd seen it for myself.

After salat and zikr, a Sufi devotional tradition of collective repetitive recitation, everyone was given the opportunity to share a personal request from God—what attendees called "my Fatiha." An elderly white woman gave her Fatiha to Yemen's famished victims of war, another woman to her friend struggling to find the means to visit her ailing grandmother overseas. Several asked God to help them find meaningful employment. Khaki himself asked for God to give him and his husband, Unity Mosque cofounder Troy Jackson, the patience to become the best fathers they could be as they began negotiating parenthood.

As Juma Circle progressed, I realized that it was modelled more on First Nations sharing circles than any Sufi tradition. Short of passing around a talking stick, congregants follow an Indigenous oral tradition that invites each to speak and obliges all to actively listen.

When it was my turn to ask God for something, I became suddenly self-conscious. I had not asked God for anything in a very long time, at least not aloud. In my mind or under my breath, sure. *Please, God, don't tell me I locked my keys inside. Please, God, make this traffic go!* Why does that come so naturally to me, and why did this feel so dramatically different?

I was way too inside my head to conjure anything from the depths of my soul the way I've heard my mom and sister pray aloud for good health. But my parents and siblings must have been on my mind when I finally offered my prayer. "My Fatiha," I said, "is that more mosques, more houses of worship, and more people of faith will become more accepting of the people in their lives with different values."

I wasn't entirely sure why that was my Fatiha. Meeting so many misfits and outliers must have reminded me of how hard it can be to relate to my family sometimes. Every few years, I say or do something that makes me wonder, *Is this the thing that gets me disowned?* Nothing has, of course, and probably nothing will, but that hasn't relaxed me enough to be straight with them about my fundamental disbeliefs.

That atheism is the source of my wickedness made me lucky compared to most of the worshippers present. Though my family finds it painful to accept my beliefs, they are just beliefs. They have little currency over my actions, my ability to live my life as I please, my capacity to love, and my right to happiness.

After the salat, sermon, and sharing circle, I went to speak to my imam—the young Black woman who led us in prayer. For her safety, I'll call her Natukunda, a Central African name that means "God loves us."

She told me that she resented Islam shortly after her parents converted the family from Christianity. Muslims chastised Natukunda for wearing shorts to the mosque on her first Salat al-Jumah. Only ten years old, modesty wasn't even a concept. "I had a perspective that Islam is strict. It holds women back, and women belong in back," she said. "You have to dress a certain way; if you don't do that then you're a sinner."

Her family suspected she was a lesbian in her teens. She escaped to Canada in 2014 after they tried to force her into a heterosexual marriage. Once here, she felt safe enough to confess. "They don't want to talk to me now," she said.

Looking for solace, she went to a mosque in Toronto. But she made the mistake of underdressing again and was reprimanded for wearing a sleeveless shirt below her headscarf. Natukunda left vowing to never allow herself to be hurt by religion again.

"I hated Islam," she said. "I stopped praying, stopped going to the mosque, stopped everything about Islam. I hated it so much because of everything I went through, because my family abandoned me, because of the message in other mosques talking about lesbians being sinners who are going to burn in hell. All that hate."

Natukunda's candidness took me aback. We were still in a sacred place, even if the prayer rugs and yoga mats quickly disappeared around us. But more than that, it was her courage to plainly say something I'd felt for many years.

My first notions of being Muslim were rooted in judgment. Being reprimanded for eating pork in preschool was a minor offence, but it set a harsh tone for the rules. The dos and don'ts only became stricter with age. The message around chastity and intermarriage churned my resentment of Islam. Why should I have to marry a Muslim woman if I don't want to? What was so horrible about dating someone from another culture, or just dating?

Obviously, being a homosexual daughter of orthodox Muslims in Central Africa is multitudes harder than being a straight son of moderate Muslims in western Canada, but I'm familiar with the performance of a Muslim's double life. I know what it's like to hide a girlfriend from your community and cover your tracks after a date. I also ran away, to Vancouver, under the guise of college. When I moved back with my parents, now in Edmonton, I felt like I'd been forced back into my double life. My resentment for Islam turned into hate—hate for the religion, hate for my affiliation, hate that begat self-hate.

I only started to let go of my hatred after getting honest with my parents, confidently speaking my mind, and expressing my values around them. I found that I'd underestimated their tolerance. Once I was living on my own again, I sat them down to tell them I was in a serious relationship with my now wife.

"Is she Muslim?" asked my mother.

"No."

"Is she white?" asked my father.

"Yes."

For a while, it seemed my worst fears were true. My dad fell silent and my mom was visibly crushed. She went through all the stages of grief in rapid succession. *It's not serious though, right? I bet she's not even that pretty. How can you do this to us? Just get it out of your system and settle down with a nice Muslim girl.*

But after about an hour, I realized we'd still be eating dinner together that night and my mom would still send me home with a week's worth of leftovers.

Though nothing nearly as traumatic as Natukunda's turning point, coming clean about my romantic relationship did feel like coming out of a closet. What I couldn't grasp about Natukunda, Ali, and the other queer Muslims I'd met was why they were still observant if so much of their pain was entwined with dogma. Being gay isn't a choice but being Muslim by definition is.

One reason, said Natukunda, was Islam was ever present in her life. Even though she hated the message, she did not have hatred for God. She felt free to continue searching for God within Islam until she found a version of Her that affirmed Natukunda's humanity. "When I came to Unity Mosque, it helped me become confident and feel supported, and it's helping me grow. This is what I actually thought mosques should be," she said. "Now I pray, I sit down and think about God. I put on a headscarf because I'm not being forced."

"Would you ever have imagined a few years ago leading a prayer for thirty people?"

"I never, *my God*," she said with a big grin.

As for Ali, who admitted much discomfort to me about Unity Mosque, his reasons for attending became clear after services had ended. I noticed him making friendly conversation with another Arab man he'd just met. Eavesdropping on them, I could tell they were hitting it off.

The boardroom crowd had dwindled from thirty people to five, including Khaki, who was busy packing prayer sheets and dishes. We stood in a circle, slowly assembling our winter layers, having a lively discussion about Islam. I wanted to know if and where they drew a line on Muslim inclusion.

"Would you accept someone who drinks and eats pork?"

Mostly yeses, but some nos.

"What about somebody who doesn't believe Muhammad or any of the prophets were divine?"

Surprisingly, fewer nos this time.

"What if I don't believe the Quran is literally the word of God, or that there even is a God in the traditional sense of how we describe Him or Her?"

After a long silence, Ali's friend said to me, "I feel that there are some criteria more important than others."

We workshopped some terms together that might describe me: *culturally Muslim, secular Muslim, agnostic Muslim.* None felt right to the ear or heart.

"I think you have to accept the religion of Islam as it is," said Ali. "You can't say I am Muslim, but I'm not convinced drinking alcohol or eating pork is wrong."

Not everyone agreed.

Ali asked me directly, "Are you Muslim?"

"Well . . ." I started.

"Are you practising?"

"No," I said.

"Are you a believer?"

"In what?"

"God, religion."

"No."

"For me," he said, "Muslim doesn't mean just your name or your upbringing. You have to be convinced by the beliefs."

Khaki suddenly chimed in: "I know Muslim atheists, people who identify *as* Muslim atheists."

"You can accept that such a thing exists?" I asked.

"Of course!" he said. "Historically, there's always been space for those people."

There was once a spirited tradition of Muslim elites publishing works that questioned dogma, prophethood, and only stopped short of trying to disprove God. Dedicated to values we might now call humanist—reason, empiricism, and free thought—these philosopher-scientists thrived during the medieval period known as the Islamic Golden Age. They've always existed, even if modern Muslim elites ignored or erased them by favouring conservative commentaries, a cover-up becoming harder to sustain in our Age of Information.

"So where does the Muslim start?" I asked Khaki.

Khaki said I was asking the wrong question. "It's 'Where does it end?'" Having a Muslim background—based not in spirituality but history, politics, culture, family—was legitimate enough for Muslim identity. With this, I believed I had a place in the ummah.

I walked with Khaki to his home ten minutes away. He shared a brick town house with his husband, Jackson, a Black-Indigenous artist, and their two-year-old son, Tajalli, who somehow resembled both of his fathers. He was almost a year older than my daughter, Noe, and his hyperactivity a preview of future mayhem. After we arrived, Khaki traded me to Jackson for their son, so that I could interview him.

Jackson cofounded Unity Mosque with Khaki and Laury Silvers, a religious scholar. He told me that he'd never met a queer Muslim before Khaki. Meeting his future husband forced Jackson to overcome some prejudices about Islam, particularly on the treatment of women. "I had the privilege of converting to *this* Islam—my Islam," he said. "I didn't have to go through Muslim angst." Jackson's Islam expanded his knowledge of the world, his politics, and himself. "The way I was brought up was very much about the Black experience—speaking truth to power, being true to yourself. I found that expressed in the Islam that I was seeing."

After a cup of tea, I went to say goodbye to Khaki and thank him for his time. He was upstairs in a den, sitting on a damask couch with his son in his lap. Tajalli watched whirling dervishes on YouTube, chanting along with the zikr to the best of his ability.

Before I left, I asked him where the idea for el-Tawhid Juma Circle came from—not the Unity Mosque but the circle in which we sang and shared together earlier that afternoon. The concept was adapted from a funeral service for his late partner in 2004, he explained. When he became terminally ill, his Catholic family made a ritual of stopping to pray for him at seven o'clock every day, regardless of where they were, what they were doing, or the fact that the man they prayed for had long been disaffected from the religion.

"I asked him whether he wanted to pray, and, if so, *how* he wanted to pray," said Khaki. "He chose salat and zikr."

So for his last weeks on Earth, their home became a mosque.

Every Thursday night, when many Shia and Sufi Muslims typically meet for dua, it filled with friends who would sing zikr and perform salat. Anyone who wished to join could join. It was a mixed congregation in every way that Juma Circle would become years later.

"He passed away in this house, and he was washed and wrapped in this house," said Khaki. "He had a Muslim funeral, but he was cremated and we had a multifaith service."

"Did he convert to Islam?" I asked.

Khaki considered the question closely. "He embraced Islam," he said. "People slip into Islam, and they slip out of Islam too."

Nobody can claim they know what Islam looks like because spirituality has no set form, he told me. Those who disagree stagnate a religion by looking to the past rather than the future, taking it out of a natural process, making it ahistorical and contaminated.

"Religion without spirituality is toxic, and that's what we've been seeing around the world. Spirituality has been stripped out of Islam," he said. "There's always been a tapestry in the Muslim tradition, even at the time of the Prophet—"

"—Zikr!" Tajalli interrupted.

Khaki shifted his full focus to his son. "You want zikr, baba? What zikr do you want, baba?" he asked. His affection for his boy made me want to get back home to my family.

I thanked them and gave them their space to enjoy the rest of their holy day together. As I walked back to my hotel, I thought about a question that Khaki had asked me earlier on the walk to his house: "So, Omar, what's your story?"

I gave him the gist. I told him about my small-town upbringing, conflicts with my family, Sunni dogma, Muslim politics, and religion itself. I shared with him my guilt for contributing in my own small ways to twenty-first-century Islamophobia, and that I now feared this monster endangered the Western world. I told him that I was finally embracing my Muslim identity out of parts protest and repentance.

I left out a lot. I didn't tell him about the spiritual transformation that already happened inside me years ago. It's not something I had shared with anyone else.

The truth is, I'd had a religious experience before I started my journey in 2017. When it happened, my marriage was in shambles. Janae and I had become so focused on our own personal happiness that we lost complete sight of each other, and with it the desire to make each other happy. We forgot our ability to love. We began to lash out at each other and acted out of spite. When we'd accumulated enough damage to flatten our marriage and hurt many friends, we found ourselves searching the wreckage for a way forward, together or alone.

Beneath all that debris, we found a metaphysical time capsule containing the life that we'd planned together. Where we would travel, how we'd support each other's wants and wishes, and what kind of parents we'd eventually become. The humans we'd raise for this world took up the majority of this capsule. In fact, within months of our first date, we'd picked out the name Noe for the daughter we might make, years before picking wedding invitations. We gave Noe a story. A personality. A future with us.

We were young, naive, but determined. Then we became less young and much less determined. When we finally gave up on our marriage, we genuinely grieved the death of the child we'd never conceived.

We mourned Noe separately and alone, yet we somehow opened that time capsule together. It showed us both that we could bring Noe back to life with immense mercy and compassion. I can't speak for where Janae found hers, but I know I derived mine from the message of Islam. That there's no hatred that can't be healed, no anger that can't be reconciled, no act that can't be forgiven, when you submit to something bigger than yourself. Islam was my framework for the radical forgiveness required of me.

It felt like our prayers had actually been answered when Janae became pregnant a few months later. Logically, I know that the baby had a one in two chance of being a Noe. We willed our daughter's name just like we willed her into existence together. But Noe is the closest thing to fate I'd ever known. She is faith itself.

Epilogue

The minaret reared its long neck as I turned off the freeway. It had been more than a year since I last stepped inside a mosque, and longer since I prayed at the Edmonton's Al Rashid. Usually when I enter "Little Lebanon," the neighbourhood where my closest relatives send their kids to Islamic school, own businesses, and buy their bread, it's to stop at my brother-in-law's bakery for a quick breakfast. But as I looked at the shops and services around me and the drivers searching for a parking spot at the mosque, I realized the neighbourhood is more of a "Little Mecca," where a majority of all local Muslims shop and worship, live and die.

And that is what brought me down this old road again, in the first few days of 2021, which, somewhat unbelievably, was already shaping up to be worse than the year before it.

I'd lost my first family member to COVID-19. It seemed inevitable for everyone in the world—not *if*, but *when* and *who*. Which of my beloveds would the virus pick off? And yet I was still shocked when the news came that Aunty Intissar was victim 3 million and some.

My mother felt it much harder, and she was grieving in a way I hadn't seen since my grandma died a long time ago. I tried to console her on the morning of the funeral, but the conversation turned into an argument. I was upset because my parents intended to actually attend the janazah *inside* the mosque.

Places of worship were reopened under very limited capacity, but I didn't think it was wise of anyone to commune indoors for my aunty's janazah, no matter how masked and socially distant, and especially not when there'd been an outbreak in their community. This was not my mother's first mourning since the pandemic. She'd lost a number of friends and acquaintances to the virus.

My mom and I played competing health experts, going back and forth about appropriate protocols during the deadlier second wave that had yet to peak.

Health measures or not, I doubted the venue's ability to stay within capacity given the community's respect for hajji Intissar. She was the rare *hafiza*, a woman who has mastered Quran memorization and an esteemed educator who cofounded an online Quran academy for adults. I remember her as the aunty who once jostled me out of bed to drink from her little gold cup of *zamzam*, holy water filled from a sacred well in Mecca—a memory I became fonder of with time.

It was impossible to convince my mom that we could honour Intissar's life outside, in the courtyard. As I put on my funeral suit and then immediately covered the whole thing in winter clothes, I felt angrier at myself for the way I spoke to my mom. I sounded as condescending as she had on the phone a few years ago after I confessed to eating pork.

I put the sound of my own voice out of my head as I parked out front and pulled on my mask. I tried to give my uncle condolences. We couldn't hear each other through our masks and the cracked window of his car, where he sat alone, a broken man in quarantine.

I joined a few of my irreligious relatives spread apart in the courtyard, where we tried to conjure up her blessed memory without sacred words. The whole event revealed to me the difference between being Muslim by conviction and being Muslim by culture. Both my parents and I were making our own critical choices. But they made a personal decision for the comfort of someone else, my aunt, whose soul deserved the mighty energy of communal prayer, while I made the decision to put myself and my family first. Never had the difference between collectivism and individualism been so clear.

It was just ten months prior that Al Rashid was begging people to stay home, shelter in place, and let the health professionals figure this all out so we could swiftly return to normal. *We're all in this together*, we said, and, quite astonishingly, it really looked that way for a while.

We all stayed home, doing our best for a righteous cause. And truly it was for Muslims. Prophet Muhammad said so himself in hadith: "If you hear of an outbreak of plague in a land, do not enter it; and if the plague breaks out in a place while you are in it, do not leave that place." So my parents stayed home, joining their community on Facebook Live for Friday worship.

When I felt spiritually compelled, I attended el-Tawhid Juma Circle on Zoom from my home office. It was touching and warm. El-Farouk Khaki led services from his computer, while Troy Jackson and his son, Tajalli, streamed from his phone app in another room of the house. The toddler's excitement for all faces popping up in gallery mode forced Jackson to hand off his duties for adhan. "I don't think this is going to work. Someone else will have to give the call to prayer," he said before muting.

A truck driver sitting behind the wheel in work clothes pulled the N-95 mask down over his chin and volunteered. The rest of us nonessential people congregated from home. There was a niqabi woman in Canada, a new "revert" (as opposed to *convert*) in a southern state, and a young person in outer space apparently. An Ojibway elder smudged God's virtual house while the chat box filled with a stream of *"Jumah mubarek!"* On occasion, a toilet flushed in one of the many, many more black boxes with cryptic names. This is still a safe space, after all.

Though we were worlds apart, I'd never felt so much closeness in a mosque before. It wasn't just the intimacy of their personal lives, but the closeness of their faces and voices.

I'll never forget the khatiba, the woman who gave the sermon about "hardship and ease." She drew from the Quran, verse 94, the Solace: "With every difficulty, there is ease."

And there *was* ease buried deep inside our fear. We'd just seen something most of us had given up on imagining in our lifetimes:

radical cooperation and transformation on a micro- and macroscale. The majority of everyone, everywhere, and of any belief, accepting the same rules for the preservation of humanity.

After seeing it with your own eyes, you can't help but imagine what else is possible with true global strength. Could we reverse climate change before it's too late, spread equity across the world, take in the neediest? The quality to improve is strong among us.

When I attempt to channel that optimism today, it's like trying to get in touch with my youth. The politicization and polarization of the pandemic have lowered my expectations dramatically. So has fatigue. In the words of a New Year's Eve meme, "What a decade 2020 has been."

I want much more for the world than the status quo, but it feels pragmatic to set the bar lower, to hope only for a return to normal.

Still, I manage to find scraps of ease when I scour for them. For one, the world feels less noisy now that Trump has been cancelled from the White House and mainstream social media. Though we'll likely have to reckon with him or someone worse making chaos in a couple of years, at least the Muslim ban is over. President Joe Biden, albeit reluctantly, lifted the cap on refugee admissions, ensuring some relief for refugee crises in Yemen, Myanmar, Somalia, and Syria.

Reports of anti-Muslim hate crimes are also declining across the English-speaking world. That's partly an indirect consequence of COVID-19 lockdowns keeping people at home, but the downward trend began earlier. And we really do seem to be pulling ourselves together for radical change on racial justice since the Black Lives Matter protests of summer 2020.

Does this give me ease? It's hard to see "progress" when anti-Asian attacks surge to terrifying levels reminiscent of anti-Muslim hate crimes after 9/11. And while there is incremental improvement for Muslim tolerance in this part of the world, there is terrifying regress on the opposite side, with millions of Muslims across the Pacific terrorized for their religion by mobs of Hindu and Buddhist extremists, by Burmese soldiers, by Chinese secret police.

When I started writing these portraits of Islamic life in early 2017, I thought that the idea of concentration camps filled with scores of Muslims was possible but highly improbable. I was called a Cassandra for suggesting the possibility—an abstract projection of current trends (and human history). It turned out quickly that we were all naive, my critics and me. Little did we know that China had already begun to execute its own version of a Muslim final solution.

As you read this, between 1 and 3 million Uyghurs have been forced into concentration camps that the government downplays in size and intent. Officially they are "vocational training schools," "poverty alleviation programs," and "reeducation camps" to assimilate Uyghurs to the dominant Han culture. Credible intelligence, eyewitnesses, and survivors tell us it's a torture factory producing tactical abuse, humiliation, sterilization, slave labour, sexual violence, starvation, medical experimentation, and murder.

Similarities to the Holocaust are undeniable. Even Jewish human rights activists and Holocaust survivors believe so. Around the world, they dedicated the cause of International Holocaust Remembrance Day 2021 to Uyghur genocide. As one Jewish activist quoted in the *Guardian* reminded us, "Nazi persecution of the Jews didn't start with the gas chambers."

If there are bright spots, it's in the increased awareness and actions taken against the atrocities. A growing boycott movement shows signs of impact on both China's economy and Western foreign policy. Since the new year, the US government and Canadian, UK, and Netherlands parliaments have recognized the atrocities as an official genocide. These declarations haven't been of much consequence, but they're making it harder for other governments to feign "neutrality," or, like Turkey and Saudi Arabia, support it in the name of "counterextremism."

It's a reminder that whether we like it or not, we of the so-called Western world are role models by citizenship and birthright. Privilege is not a choice, but what we do with it is. How we react to police executions of Black Americans has ripple effects that would not travel nearly as far if George Floyd and Breonna Taylor were South African.

The character of the people we elect to lead us can give rise to Narendra Modi, Jair Bolsonaro, and Mohammed bin Salman. The actions of Westerners have far-reaching consequences. We can't take this influence for granted.

Where I see the most brightness is within my own life.

The pandemic brought my travels to a hard stop, which forced me to slow down and spend more time—much more time—at home. At first I worried that being confined to a small house 24/7 would turn me against my wife, daughter, and pets, *Big Brother*-style, but it brought us together, along with our aging parents helping to look after Noe in our "bubble." It wasn't until I had time to count the days away that I realized I'd missed a quarter of my daughter's first two years of life. Noe is starting preschool in a few months, and I couldn't be more excited for her. I pray it will be close to a normal experience.

We also welcomed a healthy baby boy in 2020, and named him Elias, Ilyas in Arabic, after my parents' hometown in Lebanon. I pray he'll quickly acclimatize to strange people and places and maybe one day travel with his sister to touch his roots in Lebanon. He has much to look forward to now that his parents, grandparents, aunts, and uncles are vaccinated, inshallah.

I'm both extremely fearful and hopeful for their futures. It fills me with inconceivable love and unimaginable guilt when I consider the state of the world they'll inherit. On the best days, I can convince myself that their generation will be our salvation. Other days, I dread we've done something selfish and brutal. So I pray that the latter is not inevitable and that the Alpha Generation, with time, will show us the way forward.

The journey of this book helped me connect with strangers living unfamiliar lives. But it took a pandemic to teach me that we are, truly, interconnected. It's more than a clichéd turn of phrase; it's a determination for whether we live or die tomorrow. I pray we won't waste this knowledge.

Acknowledgments

From the outset, I knew I'd rely on the generosity of many people. There are too many to name, but I want to thank them for generously sharing their time, research, and knowledge with me in my quest to capture the Greater American Muslim experience. We did not always agree, and sometimes our conversations upset me, but I'm grateful for their honesty and hospitality.

I especially thank my mom, Tamam Mouallem, for being my go-to scholar on family and local Muslim history. She responded to every call and text for four years, always pointing me in the right direction if she didn't have an answer herself, and provided childcare while I was away. The same is true of my wife, Janae Jamieson, who helped me manage a mountain of research, to say nothing of her patience. I'm indebted to my mom, wife, and daughter for the sacrifices this book has asked of them.

My utmost gratitude to the family, friends, acquaintances, and complete strangers who granted me many favours: the Mouallem and Mourad clans in Brazil, Lebanon, and Alberta; Fatima Syed, Marcello Di Cintio, Michael Hingston, Brendan May, Nakita Valeirio, Mohamed Huque, and Marek Tyler, who gave their honest reactions to early excerpts and outlines; and Anna McLeod, for her university library card—seriously, that thing is a magic wand.

Finally, there are the people I plied with the most random questions: Baha Abu-Laban, Mansion Azeema, Russell Cobb, Mariam

Ibrahim, Akram Khater, Alexis Kleinen, Mack Lamoureux, Ariel Nasr, Danielle Paradis, June Kazeil, Nabil Mouallem, Sina Rahmani, Ranya Al-Sharkawi, Spencer Sekyer, Brian Singh, Zain Velji, Gianmarco Visconti, Earle Waugh, Nikki Wiart, and my sister Janine.

This is no doubt an incomplete list. I'm better at remembering my professional collaborators: the translators Katherine Alexander, Paula Laroche Humby, Houssem ben Lazreg, Flor Lopez, Sandro de Silvo, and Nadine Yousif; the producers and research assistants Mark Bassant, Asif Khan, Jalaludin Khan, Kevin Pennyfeather, Sheena Rossiter, Wilfred Spears, David Wears; the fact-checkers Karen Silva and Fatima Syed; and designers Maher Abu AlHassan and David Gee.

I received financial assistance from the Alberta Foundation for the Arts, Edmonton Arts Council, and Edmonton Heritage Council. Thank you to these institutions for their continued support of literary arts and to the granting jurors who made it possible for me to research and write this book over the past few years.

Excerpts of this book appeared as articles in the *Guardian*, the *Ringer*, the *Walrus*, *Broadview*, and *Eighteen Bridges*. Thank you to all these editorial teams.

Several editors worked on this manuscript, but none as closely as Justin Stoller. Thank you for helping me divine my own thoughts and feelings.

Thank you to Nita Pronovost, Kevin Hanson, and the Simon & Schuster Canada team. Thank you, Jackie Kaiser and Westwood Creative Artists. Thank you, readers. There are so many worthy books in the world, so I feel lucky you chose this one.

Glossary

The Five Daily Prayers

1. Fajr: "Dawn," or beginning of twilight.

2. Dhuhr: "Midday," after the sun passes its zenith; it lasts until twenty minutes before Asr.

3. Asr: "Afternoon," which officially begins when the shadow of an object is the same size as the object itself; lasts until sunset in Sunnism, though Shiites may combine Dhuhr and Asr.

4. Maghrib: "Sunset," which lasts until about twenty minutes before Isha.

5. Isha: "Night," which starts about halfway between Maghrib and Fajr.

Holidays

Ashura: A Shia holy day usually observed with a somber procession mourning the killing of Imam Hussein ibn Ali in the Battle of Karbala (680 AD). His martyrdom was the catalyst for the first schism in Islam.

Eid al-Fitr: The last day of Ramadan, which translates to "the feast festival"

Eid al-Adha: A four-day festival at the end of the annual hajj

Hosay: A uniquely Indo-Caribbean Muslim holiday that combines Ashura with Pakistani passion plays, Diwali lanterns, Sikh martial arts, and Caribbean festivals

Salat al-Jumah: Friday worship service, often simplified as "Jumah" (Friday)

Lailat al-Qadr: Usually observed on the twenty-seventh day of Ramadan, "the Night of Power," commemorates Prophet Muhammad's first revelation

Honourifics

Ayatollah: A high-ranking Shia clergyman, typically of Iranian descent.

Haj/haji: A person who has completed the hajj, the mandatory pilgrimage to Mecca.

Imam: At its most basic definition, anyone who leads prayer; this person ceases to be an imam as soon as the prayer ends. However, imam is most often reserved for trained faith leaders with an official post in a mosque. In Shia theology, imams hold more esteem as spiritual, political, and sometimes divine successors to Prophet Muhammad.

Mawlana/Moulvi: South Asian terms for a common Islamic scholar with limited authority (e.g., can't issue religious verdicts)

Mullah: A scholar of Quran, hadith, sharia, and Arabic with some limited authority

Mufti: A jurist qualified to issue nonbinding judgments on religious law

Shaykh/sheikh: A preacher

Sidi: An obscure Andalusian feudal title similar to "my lord"

Schools of Thought (Fiqh)

Fiqh, an important concept in Islam, is a variety of methods for legal interpretation of sharia, the divine and immutable religious law. As legal systems, the fiqh aspire to maintain juridical consistency. These schools of thought are more important in Sunnism because of its egalitarian structure. There are four dominant fiqh, each named for its respective founder and characterized as follows by *The Oxford Dictionary of Islam*:

- Hanafi: Predominant in Egypt, the Middle East, and Central Asia, it's the most widespread school, due largely to Ottoman dissemination, and also considered the most liberal. Hanafi adherents embrace reasoning, logic, opinion, analogy, and regional preference in the formulation of its laws.

- Hanbali: As the official jurisprudence for Saudi Arabia and Qatar, adherents of the Hanbali school are literalists when it comes to textual sources. Though socially conservative, they are fiscal liberals in the Muslim paradigm.

- Maliki: Predominant in North and West Africa, the doctrine is characterized by its emphasis on hadith, including many of those attributed to Muhammad's family and wives, and reliance on consensus opinion of the Prophet's first followers in Medina.

- Shafii: Emphasizes analogical reasoning when there are no clear directions in the Quran or hadith. It's the least common of the four main fiqh, with adherents dispersed throughout Polynesia, East Africa, and slivers of the Levant and Arabian Peninsula.

Common Words

Adhan: The call to prayer (sometimes "azaan" or "athan").

Ahmadiyya: A revivalist sect with Sunni-Sufi leanings founded in Punjab in 1889 by Mirza Gulam Ahmad, whom most followers believe is a minor prophet and the Messiah (Mahdi) appointed to usher in the End of Days. Because of their heterodoxy and progressive practices, they are often targets of government persecution and terrorist violence.

Allahu akbar: One of the most versatile phrases in Arabic, "God is Great" can express grief, joy, surprise, praise, modesty, anger, and various other feelings.

Bida: An innovation to Islamic practices that modern fundamentalists consider sacrilege or heresy.

Darqawi: A large and influential Sufi doctrine (tariqa); predominantly found in North Africa.

Dawah: Propagation of the faith, interpreted literally as proselytizing to nonbelievers, or figuratively through art and good citizenship

Deobandi: A Sunni revivalist movement established in 1866 alongside the Darul Uloom seminary in northern India. Deobandi Muslims primarily adhere to Hanafi fiqh, advocate for personal responsibility and conformity, and draw inspiration from ultraorthodox movements in the Arabian Peninsula.

Din/deen: Creed; also means the spiritual world, opposite the temporal world known as "dounia"

Druze: A mystical offshoot of the Shia subsect known as Nizari Ismailis. Adherents are divided on whether to still identify as Muslims.

Dua: A supplication or invocation usually recited after ritual prayers. It's also the basis for Thursday evening services in Twelver Shia communities.

Fatwa: A nonbinding legal opinion given by qualified scholars such as muftis. Fatwas are requested by courts, groups, or individuals, usually because of ambiguity or confusion emerging from modern issues.

Firman/farman: An edict. In the Nizari–Ismaili context, it's something between a royal decree and fatwa

Hadith: The sayings, teachings, and deeds of Muhammad and his first followers. Hadith regarded as a legitimate source of revelation.

Hafiz/Hafiza: One who can recite Quran from memory

Hijrah: Migration, usually as an act of sacrifice to escape hardship or persecution.

Iftar: The breaking of a fast

Ijtihad: Independent reasoning used in the absence of a clear directive or consensus

Imamat: A concept similar to the papacy used by Ismailis

Inshallah: "God willing"

Ismailism: A Shia offshoot with two main branches, the biggest being the Nizaris, who have maintained a lineage of living, hereditary imams known today as the Aga Khans.

Jamaat: Congregation. Early Arab immigrants used it interchangeably for "mosque" with several pronunciations (Jameah, Jima, Jamah).

Janazah: A specific prayer used in funeral services and death rites.

Jihad: Though it has many contentious and nuanced definitions, jihad simply means a struggle, which can be external ("small jihad") or internal ("big jihad").

Kaaba: The cubic temple in Mecca believed to have been built by Abraham and Ishmael.

Kafir: As opposed to a nonbeliever, a kafir is an unbeliever; that is, one who has learned but rejected the message of Islam. More recently, it's a violent term used by fundamentalists to disparage and persecute anyone who rejects their extremist views.

Khutba: A sermon following communal prayers, given by a khatib (or khatiba in women-led or gender inclusive mosques)

Mahdi: The promised messiah

Masjid: A mosque purpose-built for communal prayers

Mihrab: A semicircular niche from which imams lead prayer

Minbar: A pulpit for sermons, traditionally raised off the ground with a few steps

Muezzin/muezzina: One who makes the call to prayer (adhan)

Mujaddid: An imam sent by God to revitalize Islam at the turn of each century

Musalla: A prayer space, usually temporary or improvised

Mustahabb: A highly recommended but nonobligatory ritual

Qadiri: A Sufi doctrine rooted in the Hanbali Sunni school, predominantly found in West and Central Asia, East Africa, and Iraq.

Qibla: The shortest direction to Mecca unique to each person in worship.

Quraysh: Pre-Islamic polytheism dominant in the Arabian Peninsula.

Salafism: An ultraorthodox and ethnocentric Arab reformist movement that emerged from Saudi Arabia in the eighteenth century. It's better known as Wahhabism, which Salafis consider to be a pejorative.

Salat: Ritual worship, as in the five daily prayers.

Shahada: The proclamation that makes someone officially Muslim.

Shiism: Originally those who believed Muhammad's family to be the rightful, spiritual leaders of Islam. Shiites (meaning "partisans") have grown into a varied denomination with dozens of subsects with unique and sophisticated structures.

Shirk: Idolism or polytheism.

Shura: A traditional Islamic advisory group.

Sufi: A mystical method of practices that apply to Sunni, Shia, and other branches of the faith. Sufi doctrines emphasize God's divine presence, which can be channeled through such rituals as incantation, meditation, and song.

Sunnism: The largest branch of Islam, comprising about 85 percent of the ummah. The word is derived from "Sunnah," meaning the exemplary practices of Muhammad. Sunnism is sometimes simplified as orthodox Islam, but practices are quite varied according to different fiqh, Sufi doctrines, regional culture, and subsects such as the Nation of Islam.

Tablighi Jamaat: A modern and apolitical reformist movement that believes religious propagation is core to salvation

Taqiyyah: A once obscure concept that sanctions concealment of one's faith for self-preservation, but has been misappropriated by Islamophobes accusing racialized people of being Muslims in disguise

Tariqa: A type of Sufi doctrine and spiritual practices

Twelvers: The largest branch of Shiites, they believe the twelfth and last imam will reappear with Jesus to restore peace and justice for the world

Ulama: A committee of learned and upstanding Muslims, usually volunteers, helping community members navigate complexities in scripture and scholarship. The committee can request a fatwa on behalf of congregants when necessary.

Ummah: The Muslim community, usually in a global context, but also used regionally (e.g., Chicago ummah)

Wasat: Moderation; translates to "the middle path."

Wudu: A ritualistic cleansing, or ablution, performed before prayer.

Zakat: One of the pillars of Islam: an alms tax owed to the needy, usually 2.5 percent of the income of Muslim adults of sufficient means.

Zikr / dhikr: The act of reminding oneself of God. In Sufi contexts, this manifests as poems and transcendental rituals.

Selected Sources

Introduction

Beydoun, Khaled A. *American Islamophobia: Understanding the Roots and Rise of Fear*. Berkeley: University of California Press, 2018.

Majid, Anouar. *We Are All Moors: Ending Centuries of Crusades Against Muslims and Other Minorities*. Minneapolis: University of Minnesota Press, 2009.

"Muslim Population by Country." ChartsBin. https://chartsbin.com/view/557.

Saunders, Doug. *The Myth of the Muslim Tide: Do Immigrants Threaten the West?* New York: Vintage, 2012.

Spellberg, Denise A. *Thomas Jefferson's Qur'an: Islam and the Founders*. New York: Vintage, 2013.

Chapter 1

"Here Are the Hate Incidents against Mosques and Islamic Centers since 2013." ProPublica. https://projects.propublica.org/graphics/mosques.

Hoppe, Leslie J. *The Holy City: Jerusalem in the Theology of the Old Testament*. Collegeville, MN: Liturgical Press, 2000.

Thomas, David. "Early Muslim Relations with Christianity." *Anvil* 6, no. 1 (1989).

Chapter 2

Akande, Habeeb. *Illuminating the Blackness: Blacks and African Muslims in Brazil*. London: Rabaah Publishers, 2016.

Aydin, Cemil. "What Is the Muslim World?" *Aeon*, August 1, 2018. https://aeon.co/essays/the-idea-of-a-muslim-world-is-both-modern-and-misleading.

Curiel, Jonathan. *Al' America: Travels through America's Arab and Islamic Roots*. New York: New Press, 2008.

Diouf, Sylviane A. *Servants of Allah: African Muslims Enslaved in the Americas*. New York: NYU Press, 1998.

Garcia, Raphael T. "Under Brazil's New Government, Islamophobia Continues to Rise." *Sojourners*, April 8, 2019. https://sojo.net/articles/under-brazils-new-government-islamophobia-continues-rise.

Haselby, Sam. "Muslims of Early America." *Aeon*. Last modified May 20, 2019. https://aeon.co/essays/muslims-lived-in-america-before-protestantism-even-existed.

Lovejoy, Paul E. *Transformations in Slavery: A History of Slavery in Africa*. New York: Cambridge University Press, 2000.

Paul, Ames. "The Islamic Heritage in Portugal's Past." *The World from PRX*, September 18, 2010. https://www.pri.org/stories/2010-09-18/islamic-heritage-portugals-past.

Pavlu, George. "Recalling Africa's Harrowing Tale of Its First Slavers: The Arabs." *New African Magazine*, July 31, 2018. https://newafricanmagazine.com/16616/.

Reis, João J. *Slave Rebellion in Brazil: The Muslim Uprising of 1835 in Bahia*. London: Taylor & Francis, 1995.

Chapter 3

"About Sheikh Gilani." Fuqra Files. https://www.fuqrafiles.com /knowledgebase/about-sheikh-gilani/.

Al-Solaylee, Kamal. *Brown: What Being Brown in the World Today Means (to Everyone)*. New York: HarperCollins, 2016.

Bahadur, Gaiutra. *Coolie Woman: The Odyssey of Indenture*. Chicago: University of Chicago Press, 2013.

Benmelech, Efraim, and Esteban F. Klor. "What Explains the Flow of Foreign Fighters to ISIS?" *Terrorism and Political Violence* 32, no. 7 (2018), 1458–1481.

Claveyrolas, Mathieu. "The 'Land of the Vaish'? Caste Structure and Ideology in Mauritius." *South Asia Multidisciplinary Academic Journal*, 2015. doi:10.4000/samaj.3886.

Figueira, Daurius. *Jihad in Trinidad and Tobago, July 27, 1990*. Bloomington, IN: iUniverse, 2002.

Haracksingh, Kusha. "90 Days of Horror: The Voyage of the Fatel Razack to Trinidad in 1845." *Indo-Caribbean Heritage*, July 25, 2006. https://web.archive.org/web/20080302004135/www.indo caribbeanheritage.com/content/view/17/38/.

"A Historical Review of ASJA." *Caribbean Muslims*, April 2, 2009. https://www.caribbeanmuslims.com/a-historical-review-of-asja/.

Hollup, Oddvar. "The Disintegration of Caste and Changing Concepts of Indian Ethnic Identity in Mauritius." *Ethnology* 33, no. 4 (1994), 297. doi:10.2307/3773901.

Khan, Aisha. *Islam and the Americas*. Gainesville: University of Florida Press, 2016.

Khan, Zainol A. *Milestones in the History of Muslims in Trinidad and Tobago since 1845*. Trinidad: Momina, 2013.

"The Man Who Led the Western World's Only Islamist Coup." BBC News, March 3, 2019. https://www.bbc.com/news/stories-47419535.

Mustapha, Nasser. "The Influence of Indian Islam on Fundamentalist Trends in Trinidad and Tobago." *Sociological Bulletin* 46, no. 2 (1997): 245–265. doi:10.1177/0038022919970205.

Narbona, Maria D., Paulo G. Pinto, and John T. Karam. *Crescent over Another Horizon: Islam in Latin America, the Caribbean, and Latino USA.* Austin: University of Texas Press, 2015.

Noel, Otancia. "Yasin Abu Bakr: The Drugs Made Me Do It; Jamaat Boss on 1990 Coup." *Wired868*, April 17, 2017. https://wired868.com/2015/07/27/yasin-abu-bakr-the-drugs-made-me-do-it-jamaat-boss-on-1990-coup/.

"Foreign Fighters in Iraq and Syria: Where Do They Come From?" RadioFreeEurope/RadioLiberty, 2015. https://www.rferl.org/a/foreign-fighters-syria-iraq-is-isis-isil-infographic/26584940.html.

Rubin, Barry M. *Guide to Islamist Movements.* Armonk, NY: M. E. Sharpe, 2010.

Samaroo, Brinsley, Yvonne Teelucksingh, and Kenneth Ramchand. *Zalayhar: Life of a First Lady.* 2010.

Taylor, Patrick, and Frederick I. Case. *The Encyclopedia of Caribbean Religions.* Champaign: University of Illinois Press, 2013.

Chapter 4

"Birth of Sikhism." Islam Ahmadiyya, February 18, 2017. https://www.alislam.org/religions/sikhism/birth-of-sikhism/.

"Black Muslims Account for a Fifth of All U.S. Muslims, and About Half Are Converts to Islam." Pew Research Center, May 30, 2020. https://www.pewresearch.org/fact-tank/2019/01/17/black-muslims-account-for-a-fifth-of-all-u-s-muslims-and-about-half-are-converts-to-islam/.

Saadi El, Ra. *The Controversial Years of the Moorish Science Temple of America*. 2012.

Curtis, Edward E. *Muslim Americans in the Military: Centuries of Service*. Bloomington: Indiana University Press, 2016.

———. *Muslims in America: A Short History*. New York: Oxford University Press, 2009.

Dolinar, Brian. *The Negro in Illinois: The WPA Papers*. Champaign: University of Illinois Press, 2013.

Dorman, Jacob S. *The Princess and the Prophet: The Secret History of Magic, Race, and Moorish Muslims in America*. Boston: Beacon Press, 2020.

"Elijah Muhammad's Son Counters Farrakhan Teachings." *Baltimore Sun*, May 16, 1994. https://www.baltimoresun.com/news/bs-xpm-1994-05-16-1994136064-story.html.

Jackson, Sherman A. *Islam and the Blackamerican: Looking Toward the Third Resurrection*. Oxford: Oxford University Press, 2005.

Long, Jeff. "Fresh Mosque, New Attitude." *Chicago Tribune*, May 16, 1994. https://www.chicagotribune.com/news/ct-xpm-2008-10-20-0810190302-story.html.

Luhby, Tami. "Chicago: America's Most Segregated City." CNNMoney, January 5, 2016. https://money.cnn.com/2016/01/05/news/economy/chicago-segregated/.

Marable, Manning. *Malcolm X: A Life of Reinvention*. London: Penguin, 2011.

Miller, Sabrina L. "Orthodox Muslims Upset Over Farrakhan's Beliefs." *Chicago Tribune*, March 3, 1996. https://www.chicagotribune.com/news/ct-xpm-1996-03-02-9603020035-story.html.

Moore, Natalie Y., and Lance Williams. *The Almighty Black P Stone Nation: The Rise, Fall, and Resurgence of an American Gang*. Chicago: Chicago Review Press, 2011.

Morrow, John A. *Finding W.D. Fard: Unveiling the Identity of the Founder of the Nation of Islam*. Newcastle upon Tyne: Cambridge Scholars Publishing, 2019.

"Nation of Islam." *Encyclopedia Britannica*, February 1, 2021. https://www.britannica.com/topic/Nation-of-Islam.

Payne, Les, and Tamara Payne. " 'Well, What Do You Mean, We Can't Join the Klan?' " *Politico*, October 24, 2020. https://www.politico.com/news/magazine/2020/10/24/malcolm-x-biography-ku-klux-klan-meeting-431657.

Siddeeq, Muhammad. "Why Give Wallace Mohammed II Power and Authority over You That He Does Not Have?" *Family Siddeeq* (blog), July 12, 2011. https://siddeeq.com/2011/07/12/why-give-wallace-mohammed-ii-power-and-authority-over-you-that-he-does-not-have/.

Tate, Sonsyrea. *Little X: Growing Up in the Nation of Islam*. San Francisco: Harper, 1997.

Williams, Jennifer. "A Brief History of Islam in America." *Vox*, December 12, 2015. https://www.vox.com/2015/12/22/10645956/islam-in-america.

Zurlo, Gina A. "How Many Muslims Are There in the United States?" *Gordon-Conwell Theological Seminary* (blog), October 8, 2019. https://www.gordonconwell.edu/blog/how-many-muslims-are-there-in-the-united-states/.

Chapter 5

Abdelaziz, Rowaida, Hassan Khalifeh, Afaf Humayun, and Mathias Christopher. "The City That Bears the Brunt of the National Terror Watchlist." *HuffPost*, October 3, 2017. https://www.huffpost.com/entry/dearborn-michigan-terror-watchlist_n_59d27114e4b06791bb122cfe.

Abraham, Nabeel, Sally Howell, and Andrew Shryock. *Arab Detroit 9/11: Life in the Terror Decade*. Detroit: Wayne State University Press, 2014.

Abraham, Nabeel S., and Andrew Shryock, eds. *Arab Detroit: From Margin to Mainstream*. Detroit: Wayne State University Press, 2000.

Abu-Laban, Baha. *An Olive Branch on the Family Tree: The Arabs in Canada*. Toronto: McClelland & Stewart, 1980.

Abu-Laban, Baha, Faith T. Zeadey, and Sharon M. Abu-Laban, eds. *Arabs in America: Myths and Realities*. Wilmette, IL: Medina University Press International, 1975.

Bukhari, Zahid H., Sulayman S. Nyang, Mumtaz Ahmad, and John L. Esposito, eds. *Muslims' Place in the American Public Square: Hope, Fears, and Aspirations*. Lanham, MD: Rowman, 2004.

Curtis, Edward E. *The Columbia Sourcebook of Muslims in the United States*. New York: Columbia University Press, 2009.

"Ford Was First Company to Hire Blacks in Large Numbers." *Crain's Detroit Business*, June 1, 2003. https://www.crainsdetroit.com/article/20030601/SUB/306010874/ford-was-first-company-to-hire-blacks-in-large-numbers.

Howell, Sally. *Old Islam in Detroit: Rediscovering the Muslim American Past*. New York: Oxford University Press, 2014.

Kozlowski, Kim. "Mantra at New Mosque in Dearborn Hts.: 'Islam for All.'" *Detroit News*, April 12, 2017. https://www.detroitnews.com/story/news/local/wayne-county/2017/04/12/mission-new-mosque-dearborn-hts-islam/100354934/.

Lopez, Ian H. *White by Law: The Legal Construction of Race*. New York: NYU Press, 2006.

Maganti, Srividya. "Not So Black-and-White." *Harvard Political Review,* January 30, 2020. https://harvardpolitics.com/not-black-and-white/.

National Museum of American History. "Oral Histories of the Faris and Yamna Naff Arab American Collection."

Powell, John. *Encyclopedia of North American Immigration.* New York: Infobase Publishing, 2009.

Qazwini, Sayyid H. *American Crescent: A Muslim Cleric on the Power of His Faith, the Struggle against Prejudice, and the Future of Islam and America.* New York: Random House, 2013.

"Richard Caleal, 94, Who Helped Design Innovative '49 Ford, Dies." *New York Times,* September 23, 2006.

Saleh, Iman. "How Muslims, Often Misunderstood, Are Thriving in America." *National Geographic,* April 12, 2018. https://www.nationalgeographic.com/magazine/2018/05/being-muslim-in-america/.

Saunders, Pete. "Segregation: One of Detroit's Biggest Imports." *Metropole* (blog), January 22, 2020. https://themetropole.blog/2020/01/22/segregation-one-of-detroits-biggest-imports/.

Suleiman, Michael. *Arabs in America: Building a New Future.* Philadelphia: Temple University Press, 2010.

Chapter 6

Albrecht, Charlotte Karem. "Narrating Arab American History: The Peddling Thesis." *Arab Studies Quarterly* 37, no. 1 (2015), 100.

"Anti-Muslim Activities in the United States 2012–2018." New America. https://www.newamerica.org/in-depth/anti-muslim-activity/.

Awid, Richard A. *Canada's First Mosque: The Al Rashid.* Edmonton: High Speed Printing, 2010.

———. *Through the Eyes of the Son: A Factual History about Canada,* 2000 ed. Edmonton: Accent Printing, n.d.

Habib, Naiyer, and Mahlaqa N. Habib. *History of the Muslims of Regina, Saskatchewan, and Their Organizations: "A Cultural Integration."* Bloomington, IN: Trafford Publishing, 2015.

Johnson, Gilbert. "The Syrians in Western Canada," *Saskatchewan History* 12, no. 1 (1959): 31–32.

Kurd, Nadia. "The Mosque as Heritage Site: The Al-Rashid at Fort Edmonton Park and the Politics of Location." *Journal of Canadian Studies* 52, no. 1 (2018), 176–192.

Lorenz, Andrea W. "Canada's Pioneer Mosque." *Aramco World*, July/August 1998. https://archive.aramcoworld.com/issue/199804/canada.s.pioneer.mosque.htm.

Sherman, William C., Paul L. Whitney, and John Guerrero. *Prairie Peddlers: The Syrian-Lebanese in North Dakota.* Bismarck, ND: University of Mary Press, 2002.

Waugh, Earle H. *Al Rashid Mosque: Building Canadian Muslim Communities.* Edmonton: University of Alberta Press, 2018.

Waugh, Earle H., Baha Abu-Laban, and Regula Qureshi, eds. *The Muslim Community in North America.* Edmonton: University of Alberta Press, 1983.

——— , Sharon Abu-Laban, and Regula Qureshi, eds. *Muslim Families in North America.* Edmonton: University of Alberta Press, 1991.

Chapter 7

Afzal, Ahmed. *Lone Star Muslims: Transnational Lives and the South Asian Experience in Texas.* New York: NYU Press, 2014.

Association of Religion Data Archives. Accessed March 31, 2021. https://www.thearda.com/rcms2010/.

Bald, Vivek. *Bengali Harlem and the Lost Histories of South Asian America.* Cambridge, MA: Harvard University Press, 2013.

Duttagupta, Ishani. "How Houston Is Becoming the New Hub for Indian-American Community in Texas." *Economic Times*, April 28, 2015. https://economictimes.indiatimes.com/blogs/globalindian/how-houston-is-becoming-the-new-hub-for-indian-american-community-in-texas/.

Gray, Lisa. " 'America Has Changed Islam': A Woman Runs for the Board of Houston's Largest Muslim Organization." *Houston Chronicle*, December 9, 2018. https://www.houstonchronicle.com/news/article/America-has-changed-Islam-A-woman-runs-for-13451796.php.

Iyer, Deepa. *We Too Sing America: South Asian, Arab, Muslim, and Sikh Immigrants Shape Our Multiracial Future*. New York: New Press, 2017.

Khan, M. J. Phone interview with the author. Houston, January 9, 2019.

MacFarquhar, Neil. "Scrutiny Increases for a Group Advocating for Muslims in U.S." *New York Times*, March 14, 2007. https://www.nytimes.com/2007/03/14/washington/14cair.html.

Mejia, Brittny. "How Houston Has Become the Most Diverse Place in America." *Los Angeles Times*, May 9, 2017. https://www.latimes.com/nation/la-na-houston-diversity-2017-htmlstory.html.

Rossi, Rosemary. "US-Born Muslim Scientist Held, Forced to Unlock NASA Phone under Travel Ban." *Wrap*, February 12, 2017. https://www.thewrap.com/nasa-muslim-scientist-sidd-bikkannavar-travel-ban-muslim-ban/.

Selby, W. Gardner. "PolitiFact: Michael Sullivan Says NASA Administrator Said Main Mission is Muslim Outreach (Half-True)." *Politifact*, August 1, 2010. https://www.politifact.com/factchecks/2010/aug/01/michael-sullivan/michael-sullivan-says-nasa-administrator-said-main/.

Chapter 8

"1972 Ugandan Refugees: An Honourable Place in Canada." CBC, November 23, 2016. https://www.cbc.ca/radio/rewind/1972-ugandan-refugees-an-honourable-place-in-canada-1.3860296.

Drysdale, Alasdair, and Raymond A. Hinnebusch. *Syria and the Middle East Peace Process.* New York: Council on Foreign Relations, 1991.

Esmail, Aziz. *A Scent of Sandalwood: Indo-Ismaili Religious Lyrics.* London: Routledge, 2014.

Kahn III, Aga, and S. Shah. *The Memoirs of Aga Khan: World Enough and Time.* New York: Simon & Schuster, 1954.

Lakhani, M. Ali. *Sacred Web: A Journal of Tradition and Modernity*, no. 34 (December 2014).

Mohamed, Rahim. "A Brief History of the Ismailis in Canada." *Policy Options*, March 8, 2017. https://policyoptions.irpp.org/magazines/march-2017/a-brief-history-of-the-ismailis-in-canada/.

Molloy, Mike. Phone interview with the author. Ottawa, February 21, 2019.

Muhammedi, Shezan. "Lessons Learned from the Ugandan Asian Refugees." *Active History* (blog). September 13, 2015. https://activehistory.ca/2015/09/political-will-public-resources-and-refugee-resettlement-lessons-learned-from-uganda/.

Pirie, Madsen. "When Idi Amin Expelled 50,000 'Asians' from Uganda." *Adam Smith Institute* (blog), August 4, 2019. https://www.adamsmith.org/blog/when-idi-amin-expelled-50000-asians-from-uganda.

"Timeline: Canada and the Syrian Refugee Crisis." *Macleans*, November 24, 2015. https://www.macleans.ca/politics/ottawa/timeline-canada-and-the-syrian-refugee-crisis/.

Chapter 9

"Abuse of Iranian Immigrants Arriving in Bay Area." Bay Area Television Archive, November 6, 2019. https://diva.sfsu.edu/collections/sfbatv/bundles/232534.

Alhassen, Maytha. *Haqq and Hollywood: Illuminating 100 Years of Muslim Tropes and How to Transform Them.* New York: Pop Culture Collaborative, 2018.

Ali, Rozina. "The Erasure of Islam from the Poetry of Rumi." *New Yorker,* January 2017. https://www.newyorker.com/books/page-turner/the-erasure-of-islam-from-the-poetry-of-rumi.

Beydoun, Khaled A. *American Islamophobia: Understanding the Roots and Rise of Fear.* Berkeley: University of California Press, 2018.

Bozorgmehr, Mehdi. "No Solidarity: Iranians in the U.S." *Iranian,* May 2, 2001. https://iranian.com/Opinion/2001/May/Iranians/index.html?site=archive#3a.

DeYoung, Karen, Erin Cunningham, and Souad Mekhennet. " 'I Have Lost Hope for My Life': Iranians Describe Hardships as Trump Expands Sanctions." *Washington Post,* June 30, 2019. washingtonpost.com/world/national-security/i-have-lost-hope-for-my-life-iranians-describe-hardships-as-trump-expands-sanctions/2019/06/30/0f7d689a-9a86-11e9-8d0a-5edd7e2025b1_story.html.

Ditto, Steven. *Red Tape Iron Nerve: The Iranian Quest for US Education.* Washington, DC: Washington Institute for Near East Policy, n.d.

Hakimzadeh, Shirin. "Iran: A Vast Diaspora Abroad and Millions of Refugees at Home." Migration Policy Institute, March 2, 2017. https://www.migrationpolicy.org/article/iran-vast-diaspora-abroad-and-millions-refugees-home.

Hamilton, Matt. " 'Los Angeles Embodies Diversity.' The City's New Sculpture Celebrating Freedom is Unveiled." *Los Angeles Times,*

July 5, 2017. https://www.latimes.com/local/lanow/la-me-free
dom-sculpture-20170704-story.html.

Herszenhorn, David M. "Iran's Man Grabs Munich Spotlight." *Politico*, April 18, 2019. https://www.politico.eu/article/iranian
-foreign-minister-mohammad-javad-zarif-grabs-munich-security
-conference-spotlight/.

"International Students Top One Million, Contributing $32.8 Billion to U.S. Economy." New American Economy, December 5, 2016. https://
www.newamericaneconomy.org/feature/international-students
-top-one-million-contributing-32-8-billion-to-u-s-economy/.

Lahue, Kalton C. *Bound and Gagged: The Story of the Silent Serials*. New York: Castle Books, 1968.

Said, Edward W. *Covering Islam: How the Media and the Experts Determine How We See the Rest of the World*. New York: Random House, 1981.

Shaheen, Jack. *Reel Bad Arabs: How Hollywood Vilifies a People*. Northhampton, MA: Interlink Publishing, 2012.

United Nations High Commissioner for Refugees. USA: " 'We Are Not the Enemy': Hate Crimes Against Arabs, Muslims, and Those Perceived to Be Arab or Muslim After September 11." Human Rights Watch, November 6, 2002. https://www.refworld.org/docid
/45db101e2.html.

Chapter 10

Alfaro-Velcamp, Theresa. *So Far from Allah, So Close to Mexico: Middle Eastern Immigrants in Modern Mexico*. Austin: University of Texas Press, 2009.

Campbell, Denis. "Revealed: He Leads an Extreme and Anti-Semitic Islamic Sect, He Believes Hitler Was a Great Man—and Now He's Back in Scotland." *Scotland on Sunday*, November 4, 1995.

Curtis, Edward E. *The Bloomsbury Reader on Islam in the West*. London: Bloomsbury, 2015.

Doubleday, Simon R., and David Coleman. *In the Light of Medieval Spain: Islam, the West, and the Relevance of the Past.* London: Macmillan, 2008.

Escamilla, Gaspar M. *Bajo la bandera del Islam.* San Cristóbal de Las Casas, Chiapas, Mexico: Ediciones Pirata, 2004.

Galvan, Juan. *Latino Muslims: Our Journeys to Islam.* San Antonio, TX: LatinoMuslims.net, 2019.

Daniel Abdal-Hayy Moore. "Shaykh Dr. Abdalqadir As-Sufi Al-Murabit (1930–)." *Ecstatic Exchange,* July 9, 2015. https://www.ecstaticx change.com/2015/07/04/shaykh-dr-abdalqadir-as-sufi-al-murabit -1930/.

Rus, Jan, and Gaspar M. Escamilla. "The Urban Indigenous Movement and Elite Accommodation in San Cristóbal, Chiapas, Mexico, 1975–2008." *Enduring Reform,* 2015, 81–112.

"Searching for God and Justice in Mexico's Rebel State." *Revealer,* December 20, 2017. https://therevealer.org/searching-for-god-and -justice-in-mexicos-rebel-state/.

Chapter 11

"2018 Survey: Islamophobia in Canada, Still a Grave Problem." CJPE, n.d.

Al-Solaylee, Kamal. *Brown: What Being Brown in the World Today Means (to Everyone).* New York: HarperCollins, 2016.

Bouchard, Gérard, and Charles Taylor. *Building the Future, a Time for Reconciliation: Abridged Report.* Québec: Commission de consultation sur les pratiques d'accommodement reliées aux différences culturelles, 2008.

Edde, Alexandre, Vishwaa Ramakrishnan, and Celeste Cassidy. "McGill's 1926 Jewish Ban." *McGill Daily,* September 3, 2018. https://www .mcgilldaily.com/2018/09/mcgills-1926-jewish-ban/.

Griffeth, William E. "Quebec in Revolt." *Foreign Affairs* (October 1964). https://www.foreignaffairs.com/articles/canada/1964-10-01 /quebec-revolt.

Hisham Kabbani, Muhammad. "Ritual Prayer: Its Meaning and Manner." Islamic Supreme Council of America. Accessed November 6, 2019, http://www.islamicsupremecouncil.org/understanding-islam /legal-rulings/53-ritual-prayer-its-meaning-and-manner.html.

"How They Lived: Families Share Memories of Quebec City Mosque Attack Victims." CBC, January 29, 2018. https://www.cbc.ca /news/canada/montreal/quebec-mosque-shooting-who-were -the-victims-1.4496792.

Hussan, Syed. "I Went to the Canadian Mosque Where Six Muslims Were Killed." *Canadaland*, January 26, 2018. https://www.canada landshow.com/visiting-the-quebec-city-mosque-whesix-mus lims-were-killed/.

Majid, Anouar. *We Are All Moors: Ending Centuries of Crusades Against Muslims and Other Minorities*. Minneapolis: University of Minnesota Press, 2009.

"Nearly Half (47%) of Canadians Think Racism Is a Serious Problem in Canada Today, Down 22 Points since 1992 (69%)." Ipsos, May 21, 2019. https://www.ipsos.com/en-ca/news-polls/Half-of -Canadians-think-racism-is-a-serious-problem.

Peritz, Ingrid, and Tu Thanh Ha. "Mosque Shooting Victims: Six Men Who Sought Better Lives in Quebec." *Globe and Mail*, May 17, 2018. https://www.theglobeandmail.com/news/national/the-victims -six-men-who-sought-better-lives-in-quebec/article33835172/.

Riga, Andy. "Inside the Life of Quebec Mosque Killer Alexandre Bissonnette." *Montreal Gazette*, April 23, 2018. http://montreal gazette.com/news/local-news/alexandre-bissonnette-inside-the -life-of-a-mass-murderer.

————. "Quebec Mosque Shooting: Chilling Videos Show a Calm, Calculated Killer." *Montreal Gazette*, April 12, 2018. https://montrealgazette.com/news/local-news/quebec-mosque-shooting-sentencing-hearing-begins-for-killer-alexandre-bissonnette.

"Survey of Muslims in Canada 2016." Environics Institute, April 30, 2016. https://www.environicsinstitute.org/projects/project-details/survey-of-muslims-in-canada-2016.

Woods, Allan. " 'Trash Radio' Creates Culture of Intolerance in Quebec." *The Star*, February 5, 2017. https://www.thestar.com/news/canada/2017/02/03/trash-radio-creates-culture-of-intolerance-in-quebec.html.

Woods, Thomas E. *The Church Confronts Modernity: Catholic Intellectuals and the Progressive Era*. New York: Columbia University Press, 2004.

Chapter 12

Awid, Richard A. *Through the Eyes of the Son: A Factual History about Canadian Arabs*. Accent Printing, 2000.

Baker, Peter. *Memoirs of an Arctic Arab: A Free Trader in the Canadian North the Years 1907–1927*. Yellowknife, NT: Yellowknife Publishing Company, 1976.

Koptseva, Natalia P., and Vladimir I. Kirko. "Northernmost Islam: 'Islamic Factor' in Eastern Siberia." *Mediterranean Journal of Social Sciences* 6 (2016).

Parfitt, Tom. "Norilsk in the Far North of Russia Lives Uneasily with Its Past as Part of Stalin's Network of Gulags." *The Times* and *Sunday Times*, May 7, 2018. https://www.thetimes.co.uk/article/norilsk-in-the-far-north-of-russia-lives-uneasily-with-its-past-as-part-of-stalin-s-network-of-gulags-mr9v56z3h.

Paxton, Robin. "Arctic Mosque Stays Open But Muslim Numbers Shrink." Reuters, April 16, 2007. https://www.reuters.com/article

/us-muslims-russia-arctic/arctic-mosque-stays-open-but-muslim
-numbers-shrink-idUSL1072493620070416.

"Ramadan in the Arctic: How Do You Break a Fast at Sundown If the
Sun Doesn't Set?" *National Post*, July 13, 2015. https://national
post.com/news/religion/ramadan-in-the-arctic.

Sherman, William C., Paul L. Whitney, and John Guerrero. *Prairie Peddlers: The Syrian-Lebanese in North Dakota*. Bismarck, ND: University of Mary Press, 2003.

Tan, Avianne. "Midnight Sun: This Town in Canada Is Experiencing
Sunlight 24/7 for 56 Days Straight." ABC News, May 28, 2015.
https://abcnews.go.com/Travel/midnight-sun-town-canada-ex
periencing-sunlight-247-56/story?id=31376376.

Truth and Reconciliation Commission of Canada. *Final Report of the
Truth and Reconciliation Commission of Canada*, vol. 2: *The Inuit and
Northern Experience*. Montreal: McGill-Queen's University Press,
2015.

Chapter 13

Gillis, Wendy. "A Timeline of the Toronto Police Investigation into
Bruce McArthur and the Gay Village Serial Killings." *The Star*,
February 8, 2019. https://www.thestar.com/news/gta/2019
/02/08/a-timeline-of-the-bruce-mcarthur-case-and-the-police-in
vestigation-into-the-gay-village-killings.html.

Greenwald, Glenn. "Stop Exploiting LGBT Issues to Demonize Islam
and Justify Anti-Muslim Policies." *Intercept*, June 13, 2016. https://
theintercept.com/2016/06/13/stop-exploiting-lgbt-issues-to-de
monize-islam-and-justify-anti-muslim-policies/.

Jahangir, Junaid, and Hussein Abdullatif. *Islamic Law and Muslim Same-
Sex Unions*. Lanham, MD: Lexington Books, 2016.

Khan, Azmat. "Meet America's First Openly Gay Imam." *Al Jazeera English*, December 20, 2013. https://america.aljazeera.com/watch/shows/america-tonight/america-tonight-blog/2013/12/20/meet-america-s-firstopenlygayimam.html.

Roman, Gregg, Sam Westrop, and Opinion Contributors. "Once Again, CAIR Shows That Islamism and Civil Rights Don't Mix." *The Hill*, April 15, 2017. https://thehill.com/blogs/pundits-blog/civil-rights/328873-once-again-cair-shows-that-islamism-and-civil-rights-dont-mix.

Salter, Shahla K. "We're Queer Muslims and Allies Marching at Pride for Those Who Can't." *HuffPost Canada*, August 29, 2018. https://www.huffingtonpost.ca/shahla-khan-salter/lgbtq-muslims-pride-parade_a_23511149.

"Stances of Faiths on LGBTQ Issues: Islam." Human Rights Campaign, November 1, 2020. https://www.hrc.org/resources/stances-of-faiths-on-lgbt-issues-islam.

Zhou, Steven. "Muslim Leaders Break Bread with Toronto Queers." *NOW* magazine, July 12, 2020. https://nowtoronto.com/news/muslim-leaders-break-bread-with-toronto-queers/.

Index